ENCOUNTERING JESUS

ENCOUNTERING JESUS

Character Studies in the Gospel of John

Cornelis Bennema

MILTON KEYNES • COLORADO SPRINGS • HYDERABAD

15 14 13 12 11 10 09   7 6 5 4 3 2 1

This edition first published 2009 by Paternoster

Paternoster is an imprint of Authentic Media
9 Holdom Avenue, Bletchley, Milton Keynes, Bucks, MK1 1QR, UK
1820 Jet Stream Drive, Colorado Springs, CO 80921, USA
Medchal Road, Jeedimetla Village, Secunderabad 500 055, A.P., India
www.authenticmedia.co.uk

Authentic Media is a division of Biblica U.K., limited by guarantee, with its
Registered Office at Kingstown Broadway, Carlisle, Cumbria CA3 0HA.
Registered in England & Wales No. 1216232. Registered charity 270162

British Library Cataloguing in Publication Data
A catalogue record for this book is available from the British Library

ISBN-13: 978-1-84227-666-2

Cover design by David McNeill for Scratch the Sky Ltd. (www.scratchthesky.com)
Printed and bound in India by Primalogue Publishing & Media (www.primalogue.com)

For Susan

Contents

Preface

John's strategy for achieving the purpose of his gospel – to evoke and strengthen belief in Jesus (20:30–31) – is to put various characters on the stage who interact with Jesus. John wants his readers to evaluate the characters' responses to Jesus, join his point of view and make an adequate belief-response themselves. If we were to stop here, all characters would be reduced to their responses and hence to types (as most scholars indeed conclude). My argument is that most Johannine characters are more complex and 'round' than has been believed so far. Besides, the Johannine characters have a paradigmatic function but not in a reductionist, 'typical' sense. It is the complete character – traits, development and response – that is representative across cultures and time. This book, therefore, analyses and classifies both the characters and their responses to Jesus.

Our study of Johannine characters who encounter Jesus happens within a theoretical framework that I have described in detail elsewhere: C. Bennema, 'A Theory of Character in the Fourth Gospel with Reference to Ancient and Modern Literature', *Biblical Interpretation* 17.4 (2009): 375–421. This article provides the theoretical foundation for my understanding of character in John's gospel and is essentially an important companion to this book. At the same time, this book applies and tests the theory we have suggested. I have two reading tips. In chapter 1, the reader could skip the section 'Previous Studies on Johannine Character' and go directly to the section 'The Gaps' which sums up the lacunae in Johannine character studies. Beyond chapter 1, the reader can read selectively since each chapter is self-contained.

I thank the following people and institutions: Robin Parry, Paternoster's Editorial Director, for accepting this work and proving to be extremely helpful throughout the various stages of this project. George Korah, the director of Primalogue, for helping me realize an Indian edition. The South Asia Institute of Advanced Christian Studies (SAIACS) for allowing me a sabbatical. The Evangelical Theological Research and Writing Project of India (TETRAWPOI) for giving me a generous grant. My wife Susan for her kind and able editing – I have dedicated this book to her. God for his inspiration, guidance and sustaining grace. May this book please him and be of use for his work on earth.

Cornelis Bennema, SAIACS (www.saiacs.org)   May 2009

Abbreviations

AB	Anchor Bible
BCE	Before Common Era
BETL	Bibliotheca Ephemeridum Theologicarum Lovaniensium
Bib	*Biblica*
BibInt	*Biblical Interpretation*
BibRes	*Biblical Research*
BibSac	*Bibliotheca Sacra*
BIS	Biblical Interpretation Series
BNTC	Black's New Testament Commentaries
BTB	*Biblical Theology Bulletin*
BZ	*Biblische Zeitschrift*
CBQ	*Catholic Biblical Quarterly*
CE	Common Era
CUP	Cambridge University Press
DJG	*Dictionary of Jesus and the Gospels*. Edited by J.B. Green, S. McKnight, and I.H. Marshall. Downers Grove: InterVarsity Press, 1992.
DNTB	*Dictionary of New Testament Background*. Edited by S.E. Porter and C.A. Evans. Downers Grove: IVP, 2000.
ESEC	Emory Studies in Early Christianity
ETL	*Ephemerides Theologicae Lovanienses*
EvQ	*Evangelical Quarterly*
EvT	*Evangelische Theologie*
ExpTim	*Expository Times*
Int	*Interpretation*
IRM	*International Review of Mission*
ISPCK	Indian Society for Promoting Christian Knowledge
IVP	InterVarsity Press
JBL	*Journal of Biblical Literature*
JETS	*Journal of the Evangelical Theological Society*
JSNT	*Journal for the Studies of the New Testament*
JSNTS	Journal for the Studies of the New Testament Supplement Series
JSOT	*Journal for the Study of the Old Testament*

JTS	*Journal of Theological Studies*
JTSA	*Journal of Theology for Southern Africa*
LS	*Louvain Studies*
LTPM	Louvain Theological & Pastoral Monographs
NBD	*New Bible Dictionary.* Edited by D.R.W. Wood. 3d edn. Leicester: IVP, 1996.
NCB	New Century Bible
NCBC	New Cambridge Bible Commentary
NIB	New Interpreter's Bible
NIV	New International Version
NovT	*Novum Testamentum*
NovTSup	Novum Testamentum Supplement Series
NRSV	New Revised Standard Version
NTS	*New Testament Studies*
OUP	Oxford University Press
RevExp	*Review and Expositor*
SAP	Sheffield Academic Press
SBEC	Studies in Bible and Early Christianity
SBL	Society of Biblical Literature
SBLAB	Society of Biblical Literature Academia Biblica
SBLDS	Society of Biblical Literature Dissertation Series
SBLMS	Society of Biblical Literature Monograph Series
SBLSBS	Society of Biblical Literature Sources for Biblical Study
SBLSP	*Society of Biblical Literature Seminar Papers*
SNTSMS	Society for New Testament Studies Monograph Series
SP	Sacra Pagina
SPCK	Society for Promoting Christian Knowledge
StBL	Studies in Biblical Literature
Str.-B.	Strack, H.L., and P. Billerbeck. *Kommentar zum Neuen Testament aus Talmud und Midrasch.* 6 vols. Munich: Beck, 1922–61.
TDNT	*Theological Dictionary of the New Testament.* Edited by G. Kittel and G. Friedrich. Translated by G.W. Bromiley. 10 vols. Grand Rapids: Eerdmans, 1964–76.
TS	*Theological Studies*
TTod	*Theology Today*
TynB	*Tyndale Bulletin*
VT	*Vetus Testamentum*
WBC	Word Biblical Commentary
WJK	Westminster John Knox
WUNT	Wissenschaftliche Untersuchungen zum Neuen Testament
WW	*Word and World*

Introduction

'All the world's a stage, and all the men and women merely players' — W. Shakespeare

People are interested in people and like to hear their stories. The appeal of a good novel, movie or biography is that it draws one into the story so that we identify with one or more of the characters. Some authors write simply to entertain readers, while others write in order to persuade their readers of a particular viewpoint. The author of John's gospel falls in the latter category.[1] John explicitly states his purpose in 20:30–31:

> Now Jesus did many other signs in the presence of his disciples, which are not written in this book. But these are written so that you may come to believe that Jesus is the Messiah, the Son of God, and that through believing you may have life in his name.

In order to accomplish this purpose John deliberately puts on the stage various characters that interact with Jesus, producing an array of belief-responses. This book too has a specific purpose: to present the Johannine characters, especially their responses to Jesus, in order to challenge readers to evaluate their stance regarding Jesus.

Having studied the Gospel of John in recent years, I recognize the relevance and universality of John's appeal for his readers on the subject of Jesus. For John, Jesus is the central figure in human history who came into the world to provide divine, everlasting life and to reveal God (cf. 1:1–18). John 1:4 states that 'in him was life', and the rest of the gospel substantiates this claim. Jesus is the protagonist in John's story and various characters interact with him. Since peoples' response to Jesus is crucial we must study these characters. This book is the first full-length treatment of all the Johannine characters who encounter Jesus.

There is another important rationale for this book. In the last thirty years there has been an increased interest in the Bible as literature and story. Literary methods have been applied to John's gospel mainly in the form of narrative criticism and reader-response criticism and have proven fruitful. John's gospel, then, is the story of Jesus Christ – a story with a plot, events

---

[1] We contend that the author of this gospel is the Beloved Disciple, whom we tentatively identify as John the son of Zebedee (see ch. 21).

and characters. While much has been written on events and on the logical or causal sequence of events called 'plot', character appears to be the neglected child. There is no comprehensive theory of character in either literary theory or biblical criticism, and therefore no consensus amongst scholars on how to analyse and classify characters. Elsewhere I have developed a comprehensive theory of character in the Gospel of John that I am applying and testing in this book.[2] As we shall see, most scholars view the Johannine characters as one-dimensional ('types') and unchanging. This book aims to provide a fresh analysis of the Johannine characters and their responses to Jesus, showing that many characters are more complex, round and developing than most scholars would have us believe.

Before we start with our main task we will briefly consider what other scholars have done (and not done) on the subject of character in the Gospel of John. *[The reader who is not interested in a detailed review may skip the next section and go directly to the section 'The Gaps' which sums up the lacunae in Johannine character studies.]* Then, we shall explain how we understand, analyse and classify character in John's narrative – in short, our theory of character. After that, we will introduce John's story of Jesus in which the characters appear, and finally, we will spell out the plan and approach of the book.

Previous Studies on Johannine Character

Ours is not the first study on Johannine characters so we will examine others' contributions to the subject in order to firmly anchor our work. As Sir Isaac Newton said, 'If I have seen further . . . it is by standing upon the shoulders of giants.' This survey will help us identify the questions that have been left unanswered and issues that have been insufficiently dealt with. We will draw attention to those scholars who have provided significant commentary on the subject of Johannine characterization. Most studies on the subject have been done in the last two decades, corresponding to the increasing interest in the Gospel of John as a literary work.

One of the earliest treatises on Johannine characters is an article from 1956 by Eva Krafft.[3] Influenced by Rudolf Bultmann's commentary on John, she argues that John made his characters typically transparent and that they personify a certain attitude to Jesus. Next, Raymond Collins wrote a lengthy article on Johannine characters in 1976 (reprinted in 1990), and added a second essay in 1995.[4] He argues that the various characters in John's gospel

---

[2] C. Bennema, 'A Theory of Character in the Fourth Gospel with Reference to Ancient and Modern Literature', *BibInt* 17 (2009): 375–421. Below, we provide a summary of our theory.

[3] E. Krafft, 'Die Personen des Johannesevangeliums', *EvT* 16 (1956): 18–32.

[4] R.F. Collins, 'Representative Figures', in *These Things Have Been Written: Studies on the Fourth Gospel* (LTPM 2; Louvain/Grand Rapids: Peeters Press/Eerdmans, 1990), 1–45; repr.

represent a particular type of faith-response to Jesus; they are cast in a representative role and serve a typical function.[5] Krafft and Collins' descriptions of the characters are not very detailed and they do not classify the characters or their responses to Jesus. The reader is left with a collection of unconnected character descriptions since their studies are neither preceded by guidelines on how to analyse character nor followed by an evaluation of how the various characters relate to one another. We also question whether John's characters are as 'transparent' or 'definitely typecast' as Krafft and Collins would have us believe.

The 1980s witnessed the first book-length treatment of John's gospel as a literary work with Alan Culpepper's seminal work *Anatomy of the Fourth Gospel* in which he devotes one chapter to Johannine characters.[6] Culpepper provides a short theoretical discussion on characterization, arguing that John draws from both Greek and Hebrew models of character, although most Johannine characters represent particular ethical types (as in Greek literature). Using the modern character classifications of literary critics Forster and Harvey,[7] Culpepper, like Collins, contends that most of John's minor characters are 'the personification of a single trait' and are 'typical characters easily recognizable by the readers'.[8] For Culpepper, the Johannine characters are particular kinds of choosers: 'Given the pervasive dualism of the Fourth Gospel, the choice is either/or. *All* situations are reduced to two clear-cut alternatives, and *all* the characters eventually make their choice.'[9] He then produces, in relation to John's ideological point of view, an extensive taxonomy of belief-responses in which a character can progress or regress from one response to another.[10]

Culpepper describes almost all the relevant Johannine characters but his characterization is sketchy because his aim is to explore the entire literary 'anatomy' of John's gospel, of which characterization is merely one (though important) aspect. His presentation of John's characters may also be too simplistic: Does Nicodemus make a clear choice? Are Peter and Pilate typical characters, easily recognizable? Is Thomas simply the doubter? More importantly, Culpepper does not classify the characters themselves but only their responses, thereby reducing the characters to their typical responses and hence to types. Besides, his taxonomy of belief-responses appears to imply ranking or comparison, which raises questions: Is the response of belief in Jesus' words (the Samaritan woman, the royal official)

---

from *Downside Review* 94 (1976): 26–46; 95 (1976): 118–32; R.F. Collins, 'From John to the Beloved Disciples: An Essay on Johannine Characters', *Int* 49 (1995): 359–69.

[5] Collins, 'Figures', 8; *idem*, 'John', 361.

[6] R.A. Culpepper, *Anatomy of the Fourth Gospel: A Study in Literary Design* (Philadelphia: Fortress Press, 1983), 99–148. Culpepper does interact with Krafft and Collins.

[7] For Forster and Harvey's character classifications, see Bennema, 'Theory', 391–2.

[8] Culpepper, *Anatomy*, 102–4.

[9] Culpepper, *Anatomy*, 104 (emphasis added).

[10] Culpepper, *Anatomy*, 145–8.

superior or inferior to that of commitment in spite of misunderstandings (the disciples)?

Since the 1990s many scholars have applied the principles of literary theory to John's gospel, which explains the increasing interest in studying Johannine characters. For example, Margaret Davies undertook a comprehensive reading of John's gospel, mainly using structuralism and reader-response criticism, and dedicated one chapter to various Johannine characters.[11] She contends that most of the characters are flat caricatures, having a single trait and showing little or no development.[12] Her conclusions resemble those of Krafft, Collins and Culpepper, although surprisingly she does not interact with them.

Mark Stibbe also did some important work on characterization in John 8, 11 and 18 – 19 to show how narrative criticism can be applied to the Gospel of John, and he was the first to present a number of characters, like Pilate and Peter, as more complicated than had previously been assumed.[13] Stibbe provides brief theoretical considerations on characterization, stressing that readers must (i) construct character by inference from fragmentary information in the text (like in ancient Hebrew narratives); (ii) analyse characters with reference to history rather than according to the laws of fiction; and (iii) consider the gospel's ideological point of view, expressed in 20:31.[14] In addition, throughout his commentary, Stibbe highlights how John portrays the various characters in his gospel.[15]

In a detailed narratological analysis of John 13 – 17, François Tolmie also examines its characters.[16] He undergirds his study with the most extensive theoretical discussion up to now. He follows the narratological model of Rimmon-Kenan (who in turn draws on Chatman) and utilizes the character classification of Ewen, but also refers to Forster, Harvey and Greimas.[17] However, Tolmie only discusses contemporary fiction and does not consider character in ancient Hebrew and Greek literature. The main weakness of his study is his use of various character classifications, concluding that the models of Greimas and Ewen are the most suitable for classifying characters.[18] We contend that Greimas's classification is *not* the best model to

---

[11] M. Davies, *Rhetoric and Reference in the Fourth Gospel* (JSNTS 69; Sheffield: JSOT Press, 1992), 316–49. Elsewhere she refers to the world, 'the Jews' and Pilate (*Rhetoric*, 154–8, 313–5).

[12] Davies, *Rhetoric*, 157, 332, 338.

[13] M.W.G. Stibbe, *John as Storyteller: Narrative Criticism and the Fourth Gospel* (SNTSMS 73; Cambridge: CUP, 1992), 97–9, 106–13, 119; *idem, John's Gospel* (London: Routledge, 1994), 90–96, 121–5. Stibbe interacts with Culpepper but not with Krafft or Collins.

[14] Stibbe, *Storyteller*, 24–25, 28; *idem, John's Gospel*, 10–11.

[15] M.W.G. Stibbe, *John* (Sheffield: JSOT Press, 1993).

[16] D.F. Tolmie, *Jesus' Farewell to the Disciples: John 13:1 – 17:26 in Narratological Perspective* (BIS 12; Leiden: Brill, 1995), 117–44.

[17] Tolmie, *Farewell*, 13–28, 117–24, 141–4. The literary theories of Rimmon-Kenan, Chatman, Ewen, Forster, Harvey and Greimas regarding character in modern fiction are explained in Bennema, 'Theory', 389–92.

[18] Tolmie, *Farewell*, 141–4.

analyse characters since it concentrates on plot, thereby reducing characters to mere actants. Applying Ewen's non-reductionist classification, Tolmie, ironically, evaluates all characters (except God, Jesus and the Spirit) as flat – they have a single trait or are not complex, show no development, and reveal no inner life.[19] Tolmie probably arrives at a reductionist understanding of the Johannine characters because he examines only a section of the Johannine narrative, John 13 – 17 – although he briefly summarizes information from John 1 – 12. This is methodologically incorrect and we contend that one must analyse the entire text continuum of the Gospel of John to reconstruct its characters.

Viewing the Gospel of John as a trial, Robert Maccini focuses on the subject of women as witnesses, looking at Jesus' mother, the Samaritan woman, Martha, Mary of Bethany and Mary Magdalene.[20] Although Maccini admits that men also function as witnesses,[21] we believe his study would have been strengthened if he had studied women and men together. Due to his specific agenda, Maccini provides no theoretical discussion of character and does not classify the characters or their responses.

Another specialized contribution comes from David Beck, who studies the concept of anonymity in relation to discipleship.[22] He argues that anonymity facilitates readers' identification with characters and that only the unnamed characters serve as models of appropriate responses to Jesus.[23] Beck also provides a brief theoretical discussion on character. Rejecting three methods of character analysis (Forster's psychological model, Greimas's structuralist approach and Fokkema's semiotic approach), he adopts John Darr's model, which is influenced by the reader-oriented theory of Wolfgang Iser, and considers how characterization entices readers into fuller participation in the narrative.[24] Beck, however, overstates his case, thereby misreading various characters. First, contra Beck, the invalid at the pool in John 5 is not a model to be emulated since he does not heed Jesus' warning and instead reports him to the Jewish authorities, leading to Jesus' being persecuted (5:14–16). Second, Beck's attempt to squeeze the adulterous woman of 7:53 – 8:11 into his mould of paradigmatic discipleship (even though he admits that the narrative does not record her response or witness) is unconvincing. Third, why do the responses of Nathanael, Martha and Thomas not constitute an appropriate belief-response (so Beck) – especially when their confessions

---

[19] Tolmie, *Farewell*, 142–3.

[20] R.G. Maccini, *Her Testimony is True: Women as Witnesses according to John* (JSNTS 125; Sheffield: SAP, 1996).

[21] Maccini, *Testimony*, 243–4.

[22] D.R. Beck, *The Discipleship Paradigm: Readers and Anonymous Characters in the Fourth Gospel* (BIS 27; Leiden: Brill, 1997). Beck's monograph builds on his earlier essay, 'The Narrative Function of Anonymity in Fourth Gospel Characterization', *Semeia* 63 (1993): 143–58.

[23] Beck, *Discipleship*, 1–2, 9, 137–42; *idem*, 'Function', 147, 155.

[24] Beck, *Discipleship*, 6–8. Beck spends most time discussing the concept of anonymity and readers' identification with characters (*Discipleship*, 10–29).

closely resemble the ideal Johannine confession in 20:31? Finally, do John (the Baptist) as the ideal witness to Jesus, Andrew as a finder of people, Peter as the shepherd in the making, and Mary who expresses her affection of Jesus in an extraordinary devotional act not depict aspects of true disciple-ship? Thus, Beck is incorrect in his character analysis and too categorical in concluding that *only* the anonymous characters represent a paradigm of discipleship.

Like Maccini, Adeline Fehribach also examines the five women in John's gospel – Jesus' mother, the Samaritan woman, Martha, Mary of Bethany, and Mary Magdalene – arguing that their primary function is to support the portrayal of Jesus as the messianic bridegroom.[25] Her theoretical discussion of character is minimal, but she does draw on character-types in the Hebrew Bible, Hellenistic-Jewish literature and Graeco-Roman literature in her analysis of Johannine women.[26] If she had studied all the Johannine characters, female and male, she would have discovered that *all* characters function in various ways as supports in the portrayal of Jesus; they all act as foils, enhancing the reader's understanding of Jesus' identity and mission. Besides, as we shall see, Fehribach's understanding of the role of the Johan-nine women simply as advancing the plot and the portrayal of Jesus as the bridegroom is too reductionistic; they are important in their own right and fulfil larger roles than Fehribach ascribes to them. Finally, driven by a feminist agenda to expose the patriarchy and androcentrism of John's gospel (and the culture of that time), she tends to detect more sexual connotations in John's gospel than the text warrants.

In 2001, James Resseguie produced a monograph on point of view in the Gospel of John.[27] In his chapter on character study, he explores various characters from a material point of view and classifies them according to their dominance or social presence in society rather than their faith-response *per se*.[28] For example, Nicodemus, who represents the dominant culture, abandons his material perspective for a spiritual one, and the lame man, who represents the marginalized of society, is freed from the constraints of the dominant culture and even acts counter-culturally by violating the Sabbath.[29] Resseguie claims that the characters' material points of view contribute or relate to the gospel's overall ideology.[30] However, we contend that the gospel's overall ideology is soteriological rather than sociological because it is directly related to the gospel's purpose (20:30–31) and world-view, which are both soteriological in orientation. Any evaluation of the

---

[25] A. Fehribach, *The Women in the Life of the Bridegroom: A Feminist Historical-Literary Analysis of the Female Characters in the Fourth Gospel* (Collegeville: Liturgical Press, 1998).

[26] Fehribach, *Women*, 15–7, *passim*.

[27] J.L. Resseguie, *The Strange Gospel: Narrative Design and Point of View in John* (BIS 56; Leiden: Brill, 2001).

[28] Resseguie, *Strange Gospel*, 109–68.

[29] Resseguie, *Strange Gospel*, 127, 137–8, 167.

[30] Resseguie, *Strange Gospel*, 109–10.

characters' belief-responses to Jesus should therefore be in the light of the gospel's soteriological point of view rather than their material or socio-economic standing.

Colleen Conway produced two important but very different works on Johannine characters. In her 1999 monograph, she looks at Johannine characterization from the perspective of gender, asking whether men and women are presented differently in the Gospel of John.[31] Analysing five female and five male characters, she concludes that throughout John's gospel women are presented positively while male characters present a different, inconsistent pattern – Nicodemus, Pilate and Peter are depicted negatively; the man born blind and the Beloved Disciple positively.[32] Conway presents a brief overview of Johannine character studies but has not included the monographs of Tolmie and Beck.[33] She also provides an informed theoretical discussion of character in which she leans toward the contemporary theories of Chatman and Hochman, and includes Hebrew techniques of characterization (but leaves out character in ancient Greek literature).[34]

Conway's second contribution to Johannine characterization, in 2002, is more significant.[35] In this provocative article, she radically challenges the consensus view that the Johannine characters represent particular belief-responses. Criticizing this 'flattening' of characters, she argues that Johannine characters contain varying degrees of ambiguity and do more to complicate the clear choice between belief and unbelief than to illustrate it. Rather than positioning the (minor) characters on a spectrum of negative to positive faith-responses, Conway claims that the minor characters appear unstable in relation to Jesus as if shifting up and down such a spectrum. In doing so, the characters challenge, undercut and subvert the dualistic world of the gospel because they do not line up on either side of the belief/unbelief divide.[36] Whether Conway's conclusion that the Johannine characters resist and undermine the binary categories of belief and unbelief can be sustained needs to be seen, but her argument that the minor characters are often presented as too simplistic may be true. Conway's observation that scholars often disagree about what belief-response each character typifies or represents – which is indeed surprising if the Johannine characters are as flat, typecast and transparent as they suggest – certainly needs to be taken seriously.

---

[31] C.M. Conway, *Men and Women in the Fourth Gospel: Gender and Johannine Characterization* (SBLDS 167; Atlanta: SBL, 1999).

[32] Conway, *Men and Women*, 69–205.

[33] Conway, *Men and Women*, 42–7.

[34] Conway, *Men and Women*, 50–63.

[35] C.M. Conway, 'Speaking through Ambiguity: Minor Characters in the Fourth Gospel', *BibInt* 10 (2002): 324–41.

[36] Conway, 'Ambiguity', 339–40.

Craig Koester, in his chapter on characterization, also subscribes to the idea that each of John's characters represents a particular faith-response.[37] Koester's strength is that he interprets John's characters on the basis of the text and its historical context.[38] He sees many parallels between John's story and ancient Greek drama or tragedy, where characters are types who convey general truths by representing a moral choice.[39] However, Koester simply accepts Aristotle's view of character, whereas we have found that character in Greek tragedy could be more complex and round.[40] Moreover, many Johannine characters, such as Nicodemus, Peter, Judas and Pilate, do not fit the category of type; they are more complex, ambiguous and round.[41] Finally, Koester shows insufficient interaction with others who have studied Johannine characters – he does not refer to the works of Davies, Tolmie and Beck, he mentions but does not interact with Stibbe, Resseguie and Conway, and hardly interacts with Collins and Culpepper.

Ruth Edwards has devoted one chapter in her book to Johannine characters.[42] Although this chapter is short and sketchy, she recognizes that many Johannine characters are not stereotypical or 'flat'.[43] She, like Conway, is interested in whether John portrays women and men differently and treats them in different sections. However, while she touches on all the female characters, she neglects prominent male characters such as John (the Baptist), the lame man and Pilate. She has also left out complex characters such as 'the Jews', the crowd and the world.

Margaret Beirne examines six gender pairs of characters – Jesus' mother and the royal official, Nicodemus and the Samaritan woman, the man born blind and Martha, Mary of Bethany and Judas, Jesus' mother and the Beloved Disciple, Mary Magdalene and Thomas – and concludes that women and men are equal in terms of the nature and value of discipleship.[44]

---

[37] C.R. Koester, *Symbolism in the Fourth Gospel: Meaning, Mystery, Community* (2d edn; Minneapolis: Fortress Press, 2003), 33–77.

[38] See esp. Koester, *Symbolism*, 35.

[39] Koester, *Symbolism*, 36–9.

[40] Bennema, 'Theory', 382–9.

[41] Koester perhaps provides some corrective when he says about the Johannine characters that 'their representative roles do not negate their individuality but actually develop their most distinctive traits' (*Symbolism*, 35).

[42] R. Edwards, *Discovering John* (London: SPCK, 2003), ch. 10.

[43] Edwards, *John*, 111.

[44] M.M. Beirne, *Women and Men in the Fourth Gospel: A Genuine Discipleship of Equals* (JSNTS 242; London: SAP, 2003). Most scholars who focus on the female characters in John's gospel (Maccini, Fehribach, Conway, Edwards, Beirne), evaluate them positively. Fehribach, however, concludes that John's gospel, in its portrayal of women, supports the androcentric and patriarchal principles of that time and culture, and does not present a community of believers in which women are equal to men (*Women*, 175–9). S. van Tilborg also evaluates the portrayal of women in John's gospel negatively: in the beginning of the various stories Jesus is inviting and open to women but each time there is a phase in the story where this openness dissipates and Jesus retreats from this relation to women and returns to the male partners (*Imaginative Love in John* [BIS 2; Leiden: Brill, 1993], ch. 4 [esp. 207–8]). In our analysis of the female charac-

Although her agenda is different from ours, Beirne's analysis of Johannine characters could nevertheless serve our purpose because she recognizes that

> these gender pairs serve as a foil for Jesus' ongoing self-revelation and demonstrate a range of faith responses with which the reader may identify. In order to thus engage the reader, and thereby fulfil the gospel's stated purpose (20.31), the evangelist has portrayed them not as mere functionaries, but as engaging and varied characters.[45]

Beirne repeatedly points out that although many Johannine characters are representative of a particular belief-response, they are also characters in their own right and cannot be typecast or stereotyped.[46]

Jo-Ann Brant explores the relationship between the Gospel of John and ancient Greek tragedy.[47] She also interprets the Johannine characters against the backdrop of Greek drama.[48] For example, 'the Jews' are not actors in the Johannine drama but function as the deliberating chorus in a Greek drama – a corporate voice at the sidelines, witnesses to the action. As such the deliberation of 'the Jews' and their response of unbelief provides the believing audience an opportunity to look into the mind of the other, whose perspective it does not share. In this role as a collective, deliberating voice in the Johannine drama, 'the Jews' should not be associated with any particular historical group in Judaism.[49] Brant concludes that 'the characters of the Fourth Gospel like the characters of a tragedy . . . are not to be held accountable, to be pronounced innocent or guilty.'[50] She thus deliberately refrains from any evaluation since she contends that 'the Fourth Gospel does not invite us to line up the characters into categories of good and evil, saved and damned'.[51] Drawing parallels with ancient Greek tragedy, Brant argues that readers are not members of a jury, evaluating characters as right or wrong, innocent or guilty, or answering christological questions about Jesus' identity, but are called to join the Fourth Evangelist in commemorating Jesus' life.[52] 'Instead of asking, "Who are the children of God?" – that is, inquiring about who is in and who is out – the question that the Fourth Gospel addresses seems to be, "What does it mean to be children of God?"'[53]

---

ters in John's gospel, we shall see that the conclusions of Fehribach and van Tilborg cannot be sustained. Cf. Beirne's critique of Fehribach (*Women*, 8–9, 44–5 n. 8, 179 n. 34, 201 n. 21).

[45] Beirne, *Women*, 219; cf. 25–6.

[46] Beirne, *Women*, 65, 101, 135, 167–8, 219. It is surprising that Beirne has missed Conway's 1999 monograph on the subject.

[47] J.A. Brant, *Dialogue and Drama: Elements of Greek Tragedy in the Fourth Gospel* (Peabody: Hendrickson, 2004).

[48] Brant, *Dialogue*, 159–232.

[49] Brant, *Dialogue*, 178–87.

[50] Brant, *Dialogue*, 225.

[51] Brant, *Dialogue*, 225.

[52] Brant, *Dialogue*, 225–6; 259–60.

[53] Brant, *Dialogue*, 231.

There are a few problems with Brant's case. First, 'the Jews' do function as a character that actively participates in the Johannine drama; contra Brant, 'the Jews' hand Jesus over and then manipulate Pilate to pass the death sentence and thus achieve the premeditated outcome (11:47–53). Besides, 'the Jews' are not simply a literary construct that fulfils a particular role in the Johannine drama; we have demonstrated elsewhere that 'the Jews' are a composite group with a historical identity.[54] Second, if Brant had considered John's evaluative point of view and purpose, she would have realized that the narrative itself calls for the evaluation or judgement of the characters' responses to Jesus. The narrative and its inbuilt perspective *demand* that the reader reflect on and assess each character. Third, Brant wrongly assumes that John's purpose for writing his gospel is only to deepen the existing faith of believers when the gospel is also meant to persuade outsiders to believe in Jesus and thereby participate in the eternal life available in him.[55]

The most recent contribution to the subject comes from James Howard, who briefly looks at some minor characters and their responses to Jesus' miraculous signs, concluding that each character represents either belief or unbelief.[56] However, his findings do not go beyond the standard commentaries and his portrayal of most characters is too reductionistic: for example, he concludes that the key trait of both the royal official and Martha and Mary is a 'belief resulting from needs' and that the key trait of the blind man is 'belief in the context of signs'.[57]

In addition to the works mentioned above, there are studies on individual characters that we will interact with in the respective chapters. The commentaries provide valuable information on our subject but their verse-by-verse comments result in scattered images of the characters.

The Gaps

Our examination of recent studies on Johannine character reveals a few gaps. First, these studies either lack breadth (only looking at a few characters or at a certain aspect of character),[58] or depth (only providing a cursory

---

[54] C. Bennema, 'The Identity and Composition of *hoi Ioudaioi* in the Gospel of John', *TynB* 60 (forthcoming 2009).

[55] Cf. C. Bennema, *The Power of Saving Wisdom: An Investigation of Spirit and Wisdom in Relation to the Soteriology of the Fourth Gospel* (WUNT 2/148; Tübingen: Mohr Siebeck, 2002; repr., Eugene, OR: Wipf & Stock, 2007), 107–9.

[56] J.M. Howard, 'The Significance of Minor Characters in the Gospel of John', *BibSac* 163 (2006): 63–78.

[57] Howard, 'Significance', 77.

[58] E.g. Maccini and Fehribach study five female characters; Beck focuses on anonymous characters; Conway and Beirne examine gender pairs; others, such as Stibbe, Tolmie, Resseguie, Brant and Howard, examine only a few characters.

analysis of some characters).[59] This is obviously due to the limitations set by each author's project or emphasis. As a result, certain characters such as John (the Baptist), 'the world', Nathanael, 'the crowd', 'the Twelve' and Joseph of Arimathea have received virtually no attention in Johannine scholarship. Even the most comprehensive and significant contribution on the subject to date – that of Culpepper in 1983 – has scope for improvement. He provides a theoretical basis for his examination of the Johannine characters (although a rudimentary one), deals with all the relevant Johannine characters (except 'the world'), and provides an extensive taxonomy of faith-responses (but does not classify the characters themselves).[60] Our book, then, will deal *extensively* with *all* the relevant Johannine characters *and* their belief-responses to Jesus.

The second observation is that there is no comprehensive theory of character in the Gospel of John. Many scholars do not discuss any theory of character (Krafft, Collins, Davies, Maccini, Fehribach, Edwards, Beirne, Howard), while others provide a few theoretical considerations (Culpepper, Stibbe, Beck, Resseguie, Koester, Brant), but this is far short of a coherent, comprehensive theory of character. Only Tolmie and Conway undergird their character studies with a strong theoretical discussion. Remarkably, there is no consensus on how to analyse, classify and evaluate characters. Should we draw on ancient methods of characterization (whether Hebrew, Greek or both) or perhaps employ modern methods used in fiction?[61] As for character classification, some scholars tend to oversimplify Johannine characters and categorize them as being flat, minor or ficelles (Krafft, Collins, Culpepper, Davies, Tolmie, Koester), while others classify the characters according to gender (Conway, Edwards, Beirne), name (Beck), or dominance in society (Resseguie). Only Tolmie uses a more advanced, non-reductionist classification, but, ironically, reduces the characters to being flat.[62] Regarding characters' responses to Jesus, only Culpepper has attempted to classify them, although we disagree with his implied ranking – the evaluation of 'adequate' and 'inadequate' would have sufficed. Most scholars simply provide a string of character descriptions without collating them or classifying the characters and their responses. We contend that all the characters must be classified according to their responses to Jesus

[59] E.g. the studies of Collins, Koester and Edwards.

[60] A few others also propose a spectrum or typology of faith-responses, although incomplete and sketchy: R.E. Brown, *The Gospel according to John* (AB 29; 2 vols; London: Chapman, 1971), 1:530–31; S.C. Barton, *The Spirituality of the Gospels* (London: SPCK, 1992), 128–30; Stibbe, *John's Gospel*, 124.

[61] For example, Culpepper uses the modern character classifications of Forster and Harvey, while accepting that John draws from Greek and Hebrew models of character. Stibbe contends that John uses Hebrew narrative techniques, while Koester and Brant consider Greek tragedy for their understanding of Johannine character. Tolmie and Beck rely mainly on contemporary literary theories. Conway builds on insights from both contemporary literary theory (esp. Chatman and Hochman) and Hebrew characterization.

[62] Tolmie, *Farewell*, 141–3.

because John demands it. He wants us to evaluate the responses in the light of the purpose of his gospel, mentioned in 20:30–31. This means that we must develop a comprehensive *theoretical* framework to study the Johannine characters.

Third, the majority of scholars who deal with Johannine characterization have limited themselves to a literary approach, although Stibbe and Koester provide a corrective. We suggest that, besides the text itself, the social-historical world in which John's story occurs should also be examined. A combination of narrative and historical criticism, or historical narrative criticism would seem a more appropriate method. We will therefore take a text-centred approach but explore other sources if the text invites us to do so or if those sources can shed greater light on the text we study. Our study of Johannine characters will thus be *more grounded* in the world of first-century Judaism.

Fourth, Conway, in her 2002 article, has pointed out a glaring discrepancy: while many scholars argue that most of John's minor characters personify one single trait or belief-response to Jesus, there is surprisingly little agreement on what each character typifies or represents. She radically challenges the consensus view that 'flattens' Johannine characters to particular belief-responses, arguing that the Johannine characters portray varying degrees of ambiguity, causing instability and resulting in responses to Jesus that resist or undermine the gospel's binary categories of belief and unbelief. Any response to Conway's challenge would necessitate a fresh analysis of Johannine characters. We would have to test whether the minor Johannine characters are as flat, transparent and one-dimensional as most scholars would have us believe. If we find that the Johannine characters are more complex and ambiguous, we would need to explain how they operate in John's dualistic world which only seems to offer the two choices of belief and unbelief.

In sum, we must employ a comprehensive, non-reductionist theoretical framework in which we can analyse and classify both the characters and their responses. We must provide an in-depth analysis of all the Johannine characters that present a (verbal or non-verbal) response to Jesus, using a text-centred approach that will allow us to look at other sources too. Finally, we must explain how all the responses fit into John's dualistic worldview.

A Theory of Character

Many scholars perceive character in the Hebrew Bible (where characters can develop) to be radically different from that in ancient Greek literature (where characters are supposedly consistent ethical types). Most scholars also sharply distinguish between modern fiction with its psychological, individualistic approach to character and ancient characterization where character lacks personality or individuality. When it comes to John's gospel, as we observed in the previous sections, the majority of scholars regard most if not all Johannine characters as 'flat' or 'types'. I question these views and propose a different approach to character in the Gospel of John. What follows is a summary of a comprehensive theory of character in John's gospel, which I have explained at length elsewhere.[63] I began by examining concepts of character in ancient Hebrew and Greek literature as well as modern fiction, arguing that although there are differences in characterization, these are differences in emphases rather than kind. It is therefore better to speak of degrees of characterization along a continuum. Both ancient and modern literature can portray flat and round, static and dynamic characters, although in modern fiction character is far more developed and 'psychologized'.

I then articulated a comprehensive theory of character for John's gospel, consisting of three aspects. First, we study character in text and context, using information in the text and other sources. Since the Gospel of John is a non-fictional narrative whose author is a reliable eyewitness to the events recorded (19:35; 21:24), the Johannine characters have historical referents and must be interpreted within the socio-historical first-century Jewish context and not just on the basis of the text itself. The historical data available to us from other (literary and non-literary) sources should supplement the data that the text provides about a character. At the same time, John may have 'fictionalized' or embellished aspects of his characters by leaving out, changing or adding certain details from his sources – as historians and biographers often do. For example, John (the Baptist) appears in this gospel as an eloquent witness to Jesus while the Synoptics present him as a rough-hewn figure preaching a baptism of repentance. Was the so-called Beloved Disciple as perfect as this gospel portrays him or has he been somewhat 'idealized'? If the Gospels belong to the genre of ancient Graeco-Roman biography (as many scholars contend today),[64] they need not necessarily be historically accurate in every detail. The authors may have used literary 'creativity' but what matters is that the reader does not doubt their explicit or implicit truth claims.

Second, we analyse and classify the Johannine characters along three dimensions (complexity, development, inner life), and then plot the resulting character on a continuum of degree of characterization (from agent to type to personality to individuality). We classify the Johannine characters, using the non-reductionist classification of Jewish scholar Yosef Ewen, who advocates three continua or axes upon which a character may be situated:

---

[63] Bennema, 'Theory', 375–421 (see n. 2 for details).

[64] The compelling case for this has been made by R.A. Burridge, *What Are the Gospels?: A Comparison with Graeco-Roman Biography* (2d edn; Grand Rapids: Eerdmans, 2004; orig. SNTSMS 70; Cambridge: CUP, 1992), 213–32.

- Complexity: characters range from those displaying a single trait to those displaying a complex web of traits, with varying degrees of complexity in between.
- Development: characters may vary from those who show no development to those who are fully developed. Development is not simply the addition of a trait that the reader infers further along the text continuum or a character's progress in his or her understanding of Jesus. Development is revealed in the character's ability to surprise the reader, when a newly found trait replaces another or does not fit neatly into the existing set of traits, implying that the character has changed.
- Penetration into the inner life: characters range from those who allow us a peek inside their minds to those whose minds remain opaque.[65]

After analysing and classifying each character along these three continua, we can create a continuum showing *degree of characterization*. We can plot each character on this resultant continuum as (i) an agent, actant or walk-on; (ii) a type, stock or flat character; (iii) a character with personality; or (iv) an individual or person.[66] In the concluding chapter we shall present the results of our character analysis in the following table:

Character	Complexity	Development	Inner Life	Degree of Characterization
Character 1	–	0	–	type
Character 2	–/+	0	0	type
Character 3	–/+	0	–	personality
Character 4	+	+	–	personality
Character 5	++	+	+	towards individual
Character 6	++	++	+	individual

0 = none, – = little, + = some, ++ = much

Third, besides examining and classifying the Johannine characters, we must also analyse and classify their *responses* towards Jesus. Contra many scholars who perceive the Johannine characters as types, we argue that it is their responses to Jesus that are typical.[67] We say this because John has presented an array of responses to Jesus that are applicable in any time and context – they are human responses. But a character's typical belief-response need not reduce the entire character to a type. The responses of the Johannine characters to Jesus are part of a larger soteriological framework that is informed by the purpose and worldview of John's gospel. John's dualistic worldview only allows for the options of acceptance or rejection of Jesus,

---

[65] Ewen's works are only available in Hebrew but his theory is summarized in S. Rimmon-Kenan, *Narrative Fiction: Contemporary Poetics* (New York: Methuen, 1983), 41–2.

[66] In this study we do not analyse agents, such as the master of ceremonies in 2:9–10 and the servants of the royal official in 4:51–52, since they simply fulfil a function in the plot and do not make any response to Jesus.

[67] In ch. 25, however, we shall affirm the representative value of the Johannine characters.

and hence each response is either adequate or inadequate. We define an adequate belief-response to Jesus as a sufficiently true, Spirit-provided understanding of Jesus in terms of his identity, mission and relationship with his Father, resulting in an allegiance to Jesus.[68] We can, however, not quantify such a belief-response, i.e. we cannot determine how much authentic understanding is adequate. Instead, we determine whether or not a character's response is adequate by discerning John's evaluation of this response, which is determined by his evaluative point of view.

We therefore analyse and evaluate the characters' responses to Jesus in keeping with *John's* evaluative point of view, purpose and dualistic worldview. As the Johannine characters interact with Jesus, the author evaluates their responses according to his ideology and point of view and communicates this ideological or evaluative system to the reader with the intention that the reader embraces it. This is the author's evaluative point of view and the reader's task is to discover and reconstruct it. John's evaluative point of view corresponds to both the soteriological purpose of his narrative (20:31) and his dualistic worldview in which there is scope for only two responses to Jesus – acceptance or rejection. John's evaluative point of view therefore allows for two options – adequate and inadequate. This raises an important question. If the characters' responses to Jesus are varied and form a broad spectrum, how do they fit in with the dualistic scheme that John has adopted? How will such diverse responses fit into the binary categories of belief and unbelief, adequate and inadequate? We shall address this issue in our concluding chapter and also present the array of responses to Jesus as well as John's evaluation of each response.

John's Story of Jesus

A story consists of events and characters, held together by a plot.[69] Before we analyse the Johannine characters we must look at John's story. If plot is the logical and causal sequence of events, the plot of John's gospel is the revelation of the Father and Son – their identity, character, mission and relationship – and people's response to this revelation (see, e.g. 1:10–12, 18; 3:16–18; 14:6–10; 17:6–8).[70] John 1:4 puts the story in a nutshell, 'in him [Jesus] was (divine) life', and the rest of the gospel then expands this concept. The purpose of John's story is to persuade the reader to believe that Jesus of Nazareth is the Christ and the source of everlasting life or

---

[68] Bennema, *Power*, 124–33; *idem*, 'Christ, the Spirit and the Knowledge of God: A Study in Johannine Epistemology', in *The Bible and Epistemology: Biblical Soundings on the Knowledge of God* (ed. M. Healy and R. Parry; Milton Keynes: Paternoster, 2007), 119–20.

[69] Cf. S. Chatman, *Story and Discourse: Narrative Structure in Fiction and Film* (Ithaca: Cornell University Press, 1978), 19; Rimmon-Kenan, *Narrative Fiction*, 3, 6; Culpepper, *Anatomy*, 7.

[70] Cf. Culpepper, *Anatomy*, 87–9; Stibbe, *John's Gospel*, 34, 40–44.

salvation (20:31).[71] Through his story John wants to elicit and increase faith in the life-giving Jesus amongst his readers.

John's story world is both dualistic and symbolic. It is dualistic in that the world of the narrative is divided into two realms or spheres – the realm above or heaven and the realm below or the earth. God, Jesus, the Spirit, revelation, life, light, grace, truth, freedom and glory belong to the realm of heaven; the devil, the world, 'the Jews', flesh, darkness, blindness, death, lies and sin belong to the realm of the earth. This dualism is also found in John's presentation of salvation: people ultimately accept or reject Jesus and his life-giving revelation. John explains that people are naturally 'from below' and in order to enter into the realm 'from above' (i.e. salvation) they need to be born 'from above' (3:3–6; cf. 8:23). Jesus functions as the mediator between the two realms (1:51; 3:13, 31–36) because there is no natural contact between them (cf. 1:10; 3:6, 31; 14:17).

John's narrative world is also highly symbolic. The life-giving qualities of Jesus and his revelatory teaching are often expressed in symbols such as water (4:10–11; 7:38), bread (6:33, 35, 51), light (1:4–5; 8:12), gate (10:9), vine (15:1, 5). John also uses other symbols including flesh (3:6), darkness/night (1:5; 3:2; 8:12; 13:30) and blindness (9:1–41). Symbols, as Stibbe explains, are connecting links between two levels of meaning in a story, between two spheres – the sphere of the symbol itself and the sphere that the symbol represents.[72] The Johannine symbols are vehicles of Jesus' life-giving revelation, but their effectiveness depends on whether people perceive that the symbols are pointers to another reality.[73]

We will now outline the story within which the characters operate.[74] John paints a bleak picture of the world: it does not have a (saving) knowledge of God (7:28; 8:55; 15:21; 16:3; 17:25) and is enveloped in darkness (1:5; 12:46). His verdict in 3:19 is damning: 'the light [Jesus] has come into the world, and people loved darkness rather than light because their deeds were evil.' The world, according to John, is in need of life-giving knowledge about God (cf. 6:63; 17:3). Since people do not naturally possess this life-giving knowledge – they neither belong to the realm of God nor can they access this divine realm – the solution must come from the realm above. As John 3:16–17 states, the Father sent the Son into the world to save it. Or, as John explains in his Prologue (1:1–18), the divine response to the world's crisis was illuminating revelation; the Logos-Light came into the world to enlighten its darkness through the revelation of God. The world, however, did not recognize or accept the incarnate Logos, but those who did receive him, i.e. believe in him, became part of God's family (1:10–13).

---

[71] For a discussion of the textual variant in 20:31 ('so that you may *come or continue* to believe'), see Bennema, *Power*, 107–9 or any major commentary.

[72] Stibbe, *Storyteller*, 19, 27.

[73] J. Painter, 'Johannine Symbols: A Case Study in Epistemology', *JTSA* 27 (1979): 33, 38.

[74] For a detailed treatment of the Johannine story, see Bennema, 'Christ', 107–33.

Jesus' salvific mission is to reveal the character, identity and work of the Father and himself, and the nature of their relationship (1:18; 3:11–13, 31–36; 8:19; 14:9–11; 15:15; 17:6–8, 26). This life-giving or saving knowledge of God comes primarily through Jesus' revelatory teaching. People who encounter Jesus and his revelation must respond – either accepting or rejecting Jesus and his salvific teaching. In order to respond adequately in belief, a person must understand Jesus' teaching. However, John's characters often appear dull, tend to misunderstand Jesus or find his teaching difficult. In short, people lack understanding and hence the capacity to respond adequately in belief. The Spirit is the cognitive agent who enables people to progress in their understanding of and belief-response to Jesus. Those who are enabled to produce an adequate belief-response enter, through a birth of the Spirit, into a saving relationship with the Father and Son (1:12–13; 3:3, 5).

John's concept of saving belief is broader than a propositional knowledge of Jesus. Saving belief is not merely an initial adequate belief-response; it demands an ongoing belief expressed in discipleship. A person is not simply required to enter into a life-giving relationship with Jesus but also to remain in that relationship (cf. 8:31; 14:23; 15:1–10). The challenge is for people to stick with Jesus. As John 6:60–66 sadly reveals, many 'disciples' give up and no longer follow Jesus when they begin to realize what Jesus requires of them. Similarly, when Jesus probes the 'belief' of some of 'the Jews' it proves to have little substance – they are unable to accept his liberating truth and even turn violent (8:30–59). A continuous demonstration of discipleship – for instance, to love, remain in, testify to, and follow Jesus – is essential to sustain salvation. Saving belief for John is then *an initial adequate belief-response enabled by the Spirit and expressed in an allegiance to Jesus that is then sustained in discipleship.*[75]

Let us summarize John's story of Jesus. People do not know God and are not from God. They can know God through an understanding and acceptance of Jesus' revelatory teaching that contains this saving knowledge, and consequently become from God through a new birth. People who encounter Jesus and his teaching and signs, are required to make a response to Jesus and his revelation. John presents a broad spectrum of responses – which we will investigate in this book – but they boil down to two choices. People either accept Jesus and his revelation which brings them into a saving relationship with the Father and the Son, or they reject him which results in immediate judgement and ultimately death (3:15–18, 36; 5:24; 6:35, 53–54). Today, as we read John's gospel, we are confronted with Jesus just as the characters in the story were and face the same challenge: where do we stand in relation to Jesus?

---

[75] For a comprehensive treatment of John's understanding of salvation and the role of the Spirit, see Bennema, *Power*, chs 3–5.

Our Plan and Approach

John uses characters to achieve the stated purpose of his gospel – to evoke and strengthen belief in Jesus (20:30–31). Our task, then, is to analyse in depth the various Johannine characters, particularly their responses to Jesus. Our aim, in keeping with that of John, is to challenge the readers to identify with one or more of the characters and to discover where they stand in relation to Jesus. Consequently, in this book we shall address the following questions. How does John portray and develop his characters, and how do we classify them? How does each character respond to Jesus? From the spectrum of responses John presents to his audience which ones are acceptable? If John sometimes presents characters as being unstable, complex and ambiguous (as Conway suggests), how do they operate in a dualistic world that only offers them the choices of belief and unbelief? How does all this affect us – today?

Regarding the scope of the study, there are two important limitations. First, we shall not study the protagonist, Jesus, but only those characters that interact with him.[76] We will only examine the so-called 'active' characters – those who encounter Jesus and make a particular belief-response to him (whether verbal or non-verbal). We will therefore ignore characters such as the master of ceremonies in 2:8–10, the adulterous woman in 7:53 – 8:11 and the soldiers in John 18 – 19 (they do not produce a response); Jesus' biological brothers (the information is minimal – they simply disbelieve Jesus and are 'from below' [7:3–7]); Judas not Iscariot (he only occurs in 14:22); and Caiaphas (he is subsumed under 'the Jews'). Second, this book focuses on the study of character rather than characterization. Characterization has to do with the author's techniques of constructing character in the text, whereas we shall simply reconstruct character from the various indicators in the text.

We have two main sources of information for the analysis and reconstruction of Johannine characters: the character text (what characters say about themselves and others) and the narrator text (John's commentary about the characters). We shall examine the following aspects: (i) the character's actions; (ii) the character's speech; (iii) what other characters say about that character; (iv) the narrator's speech. In analysing the speech of the character and the narrator, we study both the content and style of that speech since *what* is said is sometimes determined by *how* it is said. It is therefore vital to recognize John's literary techniques such as irony, misunderstanding, metaphor, symbolism and double entendre in order to get the point he wants to make. Besides, characterization in ancient literature is often indirect and

---

[76] For an excellent analysis of the Johannine Jesus, see M.W.G. Stibbe, 'The Elusive Christ: A New Reading of the Fourth Gospel', *JSNT* 44 (1991): 19–37. Cf. Culpepper, *Anatomy*, 106–12. Neither will we examine God, the Spirit-Paraclete or the narrator as characters.

therefore the reader must reconstruct the character's traits by *inference* or 'filling the gaps'.[77]

We shall analyse and classify the Johannine characters along three dimensions (complexity, development, inner life) and plot the resulting character on a continuum of degree of characterization (from [agent to] type to personality to individuality). Besides analysing and classifying the characters themselves, we shall also evaluate their responses to Jesus as John calls us to do. Each chapter shall conclude with a more systematic collation of information about the character (complexity in terms of traits, development, inner life, degree of characterization and response to Jesus) that is dispersed throughout the exegetical sections of the chapter. We shall present our findings in the following table for each character:

Name of Character	
Appearances	References
Identity	Titles given
	Gender
	Age
	Marital status
	Occupation
	Socio-economic status
	Place of residence/operation
	Relatives
	Group affiliation
Speech and actions	In interaction with Jesus
	In interaction with others
Character classification	Complexity
	Development
	Inner life
Degree of characterization	
Response to Jesus	

After we have analysed all the characters, we will plot them in relation to one another – a comparative analysis (see ch. 25). We shall also categorize these characters according to their responses to Jesus since each character's response is typical, representing the response of a particular group of people – both then and now. Although many Johannine characters themselves cannot be reduced to 'types', their belief-responses function as such. These characters must therefore be analysed individually (they are not mere 'types') but also as part of John's larger theological framework in order to develop a taxonomy of responses to Jesus (the character's response to Jesus as typical). Besides, the characters in their entirety (traits, development and responses) are 'representative figures' in that they have a symbolic value or

---

[77] Cf. Bennema, 'Theory', 395, 397–8. Even in modern fiction a character's traits often has to be inferred from the text's deep structure.

paradigmatic function beyond the narrative, but not in the reductionist, 'typical' sense as most scholars maintain (see further ch. 25).

Concerning method, we will be guided primarily by the text of John's gospel as we have it today and use historical inquiry where necessary. This means that we shall use elements of literary-critical and historical-critical approaches. How we approach John's gospel is linked to the issue of where the meaning of a text is located. Traditionally, scholars approached John's gospel as a 'window' through which the reader could peer into the world behind the text. Such scholars have often used John's gospel to reconstruct the life-setting of the so-called Johannine community, which has led to many speculative theories.[78] According to those who take this approach, the characters in John's gospel represent certain historical groups of people in John's own time and setting.[79] However, with the increasing use of literary methods to read the Bible, people like Culpepper consider John's gospel as a 'mirror' in which meaning is produced by the reader in the act of reading. This book shall neither adopt nor reject these approaches in their entirety. Instead, we suggest another way of looking at John's gospel.

Although we do allow that the text shapes the reader's understanding in the act of reading, a reader cannot create any meaning she or he likes. In any intelligible verbal or non-verbal communication, the sender communicates a message to the receiver with the assumption that the receiver will understand the intended meaning of the sender. In written communication the intended meaning of the sender (the author) is located in the text itself and the recipient (the reader) must extract this authorial intention from the text. However, as modern readers we are separated from John's original audience by time, language and culture, and do not share the knowledge that John and his first readers had in common – their presupposition pool. Hence, at times we must reconstruct this presupposition pool to understand John's intended meaning. This reconstruction is possible through historical inquiry into the world of first-century Judaism from the sources available to us, which means that, where necessary, we shall go *beyond* the narrated world of the text. Our task as readers is to approach the intent of the author embedded in the text *and* its socio-historical context. This method can perhaps be called 'historical narrative criticism'.[80] Besides, since character is

---

[78] E.g. J.L. Martyn, *History and Theology in the Fourth Gospel* (3d edn; Louisville: WJK, 2003); R.E. Brown, *The Community of the Beloved Disciple* (London: Chapman, 1979). For a corrective understanding of the gospel's audience as a general Christian audience rather than a specific, geographically located community, see R. Bauckham, ed., *The Gospels for All Christians: Rethinking the Gospel Audiences* (Grand Rapids: Eerdmans, 1998); E.W. Klink III, *The Sheep of the Fold: The Audience and Origin of the Gospel of John* (SNTSMS 141; Cambridge: CUP, 2007).

[79] Brown, for instance, identifies seven historical groups of people (*Community*, 59–91).

[80] See also M.C. de Boer, 'Narrative Criticism, Historical Criticism, and the Gospel of John', *JSNT* 45 (1992): 35–48; S. Motyer, 'Method in Fourth Gospel Studies: A Way Out of the Impasse?', *JSNT* 66 (1997): 27–44; K.J. Vanhoozer, *Is There a Meaning in This Text?: The Bible, the Reader and the Morality of Literary Knowledge* (Leicester: Apollos, 1998); M. Turner, 'Historical Criticism and Theological Hermeneutics of the New Testament', in *Between Two Horizons:*

often inferred from the text, exegesis is the primary means for our character reconstruction.[81] We have now laid the groundwork and turn to the main task – the study of the Johannine characters.

Spanning New Testament Studies and Systematic Theology (ed. J.B. Green and M. Turner; Grand Rapids: Eerdmans, 2000), 44–70. Although J.L. Resseguie presents a more 'mature' form of narrative criticism, stating that the narrative critic should be familiar with the cultural, linguistic, social and historical assumptions of the audience envisioned by the implied author, he nevertheless contends that this information must be obtained *from the text itself* rather than from outside the text (*Narrative Criticism of the New Testament: An Introduction* [Grand Rapids: Baker Academic, 2005], 32, 39).

[81] Exegesis is the process of the interpreter's understanding of the author's intended meaning of the text (cf. P. Cotterell and M. Turner, *Linguistics & Biblical Interpretation* [Downers Grove: IVP, 1989], 72).

John – Witness *Par Excellence*

'Testimony is like an arrow shot from a long bow and the force of it depends on the strength of the arm from which it was shot' — Anonymous

The first human character mentioned in John's gospel is John (1:6).[1] Although John is never called 'Baptist' or 'Baptizer', the references to his baptizing activities in 1:25–33 and 3:23 assure us that he is the same person we find in the Synoptics. Virtually all scholars agree on the characterization of John in John's gospel: he is a witness. The author has stripped John of almost all details regarding his identity and actions, reducing him to a flat character whose single role is to testify to Jesus.[2] This characterization, however, is an oversimplification. Although John is primarily presented as a witness, his characterization is complex and multifaceted – his single trait is not a simple trait. We shall see that John is not a witness separate from his other roles; rather, he is a witness *in* these roles. John's other roles of baptizer, herald and forerunner, teacher, best man and 'lamp' in fact define his role as a witness.

John the Witness

The Prologue introduces John as a God-appointed witness to the divine Logos-Light – Jesus.[3] The author clarifies that John himself is not the light but the one who testifies about it (1:8). The Johannine concept of witness has strong forensic overtones in that the story of Jesus is set within the framework of a cosmic trial or lawsuit.[4] In this trial, 'the Jews' prosecute

---

[1] This chapter is a concise version of C. Bennema, 'The Character of John in the Fourth Gospel', *JETS* 52 (2009): 271–84. In this chapter, 'John' refers to John the Baptist and 'author' refers to John the author of this gospel.

[2] E.g. W. Wink, *John the Baptist in the Gospel Tradition* (SNTSMS 7; Cambridge: CUP, 1968), 89, 105; Collins, 'Figures', 10–11; *idem*, 'John', 361–2; Culpepper, *Anatomy*, 132–3; Davies, *Rhetoric*, 316; J.E. Taylor, *The Immerser: John the Baptist within Second Temple Judaism* (Grand Rapids: Eerdmans, 1997), 2, 195; Conway, 'Ambiguity', 330.

[3] The verb 'to testify' and the noun 'testimony' are used frequently with reference to John (1:7 [2x], 8, 15, 19, 32, 34; 3:26; 5:33).

[4] See esp. A.E. Harvey, *Jesus on Trial: A Study in the Fourth Gospel* (London: SPCK, 1976); A.A. Trites, *The New Testament Concept of Witness* (SNTSMS 31; Cambridge: CUP, 1977), 78–127;

Jesus for his divine claims to provide eternal life, to work on God's behalf and to have a unique relationship with him. As in any trial, it is crucial to have credible witnesses with a sustainable testimony, who will speak up and not remain silent. In this context Jesus calls up various witnesses, including John (5:31–38). John's gospel mentions 'fear of the Jews' as a major factor that causes people to withhold their testimony (7:13; 9:22; 12:42; 19:38; 20:19). As a true witness, however, John does not remain silent but openly testifies before the Judaean religious leaders when they sent a delegation to find out who he is (1:19–28). We make two observations. First, John's testimony before the religious authorities has a cosmic dimension since 'the Jews' are the primary representatives of the world (cf. ch. 4). Second, John functions as a witness in the context of his baptizing activity (1:28), which implies that John is not a witness *apart* from his role as baptizer but precisely *as* baptizer.

The purpose of John's testimony is to elicit belief (1:7) – a life-giving belief in Jesus as the immediate and wider context indicates (1:12; 3:36; 20:31). Two passages demonstrate that John's testimony does indeed cause people to believe in Jesus. First, John points his own disciples to Jesus, with the result that they start to follow Jesus (1:35–39) and soon express their belief in him (2:11). Second, after being threatened by 'the Jews', Jesus escapes to Bethany where many people believe in him as a result of John's earlier testimony (10:40–42). This salvific intention of testimony is an important Johannine theme: based on the Samaritan woman's testimony, many of her fellow-villagers believe in Jesus (4:28–29, 39); the disciples' future testimony is expected to elicit belief (17:20), and John's gospel itself (as a written testimony) intends to produce a life-giving belief among its readers (19:35; 20:31). Hence, testimony is instrumental in people coming to believe and John functions as a paradigmatic witness who is divinely authorized to testify so that people might believe in Jesus.

John the Baptizer

In contrast to the Synoptics, John is never called 'Baptist' or 'Baptizer' because the author has redefined his role from that of a baptizer proclaiming a baptism of repentance for the forgiveness of sins (Mark 1:4) to a witness proclaiming the identity of Israel's messiah (1:31). Nevertheless, John's gospel has not dismissed John's baptizing ministry, as 1:25–33; 3:23; 10:40 make clear.

John appears to move freely in the wilderness along the Jordan valley, between Bethany in Peraea (1:28; 3:26; 10:40) and Aenon in Samaria (3:23). He places himself not just literally but also theologically in the wilderness

A.T. Lincoln, *Truth on Trial: The Lawsuit Motif in the Fourth Gospel* (Peabody: Hendrickson, 2000).

by quoting from Isaiah 40:3 (1:23). In the Old Testament, the wilderness was often a place of preparation and testing, as seen in the lives of Moses and David, but particularly when Israel was led out of Egypt into the wilderness and established as God's people at Mount Sinai (Exod. 19, 24). Consequently, a return to the wilderness would naturally evoke the idea of a new exodus and the expected messianic age (Isa. 35:1–2; 40:3–5; Hos. 2:14–23; Ezek. 20:33–44; 1QS 8:12–16).[5] Since Isaiah 40:3 is placed in the context of Israel's future restoration and baptism naturally evokes the idea of cleansing, John probably viewed himself as the prophetic herald of Israel's coming restoration and his baptism was in some way preparatory for this event.[6]

Before examining how John's baptism is related to that of Jesus, we must first determine with which baptism of Jesus we must compare John's baptism since the author mentions *two* kinds of baptism that Jesus administers – one with/in the Spirit (1:33) and another with/in water (3:22, 26; 4:1).[7] Although in a comparison of John's water-baptism with that of Jesus, Jesus was apparently more successful (3:26; 4:1), I suggest that the author's intended contrast is between John's *water*-baptism and Jesus' *Spirit*-baptism (cf. 1:26 and 1:33).[8] I have argued elsewhere that Jesus' baptizing people with the Holy Spirit is a programmatic statement for Jesus' entire ministry of cleansing and saving people through his revelatory word *by means of* the Spirit.[9] Therefore, while John's water-baptism was *preparatory* for salvation and probably had an aspect of cleansing, Jesus' Spirit-baptism provided a greater cleansing – the taking away of sin – *effecting* salvation (1:29; 13:10; 15:3).

Although we suggested that John's baptism was preparatory for Israel's expected restoration and the coming Messiah, this purpose is subordinated to the main purpose of John's baptism, which we find in his testimony

---

[5] Cf. D.C. Allison, 'Mountain and Wilderness', in *DJG*, 564.

[6] Most scholars today deny an association between John and the Qumran community, which was also located in the wilderness and knew of purificatory water rites (e.g. H. Stegemann, *The Library of Qumran: On the Essenes, Qumran, John the Baptist, and Jesus* [Grand Rapids: Eerdmans, 1998], 221–5; Taylor, *Immerser*, 15–48). Nevertheless, John as a youth may have had contact with the Qumran community but later had a distinct ministry (J.C. VanderKam, *The Dead Sea Scrolls Today* [Grand Rapids: Eerdmans, 1994], 170; J.A. Fitzmyer, *The Dead Sea Scrolls and Christian Origins* [Grand Rapids: Eerdmans, 2000], 18–21).

[7] Only John's gospel mentions that Jesus baptizes with water, and I explained elsewhere that both John and Jesus baptized at different locations until John was arrested (cf. 3:24) and Jesus left Judaea at the sight of possible trouble (4:1–3) (Bennema, 'John', 275–6).

[8] Taylor only sees the continuity between John and Jesus, arguing that Jesus (and later the early church) simply continued John's teaching and baptism (*Immerser*, 297–9, 314–6). However, Acts 18:24–26; 19:1–7 reveal that John's baptism was radically different from Christian baptism.

[9] C. Bennema, 'Spirit-Baptism in the Fourth Gospel: A Messianic Reading of John 1,33', *Bib* 84 (2003): 35–60. Contra J.R. Michaels, who contends that Jesus never baptized with the Holy Spirit during his ministry but only in the manner of John ('Baptism and Conversion in John: A Particular Baptist Reading', in *Baptism, the New Testament and the Church: Historical and Contemporary Studies in Honour of R.E.O. White* [ed. S.E. Porter and A.R. Cross; JSNTS 171; Sheffield: SAP, 1999], 136, 140–41; cf. Wink, *John*, 95).

before Israel in 1:29–34 where John presents Jesus to his audience using an unmatched string of christological statements. Initially, John himself did not know the identity of the Messiah (1:31) but God revealed to him that it would be the one on whom the Spirit descends and remains (1:33). John would then be able to reveal this messianic figure to Israel – and this was exactly the purpose of his baptizing ministry (1:31). Thus, while the author implicitly preserves the traditional understanding of John's baptism, he redefines its purpose in agreement with his characterization of John as a witness. The main purpose of John's baptism was to identify Jesus as the Messiah and to reveal him as such before Israel. As we observed in 1:19–28, it is precisely *as baptizer* that John is a witness to Jesus.

John the Herald and Forerunner

John sees himself as being in tandem with Jesus, where he precedes Jesus as his forerunner (1:15, 27, 30). John enigmatically states that his successor is actually ahead because he was 'first' (1:15, 30) – first in that Jesus existed before John (1:1–2; cf. 8:58) and is superior to him (cf. 1:27).

The portrayal of John as a herald, however, is more significant. Quoting Isaiah 40:3, John declares, 'I am a voice shouting in the wilderness, "Make straight the way of the Lord."' (1:23). Isaiah 40 begins a message of consolation, hope and the promise of Israel's eschatological restoration. In this context, Isaiah 40:3 speaks of preparing and making straight the way of the Lord. To prepare or make a way in the wilderness is a picture of coming salvation, echoing the exodus where God led the Israelites 'along the way' through the wilderness (Exod. 13:21).[10] Hence, 'the way of the Lord' is the way of salvation on which God will lead his people. In John's understanding, the 'Lord' of Isaiah 40:3 now refers to Jesus as God's agent of Israel's salvation. Other passages in Isaiah, such as 35:1–10; 43:14–21; 49:8–12; and 62:1–12, also mention the wilderness-way-salvation nexus. Hence, God's transformation of the wilderness as a picture of Israel's future restoration is a dominant Isaianic motif, in which the wilderness and the new way that God constructs in it evoke the image of the exodus and salvation.

John 1:23 may allude to this complex web of ideas about Israel's eschatological salvation, where John views himself as the herald of Israel's new exodus which will be brought about by Jesus. When we combine 1:23 and 1:32–33 – 1:32 also presents an Isaianic motif since the coming and remaining of the Spirit upon Jesus alludes to Isaiah 11:2 – it is apparent that John understands Jesus to be God's messianic agent of the new exodus who will cleanse and restore Israel by means of the Spirit. Again, we find that it is precisely in his role *as herald* that John is a witness to Jesus.

---

[10] Cf. L. Ryken et al., 'Path', in *Dictionary of Biblical Imagery* (Downers Grove: IVP, 1998), 631.

John the Teacher

In 3:26, John is called 'Rabbi,' which means teacher (cf. 1:38).[11] In Judaism a rabbi had disciples, and indeed so does John (1:35; 3:25). Using his influence as a teacher, John directs his disciples to Jesus. On one occasion, John testifies to two of his disciples regarding Jesus, causing them to leave him and join Jesus, i.e. Jesus' first disciples were followers of John (1:35–39). On another occasion, John's disciples are troubled that Jesus is becoming more successful than their teacher (3:26; cf. 4:1), and in the light of 1:35–37 perhaps more of John's disciples have gone over to Jesus. John remains unconcerned and his teaching in 3:27–30 shows that this is the whole point of his ministry (cf. 10:40–42).

John's gospel does not mention the content of John's teaching, except that it appears to be the content of his testimony (1:15, 19–36; 3:27–30). It includes the following assertions: (i) Jesus is more important than he (1:15, 27, 30); (ii) he is no major eschatological figure (1:19–21; 3:28); (iii) he is the prophetic voice announcing the coming Messiah and the new exodus (1:23; 3:28); (iv) Jesus is the Lamb of God who takes away the sin of the world (1:29, 36); (v) Jesus is the Spirit-anointed Messiah (1:32); (vi) Jesus is the Spirit-Baptizer while he 'merely' baptizes with water (1:26, 33); (vii) Jesus is the Son or Chosen One of God (1:34); (viii) Jesus is the bridegroom while he is the best man (3:29); (ix) Jesus must increase while he must decrease (3:30).

The main feature of John's teaching is that he continually defines himself and his role as subordinate to Jesus. At the same time, John's testimony shows his profound understanding of Jesus. For John, Jesus is the Spirit-empowered Messiah who will take away sin and bring about the new messianic age. Although John never directly responds to Jesus, his confessions regarding Jesus are virtually belief-responses, indicating that he has an adequate understanding of Jesus' identity and mission. We must note that, *as a teacher*, John testifies regarding Jesus and points his disciples towards him.

John the Best Man

A controversy over purification causes John's disciples to complain to their master that Jesus is becoming more successful than he, but John puts himself firmly on Jesus' side (3:25–30).[12] The argument in 3:29 has most significance

---

[11] Nicodemus (3:10) and Jesus (1:38; 49; 3:2; 4:31; 6.25, 11:28; 13:13–14) are also designated as teachers.

[12] Contra those who contend that there was a rivalry between John's disciples and those of Jesus (e.g. R. Bultmann, *The Gospel of John* [trans. G.R. Beasley-Murray; Philadelphia: Westminster Press, 1971], 167–72), or between the Johannine Christians and the followers of John the Baptist

for John's characterization because he casts himself in the new role of best man. He, abruptly it seems, brings up the imagery of a wedding, saying that the one who has the bride is the bridegroom – and hence the most important one – and the best man supports the bridegroom (literally, 'the one who stands with him') (3:29). However, wedding imagery features prominently in the so-called 'from-Cana-to-Cana' section (John 2 – 4). Against the backdrop of a wedding, Jesus performs a miracle in Cana, indicating the arrival of the new messianic age.[13] Later, Jesus' encounter with the Samaritan woman symbolizes the spiritual betrothal of Jesus with those who believe in him.[14] Hence, the mention of Jesus as bridegroom and the then still unknown bride in 3:29 fits within the nuptial context of John 2 – 4 and anticipates the story of the Samaritan woman.

In Jewish tradition, the function of the best man or *shoshbin* was to be a witness at the wedding – a highly honoured position at a joyful event.[15] Four related aspects of John as *shoshbin* are highlighted in 3:29. First, John is the bridegroom's friend (cf. *m. Sanhedrin* 3:5 where the best man is called the groom's friend), denoting his intimacy with Jesus (cf. 15:13–15). Second, he stands with the bridegroom to give support. Third, John hears the bridegroom's voice, which elsewhere has salvific overtones (5:25; 10:3–4, 16). Fourth, John rejoices greatly at hearing the bridegroom's voice since it indicates that the bridegroom has consummated the marriage.[16] I have argued elsewhere that joy in John's gospel refers to a divine emotion resulting from participating in and fulfilling God's work in this world.[17] Thus, John's joy is the joy of knowing that Jesus has arrived as the messianic bridegroom who will bring God's salvation, depicted here as a marriage (cf. Isa. 62:5; Hos. 2:19–20). Jesus will symbolically 'consummate the marriage' in his encounter with the Samaritan woman. Thus, *as the best man*, John rejoices in and testifies to the arrival of Jesus as the eschatological bridegroom to gather his bride, i.e. those who believe in him.

---

in the author's own time (e.g. Brown, *Community*, 29–31, 69–71). For a critique, see Wink, *John*, 98–105. According to Taylor, John posed a problem for the early church because he was a significant person in his time; hence the gospels handle John respectfully yet deliberately reduce his significance, subordinating him to Jesus (*Immerser*, 4–5). Stegemann disagrees that the early church made John inferior to Jesus (*Library*, 216–8).

[13] C. Bennema, *Excavating John's Gospel: A Commentary for Today* (Delhi: ISPCK, 2005; repr., Eugene, OR: Wipf & Stock, 2008), 39–40.

[14] Bennema, *Power*, 182, 192.

[15] C.S. Keener, *The Gospel of John: A Commentary* (Peabody: Hendrickson, 2003), 579–80; A.J. Köstenberger, *John* (BECNT; Grand Rapids: Baker Academic, 2004), 138.

[16] D.J. Williams explains that on the first night the newly-weds retired to the bridal chamber to consummate their marriage, superintended by the *shoshbin*. The bridegroom's voice of 3:29 is probably his call for the best man to collect the *signum virginitatis* – the blood-stained cloth as a sign of the woman's virginity (cf. Deut. 22:13–21) ('Bride, Bridegroom', in *DJG*, 87).

[17] Bennema, *John's Gospel*, 178–80.

John the Lamp

Faced with opposition, Jesus calls forward various witnesses in his defence (5:31–40). Amongst them is John, whom Jesus characterizes as 'a burning and shining lamp' (5:35a). The word 'light' is never used to describe John since this is exclusively preserved for Jesus (1:4–5, 9; 3:19–21; 8:12; 9:5; 11:9–10; 12:35–36, 46) and the Prologue had already indicated that John was simply a witness to the light (1:7–8). Nevertheless, as a lamp John does provide light (5:35b) and we must examine *how* John is a light-giving lamp.

Jesus' statement, 'You sent messengers to John, and he testified to the truth' (5:33) harks back to the events described in 1:19–27. Apparently, the Jewish leaders who attack Jesus here were the ones who sent a delegation to John to find out who he was. John had testified truthfully and 'the Jews' had even rejoiced in his testimony for a while (5:33, 35b). Besides 5:33, the phrase 'to testify to the truth' also occurs in 18:37 with reference to Jesus. Jesus' testimony to the truth is shorthand for his entire ministry during which he spoke God's words, which contain truth that liberates, cleanses and saves (3:34; 6:63; 8:31–32; 15:3; 17:17). All who belong to the truth belong to Jesus and have heard his voice and accepted his life-giving words (cf. 5:25; 10:3–4, 16). Jesus is both the embodiment and dispenser of divine saving truth (1:14, 17; 14:6). John's testimony to the truth, then, is his testimony about Jesus' identity, mission and relationship with God.

Although the phrase 'to testify to the truth' only occurs twice in John's gospel, the concept comes up in other passages. First, in 5:32, God's testimony regarding Jesus is labelled as 'true'.[18] Second, Jesus mentions in 15:26 that 'the Spirit of truth' will testify regarding him – a testimony in which the disciples will partake (15:27). In fact, the Spirit empowers and prepares the disciples' testimony before the world by communicating to them the truth that is in Jesus' teaching (14:26; 16:13).[19] Third, the gospel itself claims to be a written testimony to the truth (19:35; 21:24).

In sum, *as a lamp*, John testifies to the truth, i.e. to Jesus as the embodiment and dispenser of saving truth. Moreover, *as a lamp*, John sheds light in that his testimony aims to elicit belief (1:7; cf. 1:35–37; 10:41–42). As such John functions as a model witness to be emulated. Indeed, Jesus' disciples, empowered by the Spirit of truth, are expected to testify to the truth, which should produce belief (15:27; 17:20), and John's gospel, as a written testimony to the truth, also intends to yield belief (19:35; 20:31). Thus, believers can be light-giving lamps since their testimony to the truth is potentially life-giving.

---

[18] Taking 5:37 into consideration, 'the other' who testifies about Jesus in 5:32 is most probably the Father.

[19] For a detailed treatment of the disciples' Spirit-empowered testimony, see Bennema, *Power*, ch. 5.

Conclusion

The lack of details regarding John's appearance and personal life in John's gospel heightens his characterization as a witness, in that the focus is solely on the one to whom he testifies. However, even though John is a somewhat flat character, his primary trait of a witness is complex and multifaceted. His characterization as a witness comes to the fore specifically in his other roles of baptizer, herald/forerunner, teacher, best man and 'lamp.' These roles serve to *clarify* and *define* his role as a witness. It is as baptizer that John reveals Jesus as the expected Messiah to Israel; as herald, he announces the arrival of Israel's imminent restoration through Jesus as God's salvific agent; as teacher, he testifies about and directs his disciples to Jesus; as best man, he announces the arrival of the eschatological bridegroom; and as lamp, he testifies to the divine truth embodied in Jesus aiming to bring about belief. John *never* operates as a witness apart from his other roles; rather, he is a witness *in* these roles. In addition, John displays traits of loyalty (to Jesus), courage (he testifies before the Jewish authorities), and humility (e.g. 3:27–30).

There is little evidence of John's inner life: in 1:33, he mentions his initial ignorance of the Messiah's identity and how he subsequently acquired that knowledge. Although John never makes an explicit belief-response to Jesus, there is reason to assume that he has done so. First, the author places John firmly at Jesus' side from the beginning, and it is noteworthy that he does not record the episode in prison when John has doubts about Jesus (cf. Matt. 11:2–6; Luke 7:18–23). Then, as the best man, John positions himself at Jesus' side. Second, the content of John's testimony regarding Jesus – he is the Messiah who will take away sin and bring about the new messianic age – implies his belief in him. Third, Jesus' command to testify (15:27) is a command to his disciples and presupposes that the witness has made a prior adequate belief-response. Fourth, if John's testimony aims to elicit a belief-response to Jesus, it would be natural to assume that he has responded first.

At crucial points in his ministry John does not remain silent but testifies regarding Jesus – before the potentially hostile Jewish leaders (1:19–28), Israel (1:29–34) and his disciples (1:35–37; 3:26–30). The aim of his testimony was to elicit a saving belief in Jesus (1:7) – an aim that was realized (1:35–37; 10:41–42). This salvific aim of being a witness is a major motif in John's gospel: the testimony of the Samaritan woman leads her people to believe in Jesus (4:39); the aim of the disciples' Spirit-empowered witness is belief (17:20); the author's aim is that his gospel functions as a life-giving testimony (20:30–31). In short, John is the witness *par excellence*, and in today's world where Jesus is still on trial we need witnesses like John.[20]

---

[20] We disagree with Beck's conclusion that John is inappropriate for reader emulation since he has an unrepeatable role as a contemporaneous witness to Jesus (*Discipleship*, 40). John's

John		
Appearances	References	1:6, 15, 19, 26, 28, 32, 35, 40; 3:23, 24, 25, 26, 27; 4:1; 5:33, 36; 10:40, 41 (2x)
Identity	Titles given	'a man sent from God', 'a voice in the wilderness', Rabbi, 'the friend of the bridegroom', 'a burning and shining lamp'
	Gender	male
	Age	–
	Marital status	–
	Occupation	baptizer, teacher
	Socio-economic status	a rabbi with disciples (and hence respected)
	Place of residence/operation	in the wilderness along the Jordan (Bethany in Peraea, Aenon near Salim)
	Relatives	–
	Group affiliation	–
Speech and actions	In interaction with Jesus	no direct interaction
	In interaction with others	John constantly defines his own status and role as subordinate to that of Jesus
Character classification	Complexity	little complex; his trait of being a witness is defined by his traits of being a baptizer, herald, teacher, best man and 'lamp'. John also shows traits of loyalty, courage and humility
	Development	none
	Inner life	little
Degree of characterization		type/personality
Response to Jesus		adequate: his role as an effective model witness to Jesus and the content of his testimony implies his understanding of and belief in Jesus

uniqueness does not exclude his being an example – today's believers can (and should) emulate John to a great extent (Bennema, 'John', 283; cf. Wink, *John*, 106).

The World – Enveloped in Darkness but Loved by God

'The world remains ever the same' — *J.W. von Goethe*

The term 'world' or *kosmos* occurs seventy-eight times in John's gospel, making it together with 'the Jews' one of the characters with most appearances. We shall see that 'the Jews' are partially synonymous with the world in that the former represent the latter on a micro scale. It is therefore surprising that while the world finds mention throughout the gospel (except for John 2, 5, 19 – 20), 'the Jews' are absent from the farewell discourses in John 13 – 17 (except for an isolated reference in 13:33). In fact, over half the occurrences (51%) of the term 'world' are concentrated in John 13 – 17 – especially in Jesus' prayer in John 17 (23% of all occurrences). This demands clarification.

The Identity of the World

John characterizes the world as the human habitat or realm below in contrast with heaven as God's habitat or the realm above (1:1–9; 3:16, 31; 8:23; 18:36). Scholars have observed that John depicts a cosmic trial between God/Jesus and the world, where Jesus is being prosecuted for his divine claims to judge and give life, and his intimate relationship with God.[1] The story of Jesus and the world is ongoing because after Jesus' departure from the world, the story of the disciples and the world begins.

The world is in a sense represented by 'the Jews': (i) both are governed by the devil (8:44; 12:31; 14:30; 16:11); (ii) both respond to Jesus with hostility, unbelief and rejection (cf. 1:10–11; 8:24, 43–47); (iii) Jesus accuses 'the Jews' of belonging to the world (8:23).[2] 'The Jews' as a group and the world as a system are hostile towards Jesus.

[1] See ch. 2 n. 4.

[2] Scholars recognize that the world is a metaphorically extended referent of 'the Jews' (Bultmann, *Gospel*, 86–7; J. Ashton, 'The Identity and Function of the *IOUDAIOI* in the Fourth Gospel', *NovT* 27 [1985]: 65–8; S. Motyer, *Your Father the Devil?: A New Approach to John and 'the Jews'* [Carlisle: Paternoster, 1997], 57). For the relationship between 'the Jews' and the

The world is in some sense personified or hypostatized as the great opponent of Jesus.[3] Yet, we must bear in mind Bultmann's apt warning:

> [T]he *kosmos* can be described both as the object of God's love (3.16) and receiver of the revelation (4.42; 6.33; 12.47), and also as the deceitful power which revolts against God (14.30; 16.11) and is rejected (12.31; 17.9). Both elements go to make up the concept of *kosmos*, and it is wrong to try to distinguish two separate concepts of *kosmos* in John.[4]

The world is both object – the target of God's love and salvific mission – and subject – the personified world as humanity at large which opposes God/Jesus. In effect, the world is both the *environment* in which the story of Jesus is played out and a *character* within the story. This dual aspect is reflected in 1:11, 'He [Jesus] came to what was his own [the world as environment], and his own [the people of the world] did not accept him.' It appears that Johannine scholarship has not paid much attention to the world as character but simply perceived it as the arena in which the Johannine drama is acted out.[5] This invites a fresh study of the character 'the world'.

The Condition of the World and the Divine Mission

Elsewhere I have explained that John analyses the world as being enveloped in darkness – a darkness of (saving) knowledge about God – and that God sent Jesus into the dark world to save it.[6] In the Prologue, John already paints a bleak picture: when the Light shone in the darkness (of the world), it did not grasp it; when the life-giving Light came into the world, it did not know him (1:4–5, 9–10). In fact, the world prefers (literally, 'loves') the darkness because light would expose its evil works (3:19–20). John presents the world's epistemic darkness as people's inability to 'see' and 'hear', i.e. understand, the things of God (1:18; 6:46; 8:43, 47; 9:40–41; 10:6; 12:40). The world and its people make up the realm below (3:6; 8:23) and have no natural access to the realm above (3:3, 6, 31; 8:23, 47; 17:25). The world is alienated from God – it does not know God (7:28; 8:55; 15:21; 16:3; 17:25), Jesus (1:10; 8:14; 9:29; 16:3), or the Spirit (14:17).

world, see esp. L. Kierspel, *The Jews and the World in the Fourth Gospel: Parallelism, Function, and Context* (WUNT 2/220; Tübingen: Mohr Siebeck, 2006).

[3] H. Sasse, '*Kosmeō, ktl.*', in *TDNT*, 3:894; S.B. Marrow, '*Kosmos* in John', *CBQ* 64 (2002): 99–100.

[4] Bultmann, *Gospel*, 55.

[5] The world as character is absent from Culpepper, *Anatomy*, ch. 5; Collins, 'Figures', 1–45; Koester, *Symbolism*, ch. 2; Edwards, *John*, ch. 10. Tolmie treats the world only briefly (*Farewell*, 140). The only notable treatment of the world is found in Marrow, '*Kosmos*', 90–102 and Kierspel, *Jews*, chs 3–5. However, Marrow's division of the occurrences of 'the world' into neutral, positive and negative categories are unhelpful, not least because it betrays an a priori interpretation without an explanation for putting each occurrence in one of the three categories.

[6] Bennema, 'Christ', 107–33. See also ch. 1, section 'John's Story of Jesus'.

The world is characterized by sin (defined mainly as unbelief) and evil works (1:29; 3:19–20; 7:7; 8:24, 31–36; 9:41; 15:22; 16:8–9). The driving force behind the world is the devil as 'the ruler of the world' (12:31; 14:30; 16:11). He prompts the world to do evil works (cf. the world's evil works in 3:19; 7:7 and the devil as 'the evil one' in 17:15) and hence enslaves people to sin (8:34). People thus experience a spiritual oppression since they naturally belong to the world and are subject to the devil's oppressive rule. The devil explicitly controls 'the Jews' (8:44) and is even able to gain control over one of Jesus' disciples – Judas (6:70; 13:2, 27).

The divine response to the world's darkness is light or epistemic illumination. Despite its darkness and sin, the world remains the world that was created by the Logos (1:3, 11a), the object of God's love (3:16), and hence God sends Jesus into the world to save it (3:17; 10:36; 12:47; cf. 4:42). Jesus comes into the world with the revelation of God, which expels the epistemic darkness and provides saving knowledge of God and life for those who accept it (cf. esp. Jesus as the life-giving light of the world in 1:5, 9; 8:12; 9:5; 11:9; 12:46). Despite Jesus' illuminating revelation, the world struggles to understand, misunderstands or fails to understand it – as is clear from Jesus' encounters with Nicodemus, the Samaritan woman and 'the Jews' for instance.[7] Since, by nature, people are unable to discern Jesus' words cognitively and respond adequately in belief, further divine help is needed. The Spirit is the cognitive agent 'from above' who is instrumental in the process of bringing people to knowledge/understanding, belief and hence salvation.[8]

Since the world is ruled by the devil, Jesus must also deal with him. Contra the Synoptics, John neither records Jesus' struggle with the devil in the beginning of his ministry nor any of his exorcisms. Instead, John envisages one large 'exorcism': in 12:31, Jesus announces the imminent judgement of the world as the casting out of the devil from his dominion. This cosmic judgement is accompanied by cosmic reconciliation, which happens at the cross (12:32–33; cf. 3:14–15; 6:51; 12:24; 19:30).[9] In the light of the persecution that awaits the disciples at the hands of the world, Jesus reminds them of his victory over the world (16:33; cf. 16:11).

Jesus' disciples are included in the divine mission. Patterned on Jesus' mission, the disciples are sent into the world to continue God's mission (17:18; 20:21) with the same Spirit as the driving force behind their mission (14:17, 26; 15:26–27; 16:8–15).[10] John 17:6–20 explains how Jesus envisages

---

[7] Ironically, many who are entrenched in epistemic darkness nevertheless make claims to knowledge: Nicodemus (3:2), 'the Jews' (5:38–40; 6:42; 7:27; 8:54–55), the Pharisees (9:24, 29). Even Jesus' disciples often misunderstand (12:16; 14:9; 16:18; 20:9).

[8] For the Spirit as a cognitive agent, see Bennema, *Power*, ch. 4, or *idem*, 'Christ', 115–20.

[9] John 12:32 does not depict universal salvation because a wider reading of John's gospel shows that a personal response is needed to appropriate the divine benefits flowing from Jesus' death – Jesus died for all so that all *who respond in belief* may have life.

[10] For the Spirit's role in the disciples' mission, see Bennema, *Power*, ch. 5, or briefer, Bennema, 'Christ', 118–9.

his mission to continue in the world. Jesus liberates people *from* the world through his life-giving word – not in the sense that they are taken *out of* the world (hence the need for protection against the evil one) but in that they no longer belong *to* the world (hence the hatred of the world).[11] These liberated believers – Jesus' disciples – are then sent *into* the world so that they may liberate other people *from* the world through their Spirit-informed testimony.

The Attitude of the World

Having described the condition of the world and the divine mission to save it, we must now examine the response of the world to Jesus – and his followers. When Jesus came into the world as the divine emissary of salvation, the world did not know, i.e. recognize, him, and (hence) it rejected him (1:10–11). Indeed, the world does not want its evil works to be exposed (3:19–20), which is what Jesus would do (7:7) and what the Spirit would continue to do in the disciples' mission (16:8–11). However, 1:12–13 adds that some people from the world will believe in Jesus and become part of God's family. Thus, the Prologue outlines the two basic reactions of the world: (i) as 'world' it will reject Jesus and hence its people will remain in darkness and 'from below', but (ii) some will accept Jesus and, through a spiritual birth 'from above', come out of the world and enter into the realm of God.

At his trial, Jesus clarifies that he has openly interacted with the world – teaching in synagogues and the temple (18:20; cf. 8:26). The world 'from below' does not know the God 'from above', and hence Jesus revealed him to the world during his ministry (1:18; 8:23, 26, 47, 55). The world, in its encounter with Jesus, is offered two choices – acceptance (resulting in eternal life) or rejection (resulting in immediate judgement and eventually death) (3:16–18, 36; 5:24; 12:35–36, 46). Some people from the world, such as the disciples, the Samaritan woman and her fellow-people, the royal official and his household, and the man born blind, accept Jesus. The world as 'world', however, will reject him. The world prefers darkness (3:19) and hates Jesus because he exposes its evil works (7:7).

The attitude of the world becomes especially obvious in the attitude of 'the Jews' towards Jesus. 'The Jews' are identified as 'from below' and 'from the world' (8:23), and function as the world's typical representatives. Although some of 'the Jews' respond more positively towards Jesus (e.g. 8:30; 11:45/12:11; 12:42), they largely display an attitude of rejection, hostility

---

[11] Contra Marrow's conclusion that '"the world" is within the community of believers as well as outside it' and '[t]he "world" is firmly ensconced in the community' ('*Kosmos*', 101–2). With Jesus' coming into the world, the realm above has penetrated the realm below, but the two realms and its people are mutually exclusive. Although Jesus' kingdom 'from above' and its citizens (the believers) operate within this world, they do not belong to it (18:36).

and unbelief towards him, and try to kill him on various occasions (5:18; 6:41, 52; 7:1, 19; 8:37, 40, 59; 10:31–33; 11:8) in which they eventually succeed (see ch. 4). However, while 'the Jews' *par excellence* represent the world in its rejection, hostility and unbelief, the two characters cannot simply be equated; rather, 'the Jews' are a *subset* of the world.[12] Moreover, although the world and 'the Jews' are unchanging characters who fulfil negative roles and form a hostile environment for Jesus, individuals can come out of these groups and change their allegiance to Jesus.

The crowd also represents the world in that it embodies its two basic reactions. As 'crowd' it is divided, unable to make up its mind regarding Jesus, but eventually it exhibits rejection and unbelief towards Jesus (like 'the Jews'). Nevertheless, individual people from the crowd respond to Jesus with belief (see ch. 13). In fact, all human beings start out in the world. Within the context of 3:3–8, 3:6 explains that people's starting position is the realm of the flesh or the natural world through a birth of the flesh (cf. 3:31), but a transfer from this world below to the world above is possible through another birth – a birth 'from above' or of the Spirit. Hence, the world interacts with Jesus through people – primarily 'the Jews' and the crowd, but also other characters.

Regarding the attitude of the world towards Jesus' followers, it will closely resemble the treatment meted out to Jesus since their mission is based on, and a continuation of, Jesus' mission. Indeed, Jesus warns his disciples that the world will hate them because it hated him first and they belong to him rather than to the world (7:7; 15:18–19; 17:14, 16), and that the world will also persecute them (16:2, 33). Since the disciples will not be taken out of the world but continue Jesus' mission in the world, Jesus assures them of the Spirit-Paraclete's assistance, his peace (14:27; 16:33), his victory over the world (16:33), and protection from the devil (17:11, 15). Thus, Jesus' mission to expose the evil works of the world, expel darkness and give life (7:7) is continued in the combined mission of the disciples and the Spirit-Paraclete (15:26–27; 16:8–11; 17:20). Although the world as 'world' will not change in nature or attitude and will continue to exhibit hostility, rejection and unbelief, the Spirit-empowered mission of the disciples will yield results in that some people from the world will know and believe in Jesus on the basis of the disciples' testimony and unity with the Father and Son (17:20–23).

Conclusion

The Gospel of John sets the story of Jesus within the framework of a cosmic lawsuit, in which the world brings Jesus to trial. In this trial, Jesus is prosecuted for his divine claims to judge and provide eternal life, to work on God's behalf and to have a unique relationship with him. As in any trial,

---

[12] Cf. Kierspel, *Jews*, 107–8, 153.

it is crucial to have credible witnesses and to keep the testimony going lest the case be lost. In this context we see Jesus appointing his disciples to be his witnesses in the world after his return to the Father. Besides, Jesus fore-warns his disciples that, as his representatives in this world, they too will find themselves accused by the world. John's gospel thus describes the clash between the world 'from above', represented by Jesus, and the world 'from below' (*kosmos*), represented primarily by 'the Jews'. With the coming of Jesus into the world, heaven has penetrated the earth, the divine has entered into a dark world. This causes conflict, opposition and persecution. Whereas John 5 – 12 predominantly narrates the conflict between Jesus and 'the Jews' who are the main representatives of the world, John 13 – 17 informs the reader that the same scenario awaits Jesus' followers in its conflict with the world at large.[13]

Thus, the world as 'world' or realm below will not change in its attitude but remain a hostile environment – towards both Jesus and his followers.[14] Yet, some individuals from the world will respond with belief and escape this environment. Through a birth 'from above', they will enter into the world above, the realm of God and salvation, and no longer belong to this world. The primary conflict is between Jesus and the realm above or heaven, and the devil and the realm below or the world. At the same time, the world

---

[13] The absence of 'the Jews' from John 13 – 17 (except for an isolated reference in 13:33) and Jesus' forewarning his disciples about the conflict with the world, should caution us regarding Martyn's hypothesis, reading John's gospel as a two-level drama in which the story of Jesus is retold to tell the story of a Johannine community in conflict with post-70 CE Pharisaic Judaism. Although scholars have become increasingly critical about the specifics of Martyn's hypothesis, the majority remains convinced that his understanding of John's gospel as a two-level drama is essentially correct. We maintain that John's story is the story of Jesus rather than that of a Johannine community. Besides, John intends to maintain the cosmic scope of the conflict when Jesus warns his disciples (and later generations of believers) about the hatred and persecution *of the world*. That a possible Johannine community might have faced persecution from certain Jews in the Diaspora (cf. 16:2) is beside the point. John's gospel indicates that the conflict between Jesus and the world is paradigmatic for the conflict that *all* his followers will face in *any* time and context -- whether Johannine Christians versus the Rabbis of Yavneh, Pauline Christians versus Judaizers, Christians in Rome and Asia Minor persecuted by emperors like Nero, Domitian and Marcus Aurelius, or Christians facing persecution in many countries today. Cf. C. Bennema, 'Religious Violence in the Gospel of John: A Response to the Hindutva Culture in Modern India', in *Violence and Peace – Creating a Culture of Peace in the Contemporary Context of Violence* (ed. F. Fox; Delhi: CMS/UBS/ISPCK, forthcoming 2009).

[14] Jesus' lack of prayer for the world in John 17 perhaps betrays his knowledge that the world as 'world' will not change. Jesus' intention was not to change the world into a better place but to constitute in it a new society. This community of believers (Johannine images of the 'church' are God's family [1:12–13], the flock [10:16], and the vine with many branches [15:5]) no longer belongs to the world (its source is 'from above' [cf. 18:36]) but still operates (subversively) in this world. Moreover, since Jesus demands from his followers an exclusive allegiance to himself and his rule or kingdom, it will inevitably clash with loyalties to powers, regimes and ideologies 'from this world', which essentially explains the conflict and persecution that John's gospel depicts. Cf. C. Bennema, 'The Sword of the Messiah and the Concept of Liberation in the Fourth Gospel', *Bib* 86 (2005): 54–5.

is personified, functioning as Jesus' major opponent and interacting with him through its people. Thus, the world also stands for humanity, particularly a sinful humanity estranged from God and opposed to Jesus and his saving revelation.[15] The world displays traits of ignorance (it lacks knowledge of God), intolerance (towards Jesus), hatred, wickedness, being unreceptive (1:11; 14:17), and hostility (persecution and murder [16:2]). Jesus and the narrator reveal many aspects of the world's 'inner life': it does not know God, Jesus and the Spirit (1:10; 14:17; 16:3; 17:25), it rejects Jesus (1:11), loves evil (3:19), hates (7:7; 15:18–19; 17:14), (falsely) presumes (16:2), and rejoices (16:20).

The World		
Appearances	References	1:9, 10 (3x), 29; 3:16, 17 (3x), 19; 4:42; 6:14, 33, 51; 7:4, 7; 8:12, 23 (2x), 26; 9:5 (2x), 39; 10:36; 11:9, 27; 12:19, 25, 31 (2x), 46, 47 (2x); 13:1 (2x); 14:17, 19, 22, 27, 30, 31; 15:18, 19 (5x); 16:8, 11, 20, 21, 28 (2x), 33 (2x); 17:5, 6, 9, 11 (2x), 13, 14 (3x), 15, 16 (2x), 18 (2x), 21, 23, 24, 25; 18:20, 36 (2x), 37; 21:25
Identity	Titles given	'from below'
	Gender	–
	Age	–
	Marital status	–
	Occupation	–
	Socio-economic status	–
	Place of residence/operation	–
	Relatives	–
	Group affiliation	the devil, 'the Jews', the crowd, humanity
Speech and actions	In interaction with Jesus	primarily hate, conflict, persecution, unbelief, rejection; some individuals respond positively
	In interaction with others	it hates, rejects, persecutes and even kills Jesus' followers
Character classification	Complexity	little complex; multiple traits: ignorant, hateful, evil, intolerant, unreceptive, hostile
	Development	none
	Inner life	much
Degree of characterization		type
Response to Jesus		primarily opposition, hostility, rejection, unbelief; some respond with acceptance and belief

---

[15] Cf. Marrow, '*Kosmos*', 97–100; Kierspel, *Jews*, chs 4–5.

'The Jews' – Jesus' Opponents *Par Excellence*

'Persecution is a tribute the great must always pay for pre-eminence' — *Oliver Goldsmith*

The term 'the Jews' occurs sixty-six times in John's gospel making this group an important character in John's story.[1] Bultmann saw 'the Jews' as theological symbols, representing the unbelieving world in general in its hostility towards Jesus.[2] There is a consensus within Johannine scholarship on Bultmann's views on the role of 'the Jews'.[3] Consequently, some scholars regard 'the Jews' in John's gospel as a flat, composite character, representing the evil attitudes of the world.[4] However, we shall argue that more can be said about Bultmann's definition of 'the Jews' and that they are not entirely static as a character or monolithic in their response to Jesus.[5] Before we embark on such an exercise, we must first deal with the identity and composition of this complex group of people.[6]

The Identity and Composition of 'the Jews'

Regarding the historical referent of 'the Jews', the debate centres on whether the term refers exclusively to the religious authorities (whether Judaean or Jewish in general), to a religious group within Judaism, to the religious authorities and common people, or simply to Jewish people in general. While the majority of scholars agree that 'the Jews' at least include the religious authorities, many do not specify *which* authorities are in view,

---

[1] We use 'the Jews' within inverted commas throughout the book to indicate that we refer to a specific group of people in John's gospel rather than a generic term for the Jewish race. Hence, our use of the term 'the Jews' does not carry anti-Semitic connotations.

[2] Bultmann, *Gospel*, 86–7.

[3] U.C. von Wahlde, '"The Jews" in the Gospel of John: Fifteen Years of Research (1983–1998)', *ETL* 76 (2000): 53; Ashton, 'Identity', 75; *idem*, *Understanding the Fourth Gospel* (Oxford: Clarendon Press, 1991), 134–5.

[4] E.g. Davies, *Rhetoric*, 157.

[5] See also R.A. Culpepper, 'The Gospel of John and the Jews', *RevExp* 84 (1987): 273–88.

[6] Contra Brant, who contends that 'the Jews' are not actors in the Johannine drama but function as the deliberating chorus in a Greek drama and as such should not be associated with any particular historical group in Judaism (*Dialogue*, 178–87).

whereas others argue (but sometimes simply assume) that the authorities are primarily the Pharisees.

In a recent article, I have made three contributions to this debate.[7] First, sometime during the Second Temple period (but well before the first century CE) the referent of 'the Jews' was extended from an ethno-geographic term for Judaean Jews to a geo-religious term for those who adhered to the Judaean religion (whether or not residing in Judaea). We then argued that John had this extended referent in mind – the term 'the Jews' refers to a particular religious group of Torah- and temple-loyalists found especially, but not exclusively, in Judaea. Second, 'the Jews' is a composite group with the chief priests or temple authorities as the core or in leadership and the Pharisees as the influential laity. The Sanhedrin, the Jewish Supreme Court in Jerusalem, is another subset of 'the Jews', comprising the chief priests and some notable Pharisees, with the temple police as its instrument of law-enforcement. Third, within 'the Jews', John depicts a shift in hostility towards Jesus from a religious-theological conflict with the Pharisees in the middle of Jesus' ministry, to a religious-political conflict with the chief priests later on.

The Roman authorities and the world are not part of 'the Jews' but there are important points of contact. For example, the Jewish and Roman authorities team up to arrest Jesus (18:1–12) and later the Jewish authorities openly align themselves with Rome (19:15), confirming what we know from other sources that the Jewish leaders and aristocracy collaborated with the Roman oppressors. 'The Jews' is also partially synonymous with the world, in that both represent the response of rejection (cf. 1:10–11; 8:24, 43–47) and Jesus accuses 'the Jews' of belonging to the world (8:23).[8] Both the world and 'the Jews' are governed by the devil (8:44; 12:31; 16:11), which explains the murderous intentions of 'the Jews' regarding Jesus. 'The Jews' as a group and 'the world' as a system are hostile towards Jesus.

Having clarified the identity and composition of 'the Jews', we must now examine their attitude towards Jesus. We shall argue that their responses to Jesus are more diverse than most scholars have assumed.

The Conflict between 'the Jews' and Jesus

Prior to John 5, Jesus faces little opposition from 'the Jews'. The only conflict between them is mentioned in 2:13–22, where 'the Jews' are offended by what Jesus did in, and said about, the temple. Most scholars agree that there was only one cleansing of the temple, towards the end of Jesus' ministry (as we find in the Synoptics), and that John has brought this incident

---

[7] Bennema, 'Identity' (see ch. 1 n. 54 for details).

[8] Most scholars recognize that the world is a metaphorically extended referent of 'the Jews' (e.g. Bultmann, *Gospel*, 86–7; Ashton, 'Identity', 65–8; Motyer, *Father*, 57; cf. Kierspel, *Jews*, 214–7).

forward for theological reasons. Thus, the incident mentioned here reflects a situation at the end of his ministry when the chief priests come to the fore. That the encounter occurs in the temple may also indicate that these 'Jews' are the temple authorities or chief priests. Nevertheless, Jesus is aware of the potential threat from the religious authorities quite early in his ministry, and leaves Judaea (4:1, 3) – perhaps to avoid the kind of confrontation John the Baptist had earlier (1:19, 24). In effect, John does not record a direct confrontation between Jesus and 'the Jews' prior to John 5.

With Jesus' return to Jerusalem in 5:1, the situation changes rapidly. From John 5 there is a dramatic increase in the opposition, until the end of Jesus' ministry in John 12 and eventually his death in John 18 – 19. Except for 6:1 – 7:9 and 10:40 – 11:6, all events in John 5 – 12 take place in or near Jerusalem, the religious-political headquarters of 'the Jews'. The opposition of 'the Jews', however, is not consistent since the various subgroups within 'the Jews' have periods of dominance in this conflict. We mentioned that John depicts a shift in hostility from a religious-theological conflict with the Pharisees about halfway through Jesus' ministry to a religious-political conflict with the chief priests towards the end of Jesus' ministry. We shall now examine the various stages in the conflict between 'the Jews' and Jesus.

Emerging opposition in Jerusalem (John 5). The bone of contention in John 5 is not so much that Jesus has healed a paralytic but that he did so *on the Sabbath* (5:16). Jesus' reply in 5:17 only infuriates 'the Jews' further and they accuse him of blasphemy for putting himself on a par with God (5:18). In his defence, Jesus questions the credibility of his opponents as expert interpreters of the Mosaic Law, indicating that the Scriptures and Moses are on his side rather than theirs (5:39–47). Although John does not specify the identity of 'the Jews', the religious-theological nature of the conflict seems to point to the Pharisees. Jesus' comment in 5:33 that these are the same 'Jews' who sent a delegation to John (the Baptist) supports this presumption since 1:19, 24 says that the delegation was sent by 'the Jews'/Pharisees from Jerusalem. However, these 'Jews' could also be the general Torah- and temple-loyalists in Jerusalem.

Emerging opposition in Galilee (John 6). In 6:22–40, Jesus contends with the crowd, but as the debate intensifies, 'the Jews' emerge from the crowd, disputing his claims of having a divine origin (6:41–42) and questioning the need 'to eat his flesh' (6:52). Again, John does not specify who these 'Jews' are, but I offer two alternative explanations. First, they could be the religious authorities, probably Pharisees, who had come from Judaea to Galilee. If 'the Jews'/Pharisees from Jerusalem could send a delegation to John the Baptist in Peraea (1:19, 24, 28), they could well have travelled to Galilee. Alternatively, these Galilean 'Jews' may be adherents of the Judaean religion living in Galilee – perhaps Pharisees. Pharisees were widespread in both Galilee and Judaea, and they had an influential presence in the synagogues.[9] This coheres with the setting of the dispute in John 6 between the Galilean 'Jews' and Jesus in the *synagogue* of Capernaum (6:59).[10] It is therefore plausible that some 'Jews' travelled or resided outside Judaea.

The domination of the Pharisees (John 7 – 10). The conflict between Jesus and his opponents deepens in John 7 – 10, with 8:12–59 undoubtedly being the most poignant episode; accusations fly back and forth with Jesus indicating that 'the Jews' have the devil as their father (8:44) and 'the Jews' alleging that Jesus has a demon (8:48). John 7 – 10 is dominated by 'the Jews' (18 occurrences) and the Pharisees (11 occurrences). In certain passages the Pharisees and 'the Jews' are synonymous: for example, though Jesus' audience is referred to as the Pharisees in 8:12–20 and 'the Jews' in 8:22–59, it is probably the same audience; in 9:13–41 the Pharisees are identical or belong to 'the Jews'. However, 'the Jews' and the Pharisees cannot always be equated since we have learned that the chief priests are also part of this group; in 11:45–47, for instance, it is clear that 'the Jews' must be distinguished from the Pharisees. Thus, the Pharisees are part of 'the Jews' and have a dominant presence in John 7 – 10.[11] This would explain the nature of the debates, which mostly centre on issues regarding the law (7:19, 23, 49; 8:13, 17; 10:34), Sabbath (7:23; 9:16), Moses (7:19, 22; 9:28–29), Abraham (8:33–58) and blasphemy (10:36). In short, it is a religious-theological conflict, typical of the Pharisees who were seemingly more concerned with theological than political issues. Accordingly, Jesus' opponents identify themselves as 'disciples of Moses' (9:28) and 'seed/children of Abraham' (8:33, 39).

The domination of the chief priests (John 11). Having witnessed Jesus' raising of Lazarus, many 'Jews' defect and 'believe' in Jesus (though perhaps merely as a miracle worker), but others report the incident to the Pharisees (11:45–46; cf. 12:10–11). Consequently, the chief priests and Pharisees convene the Sanhedrin, and in contrast to 7:45–52, it is the chief priests who dominate the meeting. They view the incident as a national emergency considering the possibility of everyone going over to Jesus' side thereby risking decisive military intervention by the Romans. It is clear that they are essentially concerned about their own power base (the temple) and position (11:47–48). The chief priest Caiaphas then suggests that in

---

[9] A.J. Saldarini, *Pharisees, Scribes and Sadducees in Palestinian Society: A Sociological Approach* (Grand Rapids: Eerdmans, 2001), 291–5; Taylor, *Immerser*, 161–4; J.D.G. Dunn, *Jesus Remembered* (vol. 1 of *Christianity in the Making*; Grand Rapids: Eerdmans, 2003), 306–8. The Synoptics also mention the presence of Pharisees in Galilee (Matt. 9:11; Mark 2:18, 24; 3:6; 7:1; Luke 5:17, 30) and in the synagogues (Matt. 23:2, 6; Luke 11:43).

[10] In 18:20, Jesus speaks of his common teaching in synagogues and there is no hint that only Judaean synagogues are in view.

[11] Although 10:1 introduces a new topic and the term 'Pharisees' does not occur in John 10, there is no change in audience, and hence 10:1–21 envisages the same audience of 'the Jews'/ Pharisees as in 9:13–41.

order to avert a possible disaster, Jesus must die (11:49–50), and a resolution is passed (11:53).[12] Thus, it is the religious authorities of the Sanhedrin and the chief priests in particular who plot Jesus' death because they perceive him as a political threat.

Jesus' trial and death (John 18 – 19). The passion narratives in John 18 – 19 bring 'the Jews' back on the scene. We have argued elsewhere that although the Pharisees vehemently opposed Jesus, they might not have wanted his death. In fact, the scheme to kill Jesus originates with 'the Jews' in general (5:18; 7:1, 19; 8:37, 40, 59; 10:31–33; 11:8) and the chief priests (11:47–53; cf. 12:10–11). It is 'the Jews' led by the chief priests who hand Jesus over, demand his death and witness the crucifixion (18:28–36; 19:6–7, 14–16, 20–21, 31).[13]

The Response of 'the Jews' to Jesus

Most scholars argue (but often assume) that the response of 'the Jews' is uniform – one of rejection and unbelief. This is probably because the majority of scholars have accepted Bultmann's definition of the role of 'the Jews'. Von Wahlde, for instance, asserts that 'the Jews' display a 'constant, intense hostility toward Jesus . . . which neither increases nor diminishes as the gospel progresses.'[14] We have already noticed that this is an inaccurate assessment. Although our analysis thus far has demonstrated that indeed 'the Jews' and its constituents represent hostility, rejection and unbelief, we contend that more must be said. Despite the intensity of the opposition to Jesus, we must concede that the hostility of 'the Jews' is not monolithic or impenetrable. On various occasions John shows that Jesus is able to penetrate this group with his teaching, and even win some over to his side. We will first examine the occasions where Jesus is able to divide his audience and then investigate the 'belief'-responses of 'the Jews'.

Throughout John 6 – 12, Jesus is often able to break up the hostility of his opponents. Jesus' teaching and signs occasionally cause division (*schisma*) amongst the Pharisees (9:16) and 'the Jews' (10:19–21).[15] But there are other encounters that suggest division. In 6:52, 'the Jews' contend bitterly *amongst themselves* about Jesus' teaching. Next, seeing a divided crowd (7:12, 30–31), the chief priests and Pharisees of the Sanhedrin send the temple police to arrest Jesus, but this only leads to a division amongst the religious authorities: the awe of the temple police for Jesus' teaching is quickly condemned by

---

[12] Not surprisingly, the chief priests also want to kill Lazarus, whose raising triggered off the event (12:10).

[13] Bennema, 'Identity', section 3.1.

[14] U.C. von Wahlde, 'The Johannine "Jews": A Critical Survey', *NTS* 28 (1982): 35.

[15] In fact, John speaks of such a division at a cosmic scale in the reaction of the world to Jesus' coming (1:11–12).

the Pharisees (7:46–48), and even the Pharisees disagree amongst themselves (7:50–52). Finally, 'the Jews' who have come to mourn for Lazarus are divided about Jesus (11:36–37). This division only intensifies after Lazarus is raised, causing many to desert their fellow 'Jews' and believe in Jesus (11:45; 12:11), while others report about the incident to the authorities of the Sanhedrin (11:46). We must now turn to the 'belief'-responses of Jesus' opponents.

The first 'belief'-response comes from Nicodemus, one of the Pharisaic authorities. The Nicodemus story really starts in 2:23 (cf. ch. 9), implying he is one of the 'many who believed' based on Jesus' signs (2:23) but whose belief is questioned by Jesus (2:24). The resulting dialogue with Jesus in 3:2–15 clarifies what is deficient about Nicodemus's 'belief'. Despite his sympathy towards Jesus (3:2), he is unable to grasp the spiritual reality that Jesus is speaking about and does not experience the birth from above into the realm of salvation. While Nicodemus remains sympathetic towards Jesus and willing to take risks (7:50–52; 19:39–40), John's gospel does not record an explicit belief-response from him (see further ch. 9).

The next recorded 'belief'-response is of Jesus' opponents in 8:30, which mentions that many of 'the Jews' 'believed' in Jesus. However, when Jesus probes further into their 'belief' it appears to have little substance since they are unable to take in his liberating truth and even turn violent (8:31–59). On another occasion, many 'Jews' 'believe' in Jesus after they witness Lazarus's resurrection, greatly upsetting their fellow 'Jews' and leaders (11:45–47; cf. 12:10–11). Though this 'belief' may not have been more than a belief in Jesus as a miracle worker, it shows that 'the Jews' do not consistently respond to Jesus with hostility. The identity of these 'Jews' who have come to console Martha and Mary after the death of their brother Lazarus (11:19, 31, 33, 36, 45–46) is unclear and problematic. Although they may have been common Jerusalemites, I have argued elsewhere that it is more likely that these 'Jews' are either adherents of the Judaean religion in general or the religious authorities, perhaps the influential laity as part of the religious leadership.[16]

Finally, even from amongst 'the authorities' (whether chief priests or Pharisees), some/many believe in Jesus (12:42). John indicates, however, that this 'belief' is inadequate. First, 12:42 qualifies this as a 'secret' belief

---

[16] Bennema, 'Identity', section 3.2. To explain the coming of these 'Jews' to Bethany, I suggest that Lazarus may have been a 'Jew', perhaps even a wealthy nobleman (cf. the expensive perfume that his sister could buy [12:3–5]), which would explain fellow 'Jews' coming for his funeral. Although it may be odd that Lazarus as a 'Jew' is identified as Jesus' friend (11:3, 11), 11:45 reveals that not every 'Jew' was hostile towards Jesus. In fact, these 'Jews' were divided (11:36–37, 45–46) – and not for the first time (10:19–21). Thus, it is possible that a group of 'Jews' who were already divided on the issue of Jesus had come to the funeral of their friend Lazarus, and Jesus' raising of Lazarus only reinforced their opinions about him – those who were hostile reported him to the authorities; others who were open to Jesus came to believe in him.

that is not confessed openly for fear of expulsion from the synagogue, which would virtually mean becoming a social outcast. In 9:18–34, John is implicitly critical of such an attitude when he contrasts the positive, bold testimony of the formerly blind man with his parents' unwillingness to testify because they are afraid of excommunication. Second, 12:43 provides another, related reason, that these authorities are more concerned about receiving human praise than God's, something that Jesus has already clarified is an obstacle to real belief (5:44).

A comparison with the world, which is an extended referent of 'the Jews', may corroborate our argument since the reaction of 'the Jews' is in fact prototypical or representative of the reaction of the world at large to Jesus and his followers.[17] Both the world and 'the Jews' are unchanging characters who fulfill negative roles in John's gospel forming a hostile environment for Jesus. However, this does not mean that individuals from these groups cannot change their allegiance. John describes a division of cosmic proportions in the reaction of the world towards Jesus: the world at large rejects Jesus but some people are able to respond positively to him, causing them to come out of their hostile environment (1:10–13). Similarly, 'the Jews' as an entity are 'from below', from the world (8:23), but individual 'Jews' may go over to Jesus' side. Thus, although the essential nature of the world and 'the Jews' remains unchanged, individuals may come out of these groups and start to belong to Jesus.

In sum, although 'the Jews' oppose Jesus and create a hostile environment for him, Jesus is able to get past their attitude end even elicit positive responses. In fact, by the end of his ministry Jesus is able to penetrate this group of 'the Jews' (9:16; 10:19–21; 11:45–46; 12:42). Although the 'belief'-responses of 'the Jews' appear inadequate and superficial, the point is that they do not respond negatively throughout. As a group or character, 'the Jews' represent hostility, rejection and unbelief towards Jesus, but individuals are able to respond positively and come out of these groups. Thus, Jesus was not only able to penetrate the hostile attitude of his opponents but also to win some over (whether publicly or secretly). The fact that 'the Jews' has one referent does not necessitate a single response from all its constituents.

---

[17] Hence, Jesus warns his followers in 15:18 – 16:4a not of the hate and persecution of 'the Jews' but of *the world* (cf. 17:11–19). It is surprising that the term 'the Jews' is entirely absent from the farewell discourses in John 13 – 17 (except for the isolated reference in 13:33). If Martyn's hypothesis were right that John's gospel in reality narrates the story of the conflict between Pharisaic-Rabbinic Judaism and the Johannine community, would Jesus not have warned his disciples about 'the Jews'? Viewing John's gospel as a cosmic trial, I suggest that the real conflict has Jesus and the realm above that he represents pitted against the world or realm below. This will hold true in any time and culture, whether Jesus versus the Jewish authorities of his time, Johannine Christians versus the Jewish synagogue, or Christians in general versus the world (as history confirms).

Conclusion

Most Johannine scholars agree that the term 'the Jews' refers to the religious authorities, who represent the attitude of hostility, rejection and unbelief. We have argued that this is only partially true and provided correctives on both the identity and role of 'the Jews'. With regard to its identity, 'the Jews' are a particular religious group within Judaism – the (strict) Torah- and temple-loyalists who are mainly located in Judaea but could also have been present in Galilee. 'The Jews' is a composite group, with the chief priests as the leaders and the Pharisees as the influential laity. The Sanhedrin, consisting of the chief priests and some notable Pharisees, and its instrument of law-enforcement, the temple police, are other subsets of 'the Jews'. In attempting to identify the role or function of 'the Jews' within the Johannine narrative, we argued that their response is not homogenous or uniform. Although as a group or character, they are Jesus' opponents *par excellence*, representing hostility, rejection and unbelief, some of its members react more positively towards Jesus – even with 'belief' (though this needs qualification). As such, 'the Jews' are far more complex – both in their identity and their role – than scholars have assumed so far.[18]

The main traits of 'the Jews' are ignorance (of God), enslavement (to sin [8:34]), arrogance (9:24, 28–29), resistance (8:37 translates literally, 'my word makes no progress in or among you'), hostility, rejection, murderous inclinations and unbelief, but some also display sympathy, courage (Nicodemus) and 'belief'. 'The Jews' show development in that the reader may be surprised that despite their intense and continual hostility, rejection and unbelief, Jesus is able to penetrate the group and elicit some positive (though perhaps inadequate) responses. Regarding their inner life, 'the Jews' claim to know who Jesus is (9:24, 29) but Jesus points out that they actually do not know/understand (8:14, 27, 43, 47) or believe (8:45–46); rather, they resist his teaching (8:37) and desire to imitate the devil (8:44). Besides, their style of speaking is sometimes comparable to a character carrying on an 'inner monologue' or soliloquy (6:52; 7:35–36; 9:16; 10:20–21; 11:36–37).

---

[18] T. Thatcher, for example, asserts that 'the Jews' and the crowd are background characters – anonymous voices that only perform some necessary plot function and generally illustrate the social environment ('Jesus, Judas, and Peter: Character by Contrast in the Fourth Gospel', *BibSac* 153 [1996]: 436). According to Brant, 'the Jews' is merely a background character with no particular historical referent (*Dialogue*, 178–87). Koester essentially also denies that 'the Jews' refers to a historical group; the term simply designates those who 'exhibit certain types of faith responses' (*Symbolism*, 58). Similarly, J.M. Bassler ('The Galileans: A Neglected Factor in Johannine Community Research', *CBQ* 43 [1981]: 253–6) and R. Fuller ('The "Jews" in the Fourth Gospel', *Dialog* 16 [1977]: 32–3) use 'the Jews' as a term for everyone who is hostile to Jesus.

'The Jews'		
Appearances	References	1:19; 2:6, 13, 18, 20; 3:1; 4:22; 5:1, 10, 15, 16, 18; 6:4, 41, 52; 7:1, 2, 11, 13, 15, 35; 8:22, 31, 48, 52, 57; 9:18, 22 (2x); 10:19, 24, 31, 33; 11:8, 19, 31, 33, 36, 45, 54, 55; 12:9, 11; 13:33; 18:12, 14, 20, 31, 33, 36, 38, 39; 19:3, 7, 12, 14, 19, 20, 21 (3x), 31, 38, 40, 42; 20:19. [In 3:22, 25; 18:35, 'Jew' is used in the singular; and in 4:9, the term is anarthrous in the singular and plural.]
Identity	Titles given	'the Jews', 'disciples of Moses', 'children of Abraham'
	Gender	male
	Age	–
	Marital status	–
	Occupation	Torah- and temple-loyalists
	Socio-economic status	controlling priesthood (chief priests), influential laity (Pharisees)
	Place of residence/operation	primarily Jerusalem and Judaea, but also Galilee
	Relatives	–
	Group affiliation	the adherents of the Judaean religion with the subgroups chief priests, Pharisees, Sanhedrin and temple police. Other affiliated groups: crowd, world, Romans, devil
Speech and actions	In interaction with Jesus	heated debates, hostility, unbelief, 'belief', division
	In interaction with others	feared by common people, controlled by the devil, collaborate with the Romans
Character classification	Complexity	complex; multiple traits: hostility, ignorance, enslavement, arrogance, resistance, rejection, murderousness, unbelief; some exhibit positive traits of sympathy, courage and 'belief'
	Development	despite their overall negative response, Jesus is able to penetrate the group and elicit positive responses
	Inner life	much
Degree of characterization		corporate personality
Response to Jesus		inadequate (as group): rejection, unbelief, hostility, opposition, persecution, plans to kill Jesus.

Andrew and Philip – Finders of People

'Jesus said to them, "Follow me, and I will make you fishers of people"' — Mark 1:17

Andrew and Philip have a stronger presence in John's gospel (5 and 12 occurrences respectively) than in the Synoptics, but, more importantly, they have a distinct role to play and always appear together – 1:35–51; 6:1–9; 12:20–26 – except for 14:8–9 where only Philip is present.[1] Information about the identity and social status of Andrew and Philip is sparse. Both are Galileans, originating from Bethsaida (1:44), a town near the Sea of Galilee meaning 'house of fishing'. John does not mention their profession, but if the two unnamed disciples in 21:2 refer to Andrew and Philip, they may have been fishermen – in keeping with (the name of) their hometown.[2] We know Andrew has a brother called Simon Peter (1:40), who has a prominent role in this gospel (see ch. 6), and before he joined Jesus, Andrew was a disciple of John (the Baptist) (1:35–40).

Bringing People to Jesus

The first time the duo turns up is in 1:35–51, which describes the gathering of Jesus' first disciples. John 1:35–51 contains two sections – 1:35–42 and 1:43–51 – which have remarkable parallels. First, both sections open with 'the next day' (1:35, 43). Second, in both sections people acknowledge the

---

[1] In the Synoptics, Philip only appears once – in the list of the twelve apostles (Matt. 10:3; Mark 3:18; Luke 6:14), and although Andrew has more appearances, he has no role of his own but simply operates in the shadow of his famous brother (Matt. 4:18; 10:2; Mark 1:16, 29; 3:18; 13:3; Luke 6:14).

[2] Peter seems to have been a fisherman since 21:3 can hardly imply that he went fishing for the first time or for leisure, and hence his brother Andrew was probably also one (cf. Matt. 4:18; Mark 1:16). Besides, the presence of Peter and Nathanael in 21:2 could imply the presence of their finders Andrew and Philip. However, if one of the two unnamed disciples in 21:2 is the Beloved Disciple mentioned in 21:7 (so F.J. Moloney; *The Gospel of John* [SP 4; Collegeville: Liturgical Press, 1998], 548–9; R. Bauckham, *Jesus and the Eyewitnesses: The Gospels as Eyewitness Testimony* [Grand Rapids: Eerdmans, 2006], 415), it would exclude the presence of Andrew and Philip, although the Beloved Disciple may also have been one of the sons of Zebedee in 21:2 (see ch. 21).

call to follow Jesus as a disciple (1:37, 43). Third, the invitation 'come and see' is found both in 1:39 and 1:46. Fourth, Andrew finds Peter (1:41) and Philip finds Nathanael (1:45). As an aside, 1:43 translates literally, 'The next day *he* wanted to go to Galilee and *he* found Philip. And Jesus said to him, "Follow me."' Since the subject 'he' is not specified, it could be either Jesus or Andrew. Perhaps the latter is preferable because it makes sense of the 'first' in 1:41, so that Andrew *first* finds Peter and *then* Philip.[3] Fifth, the finder (Andrew, Philip) has some perception about Jesus' identity, which he then reveals to the person found (1:41, 45). Sixth, Jesus provides revelation about the person found (1:42, 48), although John records only Nathanael's response to Jesus' revelation (1:49).

John may have recorded the two incidents with such striking similarity because he wants to highlight important aspects of discipleship. First, people are invited to come to Jesus; then follow him and remain with him as disciples. The invitation to come to Jesus is more specifically the invitation 'to come and see', i.e. to find out for themselves. In 1:39, Jesus' 'come and you will see' is an invitation to undertake empirical research – and they do. In 1:46, Philip does not argue with Nathanael but simply extends the invitation 'come and see', i.e. he invites Nathanael to investigate for himself (1:46). John has invested the verb 'to remain, to abide' with theological meaning in his gospel so that 'they remained with him' in 1:39 probably indicates the need to stick with Jesus as disciples.[4] Second, people are to testify to others and bring them to Jesus, who will do the rest. There is, in fact, a chain of testimony: John (the Baptist) testifies to Andrew and another disciple (1:35–36); Andrew testifies to Peter (and possibly Philip); Philip in turn testifies to Nathanael. There seems to be a correlation between being a disciple and a witness, in that a true disciple will bear witness to other people about Jesus.

We must further examine the Greek verb *heuriskō* ('to find') in relation to the concept of bringing people to Jesus. Besides Jesus himself finding people (5:14; 9:35; cf. 11:17), the only instances of people finding others in order to testify about Jesus and bring them to him are found in 1:41, 43, 45. Andrew finds his brother Peter, testifies to him and introduces him to Jesus (1:41–42). Next, we tentatively suggested that Andrew also finds Philip and brings him to Jesus (1:43). In turn, Philip finds Nathanael, testifies about Jesus and invites him to come to Jesus – and he does (1:45–47). Later, when Jesus sends his disciples into the world (17:18) to testify about him (15:27) so that people may come to believe in him (17:20), the same dynamic is at work because the disciples' mission is 'to find' people and bring them to

---

[3] Cf. D.A. Carson, *The Gospel according to John* (Leicester: IVP, 1991), 157–8; C.R. Matthews, *Philip: Apostle and Evangelist. Configurations of a Tradition* (NovTSup 105; Leiden: Brill, 2002), 107–8. K. Quast, however, argues that 'first' in 1:41 simply means that Andrew found Peter before he did anything else (*Peter and the Beloved Disciple: Figures for a Community in Crisis* [JSNTS 32; Sheffield: JSOT Press, 1989], 32–5).

[4] Cf. the discipleship terminology in 1:38: to follow (as a disciple) and to seek (Jesus).

Jesus. Indeed, Jesus' command to his disciples to cast the net where they would *find* fish (21:6) is symbolic of the disciples' future mission – to find people. The miraculous catch of fish also foreshadows the success of the disciples' impending mission. Thus, from the time they start following Jesus, Andrew and Philip set an example of finding people who in turn become Jesus' followers.

We also note that the finder (Andrew, Philip) has some perception about Jesus' identity, which he then reveals to the person found (Peter, Nathanael). Andrew perceives Jesus as the expected Messiah (1:41), which he probably infers from John's revelation of Jesus in 1:29–34 since 1:32 alludes to the Spirit-endowed messiah of Isaiah 11:2. Perhaps Isaiah 42:1 is also in view if the textual variant 'the chosen one of God' in 1:34 is the original reading. Philip probably perceives Jesus' identity in terms of the Prophet like Moses mentioned in Deuteronomy 18:15–18 (1:45). Hence, both Andrew and Philip view Jesus as an important end-time figure and their testimony reflects their understanding of Jesus' true identity. The finder first needs to grasp Jesus' identity before he can testify and bring others to him.

The Challenge to Think 'from Above'

John 6 contains the story of Jesus miraculously feeding a multitude followed by a discourse in which he reveals himself as the true bread from heaven who gives life to the world. A large crowd follows Jesus (6:2) but before he tests the crowd's sincerity and potential for discipleship (cf. ch. 13), he first tests his disciples, represented by Philip and Andrew (6:3–9).

Jesus poses a challenge to Philip about feeding the large crowd because he wants to test him (6:5–6). The disciples have been with Jesus for just over two years, seen him perform several miracles and heard most of his teaching.[5] Hence, Jesus may have wanted to test them regarding their ability to think about a situation from a divine perspective – a challenge to think in terms of Jesus' identity and potential. Philip, it appears, has not made progress in this regard since he sees no viable solution to the situation (6:7). Andrew is more inquiring and resourceful – he finds a boy with some bread and fish – but he also approaches the situation from a human perspective and reasons that the boy's resources are clearly insufficient for the large crowd (6:8–9). Both Philip and Andrew think in human terms and fail to see the situation from a divine perspective. Indeed, within John's dualism of the realm above and the realm below, they fail the challenge to think

---

[5] Both 2:23 and 6:4 mention the Passover, occurring in March/April, and 5:1 may refer to the Feast of Weeks around May/June. Then, 4:35 mentions that the summer harvest in May/June is four months away, putting the context of 4:35 around January/February. Hence, another, unrecorded Passover must have gone by between 4:35 and 5:1 so that the period between 2:23 and 6:4 is two years.

'from above'. Perhaps Jesus even wants to develop Philip and Andrew's 'finding' qualities in that finding a solution for this situation requires an approach 'from above'.

Thinking 'from above' is thinking as one who belongs to the realm above and realizes its potential and resources. The realm above is characterized by or as heaven, Father, Son, Spirit, revelation, knowledge, freedom, light, love, truth, life (e.g. 1:32; 3:13, 31; 6:38; 12:28). Later on, Jesus reveals to his disciples that they will receive the Spirit to assist them to think 'from above' (14:16–17) and that the resources 'from above' are available to them if they ask the Father in his name (14:13–14; 15:7; 16:23–24).[6]

Bringing More People to Jesus

The last appearance of Andrew and Philip is in 12:20–22, towards the end of Jesus' public ministry. The Passover is approaching and, besides the expected Jewish multitude, many Gentile proselytes or God-fearers would have attended the festival. Therefore, the presence of some 'Greeks' or Gentiles is not surprising (12:20). What is surprising is that they wish to see Jesus (12:21) – perhaps they had heard stories about him or witnessed the crowd's 'coronation' of Jesus in 12:12–13.

When this is reported to Jesus, he understands it as the arrival of the hour of his glorification, i.e. the hour of his coming death and departure from this world (12:22–23). Jesus' perception of the event is somewhat puzzling but I suggest two explanations. First, in 12:9–18, a great crowd enthusiastically welcomed Jesus as the expected Messiah (though with the misplaced notion of Jesus as a military leader), causing the Pharisees to sneer that the world is following him. Ironically, their mocking suggestion is realized when a representation of the world – the Jewish crowd and the non-Jewish God-fearers in 12:20–21 – indeed 'follows' him (cf. the drawing of all people to himself in 12:32). Second, Jesus may have had in mind a previous conversation with 'the Jews' (7:32–36) – the only other passage where the word 'Greek' or 'Gentile' occurs. There Jesus had announced to 'the Jews' that his departure from this world was imminent, to which they replied sarcastically that surely he was not going into the Diaspora to teach the Gentiles. Ironically, the mock prediction of 'the Jews' now appears to be fulfilled; but, instead of Jesus going into the Diaspora to teach the Gentiles, they come to him.

It is important to note that, once again, Andrew and Philip play a role in bringing people to Jesus. Strictly speaking Philip does not find these Gentiles – they approach him – but he is the first link in the chain of events (12:21). Philip goes and tells Andrew, and then both of them go and tell

---

[6] For the Spirit's cognitive aid, see Bennema, *Power*, ch. 5, or briefer, Bennema, 'Christ', 116–9. For the concept 'to ask in Jesus' name', see Bennema, *John's Gospel*, 154–6, 166, 179.

Jesus (12:22). Perhaps Philip goes to Andrew first rather than Jesus because Andrew may have found Philip (1:43), and hence Philip perceives Andrew as his mentor or senior. The text does not clarify whether Andrew and Philip are surprised that non-Jews are looking for Jesus – perhaps they have been conditioned to the universal scope of Jesus' mission through his encounters with the Samaritans and the (possibly non-Jewish) royal official. Thus, Andrew and Philip continue to play their role of 'finding' people and introducing them to Jesus.[7] Besides, if bringing these Gentiles to Jesus reflects their understanding of Jesus' mission beyond Israel's ethnic borders, Andrew and Philip's 'finding' abilities show development. Philip makes one more appearance, to which we now turn.

Philip's Misunderstanding

Philip's last appearance in the gospel does not depict him in his typical role as 'finder' but shows him misunderstanding Jesus' assertion that the disciples have seen the Father (14:7–8). Krafft argues that since Philip has not understood that the Father is present in Jesus, he has not understood the concept of discipleship because, rather than bringing people externally to Jesus, discipleship is letting people meet Jesus who indwells the believer.[8] Nevertheless, misunderstanding is not characteristic of Philip alone; rather, Jesus' disciples frequently misunderstand him (see ch. 14).[9]

Conclusion

John has paired Andrew and Philip because they have a similar role as 'finders' where they testify about Jesus and bring people to him. If 1:35–51 depicts a paradigm for making disciples – coming to and remaining with Jesus, testifying about him, bringing people to him – then Andrew and Philip are exemplary disciplemakers. In their ability to find people, testify about Jesus and introduce them to him, Andrew and Philip also foreshadow the

[7] Köstenberger suggests that these 'Greeks' single out Philip (and Andrew) because of their Greek names (*John*, 377–8). It seems far-fetched to say that Philip 'represents the Greek believer who introduces others to Jesus' because of his Greek name (so Collins, 'Figures', 25; cf. T.L. Brodie, *The Gospel according to John: A Literary and Theological Commentary* [New York: OUP, 1993], 165–6; Keener, *Gospel*, 480). Matthews contends that there are allusions to Philip's mission to non-Jews in Acts 8 and the later *Acts of Philip* (*Philip*, 116–7). G.R. O'Day understands the Greeks' request to 'see' Jesus as their desire to become disciples and hence sees a connection between the call of the first Jewish disciples, including Andrew and Philip (cf. 'come and see' in 1:39, 46), and the arrival of the first Gentile disciples (*The Gospel of John* [NIB 9; Nashville: Abingdon Press, 1995], 710).

[8] Krafft, 'Personen', 28–9.

[9] *Pace* Collins, who views Philip as *representing* the disciples' misunderstanding (both in 6:5–7 and 14:8–9) ('Figures', 24).

disciples' future mission, symbolized by the miraculous 'finding' of 153 fish in John 21.[10] Although their main trait is the ability to find people and bring them to Jesus, they also display traits of being inquiring (1:39), perceptive (1:41, 45) and resourceful (6:8–9) but sometimes dull (6:7–9; 14:8–9). We can possibly trace a little character development since their early traits of perception and being keen to inquire are somewhat negated by their later lack of perception and understanding. If one has to compare Andrew with Philip, Andrew seems to come off somewhat better: he possibly found Philip (1:43); is more resourceful than Philip (6:8–9); Philip reports to him (12:22); Philip shows poor understanding (14:8–9).[11]

Andrew and Philip		
Appearances	References	Andrew: 1:40; 1:42; 6:8; 12:22 (2x); Philip: 1:43; 1:44; 1:45; 1:46; 1:48; 6:5; 6:7; 12:21; 12:22 (2x); 14:8; 14:9
Identity	Titles given	–
	Gender	male
	Age	–
	Marital status	–
	Occupation	probably fishermen
	Socio-economic status	–
	Place of residence/operation	both come from Bethsaida in Galilee
	Relatives	Andrew is Peter's brother
	Group affiliation	both belong to 'the Twelve'; Andrew was a former disciple of John
Speech and actions	In interaction with Jesus	coming to and remaining with Jesus
	In interaction with others	testifying about Jesus, bringing people to him
Character classification	Complexity	uncomplicated; main trait: the ability of finding people and introducing them to Jesus; other traits: perceptive, inquiring, resourceful, dull
	Development	little
	Inner life	none
Degree of characterization		type
Response to Jesus		adequate: exemplary disciples

---

[10] Cf. Edwards' portrayal of Andrew and Philip as 'model "missionaries"' (*John*, 100).

[11] Culpepper's depiction of Philip as less perceptive than Andrew because Philip failed both the 'bread' test and the 'Greek' test (*Anatomy*, 120) is untenable since both did not think 'from above' in 6:7–9, and 12:20–22 makes no distinction between the actions of Andrew and Philip.

Simon Peter – A Shepherd in the Making

'Leaders aren't born, they are made' — Vince Lombardi

Peter is probably the disciple we know and like best – perhaps because many sympathize with him.[1] Although John's gospel mentions Simon Peter more often than all the disciples, it only provides few details about his identity. First, he is from the town of Bethsaida (1:44), at the Sea of Galilee. Bethsaida means 'house of fishing' or 'fisherman's house'. John 21:2–3 suggests that Peter was probably a fisherman before he joined Jesus – perhaps even owning a boat.[2] Second, Peter had a brother Andrew and their father was called 'John' (1:40–42). Third, his original name was 'Simon' but Jesus renames him 'Peter' (1:42). A change of name was a significant event since, in ancient thought, the name usually reflected aspects of the person's character. The Greek 'Peter' and its Aramaic equivalent 'Cephas' play on the word 'rock' or 'bedrock' in Greek (*petra*) and Aramaic (*kepha*) respectively. Simon's change of name very likely reflects the tradition recorded in Matthew 16:13–20 but John does not expand on its significance.[3] Peter's true significance is revealed only in John 21 – an account only preserved in this gospel.

Peter's story is one about leadership and there are various indications that he has a leading position among 'the Twelve': he speaks on their behalf

---

[1] According to most scholars, however, Peter does not fare well in John's gospel (B.B. Blaine, *Peter in the Gospel of John: The Making of an Authentic Disciple* [SBLAB 27; Leiden: Brill, 2007], 1 n. 1). Blaine himself argues for a very positive portrayal of Peter.

[2] Cf. the Synoptic tradition (Mark 1:16; Matt. 4:18; Luke 5:2–3).

[3] Although A.J. Droge is right that we should not impute the characterization of Peter as a 'rock' in Matt. 16:18–19 to John's gospel (contra R. Schnackenburg, *The Gospel according to St John* [3 vols; London: Burns & Oates, 1968–82], 1:312), his explanation that Peter is a 'rock' because of his obtuseness and persistent inability to understand Jesus is unwarranted ('The Status of Peter in the Fourth Gospel: A Note on John 18:10–11', *JBL* 109 [1990]: 308). The mention of Simon's new name may simply reflect John's awareness of the Peter tradition, on which he does not want to expand because he will develop the character of Peter in terms of a shepherd (as we shall see). Cf. D. Tovey, who states that Jesus' giving Peter a new name in 1:42 signals that Peter embarks upon a process of becoming a new person – he *is* Simon, he *will be* called Cephas (*Narrative Art and Act in the Fourth Gospel* [JSNTS 151; Sheffield: SAP, 1997], 135). Similarly, Blaine argues that Peter does not receive his new name because he is *presently* 'rock-like' but in anticipation of who he will become (*Peter*, 38).

(6:68–69 uses plurals); he takes initiative (13:24; 18:10; 21:3); he is sometimes approached or named first (18:15; 20:2; 21:2); he often responds first (6:68–69; 13:6, 36; 21:11).

Peter's Confession of Jesus

Although Peter is also among the first of Jesus' disciples in John's gospel, he does not immediately acquire the high profile that he receives in the Synoptic tradition.[4] First, Peter is introduced to Jesus by his brother rather than being called directly by Jesus (1:40–42). Then, Jesus' revelatory insight into Peter's life and his change of name do not elicit a faith-confession from him (1:42), whereas Andrew, Philip and Nathanael all display a true understanding of Jesus' identity (1:41, 45, 49). However, John may intentionally have delayed Peter's confession until 6:68–69, where he functions as the spokesman of 'the Twelve', as the use of the plurals in 6:68–69 indicate.

Peter's profession comes at a crucial junction in Jesus' ministry since John 6 is a story of rejection and sifting. First, the crowd fails to live up to the expectation that is created (6:2, 26, 36). Then, 'the Jews' emerge from the crowd as a hostile subgroup who rejects Jesus (6:41–59). Finally, many of Jesus' disciples find his teaching too hard or scandalous to accept and they defect (6:60–66). After this, Jesus asks 'the Twelve' whether they also want to leave – although the Greek indicates that Jesus expects the answer 'no' (6:67). Indeed, Peter's declaration on behalf of 'the Twelve' affirms that they will stick to Jesus (6:68–69). Yet, Jesus has greater insight than Peter, indicating that even amongst 'the Twelve' one will eventually defect (6:70–71).[5]

Peter's rhetorical question, 'Lord, to whom shall we go?', indicates that, for him, there was no alternative and hence defection was not an option. Peter's question is accompanied by a twofold confession: (i) Jesus has words of eternal life; (ii) Jesus is the Holy One of God. The first part harks back to Jesus' own assertion in 6:63 that his words are Spirit and life, indicating that the Spirit gives life by revealing the meaning of Jesus' life-giving teaching.[6] This is probably more than an intellectual assent to a proposition (although it is this also); Peter (and the others) have probably already experienced the Spirit and the life that is available in Jesus during his ministry (cf. 14:17).[7]

The second part of Peter's confession – Jesus is 'the Holy One of God' – only occurs once in John's gospel and differs from Peter's confession of Jesus as *the Christ* (at Caesarea Philippi) in the Synoptic tradition (Mark 8:29;

---

[4] Cf. A.H. Maynard, 'The Role of Peter in the Fourth Gospel', *NTS* 30 (1984): 543; Quast, *Peter*, 40–41.

[5] O'Day remarks that a confession of faith will always be tested and hence is always in jeopardy – even among the Twelve, the drama of belief and unbelief is acted out (*Gospel*, 611).

[6] Bennema, *Power*, 204; idem, *John's Gospel*, 84.

[7] Peter's use of 'to believe' and 'to know' in tandem and in the perfect tense in 6:69 may indicate that he, and the others, have had a personal, experiential knowledge (or 'knowing belief') of Jesus and his life-giving abilities (cf. Bennema, 'Christ', 122–5).

Matt. 16:16; Luke 9:20).[8] Since the title 'the Holy One of God' occurs in the Synoptics only on the lips of the demon-possessed (Mark 1:24; Luke 4:34) and since Peter's confession in the Synoptics is followed by Jesus' rebuke 'Get behind me Satan', a few scholars contend that Peter's declaration in 6:69 places him in the role of the devil and that Jesus' rebuke of Peter is transferred to Judas as a devil in 6:70b.[9] However, we should be careful about interpreting John through a Synoptic lens. More importantly, the adjective 'holy' is only used in John with reference to the Spirit (1:33; 14:26; 20:22), Jesus (6:69; cf. 10:36; 17:19) and the Father (17:11). 'Holy' essentially is an attribute of God and if 'holy' qualifies objects, places or people it is to be understood in proximity or relationship to this holy God – set apart for God's use.[10] 'The Holy One' is a frequent designation of God in the Old Testament (e.g. 2 Kgs 19:22; Job 6:10; Pss 71:22; 78:41; Prov. 9:10; Isa. 1:4; 5:19; Jer. 50:29; Ezek. 39:7), and Peter's assigning this title to Jesus implies his unity with God.[11] Thus, Peter perceives Jesus as being closely related and dedicated to the holy God, and perhaps even on a par with him.[12]

Thus, in contrast to many disciples who leave Jesus, Peter declares that he (and the others among 'the Twelve') will stick to him because they have experienced his words as life-giving. Connecting the two aspects of Peter's confession, he views Jesus as the one who provides divine life *because* he is consecrated and closely related to the holy God (cf. 3:34–36; 5:26; 10:30).[13] Peter displays traits of perceptiveness, outspokenness, zeal and loyalty.[14]

[8] Consequently, various Greek manuscripts have inserted 'the Christ' in 6:69 to bring John in line with the Synoptics.

[9] Droge, 'Status', 308 n. 7; G.F. Snyder, 'John 13:16 and the Anti-Petrinism of the Johannine Tradition', *BibRes* 16 (1971): 11. J. Painter briefly considers the possibility but then rejects it (*The Quest for the Messiah: The History, Literature and Theology of the Johannine Community* [2d edn; Edinburgh: T&T Clark, 1993], 283–4; cf. Quast, *Peter*, 50–51). Thatcher also evaluates Peter's confession negatively, arguing that Jesus emphatically rejected Peter's confession because (i) he had chosen 'the Twelve' rather than vice versa, and (ii) Peter was unaware that a devil lurked in their midst ('Jesus', 441).

[10] K.E. Brower, 'Holiness', in *NBD*, 477; H.N. Ridderbos, *The Gospel according to John: A Theological Commentary* (trans. J. Vriend; Grand Rapids: Eerdmans, 1997), 250.

[11] Cf. D. Kim, *An Exegesis of Apostasy Embedded in John's Narratives of Peter and Judas against the Synoptic Parallels* (SBEC 61; Lewiston: Edwin Mellen Press, 2004), 85.

[12] Cf. Blaine, *Peter*, 45. Moloney remarks that Peter also confesses Jesus' true origins – he is *of God* (*Gospel*, 229).

[13] J.H. Neyrey is mistaken when he asserts that Peter's confession is marked by his 'lacklustre and low-density understanding of Jesus', compared with his confession at Caesarea Philippi in the Synoptics ('The Sociology of Secrecy and the Fourth Gospel', in *What is John? Vol. II: Literary and Social Readings of the Fourth Gospel* [ed. F.F. Segovia; Atlanta: Scholars Press, 1998], 103). Others also view Peter's confession as an inadequate understanding of Jesus' identity (S.M. Schneiders, 'Women in the Fourth Gospel and the Role of Women in the Contemporary Church', *BTB* 12 [1982]: 41; H.C. Waetjen, *The Gospel of the Beloved Disciple: A Work in Two Editions* [New York: T&T Clark, 2005], 16–7). However, Peter's confession in John is as bold, public and displays as profound an insight into Jesus' identity as in the Synoptics.

[14] T. Wiarda, *Peter in the Gospels: Pattern, Personality and Relationship* (WUNT 2/127; Tübingen: Mohr Siebeck, 2000), 115.

Peter's Misunderstandings

Peter frequently misunderstands the actions and mission of Jesus. His first misunderstanding occurs in John 13 when Jesus washes his disciples' feet during their final meal. Jesus' actions of 'taking off' and 'putting on' his robe (13:4, 12) are unmistakeable allusions to the laying down and taking up of his life in 10:17–18 since the same verbs are used. Jesus thus enacts his ability to lay down and pick up his life at will, foreshadowing the cross and the resurrection where he will ultimately demonstrate this. When it is Peter's turn to have his feet washed by Jesus, his question regarding the propriety of Jesus' action (13:6), his reprimand of Jesus (13:8a), and his overreaction (13:9) show his misunderstanding of Jesus' action. While Peter reasons at an earthly/material level, Jesus is speaking of a spiritual cleansing that is necessary for people to have a relationship with him (13:8b, 10). Although Jesus assures Peter that he has been cleansed, the cleansing needs completion – Jesus must still die for Peter (and the others) on the cross.[15]

After this Jesus announces his imminent departure and gives a new commandment (13:33–35). Shocked at the news of Jesus' departure, Peter interrupts him (13:36a). Jesus' reply that where he is going Peter can only follow later (13:36b) must have seemed enigmatic. The reader, however, may observe that Jesus refers to the way of the cross, where Peter is not yet ready to follow. Only later – after the resurrection and Peter's reinstatement – Peter will follow Jesus on that same road (cf. 21:18–19). Peter, however, claims to be ready immediately to demonstrate the highest principle of loyalty and discipleship, namely, to lay down his life for Jesus (13:37; cf. 10:11; 15:13). Jesus then painfully points out that Peter is not yet the disciple he thinks he is: Peter will deny or disown Jesus three times (13:38).

Peter's third misunderstanding occurs at Jesus' arrest. Although Jesus is in control (18:5–6), Peter tries to take matters into his own hands and violently attacks Malchus, the servant of the high priest (18:10). Perhaps Peter clings to the idea of a warrior-messiah who will liberate Israel from the Romans, or was serious about his willingness to lay down his life for his master (13:37). Whatever his reasons for carrying a weapon and for his violent act, Peter still cannot conceive the path Jesus has to take. Jesus therefore rebukes Peter (18:11).[16] Like Andrew and Philip, Peter is not able to think 'from above' (see ch. 5).

Peter's last recorded misunderstanding is about Jesus' resurrection. When Mary reports that Jesus' body is missing, Peter and the Beloved Disciple run to the tomb to investigate the matter for themselves (20:1–7). It is ambiguous whether the Beloved Disciple's 'belief' mentioned in 20:8 is a

---

[15] B. Lindars's assessment of Peter as one who 'represents faith without understanding' is too harsh (*The Gospel of John* [NCB; London: Oliphants, 1972], 450). Keener's evaluation of Peter as misunderstanding mitigated by his loyalty to Jesus seems more appropriate (*Gospel*, 909).

[16] Droge's judgement on Peter, denying that he is one of Jesus' own, is too harsh ('Status', 311).

belief that Jesus had risen (see ch. 21), but the text certainly does not indicate that Peter reached resurrection faith.[17] In fact, 20:9 explains that neither of them understood that, according to the Scriptures, Jesus must rise from the dead. That they returned to their homes may also indicate that they were puzzled and distressed rather than convinced that Jesus had risen – otherwise they would surely have testified to the others (cf. 20:18).

Although Peter frequently misunderstands Jesus and the events surrounding him, he is not unique – many characters, including 'the Twelve', frequently struggle to understand, misunderstand or fail to understand Jesus. Besides misunderstanding, Peter also displays traits of outspokenness, zeal, loyalty and taking initiative.[18] In fact, Peter's misunderstandings are caused in part by his being too enthusiastic and impulsive, and over-confident of his loyalty his master.[19]

Peter's Defection

Peter's denial of his belonging to Jesus is narrated in 18:15–27. Peter and the Beloved Disciple follow Jesus to Annas's house – as loyal disciples (18:15a).[20] However, while the Beloved Disciple goes with Jesus into the courtyard, Peter must remain outside until the Beloved Disciple arranges for Peter to come in (18:15–16). The Greek word for 'courtyard' in 18:15 also occurs in 10:1, 16 where it refers to the sheepfold, and just as there is a gate to the courtyard (18:16), so there is a gate for the sheepfold (10:1–2, 7, 9). The significance of John's allusion to John 10 is that the Beloved Disciple, contra Peter, is the true or ideal disciple. The former can freely go in and out and stays close to Jesus (cf. 10:9), whereas Peter has to remain at the gate and can only get in with the help of the Beloved Disciple. Unlike the Beloved Disciple, Peter is not able to follow Jesus closely and it only gets worse.

In 18:17, Peter denies being a disciple for the first time.[21] The mention of the charcoal fire in 18:18 seems unimportant, but it will gain significance when we reach 21:9 (see below). After an interlude with Jesus before the

---

[17] Krafft's assertion that Peter reached resurrection faith when he saw the empty tomb and the burial cloths is unwarranted ('Personen', 25).

[18] Cf. Wiarda, *Peter*, 107–10.

[19] Neyrey's argument that Peter, as an insider, is 'not in the know' and enjoys no high status within the Johannine group is overstated ('Sociology', 103–4). Peter may have been less 'in the know' than the Beloved Disciple but certainly not less than any others among 'the Twelve'. Thatcher's conclusion that '[b]efore Jesus' death, Peter was the pinnacle of ignorance' is also exaggerated ('Jesus', 448).

[20] In the light of 20:2, the 'other' disciple in 18:15a is probably the Beloved Disciple.

[21] Unlike in the Synoptics, in John's gospel Peter does not so much deny knowing Jesus as being a *disciple* of Jesus (Krafft, 'Personen', 24; Brown, *Gospel*, 2:824; Culpepper, *Anatomy*, 120; Resseguie, *Strange Gospel*, 153; Conway, *Men and Women*, 174). As Brant remarks, Peter's denials are denials of identity – he is no longer a disciple – and his 'I am not' is the antithesis to Jesus' 'I am' (*Dialogue*, 197–8).

high priest in 18:19–24, the camera swings back to Peter. Peter is asked again whether he is one of Jesus' followers, and as in 18:17, Peter denies it – this is the second time (18:25). Finally, a relative of Malchus, whose ear Peter had chopped off, challenges him and Peter denies any association with Jesus – the third time (18:26–27).[22]

This episode would probably rate as the most tragic in Peter's life. First, he is unable to follow Jesus as closely as the Beloved Disciple, and worse, when the heat is on, he becomes disloyal – a defector or non-disciple. Peter's bravado in 13:37, sadly, amounts to nothing, as Jesus has foretold (13:38). By denying his association with Jesus, Peter essentially denies his discipleship.[23] Peter is not (yet) able to follow Jesus the whole way.

Peter's Restoration and Commission

Although there is considerable debate whether John 21 was part of the original gospel, an important reason for accepting it – even if it was added at a later stage – is that it concludes the story of Peter. Peter's denial that he belongs to Jesus in John 18 has probably left the reader wondering how things will be resolved (for the Synoptics do not settle it).[24]

John 21:2–3 tells us that seven of Jesus' disciples are in Galilee, where Peter resumes his old profession (only mentioned here in John) and is joined by the others. Why did they return to fishing after having met the risen Jesus and being commissioned (20:19–29)? The text does not provide answers. Perhaps Peter is still ashamed and feels inadequate to carry out the mission that Jesus has called him to, and, as the leader, he drags the others with him.[25] Or, if a comparison with Mark 16:7 can be made, the disciples might have gone to Galilee in obedience to Jesus' command and their decision to go fishing is simply an effective use of their waiting period.[26]

---

[22] In Greek, the questions in 18:17, 25 are tentative suggestions, but the question in 18:26 expects an affirmative answer.

[23] Contra Quast, who suggests that Peter's denials are more denials of his violence in the garden, afraid of retribution for cutting off Malchus's ear (*Peter*, 87). Kim also diminishes the significance of Peter's denials, claiming that he does not deny Jesus directly and publicly, and hence there is no need for repentance (and restoration) (*Apostasy*, 59–67). Others go too far, claiming that Peter's denial is his confession/testimony (Droge, 'Status', 311; Beck, *Discipleship*, 141), but they have neglected 6:68–69. NB while John did not deny but testified in 1:20 (an aspect of discipleship), Peter denies and fails to testify – and hence fails in discipleship.

[24] Cf. D.A. Lee, 'Partnership in Easter Faith: The Role of Mary Magdalene and Thomas in John 20', *JSNT* 58 (1995): 40; T. Wiarda, 'John 21.1–23: Narrative Unity and Its Implications', *JSNT* 46 (1992): 53–71; R. Bauckham, 'The Beloved Disciple as Ideal Author', *JSNT* 49 (1993): 27–8; Stibbe, *John*, 206.

[25] Cf. Stibbe, *John*, 210.

[26] Carson, *Gospel*, 669; G.R. Beasley-Murray, *John* (WBC 36; Milton Keynes: Word, 1991), 399; Köstenberger, *John*, 588. C.K. Barrett overinterprets Peter's proposal in 21:3 as a reference

After the account of the miraculous catch of fish, Jesus is seen having breakfast with his disciples (21:4–14).[27]

Only in John's gospel do we learn that Peter's fellowship with Jesus is restored (21:15–17). We may safely interpret this encounter between Jesus and Peter as reconciliation when we observe the parallels between the accounts in John 18 and John 21: (i) the mention of a charcoal fire on both occasions (18:18; 21:9); (ii) both the denial and the restoration happen in the presence of others ('they' in 21:15 probably refers to all disciples present);[28] (iii) Peter's threefold denial is matched by Jesus' threefold repetition of a question in 21:15–17. The three verses follow the same pattern – Jesus asks Peter a question, Peter replies, Jesus gives Peter a commission – and are virtually identical in content.

Some people make too much of the different uses of the verb 'to love'. A popular theory, not just based on this episode, is that John distinguishes between divine or 'agape' love (based on the verb *agapaō*) and human love (based on the verb *fileō*). A quick examination of John's gospel, however, would reveal that such a theory does not stand scrutiny. The verb *fileō* is used to denote the love between the Father and Son (5:20), as well as the Father's love for the disciples (16:27). On the other hand, the verb *agapaō* is used to express people's love of the darkness (3:19) and the love of the Jewish authorities for human glory (12:43). In essence, John varies his style, using the verbs *agapaō* and *fileō* interchangeably, just as he uses two verbs for 'to know' and four verbs for 'to see' without any substantial variation in meaning.[29]

With this insight, we return to 21:15–17. In the first two questions, Jesus uses the verb *agapaō*, but in the third question he employs *fileō*, whereas Peter uses the verb *fileō* in all his replies. We can hardly hold to the position that Jesus asks Peter twice whether he loves him with a divine, sacrificial love, and goes down to Peter's level in the third question because Peter replies that he merely loves Jesus with a human, friendly love. This view does not make sense of Peter's sadness at the third question. In all likelihood, Peter's sadness is caused by the fact that he knows all too well that he had claimed to love Jesus (cf. 13:37 and 15:13) but then denied his association with Jesus three times; Jesus' threefold repetition of his question serves as a painful reminder.[30] Besides, the text does not indicate that Jesus is disap-

---

to 'the apostolic mission of "catching men"' (*The Gospel according to St John: An Introduction with Commentary and Notes on the Greek Text* [2d edn; London: SPCK, 1978], 579).

[27] Peter's act of jumping into the water (21:7) may make it evident that his affection, loyalty and priority really lie with Jesus (Wiarda, 'John 21.1–23', 59).

[28] Cf. Wiarda, 'John 21.1–23', 55. Contra Thatcher, 'Jesus', 446.

[29] Cf. K.L. McKay, 'Style and Significance in the Language of Jn 21.15–17', *NovT* 27 (1985): 319–33; Quast, *Peter*, 144–6. Contra Maynard, 'Role', 542.

[30] Thatcher believes that Jesus' reference to Peter as 'Simon son of John' echoes their initial encounter in 1:42, indicating the need to redefine their relationship ('Jesus', 447). Whereas the second and third question ask, 'Do you love me?', the first question has added the words

pointed with Peter's replies; on the contrary, each time Jesus affirms Peter by giving him a commission. In the threefold repetition of Peter's commissioning – 'Feed my lambs', 'Tend my sheep', 'Feed my sheep' – there is very little or no difference in meaning. It becomes evident in his first Epistle that Peter has understood and realized his mission, and that, in turn, he is able to exhort others to follow in his footsteps and humbly tend God's flock (1 Pet. 5:1–4).

After commissioning him, Jesus prepares Peter for his future mission by warning him about what lies ahead (21:18). In fact, Jesus is foretelling how Peter will die – probably on a cross (21:19a; cf. 16:2; 2 Pet. 1:14). Next, Jesus encourages Peter to follow him (21:19b). Earlier, Peter pledged that he would follow Jesus and even lay down his life for him, but he was not able to stick by Jesus when it mattered (13:36–38; 18:15–27). Now Jesus ensures that he is ready to follow him all the way – even unto death. Thus, Peter's commission and his impending death are conceptually linked: *as a shepherd*, he will eventually lay down his life for the sheep – quite literally. In this, Peter's life is patterned on the life of the good shepherd himself as outlined in 10:1–18.[31]

Peter and the Beloved Disciple

The Gospel of John seems to portray a rivalry between Peter and the Beloved Disciple, where most often the Beloved Disciple outclasses Peter. First, the Beloved Disciple seems to be more intimate with Jesus than Peter (13:23–25).[32] Second, the Beloved Disciple is able to follow Jesus farther than Peter (18:15–16). Third, Peter denies Jesus and stops following (18:17–27), whereas the Beloved Disciple remains with Jesus (19:26–27). Fourth, the Beloved Disciple outruns Peter on the way to the tomb (20:4) and 'believes' (20:8). Fifth, the Beloved Disciple recognizes Jesus first (21:7). This rivalry has led some scholars to suggest that John depicts a tension between Jewish Christians (represented by Peter) and Gentile Christians (represented by

'more than these'. While most commentators favour the interpretation 'Do you love me more than these others do?', Wiarda argues persuasively for the understanding 'Do you love me more than these things?', where 'things' refer to the fish or fishing equipment. The significance being that Jesus' question is about *occupation*, forcing Peter to choose between fishing and discipleship ('John 21.1–23', 60–65). However, Wiarda is mistaken when he claims that 21:15–17 is not about Peter's rehabilitation but only about his commission ('John 21.1–23', 65; *Peter*, 113–4 n. 154; cf. Conway, *Men and Women*, 176–7; Kim, *Apostasy*, 136–40). Jesus' threefold question and the mention of the charcoal fire unmistakably connects 21:15–17 with 18:15–27.

[31] Cf. Culpepper, *Anatomy*, 120; A.J. Köstenberger, *The Missions of Jesus and the Disciples according to the Fourth Gospel: With Implications for the Fourth Gospel's Purpose and the Mission of the Contemporary Church* (Grand Rapids: Eerdmans, 1998), 158–9; Bauckham, 'Beloved Disciple', 35–6.

[32] The Beloved Disciple was not simply close to Jesus physically; 13:23 says that he was 'in the bosom of Jesus', echoing 1:18 where Jesus' intimacy with his Father is phrased similarly.

the Beloved Disciple),[33] or between 'Apostolic Christians' and the Johannine community,[34] while others see an anti-Petrine bias in the Gospel of John.[35] However, we suggest that the 'rivalry' between Peter and the Beloved Disciple should be understood as their having corresponding rather than competitive roles.

After his restoration and commission, Peter spots the Beloved Disciple and immediately asks, 'Lord, what about him?' (21:20–21). In response to this petulant question, Jesus reprimands Peter saying he should mind his own business, focus on following him and not be distracted by what is in store for others (21:22). Peter may perceive a rivalry between himself and the Beloved Disciple, but they actually have complementary roles. While the Beloved Disciple is the paradigm of a loyal and credible witness for Jesus, who is intimate with him (see ch. 21), Peter exemplifies self-sacrifice in following Jesus. Both Peter and the Beloved Disciple demonstrate love, the ultimate expression of discipleship (13:34–35) – Peter will lay down his life for his friend (cf. 15:3) and the Beloved Disciple has a relationship with Jesus characterized by love. Thus, both the Beloved Disciple and Peter function as paradigms of discipleship, stressing different characteristics of a true follower of Jesus.[36]

Conclusion

Peter is a complex character whose traits include outspokenness and zeal (6:68–69; 13:6, 36), impetuousness (13:6–9; 18:10; 21:7), loyalty (6:68–69; 13:37), love (21:15–17), perceptiveness (6:68–69), misunderstanding (13:8–9, 37; 18:10), ambition (cf. his rivalry with the Beloved Disciple), failure/disloyalty (18:15–27), and the ability to take initiative (13:24; 21:3, 11). Peter is unstable and presents conflicting traits, making room for considerable character

---

[33] Bultmann, *Gospel*, 483–5, 685.

[34] Brown, *Community*, 81–8.

[35] Snyder, 'John 13:16', 5–15; Waetjen, *Gospel*, 24. Cf. Maynard, 'Role', 546; P. Perkins, *Peter: Apostle for the Whole Church* (Edinburgh: T&T Clark, 2000), 98–103. For an overview of opinions on the relationship between Peter and the Beloved Disciple, see Köstenberger, *Missions*, 155–7.

[36] Amongst those who see the relationship between Peter and the Beloved Disciple as complementary rather than competitive are Culpepper, *Anatomy*, 121; Quast, *Peter*, 153–70; Brodie, *Gospel*, 560–64, 580–86; Bauckham, 'Beloved Disciple', 34–9; Köstenberger, *Missions*, 158–61; Blaine, *Peter*, 186–90. T.V. Smith argues that John's gospel responds to the polemic from pro-Peter groups by asserting the importance of the Beloved Disciple while acknowledging Peter's authority (rather than being anti-Petrine) (*Petrine Controversies in Early Christianity* [WUNT 15; Tübingen: Mohr Siebeck, 1985], 143–50). Although Tovey does not view them in competition, he perceives Peter as representing pre-Easter discipleship, marked by loyalty, partial comprehension, misunderstandings and failure, whereas the Beloved Disciple also features post-Easter discipleship, marked by intimacy with Jesus, faithfulness, belief and witnessing (*Art*, 135–8). Blaine's case for Peter as the inspirational co-founder (the other being the Beloved Disciple) of the Johannine community is unpersuasive (*Peter*, 2, 190–92).

development. While he displays profound insight into Jesus' identity he also frequently misunderstands him. He functions as spokesman and leader of 'the Twelve' but fails surprisingly when he denies being Jesus' disciple. His initiative to go fishing after he had been commissioned in 20:21–23 may also be unexpected. He thus exhibits insight, confidence, discipleship and leadership but also dullness, failure and disloyalty. As Collins aptly states, 'Simon Peter appears as a man of contradictions and ambivalence.'[37] Peter represents the Christian in the making: those who are zealous for Jesus but sometimes fail miserably; those who can see Jesus for who he is but who can also misunderstand profoundly. Regarding his inner life, Peter knows Jesus' identity (6:69) and asserts that he loves him (21:15–17), Jesus unmasks Peter's bravado (13:36–38), and the narrator mentions that Peter was saddened (21:17).

Peter functions as a leader early on but his skills need to be honed. He must go through a crisis experience before he can be the kind of leader that Jesus wants him to be. Peter was overconfident of his ability to follow Jesus. Rather than affirming his discipleship, Peter negated it by denying any association with Jesus. He became a non-disciple, a defector, but unlike Judas this was temporary. Only when Peter's threefold denial of Jesus is matched by Jesus' threefold affirmation of Peter, he is ready to truly follow Jesus – even unto death – and to fulfil his earlier promise to lay down his life for his master (13:37). Peter, like the Beloved Disciple, is a paradigm of discipleship in that his love for and devotion to Jesus will ultimately be demonstrated in his laying down his life for his friend.

The story of Peter is essentially the story of *a shepherd in the making*. Both in his commission (21:15–17) and in the foretelling of his death (21:18–19), the shepherd imagery comes to the fore. In his commission, Jesus commands Peter to look after the flock – the one flock of which Jesus is the chief shepherd (10:16; cf. 1 Pet. 5:4). In foretelling Peter's death, Jesus indicates that Peter, like him, will also lay down his life for the sheep – literally (10:11, 14) – and thus will demonstrate his love for his master (cf. 15:13). In effect, Peter, under the chief shepherd, will shepherd Jesus' flock and ultimately lay down his life for his master and the flock.[38]

---

[37] Collins, 'John', 365. Cf. Wiarda, *Peter*, 116–7. Tolmie's evaluation of Peter's characterization as 'not complex' and showing 'no development' is rather surprising and probably due to not taking sufficiently into account 6:68–69 and John 18, 20 – 21 (*Farewell*, 142). Davies also evaluates Peter as a flat character (*Rhetoric*, 332). Kim's evaluation of Peter as a rock-like character who remained loyal to Jesus throughout is too one-sided (*Apostasy*, 74–6, 143–7). In his attempt to rehabilitate Peter's characterization in John's gospel and present him as an inspirational co-founder of the Johannine community, Blaine's portrayal of Peter as consistently positive is perhaps too positive, minimizing his misunderstandings, failures and instability (*Peter*, 78–9, 183–93).

[38] Köstenberger argues that besides the obvious pastoral aspect of Peter's role as a shepherd (to nurture believers), there is also an evangelistic aspect, namely to reach out to unbelievers and bring them to the flock (cf. 10:16) (*Missions*, 159–60).

Simon Peter		
Appearances	References	1:40; 1:41; 1:42 (2x); 1:44; 6:8; 6:68; 13:6; 13:8; 13:9; 13:24; 13:36; 13:37; 18:10; 18:11; 18:15; 18:16 (2x); 18:17; 18:18; 18:25; 18:26; 18:27; 20:2; 20:3; 20:4; 20:6; 21:2; 21:3; 21:7 (2x); 21:11; 21:15 (2x); 21:16; 21:17 (2x); 21:20; 21:21
Identity	Titles given	Peter
	Gender	male
	Age	–
	Marital status	–
	Occupation	probably a fisherman
	Socio-economic status	possibly owned a boat (21:3)
	Place of residence/operation	from Bethsaida in Galilee
	Relatives	brother Andrew, father John
	Group affiliation	'the Twelve'
Speech and actions	In interaction with Jesus	adequate belief, frequent misunderstanding, loyal to Jesus, temporary defection
	In interaction with others	in rivalry with the Beloved Disciple
Character classification	Complexity	complex; multiple traits: outspoken, impetuous, zealous, initiatory, loyal, showing love, ambitious, fallible, perceptive, dull
	Development	much
	Inner life	some
Degree of characterization		individual
Response to Jesus		adequate but marked by frequent misunderstandings; inadequate during Jesus' arrest and trial

Nathanael – The Genuine Israelite

'Achievement is not the most important thing – authenticity is' — *Anonymous*

Nathanael's Identity

Nathanael appears only in John's gospel and very little is known about him. We learn from 21:2 that his hometown is Cana in Galilee – probably in the hill country about fifteen kilometres west of the Sea of Galilee. Hence, Nathanael was not a fisherman like Andrew and Peter.

'Nathanael' is a Hebrew name, meaning 'gift of God' or 'God has given'. This has led a few scholars to argue that Nathanael is symbolic of the disciples that have been *given* by the Father to Jesus rather than a real disciple (6:37; 17:2, 6).[1] However, this requires the reader to know the meaning of Nathanael's name, and normally John provides a translation if he wants to draw attention to Semitic terms (e.g. 9:7).[2] Indeed, 1:35–51 explains three other Semitic terms: rabbi (1:38), messiah (1:41) and Cephas (1:42). Moreover, there is evidence that Nathanael was Jesus' disciple independent of John's gospel. The Babylonian Talmud mentions 'Nittai', a possible diminutive of Nathanael, as a disciple of Jesus (*b. Sanhedrin* 43a),[3] and the second-century *Epistula Apostolorum* mentions Nathanael in its list of apostles.[4] Thus, Nathanael is very likely a historical rather than a fictitious disciple of Jesus.

There is considerable debate whether Nathanael is one of 'the Twelve' – Jesus' inner circle of disciples. Comparing the disciples named in John's gospel with the lists of the twelve disciples in the Synoptics and Acts, scholars have suggested that Nathanael could be Bartholomew,[5] Matthew,[6]

---

[1] E.g. Barrett, *Gospel*, 179, 184.

[2] Carson, *Gospel*, 159.

[3] R. Bauckham, 'Nicodemus and the Gurion family', *JTS* 47 (1996): 34–6. This evidence is late but may reflect earlier tradition.

[4] C.E. Hill, 'The Identity of John's Nathanael', *JSNT* 67 (1997): 50–51. Hill also mentions *Didascalia Apostolorum* 3 and the *Apostolic Church Order* ('Identity', 52–3).

[5] Schnackenburg, *Gospel*, 1:314; Carson, *Gospel*, 159; Ridderbos, *Gospel*, 87–8; Keener, *Gospel*, 482 (though tentatively); Köstenberger, *John*, 79–80.

[6] Bultmann, *Gospel*, 103 n. 4 (mentioned as one option); M. Hengel, *The Johannine Question* (London: SCM, 1989), 19–20.

James of Alphaeus,[7] or a disciple other than the Twelve.[8] Although Bartholomew is the favoured option, Hill's argument for James of Alphaeus is more convincing since he provides both external and internal evidence. Based primarily (but not solely) on the second-century document *Epistula Apostolorum*, he argues that Nathanael has been substituted for James of Alphaeus. According to Hill, the allusions in 1:45–51 to the Jacob narrative of Genesis suggest that Nathanael was also known by the name James or *Iakōbos* (the Greek transliteration of the Hebrew 'Jacob').[9] However, since there were many other apostle lists available in the early church, we need more evidence for Hill's proposition. Although Nathanael compares to Jacob (see below), this is not conclusive evidence that Nathanael must be James of Alphaeus.[10] Besides, when someone is known by another name, John usually mentions both: Simon called Peter/Cephas (1:42); Thomas called Didymus/Twin (11:16; 20:24). It also remains problematic that someone should bear two Hebrew names (this is the same problem for any identification with Bartholomew and Matthew),[11] although Hill provides some explanation.[12]

Although it is tempting to identify Nathanael with one of the Twelve, it is by no means necessary. John's gospel depicts a broader concept of discipleship than merely the twelve apostles. Anyone who believes in Jesus and remains with him is a disciple: for example, the Samaritan woman, the disciples mentioned in 6:60 (although many give up), the man born blind, Lazarus and his sisters, Joseph of Arimathea (though he is a secret disciple [19:38]). If we consider that the identification of Nathanael with one of the twelve disciples is not required and that all attempts to do so are speculative, it might be safest to conclude that Nathanael was not one of them. If he was one of the Twelve, he was likelier James of Alphaeus than anyone else.

Nathanael's Interaction with Jesus

We will now examine what aspect of discipleship Nathanael represents by turning to 1:45–51 which describes his interaction with Jesus. Philip testifies to Nathanael that Jesus is the one Moses wrote about in the law and to whom the prophets also testified (1:45). Since 'Moses and the prophets' is usually shorthand for the Hebrew Scriptures (the Old Testament), Philip essentially conveys that he has encountered the one whom the Old

---

[7] Hill, 'Identity', 45–61.

[8] Brown, *Gospel*, 1:82–3; Beasley-Murray, *John*, 27.

[9] Hill, 'Identity', 50–57.

[10] Hill admits this also and hence renders his theory 'possible – though not at all certain' ('Identity', 58–9, 61).

[11] Brown, *Gospel*, 1:82 n. 45. Cf. Keener, *Gospel*, 482.

[12] Hill, 'Identity', 57.

Testament anticipates – probably a veiled expression for the expected Messiah.[13] Nathanael's sceptical reaction is met with Philip's 'come and see' (1:46; cf. 1:39) – an invitation to investigate matters for himself – and despite his doubts, Nathanael accepts Philip's invitation and goes out to meet Jesus (1:47).[14]

Jesus' remark about Nathanael, 'Here we really have a genuine Israelite!' (1:47), typifies him as an Israelite in whom is no 'treachery', 'deceit' or 'guile'. The same word occurs in Genesis 27:35 (LXX) to describe Jacob, whose name means the supplanter or deceiver (Gen. 27:36). If this allusion is intended, then Nathanael is *contrasted* to Jacob in that Nathanael represents the new Jacob or true Israel.[15] Trudinger suggests that the use of Jacob's new name 'Israel' in Jesus' greeting of Nathanael signifies something like, 'Look, Israel without a trace of Jacob left in him!'[16]

Jesus' insight into his character startles Nathanael and in response to his question Jesus provides further revelation (1:48). Although scholars have discussed the (symbolic) meaning of Jesus' statement that he saw Nathanael under a fig tree, it may simply have been a demonstration of Jesus' insight into people to extract the desired response (cf. 4:17–19).[17] Indeed, Jesus' revelation elicits a response from Nathanael (1:49), which Jesus identifies as belief (1:50).

In Nathanael's twofold belief-response he declares that Jesus is the Son of God and the king of Israel. In Judaism, the title 'Son (of God)' in itself does not necessarily denote divinity – angels/heavenly beings are called 'sons of God' (Gen. 6:2; Job 38:7), but also Israel (Exod. 4:22–23), righteous people (Sir. 4:10) and the Davidic king (Ps. 2:7).[18] In John, 'Son (of God)' denotes Jesus' intimate relationship with God the Father and his authority

---

[13] Cf. Bultmann, *Gospel*, 103; Carson, *Gospel*, 159; Keener, *Gospel*, 482–3.

[14] Keener comments that 'come and see' was a standard phrase in rabbinic literature for halakic investigation, and hence the invitation reflects a contrast between the synagogue leadership which investigates the written Torah, and Jesus' disciples who are invited to investigate/experience Jesus as the Torah made flesh (*Gospel*, 485).

[15] Cf. Carson, *Gospel*, 160–61; Beasley-Murray, *John*, 27; Hill, 'Identity', 56; Stibbe, *John*, 40; Brodie, *Gospel*, 169; Keener, *Gospel*, 485–6; A.T. Lincoln, *The Gospel according to Saint John* (BNTC 4; London: Continuum, 2005), 120. Contra Schnackenburg, *Gospel*, 1:316; R.M. Chennattu, *Johannine Discipleship as a Covenant Relationship* (Peabody: Hendrickson, 2006), 37.

[16] L.P. Trudinger, 'An Israelite in Whom There Is No Guile: An Interpretative Note on John 1:45–51', *EvQ* 54 (1982): 117.

[17] For the various views on Jesus' statement to Nathanael in 1:48, see Keener, *Gospel*, 486. C.R. Koester argues that it alludes to the messianic Branch of Zech. 3:8–10 ('Messianic Exegesis and the Call of Nathanael [John 1.45–51]', *JSNT* 39 [1990]: 23–34). Although Koester's view is one of many speculative theories, a messianic interpretation nonetheless accounts for Nathanael's recognition of Jesus *as Messiah* in 1:49. However, Nathanael may have been predisposed to consider Jesus' messianic status because of Philip's testimony in 1:45. Cf. Lindars, who remarks that although Nathanael's *belief* has been evoked by Jesus' revelatory insight, its *content* is derived from Philip's announcement (*Gospel*, 119).

[18] Cf. Keener, *Gospel*, 294–6.

to act on God's behalf.[19] The title 'Son (of God)' is primarily used by Jesus himself, but also occurs on the lips of three people to refer to Jesus: John (1:34), Nathanael (1:49) and Martha (11:27). It arguably has messianic overtones because: (i) John has recognized that Jesus is the coming Messiah (1:29–34); (ii) the title 'king of Israel' in 1:49 is a messianic title; (iii) 'Son of God' is juxtaposed with 'Christ' in 11:27 and 20:31.

Regarding the designation 'king of Israel', most scholars agree that this is a messianic title, referring to the expected Davidic messiah. 'Messiah' does not indicate divinity but denotes a human agent chosen by God and anointed with God's Spirit to accomplish God's purposes. In first-century Judaism, many Jews expected a royal-political messiah who would liberate Palestine from the Roman oppressors and establish a new age of peace and justice. John, however, presents Jesus primarily as a *Teacher-Messiah* who liberates people from the spiritual oppression of sin and the devil through his Spirit-imbued teaching.[20]

Nathanael thus understands something of Jesus' true identity and his twofold exclamation, 'You are the Son of God! You are the king of Israel!', is essentially his belief-response (cf. 1:50). If we consider the purpose of John's gospel, 'that you may believe that Jesus is the Messiah, the Son of God' (20:31), we see that Nathanael's response virtually echoes the ideal Johannine belief-response. Thus, Nathanael responds to Jesus' revelation in the way the author desires, namely he perceives Jesus' true identity on the basis of the revelation Jesus provides and responds with adequate belief. For John, Nathanael represents the genuine or ideal Israelite who produces the intended christological confession.[21] In response to Nathanael's confession, Jesus promises him further and greater revelation (1:50–51), alluding to Jacob's vision of God at Bethel in Genesis 28:12.[22]

---

[19] Cf. Carson; *Gospel*, 162; B. Witherington III, *The Many Faces of the Christ: The Christologies of the New Testament and Beyond* (New York: Crossroad, 1998), 183.

[20] See Bennema, 'Sword', 35–58.

[21] Cf. Collins, 'Figures', 13; Culpepper, *Anatomy*, 123. Brodie even sees a parallel with Romans 9 – 11 in that Nathanael represents alienated Israel which eventually returns to Jesus and God (*Gospel*, 169–70). Contra Moloney, who contends that Nathanael's confession 'falls short of the mark' since it simply expresses first-century messianic hopes (*Gospel*, 56). Since both Collins and Culpepper interpret 'under the fig tree' (1:48) as a traditional place for the study of Torah, they see Nathanael in contrast to 'the Jews' who study the Torah but react negatively. However, C.F.D. Moule's comment that the phrase simply indicates accurate knowledge of Nathanael's whereabouts and movements seems to be more on target ('A Note on "Under the Fig Tree" in John 1.48, 50', *JTS* 5 [1954]: 210–11). R. Rhees's explanation of Nathanael's christological confession that he had been stirred up by the preaching of John the Baptist is unwarranted since there is no indication that Nathanael knew John ('The Confession of Nathanael, John i.45–49', *JBL* 17 [1898]: 23–8). An easier explanation would be that Philip's testimony to Nathanael, which was messianic in content, perhaps contained more than what is recorded in 1:45 and hence prepared Nathanael's messianic confession.

[22] Jesus' promise is for the disciples in general since the 'you' in 1:51 is plural (Carson, *Gospel*, 163; Keener, *Gospel*, 489).

Conclusion

Based on the little material on Nathanael, we have been able to build up a picture of him. Regarding his identity, we cannot be certain that he is one of the Twelve, but if he was, he is most likely be identified as James of Alphaeus. Regarding his role in the Johannine narrative, the allusions to the Jacob narrative in Genesis in 1:47, 51 indicate that Nathanael is like and unlike Jacob. Like Jacob, he also sees God – in Jesus (1:49–51) – but unlike Jacob, there is no deceit in him (1:48) and he responds to Jesus as an authentic Israelite (1:49). Nathanael responds adequately to Jesus' revelation (1:48b–49), and his declaration of Jesus as the Son of God and king of Israel matches the ideal Johannine confession mentioned in 20:31 – and indeed Jesus identifies Nathanael's confession as (adequate) belief (1:50). Thus, Nathanael displays the traits of Israel rather than Jacob and hence is the ideal or archetype Israelite – 'an Israelite without guile'. Nathanael's traits include being sceptical, inquiring and responsive (he takes up Philip's invitation in 1:46), perceptive and genuine. Jesus reveals one aspect of Nathanael's inner life, namely his authenticity (1:47). To Nathanael, and those who make similar confessions, Jesus promises further and greater revelation of the divine reality (1:51; cf. 16:12–15).

Nathanael		
Appearances	References	1:45; 1:46; 1:47; 1:48; 1:49; 21:2
Identity	Titles given	'a genuine Israelite' (1:47)
	Gender	male
	Age	–
	Marital status	–
	Occupation	–
	Socio-economic status	–
	Place of residence/operation	from Cana (Galilee)
	Relatives	–
	Group affiliation	uncertain – either one outside the Twelve or James of Alphaeus
Speech and actions	In interaction with Jesus	responds to Jesus' revelation with belief
	In interaction with others	sceptical towards Philip but still responsive
Character classification	Complexity	uncomplicated; multiple traits: sceptical but responsive, inquiring, perceptive, guileless/genuine
	Development	none
	Inner life	little
Degree of characterization		type
Response to Jesus		adequate belief, ideal Johannine confession

The Mother of Jesus – A Catalyst in His Ministry

'Catalyst: a person or thing that precipitates an event' — Oxford English Dictionary

In the Gospel of John, Jesus' mother is an anonymous character, married to Joseph (6:42), and she has, besides Jesus, other sons (2:12; 7:3).[1] She has an unnamed sister, and probably knows Mary the wife of Clopas, Mary Magdalene and the Beloved Disciple (19:25). Jesus' family lives in Nazareth (1:45; 18:5; 19:19) but Jesus' mother seems to accompany her son at various points during his ministry – in Cana (2:1–5), Capernaum (2:12) and Jerusalem (19:25–27). This coheres with the Synoptic accounts which show that various Galilean women accompanied and provided for Jesus during his ministry, who were also present during his passion – including Mary Magdalene and Jesus' mother herself (Matt. 27:55–56; Mark 15:40–41; Luke 8:1–3; 23:49). In John's account, Jesus' mother has a noticeable presence only on two occasions – in Cana, at the beginning of Jesus' ministry (2:3–5), and at the foot of the cross towards the end of Jesus' ministry (19:25–27).

At the Wedding in Cana

The story of the wedding at Cana is found in 2:1–11. Most scholars struggle with the enigmatic exchange between Jesus and his mother in 2:3–5 but Ritva Williams's insightful analysis helps us make sense of this conversation. She draws attention to three social conventions of first-century Mediterranean culture. First, men were associated with open, public space, while women were limited to domestic, private space. A first-century Mediterranean wedding took place in the public realm since it formalized the union of two households and their honour rather than two individuals. Second, while the father operated in the public realm, the mother's task was to raise the children in the private space, until, in case of a male child, the boy would join the father in the public space at the age of seven or eight.

---

[1] T.W. Martin finds that ancient authors most often use the epithet 'mother of X' when the name of a mother is well known to the readers. Martin thus concludes that Jesus' mother is anonymous in John's gospel *precisely* because the community was familiar with her name ('Assessing the Johannine Epithet "the Mother of Jesus"', *CBQ* 60 [1998]: 63–73).

The bond between mother and son, however, was the closest of Mediterranean relationships, and when the son grew up he became her supporter
and defender. Third, honour served as a kind of indicator of a person's social
status within the community, and came with corresponding rights and
obligations. The male head of the family was responsible for representing,
defending and if possible enhancing the family's honour in the public space,
sometimes by establishing a patron-client relationship through a broker.[2]
Williams then suggests reading 2:1–12 as 'a story about a widowed mother
at a wedding who brokers from her son a favor that preserves the honor of
the groom's family and enhances her son's honor in an unexpected way.'[3]

Jesus mother's statement in 2:3, 'they have no wine', reveals that she is
observant and practical. Running out of wine would mean a loss of honour
– not only does the groom's family lack an adequate supply of wine but
also the necessary social connections to preserve the family's honour.[4] The
statement of Jesus' mother is actually a request for Jesus to do something
about the situation. Williams explains that Jesus' mother probably sees the
embarrassing situation as an opportunity to enhance the honour of her
family and extend the family's web of reciprocal relationships. Jesus' mother
thus takes on the role of a broker, providing the groom's family privileged
access to her son as the patron.[5] The text provides no information how
much Jesus' mother understands about her son's identity and mission at
this stage, but it would be unlikely that she expected him to perform a
miracle.[6] Besides, within the story world of John's gospel, the first miracle
is only about to happen now (2:11). Nevertheless, she believes her son can
do something and her request may be an implicit reminder to him of his
family obligations.[7]

Jesus' reply in 2:4 is puzzling and complex. First, in addressing his mother
as 'woman' (he does so again in 19:26) Jesus is not rude but seems to use
an acceptable form of address – he speaks similarly to other women (4:21;
8:10; 20:15; cf. 20:13).[8] Nevertheless, Jesus' use of this impersonal address
for his biological mother may suggest that he distances himself from her

---

[2] R.H. Williams, 'The Mother of Jesus at Cana: A Social-Science Interpretation of John 2:1–12',
CBQ 59 (1997): 680–84.

[3] Williams, 'Mother', 680. Independent of Williams, Fehribach provides a similar analysis
of 2:1–11 (*Women*, ch. 2). While Williams does not explain why Jesus' mother is a widow,
Fehribach contends that her request to Jesus (rather than her husband) to meet the need (2:3)
suggests widowhood (*Women*, 38). Cf. R.E. Brown et al., *Mary in the New Testament: A
Collaborative Assessment by Protestant and Roman Catholic Scholars* (Philadelphia: Fortress Press,
1978), 64, 195.

[4] Williams, 'Mother', 684.

[5] Williams, 'Mother', 685. Cf. Fehribach, *Women*, 28.

[6] Cf. Williams, 'Mother', 686; B.R. Gaventa, *Mary: Glimpses of the Mother of Jesus* (Edinburgh:
T&T Clark, 1999), 83. Contra Collins, 'Figures', 31; Maccini, *Testimony*, 99–100.

[7] Williams, 'Mother', 686.

[8] J.M. Lieu, 'The Mother of the Son in the Fourth Gospel', *JBL* 117 (1998): 65; cf. Williams,
'Mother', 688.

and rejects any claim she might make on him because of her family relationship.[9]

The second issue is Jesus' question, 'What has this to do with us?' Williams explains that Jesus' mother acts as the broker on behalf of the groom's family (whether they have asked her or not), which is in need of patronage – a share in someone else's honour. By doing so, however, she has made someone else's problem her own and intrudes Jesus' social space. Jesus' question should read something like: What concern is that (the shortage of wine) to us? It is the groom's problem. Why should we get involved?[10] Jesus thus dissociates himself from his mother's interests.[11]

Third, Jesus' statement that his 'hour' has not yet come is also enigmatic.[12] We have argued elsewhere that Jesus' hour has two separate referents in John's gospel – the hour of Jesus' messianic ministry (2:4; 4:23; 5:25) and the hour of his passion or glorification (7:30; 8:20; 12:23; 13:1; 17:1).[13] Although Jesus indicates in 2:4b that the time of the messianic age, i.e. the new age of justice and peace ('salvation') that God would initiate through his Messiah, has not yet begun, his subsequent action of turning water into wine serves to lift the 'not yet' from the messianic hour. The events at the wedding at Cana thus marks Jesus' inauguration of the messianic age (cf. the phrase 'an hour is coming, *and is now*' in 4:23 and 5:25).[14]

Williams correctly observes that Jesus and his mother appear to be at cross-purposes. Jesus' mother uses her privileged access to her son, seeking to broker a favour from him and reminding him of his obligations as

[9] Brown et al., *Mary*, 188–9. Cf. E. Schüssler Fiorenza, *In Memory of Her: A Feminist Theological Reconstruction of Christian Origins* (London: SCM, 1983), 327; Carson, *Gospel*, 170; Beck, *Discipleship*, 55; M. Scott, *Sophia and the Johannine Jesus* (JSNTS 71; Sheffield: JSOT Press, 1992), 180; O'Day, *Gospel*, 536; Maccini, *Testimony*, 102; Lieu, 'Mother', 65; Fehribach, *Women*, 29, 37; Keener, *Gospel*, 505.

[10] Williams, 'Mother', 687–8. Contra Conway, who argues that Jesus' mother pushes Jesus before his time, trying to force a miracle, and Jesus' sharp response complicates the characterization of his mother ('Ambiguity', 337–8).

[11] Brown et al., *Mary*, 191. Cf. Köstenberger, *John*, 95.

[12] It seems inappropriate to take 2:4b as a question, 'Has not my time come?', as Williams suggests ('Mother', 689). For a critique, see Brown et al., *Mary*, 191–2.

[13] Bennema, *John's Gospel*, 38–9. In contrast, Maccini contends that the 'hour' in 2:4 refers to Jesus' death (*Testimony*, 104–6). While Fehribach also perceives 2:4 as a reference to the messianic hour, she does not recognize that there is another hour too (*Women*, 30–31). Although we differentiate between these two uses of 'hour', we should not dichotomize Jesus' ministry and his glorification as if the former was devoid of glory. On the contrary, Jesus' miracle at Cana reveals his glory (2:11); the resurrection of Lazarus results in glorification (11:4, 40); Jesus glorifies his Father during his ministry (17:4) and Jesus receives glory through his disciples (17:10). Hence, Jesus' earthly ministry is one of glory and glorification, but, in a narrower sense, his glorification refers specifically to his death, resurrection and ascension.

[14] For an explanation how the miracle signifies the start of Jesus' messianic ministry, see Carson, *Gospel*, 172–5; Stibbe, *John*, 43–6; Fehribach, *Women*, 29–30; Bennema, *John's Gospel*, 39–40. Williams points out that although the wedding occurred in the public space, only Jesus' *private* circle realizes that Jesus' honour is enhanced (but different from what Jesus' mother intended), and consequently believes in him (2:11) ('Mother', 690).

head of her family, thereby enhancing the family's honour and reciprocal networks. Jesus' answer in 2:4 shows that he realizes his mother is drawing him into the local game of honour and patronage, whereas his concern is the mission that God had given him.[15] Jesus' reply should thus be seen as a mild rebuke that his mother's 'earthly' motivations do not correspond to his 'heavenly' mandate.[16]

We can hardly assume that Jesus' mother grasped the significance of what her son was saying in 2:4, and hence her reaction in 2:5 should be evaluated with caution. According to Williams, she may have viewed her son's reply as typical male grumbling, while expecting him to do what was necessary because it was a question of honour – a confidence that came from her privileged relationship with her son.[17] Beck, however, contends that her response shows that she has re-evaluated her relationship with him, accepting the newly revealed hierarchy in which Jesus' role is defined exclusively in terms of his Father's sovereignty, with no place for human familial obligation.[18] Be that as it may, when she tells the servants to do whatever Jesus says, it is in fact a directive to obey Jesus' word, and it is possible that she has accepted (and perhaps understood something of) Jesus' correction.[19] In the Johannine narrative, people are encouraged to trust Jesus' word (above miraculous signs) (4:48–50; 6:68; cf. 20:29), as well as to adhere continually to his word (15:7). Thus, while Jesus' mother may not have understood the mission of her son and hence the true meaning of his reply in 2:4, her directive in 2:5 is a true Johannine command.[20]

In sum, at a wedding celebration, Jesus' mother witnesses the symbolic inauguration of her son's messianic ministry. In fact, she plays an active role in precipitating this important event because of her powers of observation, her implicit request to Jesus and her instruction to the servants to obey Jesus' word.[21] Many scholars connect the wedding at Cana with the scene at the foot of the cross, and diminish the significance of the part of Jesus' mother in the former event. They argue that she had no role in Jesus' ministry because his hour had not yet come (2:4) and only gains significance

---

[15] Williams, 'Mother', 689. Cf. Fehribach, *Women*, 31–6; Scott, *Sophia*, 180.

[16] Contra Williams, who contends that 2:4, rather than a rebuke or rebuff, is merely a signal that Jesus recognizes what his mother is asking of him ('Mother', 689).

[17] Williams, 'Mother', 689–90. Cf. Fehribach, *Women*, 31–2.

[18] Beck, *Discipleship*, 57. Cf. Brown, *Gospel*, 1:109; Bultmann, *Gospel*, 117.

[19] Cf. Beck, *Discipleship*, 61; Moloney, *Gospel*, 67–8; Beirne, *Women*, 57.

[20] Williams thus misses the significance of the command of Jesus' mother in the light of John's theology. However, to treat her action in 2:5 as a belief-response (so J.A. Grassi, 'The Role of Jesus' Mother in John's Gospel', *CBQ* 48 [1986]: 78; Howard, 'Significance', 67–8; Beirne, *Women*, 57–9; cf. Scott, *Sophia*, 181–2; Beck, 'Function', 150; *idem*, *Discipleship*, 58, 61; Moloney, *Gospel*, 68) concludes more than the text warrants. Conway's reading that it is Jesus' mother rather than Jesus who is attuned to the Father's will (*Men and Women*, 77–8) is unconvincing.

[21] Cf. Fehribach, *Women*, 37; Keener, *Gospel*, 501; Beirne, *Women*, 52–3, 61; Howard, 'Significance', 66.

when that hour comes (19:26–27).[22] However, that Jesus' mother makes only two appearances in the Johannine narrative does not mean that the two events interpret one another. Besides, the 'hour' in 2:4 and 19:27 do not have the same referent. The 'hour' in 2:4 denotes the messianic hour whose 'not yet' aspect is removed in the subsequent miracle, whereas the 'hour' in 19:27 lacks theological significance and simply means 'from that moment' (cf. 'hour' in 5:35; 16:2). Jesus' mother did not have to wait till 19:27 to experience the messianic blessings or be assigned a role; she was a catalyst for Jesus' messianic ministry in John 2.

At the Foot of the Cross

Standing at the foot of the cross and watching Jesus being crucified, were, among others, four women – Jesus' mother, her sister, Mary (the wife or mother) of Clopas, and Mary Magdalene – and the Beloved Disciple (19:25–26).[23] When Jesus sees his mother and the Beloved Disciple standing together, he says to her, 'Woman, see, your son', and to the Beloved Disciple, 'See, your mother' (19:26–27a). From that 'hour', the Beloved Disciple takes Jesus' mother into his own home (19:27b). How must we interpret this incident? Most Johannine scholars interpret 19:26–27 symbolically as the constitution of the church or the community of believers, in which Jesus' mother represents Judaism,[24] Jewish Christianity finding a home in Gentile Christianity,[25] faithful Israel finding a home in the Christian community,[26] or the spiritual mother or new Eve of all believers.[27] Brown later modified his position (see n. 27), arguing that Jesus reinterprets who his mother and his brothers are in terms of discipleship: Jesus' mother and the Beloved Disciple (who is now Jesus' brother) become models for Jesus' true family of disciples.[28]

---

[22] R.E. Brown, 'Roles of Women in the Fourth Gospel', *TS* 36 (1975): 697; Collins, 'Figures', 32–3; Culpepper, *Anatomy*, 133; Beck *Discipleship*, 62; M.L. Coloe, *Dwelling in the Household of God: Johannine Ecclesiology and Spirituality* (Collegeville: Liturgical Press, 2007), 54–5. Cf. those who connect the 'hour' in 2:4 and 19:27 (Davies, *Rhetoric*, 340; Lieu, 'Mother', 67; Gaventa, *Mary*, 89; Conway, *Men and Women*, 73, 79).

[23] For a discussion about the exact number of women in 19:25, see Lieu, 'Mother', 68; Maccini, *Testimony*, 185–6.

[24] Krafft, 'Personen', 18–9; Waetjen, *Gospel*, 116, 397.

[25] Bultmann, *Gospel*, 673.

[26] Schnackenburg, *Gospel*, 3:278–9.

[27] Brown, *Gospel*, 1:107–9; 2:926–7; Grassi, 'Role', 73. Cf. Lieu, 'Mother', 71–6. Fehribach also interprets 19:25–27 symbolically as the constitution of the believing community but she gives pre-eminence to the Beloved Disciple; Jesus' mother is merely the exchange object to accomplish this spiritual transaction (*Women*, ch. 5). For a detailed (but older) review of the various interpretations, see R.F. Collins, 'Mary in the Fourth Gospel: A Decade of Johannine Studies', *LS* 3 (1970): 99–142.

[28] Brown, 'Roles', 698–9; *idem, Mary*, 213–4; *idem*, 'The "Mother of Jesus" in the Fourth Gospel', in *L'Evangile de Jean: Sources, redaction, théologie* (ed. M. de Jonge; BETL 44; Leuven: Leuven

Many of these symbolic interpretations seem speculative and far-fetched.[29] Moreover, the obvious lack of consensus amongst scholars who interpret the scene at the foot of the cross symbolically makes us question the validity of this approach.[30] There are several problems with a symbolic understanding of 19:25–27 as the inception of the church or family of believers. First, such understanding would require the Beloved Disciple to be addressed as 'man', and them to be given to each other as brother and sister, not as mother and son.[31] Second, Jesus dissociates himself from this new relationship – the woman is no longer *his* mother but the Beloved Disciple's. Third, the Beloved Disciple takes Jesus' mother into *his* home rather than together becoming part of *Jesus'* home (which would fit a symbolic interpretation).[32] Fourth, Jesus has already begun to constitute a spiritual family during his ministry when people believed in and remained with him.[33]

This leads us to an alternative interpretation. I suggest that Jesus fulfils his filial obligations with a practical solution: he constitutes a new earthly family consisting of his mother and his most intimate disciple. Knowing that he will no longer be able to care for his mother, he provides a home for her with the disciple he was closest to.[34] Jesus' command suggests that his father Joseph had died – perhaps before the wedding at Cana took place (see n. 3) –

University Press, 1987), 310. Cf. Culpepper, *Anatomy*, 134; Scott, *Sophia*, 219–20; Beirne, *Women*, 170–94; Coloe, *Household*, 55–6, 112–3, 145.

[29] E.g. Grassi concludes that Jesus' mother 'could represent the church as a concerned mother asking for the new wine of the spirit and presenting obedience to Jesus' word understood in the light of his death as a means to obtain it' ('Role', 79).

[30] Cf. Conway, *Men and Women*, 81.

[31] Lieu, 'Mother', 69–70. Beirne's assertion that the particular role of Jesus' mother as 'mother' is 'to give birth to and nourish this new family of the children of God', and that the Beloved Disciple's role is to model a sonship of total obedience to Jesus' mother's advice 'Do whatever he tells you' (2:5) (*Women*, 180), is difficult to understand, especially since it is the Spirit that provides new birth and true nourishment in his teaching role. Besides, Beirne's claim that Jesus pours out the Spirit upon his newly constituted family (*Women*, 184, 191–2) is unwarranted by the text (see C. Bennema, 'The Giving of the Spirit in John's Gospel – A New Proposal?', *EvQ* 74 [2002]: 200–201).

[32] Hence, the argument that by implication the Beloved Disciple becomes Jesus' brother is not sufficiently persuasive. Only in 20:17 and 21:23 we can safely interpret 'brothers' as the community of faith (including male and female believers).

[33] A more suitable Johannine picture of the church or family of believers is the one flock, made up of Jews and Gentiles who have responded to the voice of the good shepherd (10:2–4, 16), or the vine with the branches (15:1–5). This flock has already been constituted during Jesus' ministry and included sheep such as the Twelve, the Samaritan woman and her fellow-villagers, the royal official and his household, the man born blind and the Lazarus family. For a critical assessment of the symbolic interpretations, see Martin, 'Epithet', 64–6; Lieu, 'Mother', 71; Gaventa, *Mary*, 90–91; J.G. van der Watt, *Family of the King: Dynamics of Metaphor in the Gospel according to John* (BIS 47; Leiden: Brill, 2000), 333–5.

[34] Cf. Barrett, *Gospel*, 350; Williams, 'Mother', 690; Edwards, *John*, 109. Van Tilborg relates Jesus' act to a son's obligations to support his parents, prescribed in the Mishnah and Talmud (based on Exod. 20:12; Lev. 19:3) (*Love*, 9–12). Besides, Jesus puts his mother in the care of the Beloved Disciple rather than of his brothers because there was a distance between them (7:1–9) (Williams, 'Mother', 690–91; Keener, *Gospel*, 1145).

and hence someone would have to provide for his mother. This incident illustrates how the community of believers that Jesus had already constituted during his lifetime (namely those who adequately responded to him and followed him) should function – with practical care for one another's needs. There is one more dimension: Jesus' address of his mother as 'woman' is possibly meant to create some distance between them (cf. 2:4). Being in the process of returning to his Father (starting with the cross and culminating in the ascension), Jesus can no longer maintain links with this world or his biological family.[35]

Conclusion

Jesus' mother figures as a witness to two important events. First, she is present at the launch of her son's messianic ministry; and later, she witnesses the climax of her son's mission at the cross. She appears to be practical, observant, caring, shows initiative and plays (perhaps unknowingly) an important role in Jesus' ministry. In the first instance, she precipitates the inauguration of Jesus' messianic ministry by her request in 2:3, and the resulting first sign elicits belief from the disciples. Besides, in keeping with the thrust of John's gospel, she directs people to obey Jesus' word in 2:5. The mother of Jesus thus functions as a catalyst in leading people to an authentic belief-response in Jesus. At the end of his life, Jesus makes of his mother (and the Beloved Disciple) an example of how the community of believers should care for one another. Besides, the phrase 'After this, when Jesus knew that everything was now finished' (19:28) indicates that, *inter alia*, 19:26–27 was vital or contributed to the completion of Jesus' mission.[36] She thus functions (largely unknowingly) as a catalyst for both the beginning and end of Jesus' ministry, and while she initially tries to draw her son into her plans, she is ultimately drawn into his.[37] Although John does not record an explicit belief-response from her, it would not be too wide of the mark to suggest that she was on Jesus' side.[38]

The connection between 2:3–5 and 19:25–27 is not the occurrence of the 'hour' but the issue of filial obligations. Jesus' addressing his mother as 'woman' on both occasions indicates that his loyalty lies primarily with his family 'from above'. At the wedding in Cana, Jesus distances himself from his mother's plans because his primary concern is his Father's mission – though he implicitly fulfils his filial obligations to his mother. At the cross,

---

[35] Gaventa, *Mary*, 91; Resseguie, *Strange Gospel*, 159. Cf. Lieu, 'Mother', 69–70.

[36] Cf. Lieu, 'Mother', 69; Conway, *Men and Women*, 84.

[37] Scott's evaluation of Jesus' mother as 'a symbol of true discipleship in her service and faithfulness' is overrated (*Sophia*, 220).

[38] Contra Maccini, who only attributes a miracle faith to Jesus' mother because she requests a miracle from Jesus in 2:3 (an interpretation we denied) (*Testimony*, 113, 199).

Jesus fulfils his filial obligations to his mother but once again distances himself from his family below in order to return to his Father above.[39]

The Mother of Jesus		
Appearances	References	2:1, 3, 5, 12; 6:42; 19:25 (2x), 26 (2x), 27.
Identity	Titles given	–
	Gender	female
	Age	–
	Marital status	married (perhaps widowed)
	Occupation	–
	Socio-economic status	–
	Place of residence/operation	Nazareth (but travelled in Galilee), Jerusalem
	Relatives	various sons, including Jesus
	Group affiliation	her family, her sister, Mary the wife of Clopas, Mary Magdalene, the Beloved Disciple
Speech and actions	In interaction with Jesus	she initially tries to rope Jesus into her plans but eventually finds herself part of his plan
	In interaction with others	directs people to obey Jesus' word
Character classification	Complexity	uncomplicated; multiple traits: practical, caring, observant, showing initiative, being a witness
	Development	none
	Inner life	none
Degree of characterization		type
Response to Jesus		no belief-response is recorded, but her attitude and catalysing role indicates that she is on Jesus' side

[39] Cf. Jesus' emphasis on the family 'from above' (3:3–5 [elaborating 1:12–13]; 8:39–47; 20:17; 21:23) over his family 'from below' (in 7:1–9, Jesus distances himself from his disbelieving, biological brothers). Williams misses the theological dimension of Jesus' twofold distancing himself from his mother ('Mother', 692). Conway dismisses the 'distancing' theory for an interpretation that Jesus' address of his mother as 'woman' points to the significant role that women play in this gospel (*Men and Women*, 78, 83).

Nicodemus – In the Twilight Zone

*'To rid ourselves of our shadows – who we are – we must step
into either total light or total darkness' — Jeremy P. Johnson*

One of the most intriguing characters in John's gospel is Nicodemus, not
least because scholars have evaluated him in different and contrasting
ways: from being someone who became Jesus' disciple,[1] to 'the true
Israelite',[2] 'a well-intentioned representative of the ruling classes',[3] a fearful
'secret believer',[4] a *tertium quid*,[5] a pathetic character lacking courage and
conviction,[6] one who has come 'to a dead end',[7] or even the typical
unbeliever.[8] Everything about Nicodemus is intriguing and mystifying –
his identity, his dialogue with Jesus in John 3, the argument with his
colleagues in John 7, and his appearance at Jesus' burial in John 19.

The Identity of Nicodemus

The first two clues to Nicodemus's identity appear in 3:1. First, Nicodemus
was a Pharisee. Pharisees were laity – they did not belong to the priesthood
– and were regarded as experts on Mosaic law. According to the Jewish
historian Flavius Josephus, they were the most influential sect, enjoying the
general support of the populace (*Antiquities* 13:298; 18:15–20; *Jewish War*
2:162, 411). There seems to be a growing consensus among scholars that
in Jesus' time the Pharisees had the power of *influence* rather than control.

---

[1] Lindars, *Gospel*, 149; Ridderbos, *Gospel*, 285; Moloney, *Gospel*, 511; Bauckham, 'Nicodemus',
29–32; Keener, *Gospel*, 533.

[2] S.M. Schneiders, 'Born Anew', *TTod* 44 (1987): 191.

[3] Schnackenburg, *Gospel*, 1:363.

[4] Martyn, *History*, 88, 113; Brown, *Gospel*, 2:959–60; Culpepper, *Anatomy*, 136, 146.

[5] J.M. Bassler, 'Mixed Signals: Nicodemus in the Fourth Gospel', *JBL* 108 (1989): 646. Cf.
Köstenberger, *John*, 119.

[6] Conway, *Men and Women*, 103.

[7] M. de Jonge, 'Nicodemus and Jesus: Some Observations on Misunderstanding and
Understanding in the Fourth Gospel', in *Jesus: Stranger from Heaven and Son of God. Jesus Christ
and the Christians in Johannine Perspective* (ed. and trans. J.E. Steely; SBLSBS 11; Missoula:
Scholars Press, 1977), 32–4. Cf. Krafft, 'Personen', 20.

[8] Collins, 'Figures', 15.

They were not only able to influence the common people but also those who had the power of control and policymaking. We can therefore count the Pharisees among the religious authorities though they were not the main leaders.[9]

Second, the phrase 'a ruler of the Jews' indicates that Nicodemus was probably a member of the Sanhedrin – the Jewish Supreme Court in Jerusalem. In 7:45–52, Nicodemus is present at a meeting of the chief priests and Pharisees, and such a meeting is explicitly called *sunedrion* ('council') in 11:47. Although *sunedrion* could simply refer to a local city council, the meetings in 7:45–52 and 11:45–53 are set in Jerusalem and the high priest, who presides over the Sanhedrin, is present in 11:49. Therefore, 7:45–52 and 11:45–53 very likely describe meetings of the Sanhedrin of which Nicodemus was a member. We have argued elsewhere that prominent (and probably wealthy) Pharisees could belong to the Sanhedrin,[10] and Nicodemus fits the profile.

A third pointer to Nicodemus's identity appears in 3:10, where Jesus calls him 'the teacher of Israel'. The Greek *didaskalos* ('teacher') is equivalent to the Hebrew *rabbi* (cf. 1:38; 3:2). In addition, the explicit use of the Greek *su* ('you') in 3:10 adds emphasis – Nicodemus is *the* teacher or 'top theologian' of Israel. Moreover, his reply to Jesus, 'How can a man be born when he is an old man?' (3:4), seems to imply that he was advanced in age.[11] Nicodemus very likely resided in Jerusalem since that is where he appears to be in John 3, 7 and 19. He was almost certainly wealthy, considering that the extraordinary amount of spices he brought for Jesus' burial was worth a fortune.

Nicodemus therefore appears to be a wealthy, leading Pharisaic scholar in Jerusalem and a member of the Sanhedrin. As such he would have enjoyed a prominent social, economic and religious status. Regarding the historical referent of Nicodemus, some scholars have seen a connection with a wealthy Jerusalem aristocrat called Naqdimon ben Gurion.[12] However, since Naqdimon ben Gurion was around during the Jewish War in 66–70 CE, Carson points out that it would mean Nicodemus was a very young man at the time of his conversation with Jesus, which is very unlikely.[13] Bauckham presents a more convincing case for the Gurion connection and suggests that Nicodemus may have been the uncle of Naqdimon ben Gurion.[14]

---

[9] For the Pharisees in general, see Saldarini, *Pharisees*. For the Pharisees' role in John's gospel, see Bennema, 'Identity', section 3.1.

[10] Bennema, 'Identity', section 3.1.

[11] Contra Schnackenburg, *Gospel*, 1:368.

[12] E.g. Taylor, *Immerser*, 187–8. Cf. Barrett, *Gospel*, 204.

[13] Carson, *Gospel*, 186.

[14] Bauckham, 'Nicodemus', 1–37.

Nicodemus and Jesus

We contend that the Nicodemus pericope starts in 2:23 and ends at 3:15.[15] The dialogue between Nicodemus and Jesus only starts at 3:2, but 2:23 – 3:1 sets the stage. While Jesus was in Jerusalem during the Passover festival, he performed miracles ('signs') which caused many people to believe (*pisteuein*) in him (2:23). Jesus, however, distrusted their belief-response – he did not 'believe' or entrust himself to them (*ouk episteuen*) because he knew people and their motivations (2:24–25). Although the text does not clarify in what way the people's belief-response was defective or deficient, it was nevertheless inadequate. Jesus did not question their belief because it was based on signs for on another occasion he commends such belief (10:38; cf. 20:30–31).[16] What was lacking in the people's response to Jesus in 2:23 will be clarified in the story of Nicodemus because he is included in this group – not socially but in the way he was drawn to Jesus and responded to him.[17]

Scholars frequently give the impression that Nicodemus came to Jesus alone, secretly at night, which could lead to the idea that Nicodemus was an anonymous or secret disciple.[18] A more likely scenario, however, is that Nicodemus, accompanied by his disciples, came one evening to have a discussion with Jesus and his disciples (cf. the use of plurals in 3:2, 11–12). Theological discussion between rabbis and their followers frequently occurred 'at night', i.e. in the evening, after dark.[19] Hence, at the level of story, Nicodemus may speak for himself and his disciples, while at the level of narrative, John casts him as the representative of a larger group with the same faith-stance.[20]

[15] The reason for viewing 2:23 as the start of the Nicodemus story is threefold: (i) 'a man' in 3:1 alludes to its double use in 2:25; (ii) the antecedent of 'him' in the phrase 'he came to him at night' in 3:2 is Jesus in 2:24; (iii) the phrase 'the signs that he was doing' in 2:23 is repeated by Nicodemus in 3:2. The conversation seems to end at 3:15 (rather than at 3:12 or 3:21) and 3:16–21 is the narrator's comments because: (i) 3:12–13 is one sentence in Greek so that 3:12 has no break; (ii) the phrase 'Son of man' used in 3:13–14 is Jesus' self-designation and the switch to 'Son (of God)' in 3:16–18 may indicate that the narrator has started speaking.

[16] Elsewhere I have argued that signs can be a basis for adequate belief, contra many scholars who regard signs-faith as incomplete, inadequate or unacceptable (Bennema, *Power*, 10–12, 145–7).

[17] Bultmann denies this connection (*Gospel*, 133).

[18] Cf. Painter, *Quest*, 197; Koester, *Symbolism*, 45; Ridderbos, *Gospel*, 123; Moloney, *Gospel*, 510.

[19] F.P. Cotterell, 'The Nicodemus Conversation: A Fresh Appraisal', *ExpTim* 96 (1984–85): 238; Bauckham, 'Nicodemus', 31; Beirne, *Women*, 73. See also Str.-B., 2:419–20. The Qumran community also knew a similar practice (1QS 6:6–7). Carson, however, rejects this view (*Gospel*, 187, 198).

[20] Contra scholars who contend that the use of plurals indicates that Nicodemus represents the Pharisees, the Sanhedrin or official Judaism in Jesus' time (so, e.g. Bultmann, *Gospel*, 133; Lindars, *Gospel*, 149; Carson, *Gospel*, 187) or the secret believers in the synagogue in John's time (so, e.g. Martyn, *History*, 88, 113; Brown, *Gospel*, 2:959–60; D.K. Rensberger, *Overcoming*

Nicodemus was thus attracted to and even 'believed' in Jesus on the basis of his signs but Jesus was critical of his response. His coming 'at night' (3:2) might also symbolize Nicodemus's spiritual position – for John, Nicodemus is still in the dark.[21] This was most likely not Nicodemus's evaluation of himself since he came with his disciples to establish who Jesus was – his assertion in 3:2 is in essence a question about Jesus' identity and authority (cf. 1:19, 22, 25). Nicodemus accepts that Jesus is a teacher and miracle worker from God but his identity eludes him.

Jesus, instead of satisfying his curiosity, talks about entry into the kingdom of God through a new birth 'from above' (3:3). Nicodemus accepts this topic but misunderstands what Jesus is saying (3:4). Nicodemus thinks 'from below' – he understands the new birth literally and thus misses its metaphorical meaning (cf. 3:6, 31). To clear up this misunderstanding, Jesus provides further revelation in 3:5–8.[22] Nicodemus, however, is unable to keep pace with Jesus, as his question 'How can these things be?' in 3:9 shows. Jesus' rebuke in 3:10 reveals that he expected Nicodemus to understand at least some of what he is saying (cf. 3:11–12). Nicodemus thus has a cognitive problem – he fails to understand or think 'from above' and therefore cannot become part of this saving realm. Although he recognizes that Jesus is 'from God' on the basis of his signs, Nicodemus is unable to grasp the real significance of these signs. He fails to see the realm 'from above' that the signs point to and to which Jesus belongs. Consequently, he remains 'from below'.

In spite of a promising start, Nicodemus simply fades out of the conversation and disappears into the darkness from which he came (cf. the rapid decrease in the number of words from 3:2 to 3:4 to 3:9). He remains ambiguous and as readers we must look at his two later appearances to determine whether he is able to progress in his understanding of Jesus.[23]

Nicodemus and His Colleagues

Nicodemus reappears in 7:45–52, where we read about a gathering of the chief priests and the Pharisees – probably a meeting of the Sanhedrin. During the feast of Tabernacles, a discussion arises among the crowds regarding

---

the World: Politics and Community in the Gospel of John [London: SPCK, 1988], 54–61). Rather, Nicodemus represents a particular type of belief-response mentioned in 2:23. Koester probably overstretches Nicodemus's representative function, saying that Nicodemus represents 'humanity estranged from God' or 'the world' (*Symbolism*, 46–7).

[21] Cf. Beirne, *Women*, 73. Edwards disagrees, suggesting that Nicodemus came out of the darkness into the true light (*John*, 105; cf. Barrett, *Gospel*, 205). However, she disregards the fact that towards the end of the conversation Nicodemus slips back into the darkness.

[22] For an elaborate explanation of the birth of water-and-Spirit, see Bennema, *Power*, 169–72.

[23] For a detailed exegesis of the Nicodemus story in John 3, see Bennema, *Power*, 168–81; idem, *John's Gospel*, 43–9.

Jesus' identity and origin, provoking the chief priests and Pharisees to send temple guards to arrest Jesus (7:25–32). However, this delegation fails to arrest him and their excuse angers the Sanhedrin (7:44–49). At this point, Nicodemus throws himself into the debate (7:50–51).

We determined from 2:23 – 3:1 that Nicodemus's initial 'belief' was deficient but now it also appears anonymous or secret. The same could not be inferred from John 3 – we rejected a scenario in which Nicodemus came to Jesus secretly, alone and in the middle of the night – but is suggested here in John 7. The question, 'None of the authorities or Pharisees have believed in him, have they?' (7:48),[24] reveals that the Sanhedrin is unaware that one of them, Nicodemus, 'believes' in, or is sympathetic to Jesus. Nicodemus shows courage when he defends Jesus by confronting his colleagues on judicial procedure but his challenge is rudely suppressed (7:51–52).[25] Although Nicodemus has apparently remained sympathetic to Jesus, he seems hesitant to associate himself openly with him. He does not answer the Sanhedrin's question in 7:48 and the ferocious response of his colleagues in 7:52 may have robbed him of any courage to ally himself publicly with Jesus. Once again, Nicodemus starts well but fails to follow through and vanishes.[26]

Hence, Nicodemus remains ambiguous. On the one hand, he remains sympathetic to Jesus, to the point of defending him and triggering off an angry reaction from his colleagues. On the other hand, he appears unwilling to associate himself openly with Jesus and take the kind of stand that John would recommend. We learn later that the parents of the man born blind failed to testify because of fear of the Jewish religious authorities, who had decided to excommunicate anyone who confessed Jesus to be the Messiah (9:22). Nicodemus would certainly have known of this edict and may have been afraid of his colleagues.[27] In John 3 we were uncertain about Nicodemus's attitude and what he had grasped of Jesus' identity, and this incident only adds to his ambiguity.

[24] In the Greek, the question expects a negative answer.

[25] The description of Nicodemus as being 'one of them' (7:50) may indicate that he has not sided with Jesus. Alternatively, it may be a challenge to the Pharisees' claim in 7:48 that *not one of them* had believed in Jesus (so Moloney, *Gospel*, 255). Brant remarks that Nicodemus identifies himself with the authorities ('Our law' [7:51]), but that by their question in 7:52 they distance themselves from him (*Dialogue*, 191).

[26] Brown (*Gospel*, 1:325), Beirne (*Women*, 95) and Edwards (*John*, 105) conclude too much, contending that Nicodemus here reaches mature faith.

[27] Cf. the 'secret believers' among the Jewish 'rulers' in 12:42. Some scholars, however, deny any element of fear, secretiveness or anonymity on the part of Nicodemus (Ridderbos, *Gospel*, 123, 284–5). Nevertheless, to say that Nicodemus's attitude showed elements of secretiveness or anonymity is not the same as labelling Nicodemus a 'secret believer' because nowhere does the text indicate that Nicodemus reached true belief. Rather, he is a sympathetic seeker, who is still seeking (Stibbe, *John*, 54).

Nicodemus and Joseph of Arimathea

Nicodemus's final appearance is at Jesus' burial in 19:38–42. Narratologically, Joseph and Nicodemus are clubbed together – even though Joseph makes the request to Pilate and Nicodemus brings the spices there is unity in their actions. Nicodemus's association with Joseph of Arimathea, who is described as a secret disciple of Jesus because of his fear of the Jews, may confirm the secrecy of Nicodemus's 'belief' or convictions that we noted earlier. Nevertheless, Joseph's request to Pilate for Jesus' body speaks of courage, especially when one considers that bodies of crucified people were normally not buried but left on the cross to decay or thrown into a common grave.[28] It was especially unusual to bestow honour on a 'criminal' as Joseph and Nicodemus did.

The significance of Nicodemus's involvement in Jesus' burial is a debated issue. Some argue that Nicodemus was preoccupied with death or did not find life in Jesus' death and hence remained in the darkness.[29] Others, however, view Nicodemus positively considering that such an extraordinary amount of expensive spices (weighing approximately 32.5 kilograms) was only used for a royal burial (cf. 2 Chr. 16:14; Josephus, *Antiquities* 15:61; 17:199).[30] The Talmud narrates that Onkelos burned about 40 kilograms of spices at the funeral of Gamaliel the Elder, around 50 CE. When asked why he had done so, he replied, 'Is not R. Gamaliel worth more than a hundred useless kings?' (*b. Semaḥoth* 47a).[31] Perhaps Nicodemus did recognize Jesus' kingship – a theme that incidentally comes to the fore in John 18 – 19. Besides, Nicodemus achieves what Mary did proleptically (12:3–7), and if her deed received approval, then Nicodemus's act could also be interpreted positively. Finally, it is unlikely that Joseph and Nicodemus acted secretly; it is almost certain that 'the Jews' knew who buried Jesus.

It appears that Nicodemus has made progress since John 3 and 7. But does the text give enough indication that Nicodemus in 19:38–42 openly takes Jesus' side and has grasped who Jesus really is? Nicodemus shows a curious mix of boldness and fear, both in John 7 and John 19. He is bold enough to speak up for Jesus in the Sanhedrin and to take a risk in burying Jesus, but at the same time he is afraid to ally himself openly with Jesus and he is seen associating with another fearful disciple. We conclude that John does not provide sufficient evidence that Nicodemus's actions or understanding

---

[28] Carson, *Gospel*, 629; Beasley-Murray, *John*, 358. Cf. Mark 15:43.

[29] Krafft, 'Personen', 20; W.A. Meeks, 'The Man from Heaven in Johannine Sectarianism', *JBL* 91 (1972): 55; de Jonge, 'Nicodemus', 32–4; D.D. Sylva, 'Nicodemus and His Spices (John 19.39)', *NTS* 34 (1988): 148–51. In addition, Nicodemus and Joseph's burying Jesus according to the custom of 'the Jews' (19:40) may also indicate that they are still siding with 'the Jews'.

[30] E.g. Schnackenburg, *Gospel*, 3:295; O'Day, *Gospel*, 836; Beirne, *Women*, 85–6, 96–7; Koester, *Symbolism*, 229–30.

[31] Cf. Bauckham, 'Nicodemus', 32 n. 123.

of Jesus is adequate for salvation. Although Nicodemus remains sympathetic to Jesus, it is uncertain what he understands of Jesus and his mission.[32]

Conclusion

We have inferred that John does not provide a clear picture of Nicodemus, and yet, at another level, we shall see that the picture is clear. In John 3, attracted by Jesus' signs, Nicodemus 'believed' in Jesus and came to learn more about him. However, by including him among those to whom Jesus did not entrust himself, John indicates that Nicodemus's 'belief' was deficient. Playing on the word 'at night', John hints that Nicodemus is essentially still in the dark. In his conversation with Jesus it becomes clear that Nicodemus's 'belief' was not deficient because it was based on signs but because he was thinking 'from below' – unable to grasp Jesus' teaching and hence unable to enter into the saving realm 'from above' through a birth 'from above'. Nicodemus gradually fades out of the conversation and disappears into the shadows from which he came.

Later, in John 7, Nicodemus speaks up in a meeting of the Sanhedrin, showing that he is still sympathetic to Jesus, but there is no indication whether he has progressed in his understanding of him. Despite his show of courage, Nicodemus seems afraid to be openly associated with Jesus and remains ambiguous and secretive about his beliefs. The last appearance of Nicodemus, in John 19 at Jesus' burial, does not provide clarity about his stance towards Jesus either. Nicodemus ultimately remains who he is – sympathetic but ambiguous.[33]

Nicodemus displays a complex set of traits. Although he shows initiative and remains sympathetic to Jesus, he also continues to be ambiguous and indecisive – there is no evidence of adequate belief or open commitment. It is unclear whether he was able or willing to profess allegiance to Jesus, whether a lack of understanding or fear of his colleagues in the Sanhedrin prevented him from arriving at or expressing an adequate belief in Jesus. He shows courage and risks being associated with Jesus but he displays secrecy and fear at the same time.

Nicodemus reveals a glimpse of his inner thoughts in 3:2, when he claims knowledge of Jesus. There is also development in Nicodemus's character.

---

[32] Cf. G. Renz, who concludes after an extensive comparison of a positive and negative reading of 19:38–42 that 'Nicodemus's last appearance can legitimately be interpreted in either direction' ('Nicodemus: An Ambiguous Disciple? A Narrative Sensitive Investigation', in *Challenging Perspectives on the Gospel of John* [ed. J. Lierman; WUNT 2/219; Tübingen: Mohr Siebeck, 2006], 274–9 [quotation from p. 279]). Contra Bauckham ('Nicodemus', 31–2), who argues that Nicodemus's acknowledgement of Jesus' kingship became full Christian faith after the resurrection, and Beirne (*Women*, 97–8), who contends that Nicodemus's act reflects his growth in faith and discipleship.

[33] Cf. Bassler's article 'Signals', which illuminates Nicodemus's ambiguity.

The reader is probably surprised that the intellectual Nicodemus, steeped in Israel's religious tradition, is a bit slow when it comes to understanding spiritual realities and does not seem to progress. After each initiative (3:2; 7:50–51), Nicodemus is reprimanded and quietly leaves the stage (3:10; 7:52), but returns unexpectedly (7:50; 19:39). Besides, Nicodemus's traits of showing initiative and courage are in tension with his secrecy, possible fear and silent exit from each scene when he is reprimanded. Surprisingly, Nicodemus's intellect and courage do not take him all the way to a public confession of Jesus (in contrast to the Samaritan woman and the man born blind).

John implicitly gives a negative evaluation of Nicodemus's ambiguity – to stay in the twilight zone is not acceptable. First, Nicodemus makes little or no cognitive progress in any of his appearances, and hence John's evaluation of Nicodemus's starting position (which is inadequate) remains valid. Second, Nicodemus remains ambiguous and secretive regarding his beliefs about Jesus. If fear of his colleagues keeps Nicodemus from a public allegiance to Jesus, then, in the light of Jesus' command to his disciples when faced with persecution – 'You must also testify' (15:27) – Nicodemus's stance would be inadequate.[34] Elsewhere John is also implicitly critical of such an attitude when he contrasts the bold testimony of the man born blind in the face of persecution with his fearful parents' failure to testify (9:13–34; cf. 12:42). To testify is an expression of discipleship, and discipleship is essential to remain in a life-giving relationship with Jesus (cf. ch. 1, section 'John's Story of Jesus').

It remains unclear whether Nicodemus experienced the new birth that would have brought him into the kingdom of God. Besides, there is no evidence of any form of confession or discipleship. John's implicit message to the reader is that anonymous discipleship or secret Christianity will not suffice.[35] A public confession of some kind that Jesus is the Christ seems appropriate and necessary. For John, remaining in the twilight zone, i.e. continual ambiguity, anonymity or secrecy, is not a valid option. Nicodemus is attracted to the light but does not remain in the light; he keeps moving in and out of the shadows, and within John's dualism, there is no place for a twilight zone. Too often, people feel compelled to put Nicodemus on one or the other side of John's dualistic world, but John does not redeem Nicodemus of his ambiguity. The point John wants to make is that continual ambiguity is not an acceptable attitude.[36]

[34] Even if Nicodemus's speech in 7:50 can be called 'testimony', he did not sustain it after his colleagues attacked him in 7:52.

[35] Cf. Culpepper, *Anatomy*, 136, 146; Bassler, 'Signals', 645–6; Beck, *Discipleship*, 69. Contra some overly positive conclusions of Nicodemus's being a believer, disciple and example to follow (Lindars, *Gospel*, 149, 304; Schnackenburg, *Gospel*, 1:364–5; W. Munro, 'The Pharisee and the Samaritan in John: Polar and Parallel', *CBQ* 57 [1995]: 716, 727; Ridderbos, *Gospel*, 285; Moloney, *Gospel*, 511; Edwards, *John*, 105). Collins' analysis that Nicodemus is the type of an unbeliever, however, seems too negative ('Figures', 15–6; 'John', 363).

[36] Similarly, to be a 'seeker' today is encouraging but John's warning is that one should not remain one.

Nicodemus		
Appearances	References	3:1, 4, 9; 7:50; 19:39
Identity	Titles given	Pharisee, member of the Sanhedrin, leading rabbi in Israel
	Gender	male
	Age	advanced
	Marital status	presumably married
	Occupation	Pharisaic scholar
	Socio-economic status	wealthy, respected, highly educated
	Place of residence/operation	Jerusalem
	Relatives	possibly part of the aristocratic Gurion family in Jerusalem
	Group affiliation	Pharisees, Sanhedrin, Joseph of Arimathea
Speech and actions	In interaction with Jesus	shows initiative but lacks understanding; sympathetic but no open commitment; ambiguous
	In interaction with others	ambiguous, secretive, boldness combined with fear
Character classification	Complexity	complex; multiple traits: ambiguous, indecisive, showing initiative, sympathetic to Jesus, fearful, secretive, courageous, intellectual, risk-taking
	Development	some development: he shows initiative, courage and willingness to be associated with Jesus but these traits seem curbed by fear, secrecy, an inability to sustain an argument, and silent disappearance from the scene
	Inner life	little
Degree of characterization		personality
Response to Jesus		inadequate: sympathetic but ambiguous; attracted to Jesus but no open commitment

10

The Samaritan Woman – An Unexpected Bride

'[T]he marriage of the Lamb has come, and his bride has made herself ready' — *Revelation 19:7*

After the intriguing account of Nicodemus, we come to the unexpected encounter between Jesus and the Samaritan woman. Since both stories are about belief-responses, and have common themes including water, Spirit, eternal life and testimony, it becomes evident that John wants his readers to compare the woman with Nicodemus.[1] Like Nicodemus, she is an individual character but also representative of a larger group. Despite the similarities, Nicodemus and the Samaritan woman stand in great contrast. While Nicodemus is a well-known, well-to-do, well-educated Jewish religious leader, the woman is anonymous and, as a Samaritan, belongs to a community despised by the Jews (cf. 4:9).[2] Even her own people may have treated the woman as a social outcast because of her questionable lifestyle (mentioned in 4:16–18). This would explain why she came to draw water alone (4:7), and at such an unusual time – 4:6 mentions that it was noon, the hottest part of the day.[3]

Setting the Stage

The stage for Jesus' encounter with the Samaritan woman is set in 4:1–7a. Jesus has left Judaea – perhaps to avoid a confrontation with the Pharisees (cf. 1:19–28) – for the more receptive Galilee in the north (4:1–3). Although

---

[1] Contra Stibbe, who argues that the focus of John 4 is true worship (*John*, 63).

[2] For detailed information on the Samaritans, see J. Jeremias, *Jerusalem in the Time of Jesus* (London: SCM, 1969), 352–8; R.J. Coggins, *Samaritans and Jews* (Oxford: Blackwell, 1975); A.D. Crown, ed., *The Samaritans* (Tübingen: Mohr Siebeck, 1989); R.T. Anderson, *The Keepers: An Introduction to the History and Culture of the Samaritans* (Peabody: Hendrickson, 2002).

[3] D.A. Lee contends that the woman does not come at an unusual hour because of her marginal social status but because the narrative simply demands that she meets Jesus alone (*The Symbolic Narratives of the Fourth Gospel: The Interplay of Form and Meaning* [JSNTS 95; Sheffield: JSOT Press, 1994], 68 n. 3). However, women usually fetched water in groups, either early or late in the day – when it was cooler (Carson, *Gospel*, 217). For alternative explanations, see J.N. Day, *The Woman at the Well: Interpretation of John 4:1–42 in Retrospect and Prospect* (BIS 61; Leiden: Brill, 2002), 160–63. See also nn. 17 and 28, below, for an argument that the woman is perhaps not (willingly) immoral.

Jews going from Judaea to Galilee might travel east of the Jordan to avoid Samaria, Josephus records that for the festivals Galileans would usually travel through Samaria to Jerusalem (*Antiquities* 20:118).[4] Jesus, however, seems to be under a divine imperative: he *had to go* through Samaria (4:4).[5] He crosses geographical, ethnic, religious, social and gender barriers in order to meet this complex character – a Samaritan, a woman and a social outcast.

The reader may wonder why John includes so many details in 4:5–7a. Most scholars have recognized that, by drawing attention to the patriarchs, a well and a woman, John intends to evoke an Old Testament betrothal-type scene, such as we find in Genesis 24 (Abraham's servant [on behalf of Isaac] and Rebekah), Genesis 29 (Jacob and Rachel) and Exodus 2:15–22 (Moses and Zipporah).[6] The significance or effect of this is to create a certain expectation: Will this Samaritan woman also function as a bride, and if so, for whom? We shall see that this betrothal imagery will shape the bigger story in which Jesus' dialogue with the Samaritan woman takes place.

The Woman's Interaction with Jesus – Part I

Jesus starts the conversation with a simple request (4:7b), but it startles the woman (4:9). This, the narrator explains, is due to the hostile relations between Jews and Samaritans (4:9b).[7] Jesus then introduces two, related topics: the gift of 'living water' and the identity of the giver (4:10).[8] Each topic forms the core of one half of the dialogue – 4:7b–15 and 4:16–26.

Jesus quickly moves from a literal level (the request for physical water in 4:7b) to a metaphorical level (the offer of 'living water' in 4:10), leading us to ask what this 'living water' refers to. Judaism knew of four possible referents for 'living water': (i) life or salvation (Isa. 12:3; 35:6–7; 55:1–3; Jer. 17:13; Zech. 14:8; 1QH 16:4–23); (ii) cleansing or purification (Lev. 14:5–6; Num. 19:17ff.; 1QS 3:4–9; 4:21); (iii) the Spirit (Isa. 44:3; 1QS 4:21); (iv) divine wisdom or teaching (Prov. 13:14; 18:4; Isa. 11:9; Sir. 24:23–29; 1QH 12:11).[9] It is likely that

---

[4] Cf. Brown, *Gospel*, 1:169; Barrett, *Gospel*, 230.

[5] Cf. Moloney, *Gospel*, 116; Beck, *Discipleship*, 71–2; Day, *Woman*, 158.

[6] E.g. Culpepper, *Anatomy*, 136; J.E. Botha, *Jesus and the Samaritan Woman: A Speech Act Reading of John 4:1–42* (NovTSup 65; Leiden: Brill, 1991), 109–12; Scott, *Sophia*, 185–6; Stibbe, *John*, 68; Lee, *Narratives*, 67; Koester, *Symbolism*, 48–9; Beck, *Discipleship*, 72; Fehribach, *Women*, 49–51; Keener, *Gospel*, 586.

[7] The woman's question in 4:9 is an implicit refusal or hesitation to fulfil Jesus' request in 4:7, although she remains cooperative, as the narrative shows.

[8] The chiastic structure of 4:10 already provides the clues that the gift of God corresponds to the 'living water' and that Jesus is the giver. Contra Botha, who contends that the gift of God refers to Jesus (*Jesus*, 123). Lee also observes that Jesus reverses the roles of giver and receiver set up in 4:7, so that *he* becomes the water-giver and *the woman* the one who is thirsty (*Narratives*, 71).

[9] Cf. Bennema, *Power*, 182–4.

all these referents are in view and I suggest that 'living water' is a metaphor for Jesus' Spirit-empowered wisdom teaching that cleanses and gives life to those who accept it.[10] This understanding is in line with the rest of the gospel. In 1:32–34 and 3:34–36, John indicates that Jesus is endowed with the Spirit to speak God's words, i.e. to provide divine teaching. In 6:63, Jesus states that his teaching is Spirit-empowered and produces eternal life. Then, in 7:38–39, John identifies the Spirit as being the referent of 'living water'.[11] Finally, in 15:3, Jesus confirms the cleansing abilities of his teaching (cf. 17:17).

Like Nicodemus, the woman does not recognize that Jesus is now speaking of spiritual issues – she remains at an earthly level. She misunderstands Jesus and the nature or referent of 'living water', thinking that he is talking about literal, running water (4:11).[12] She then mockingly asks Jesus whether he is superior to their patriarchal ancestor Jacob (4:12).[13] The careful reader will detect the irony in such a question, having learned in 3:22–36 about the supremacy of Jesus.[14] The woman's misunderstanding provides an opportunity for further revelation: Jesus explains in 4:13–14 that he is the source of 'living water', that this 'living water' is actually *life-giving* water, and that 'drinking' from this water will quench one's spiritual thirst forever.[15] If 'living water' is a metaphor, then 'to drink' from this water would, naturally, also be metaphorical. 'To drink' the living water, then, is to believe in Jesus and accept his life-giving teaching. In 4:14, Jesus goes on to explain that whoever accepts him and his gift of life will become a secondary source of 'living water' (Jesus being the primary source). Although 4:15 reveals that the woman progresses in understanding – her request shows that she has grasped the superiority of the water that Jesus has to offer – she remains at an earthly level, struggling to understand Jesus' revelation. Nevertheless, she is more responsive and advances further than Nicodemus.

---

[10] Cf. M. Turner, *The Holy Spirit and Spiritual Gifts – Then and Now* (rev. edn; Carlisle: Paternoster, 1999), 61–3. See also Lee, *Narratives*, 77.

[11] F.J. Moloney denies a reference to the Spirit in 4:10–11 because the implied reader has not yet reached 7:38–39 (*Belief in the Word – Reading the Fourth Gospel: John 1 – 4* [Minneapolis: Fortress Press, 1993], 140–41). This is somewhat naive since the reader will be familiar with the explicit reference to the Spirit in any *re*-reading of the gospel.

[12] We should probably not attach too much significance to the different words used for well/spring by the woman (*frear*) and by Jesus (*pēgē*) because *pēgē* is also used by the narrator in 4:6 (cf. Carson, *Gospel*, 217). The real ambiguity lies in the meaning of the metaphor 'living water'. Contra Fehribach, who detects sexual imagery, in that *frear* connotes the female element of sexual intercourse, and water and *pēgē* sometimes connote the male element, so that the Samaritan woman as a *frear* is capable of receiving the 'living water' that Jesus provides as *pēgē* (*Women*, 54–5).

[13] In Greek, the woman's question is phrased to expect the answer 'no'. Contra Day, *Woman*, 165, who detects no mockery.

[14] Cf. Culpepper, *Anatomy*, 172.

[15] Alluding to Sirach 24:21, Jesus makes a greater claim than divine Wisdom – those who drink of the divine wisdom that Jesus gives will not thirst for more but are permanently satisfied.

The Woman's Interaction with Jesus – Part II

Seeing that the woman has not fully understood the nature of his gift, Jesus changes tactics and focuses on his identity. Some scholars think that the conversation has failed, or that the two parts of the dialogue are disjointed seeing how Jesus makes a radical shift from the topic of water to that of worship.[16] However, there is coherence when we recognize the overarching purpose of the encounter. Jesus' desire is that the woman will come to belief by recognizing who he is and by accepting his offer of life-giving water. When the woman fails to grasp the nature of Jesus' offer, he starts to focus on his identity, hoping that when she recognizes the true identity of the giver she will also recognize the true nature of the gift. Having introduced both topics – the gift and the giver – in 4:10, Jesus now simply picks up on the second topic.

Therefore, in 4:16–18, Jesus' aim is not so much to discuss ethics or the woman's lifestyle as it is to show his revelatory knowledge, so that the woman would begin to recognize his identity.[17] Indeed, the woman shows progress: she goes from addressing Jesus as 'Sir' (4:11, 15) to regarding him as a 'prophet' (4:19), to introducing the spiritual topic of worship (4:20). Nevertheless, she continues to think at an earthly level and hence more revelation is needed.

After Jesus replies to the woman's implicit question about the right place to worship God (4:21–24), the conversation moves toward the climax. The woman recognizes that Jesus is talking about important issues and brings up the subject of the Messiah who will reveal everything (4:25). While perceiving the metaphorical nature of Jesus' statements, she nevertheless misses the significance of the 'and is now' of 4:23 and stays focused on the future.[18] In reply, Jesus tells her directly that he is the Messiah she is expecting (4:26).[19]

---

[16] Bultmann, *Gospel*, 187; Botha, *Jesus*, 127; Moloney, *Belief*, 132–4, 145; Stibbe, *John's Gospel*, 18; Day, *Woman*, 166. Surely, Botha is mistaken when he asserts that '[t]he author does not intend the woman to grasp the meaning of the words. since the aim is actually the *failure* of the conversation in 4:10–15' (*Jesus*, 133 [original emphasis]).

[17] Cf. Lee, *Narratives*, 75; Edwards, *John*, 107. Lee comments that Jesus' question about the woman's marital status reveals the restlessness of her relationships, her 'thirst' for life (*Narratives*, 75). Some scholars interpret 4:18 allegorically/symbolically of the idolatry of the Samaritans (e.g. S.M. Schneiders, 'Inclusive Discipleship [John 4:1–42]', in *Written That You May Believe* [New York: Herder & Herder], 139–40), but this view has serious problems (Schnackenburg, *Gospel*, 1:433; Lee, *Narratives*, 75–6 n. 5). Although most scholars perceive the woman as immoral, a few have argued that the woman was possibly hard hit by life and that her present relationship (whether or not immoral) was a matter of necessity/survival rather than choice (Munro, 'Pharisee', 718; Day, *Woman*, 166–72). Viewing the woman as a 'serial fornicator' (Köstenberger, *John*, 152) or leading a 'scandalous way of life' (Lindars, *Gospel*, 186) is certainly excessive. Cf. the extended discussion on the woman's morality in Keener, *Gospel*, 605–8.

[18] Lee, *Narratives*, 83.

[19] In Samaritan theology, the expected figure was a prophetic person called the *Taheb* ('Restorer'), in fulfilment of Deut. 18:18.

Jesus' words in 4:26 literally translate, 'I am, the one who is speaking to you'. Although this is not one of the seven 'I am' sayings, John may have intended a parallel between Jesus' self-revelation to the woman and God's self-revelation to Moses in Exodus 3:14. Surely, we would expect the woman to make a confession at this point, but we are held in suspense because the disciples, who had gone to the village to get some food (4:8), intrude (4:27). This is no coincidence. John is a skilled storyteller, and we shall see that Jesus' interaction with his disciples in 4:31–38 serves to enhance the climax.

The Response of the Woman

In 4:27–42, John describes the response of the woman. Although the text is not explicit, there are several indications that she has begun to understand Jesus' identity and the meaning of his gift, and that she responds positively to Jesus, in faith. First, she leaves her water jar behind (4:28), possibly indicating that her thirst has been quenched.[20] Then, she invites her fellow-villagers to 'come and see' this man who she tentatively believes is the Messiah (4:28–29; cf. 1:46). We translate the question in 4:29 as 'Is he perhaps the Christ?', cautiously expecting an affirmative answer rather than expressing doubt.[21] The woman tentatively suggests that Jesus is the Messiah and invites her people to find out for themselves – and they do (4:29–30).[22] Subsequently, many Samaritans believe in Jesus on the basis of the woman's testimony (4:39),[23] and their climactic confession of Jesus as 'the Saviour of the world' in 4:42 probably includes the woman's confession.[24] The woman struggles for

---

[20] Cf. Beck, *Discipleship*, 74–5; O'Day, *Gospel*, 569; Beirne, *Women*, 91; Day, *Woman*, 173.

[21] Contra Conway, who states that the grammatical construction typically expects a negative reply ('Ambiguity', 335). The Greek word *mē(ti)* is used both in negative and hesitant questions, and the context must decide which question is in view. Considering her successful mission in 4:28–30, 39–42, it is unlikely that her community grasped who Jesus was while she was uncertain.

[22] Cf. T. Okure, *The Johannine Approach to Mission: A Contextual Study of John 4:1–42* (WUNT 2/31; Tübingen: Mohr Siebeck, 1988), 174; H. Boers, *Neither on This Mountain nor in Jerusalem: A Study of John 4* (SBLMS 35; Atlanta: Scholars Press, 1988), 183–4; Botha, *Jesus*, 164–5; Lee, *Narratives*, 85–6.

[23] Stibbe observes that this is a proleptic echo of 17:20, where Jesus indicates that others will come to believe on the basis of the disciples' words (*John*, 67). Thus, the believer's testimony aims to evoke a belief-response from others – whether oral testimony (4:39; 17:20) or written (20:30–31; cf. 19:35; 21:24). Contra Maccini, who argues that the Samaritans progress from a miracle faith in 4:39 to a mature faith in 4:41–42 since in John's gospel no one arrives at a mature faith in Jesus based only upon someone's testimony (*Testimony*, 122–6). However, even if the Samaritans' faith deepened or progressed between 4:39–42, due to Jesus' two-day teaching, we contend that their faith in 4:39, based on the woman's testimony, was already a saving faith. NB the knowledge that the Samaritans gain ('we know that' in 4:42) stands in sharp contrast to that of Nicodemus in 3:2.

[24] Contra those who contend that the woman does not reach adequate belief. For example, Boers asserts that 4:42 does not include the woman's confession and that she never comes to full faith in Jesus; she simply is an example of obedience – one who partakes in Jesus' mission of doing the Father's will (*Mountain*, 165–91). Moloney contends that the Samaritan woman merely reaches incomplete/partial belief (over against the complete belief of the Samaritan villagers)

understanding throughout the dialogue but Jesus helps her progress. This progress is reflected in the titles she uses for Jesus: she goes from 'a Jew' (4:9) to 'Sir' (4:11, 15, 19), 'prophet' (4:19), 'Messiah' (4:29) and lastly 'Saviour' (4:42).

The intrusion of the disciples does not merely delay the climax of the story but heightens it. Jesus' dialogue with the disciples in 4:31–38, like his conversation with the Samaritan woman earlier, starts at a material level and moves to a spiritual or symbolic level. Jesus explains to his disciples that his 'food' is his mission, namely, to do the will of his Father and to complete the task that the Father has assigned to him. He then invites them to participate in his mission. That the fields are 'white' for the harvest may indicate that they are *over*ripe. There is an urgency 'to reap' those people who are ready to confess faith in Jesus, and bring them into the kingdom of God. In 4:35–36, Jesus indicates that the disciples can start with this harvesting process *immediately*. Ironically, it is the *woman* – not the disciples – who participates in Jesus' mission. The disciples do not bring anything from the village, except physical food, but the woman brings the entire village.[25] Thus, the disciples' intrusion in 4:27 and their conversation with Jesus in 4:31–38 enhance the reader's understanding of true discipleship, which is exemplified by the woman.

Conclusion

The Samaritan woman struggles to understand Jesus' revelation, but she gradually overcomes the cognitive barriers, eventually confesses adequate belief and acts as a true disciple. Initially, she hesitates to participate in this unusual and culturally unacceptable conversation (4:7–9), even though she remains cooperative. Then, misunderstanding Jesus' statement in 4:10, the woman mockingly challenges him (4:11–12), but Jesus is able to arouse her interest and she seems keen and open-minded – even though she still does not understand (4:13–15). In the remaining conversation, she appears to

(*Belief*, 156–8; *John*, 131, 148; cf. Köstenberger, *John*, 143). Maccini also distinguishes between the woman's miracle faith and the mature faith of her fellow-villagers (*Testimony*, 127–9).

[25] Cf. Stibbe, *John*, 65. Culpepper even states that the woman is given 'an apostolic role' (*Anatomy*, 137). Contra Fehribach, who contends that the Samaritan woman is one of the fields that Jesus has sown rather than her sowing seeds of faith in her kinsfolk (*Women*, 56–8). Fehribach seems to neglect the woman's role as a witness to her community in 4:28–30, 39, where it would be more natural to understand Jesus 'harvesting' the woman first, and then the woman and Jesus co-'harvesting' the Samaritan village. In addition, Fehribach's reduction of the woman's role to 'the passive recipient of the seed' and 'the nurturing "space" for the male seed to mature' (*Women*, 72), does injustice to the text. The woman actively participates both in the dialogue with Jesus and in his mission. Maccini also underrates the woman's role as a witness when he argues that even though she is a prominent, credible witness leading others to Jesus, she only testifies that he is a miraculous prophet and hence her fellow-villagers only reach a miracle faith. According to him, the woman is ignorant of Jesus' true identity and cannot be labelled as a believing disciple, apostle or missionary (*Testimony*, 137–44).

be theologically perceptive, able to argue and progress (4:19–20, 25, 29b).[26] Finally, in abandoning her water jar, her testimony, and the Samaritans' confession (which most probably includes hers) she shows that she has drunk of the 'living water' and consequently become a source of living water for her community (cf. 7:37–38). The woman's belief and her expression of discipleship (she testifies and 'gathers' the village) are two integrated aspects of salvation – her discipleship *is* her belief-response. The woman thus displays the traits of being cooperative, open-minded, perceptive, initiating, responsive and a witness. She also shows some character development since it is rather surprising that a marginalized woman turns out to be a keen theological thinker and a successful missionary. Regarding her inner life, Jesus observes in 4:17 that she is truthful in her statements.

The Samaritan woman is depicted as model disciple: She testifies and brings people to Jesus (cf. Andrew and Philip in ch. 5), and in doing so, actualizes the challenge in 4:35–38 to participate in Jesus' mission. She thus becomes a source of living water for her community. Ironically, the woman does what the leading theologian Nicodemus was unable to do (to confess adequate belief in Jesus) and what the 'professional' disciples were unable to do (to participate in Jesus' mission and so display true discipleship). The outsider becomes an insider whereas the supposed insiders either remain in the dark (Nicodemus) or are outclassed (the disciples).[27] The Samaritan woman represents those who initially hesitate and struggle for understanding but finally come to an adequate belief in Jesus and display true discipleship.[28]

Coming back to the betrothal imagery in 4:5–7a, we are now in a position to see that Jesus indeed functions as a sort of bridegroom (cf. the nuptial imagery in 2:1–11; 3:29) and the Samaritan woman as a bride – in that the woman's confession of faith in Jesus symbolizes a spiritual betrothal.[29] It is

---

[26] Cf. Edwards, who characterizes her as 'practical (4.11); trusting and enthusiastic, if a little naive (4.15); impetuous and prone to exaggeration (4.28f.), but also theologically aware, perceptive, and persistent (4.19f., 25, 29b)' (*John*, 108).

[27] Contra Munro, who argues that Nicodemus and the Samaritan woman are parallel rather than polarized figures ('Pharisee', 710–28).

[28] Cf. Schneiders, 'Inclusive Discipleship', 143–4; Stibbe, *John*, 67; Day, *Woman*, 174. Day's conclusion that, prior to her encounter with Jesus, the woman already was a faithful child of God, albeit within the limits of the Samaritan belief-system, and one of good character appears somewhat overrated. However, her remark that the woman's fellow-villagers would certainly not have responded as they do were she a sinful, promiscuous woman remains a challenge (*Woman*, 173–5). It is surprising that van Tilborg, who first evaluates the Samaritan woman positively, later asserts that Jesus withdraws from her when she is made anonymous in 4:39–42 (*Love*, 178–83, 208). Fehribach even argues that the woman is not important in her own right but is important only to the extent that she is a 'woman' and a 'Samaritan' and as such simply fulfils her symbolic role of bride in order to re-establish familial relations between God and the Samaritans (*Women*, 80). Without denying her symbolic role as bride, the woman is nevertheless important in her own right in that she exhibits true discipleship and thus functions as an example for others. The corporate and individual dimensions of the woman's role are not mutually exclusive.

[29] Nevertheless, a comparison between the Samaritan woman who had five husbands and now lived in an extra-marital relationship and the virgins in the Old Testament betrothal scenes

through this meta-narrative that John provides a significant corrective to Jewish thinking that the Jewish people are the people of God, envisaged as God's 'bride' (Isa. 62:5; Jer. 13:10–11). First, John 3 explains that a spiritual birth, rather than physical birth as a Jew, determines who become the true people of God. Second, instead of a Jewish 'bride', John 4 presents a Samaritan one: the betrothal between Jesus and his people is not based on ethnic but on spiritual birth.[30] The Spirit-born disciples of Jesus are the real bride.[31]

The Samaritan Woman		
Appearances	References	throughout 4:7–42
Identity	Titles given	–
	Gender	female
	Age	–
	Marital status	unmarried – living with a man
	Occupation	–
	Socio-economic status	marginalized
	Place of residence/operation	Sychar in Samaria
	Relatives	–
	Group affiliation	Samaritan
Speech and actions	In interaction with Jesus	initial resistance and mocking, then keen participation, resulting in understanding and belief
	In interaction with others	testifying to her community and challenging them to verify her findings for themselves
Character classification	Complexity	complex; multiple traits: cooperative, open-minded, perceptive, initiating, responsive, being a witness
	Development	some
	Inner life	little
Degree of characterization		personality
Response to Jesus		adequate belief-response: she believes and testifies

is not wrinkle free (Lee, *Narratives*, 67 n. 3; Koester, *Symbolism*, 49). Although Schneiders also perceives the Samaritan woman as Jesus' spiritual bride, she argues that this episode is not a historical event in the life of Jesus but a reading back into the public ministry of Jesus the Johannine community's post-resurrection experience of the Samaritan mission and the entrance of the Samaritans into the Johannine community in order to legitimate the Samaritan mission ('Inclusive Discipleship', 134–43; cf. Schüssler Fiorenza, *Memory*, 327). However, the argument for a Samaritan integration into the Johannine community is weak and merely a possibility. Besides, we contend that although John wrote this story from a post-resurrection perspective, he narrates a historical event in Jesus' ministry.

[30] The Samaritans' confession of Jesus as 'the Saviour *of the world*' stresses the universal scope of Jesus' mission (cf. 3:16; 12:32).

[31] The book of Revelation, perhaps not written by John himself but certainly standing in the same tradition, picks up on this imagery in its portrayal of the future wedding between the church and Jesus (Rev. 19 – 22).

The Royal Official – His Word Is Enough for Me

'Faith is not belief without proof, but trust without reservation' — *Elton Trueblood*

The royal official only appears in 4:43–54, closing the larger section 'from Cana to Cana' of John 2 – 4. Culpepper observes that the royal official is 'one of the overlooked characters of the gospel' – but then devotes merely a short paragraph to him.[1] We shall provide a more detailed examination, showing that the royal official undergoes a three-stage development in his faith.

The royal official resides in Capernaum, a city on the north-west shore of the Sea of Galilee (4:46). We may assume he is married, since the narrator tells that he has a son (4:46–47), who has not attained adolescence because he is designated as 'a child' (*paidion*) (4:49). The identity of the royal official (*basilikos*) is unclear. The term *basilikos* refers either to someone in the service of the king – a civil servant or military official – or to a relative of the king.[2] The 'king' here is probably Herod Antipas, who was the tetrarch of Galilee and Peraea from 4 BCE to 39 CE. Hence, the official could have been a member of the Herodian family or someone in the service of the king – a court-official or a Roman centurion.[3] Whatever his identity, he appears to be a prominent, well-to-do person, with authority over others (he had slaves [4:51]). If he is a Gentile (cf. the parallel story in Matt. 8:5–13; Luke 7:1–10), he would be despised by the Jewish populace. If he is a Jewish nobleman, he would be similarly shunned by the populace since the Jewish aristocracy and Herodians often collaborated with the Romans. Nevertheless, Jesus does not turn his back on him.

[1] Culpepper, *Anatomy*, 137.

[2] Cf. Bultmann, *Gospel*, 206 n. 7.

[3] Scholars are divided about the man's identity: a Jewish official in service of Herod Antipas (Bultmann, *Gospel*, 206; Carson, *Gospel*, 234, 238); a Gentile officer in service of Herod Antipas (Köstenberger, *John*, 166, 169; A.H. Mead, 'The *basilikos* in John 4.46–53', *JSNT* 23 [1985]: 69–72); an officer in the army of Herod Agrippa (Beasley-Murray, *John*, 69); a Galilean aristocrat (Keener, *Gospel*, 630–31). An argument for a Jewish identity may be that the official is included in the plural 'you' in 4:48 where Jesus addresses the Galilean audience of 4:45. However, he may have been included because he had heard about Jesus' ability to perform miracles from these Galileans.

The Royal Official's Interaction with Jesus

After his two-day stay with the Samaritans, Jesus leaves for Galilee (4:40, 43), resuming the journey he started in 4.3. John 4.43–45 functions as a narrative bridge between Jesus' encounter with the Samaritans and his encounter with the royal official. John 4:46a reveals that Jesus has come full circle since 2:1 with his return to Cana (cf. the mention of Jesus' first and second sign in 2:11 and 4:54). The narrator immediately introduces the next character: a certain royal official whose son was sick and close to death (4:46b–47). We must bear in mind that the focus is on the official and not on his ill son. The boy's healing, though significant, is simply a foil for the official's response to Jesus. The desperation of the royal official to meet Jesus becomes clear when we read that he came all the way from Capernaum to Cana where Jesus was. Since it was an uphill journey, it took approximately a full day to cover the distance of about twenty-seven kilometres.

The royal official asks Jesus to come to Capernaum and heal his son who is about to die (4:47). The official's request shows that he knows or has heard about Jesus' ability to perform miracles. In 4:45, John mentions that the Galilean people welcomed Jesus because they had seen for themselves 'everything that he had done in Jerusalem at the festival'. This most probably refers to 2:23, which mentions that Jesus performed miraculous signs during the Passover festival in Jerusalem. Either the official had heard about Jesus' ability to perform miraculous signs from these Galileans or he (if he were a Jew) had been to the Passover festival mentioned in 2:23.

Jesus' reply to the official in 4:48, 'Unless you see signs and wonders, you will never believe', is somewhat puzzling. Who is Jesus addressing using the plural 'you' and why is he so exasperated? I suggest it is the Galilean audience that Jesus is addressing. In 4:45, John states that the Galileans had seen everything Jesus had done in Jerusalem, probably referring to the miraculous signs mentioned in 2:23. We also know from 2:24–25 and the Nicodemus story that the people's 'belief' in Jesus on that occasion was somehow deficient (see ch. 9). Therefore, despite the welcome they gave Jesus, the Galileans' 'belief' was probably also lacking.[4] Consequently, Jesus seems to exhort these people towards a belief that is less dependent on signs. Later, Jesus issues a similar challenge (20:29) in response to Thomas's demand for a sign (20:25).

Nevertheless, included in the address is the royal official, since the 'Therefore, Jesus said to him' indicates that Jesus' critical remark is in response to the official's request for a miracle in 4:47.[5] In which case, Jesus

[4] Cf. Koester, *Symbolism*, 51–2.

[5] Contra those who contend that the 'you' addresses the royal official and the reader (Barrett, *Gospel*, 247; Beck, *Discipleship*, 80).

also challenges him towards a more stable belief.[6] I have argued elsewhere that although signs can be a basis for adequate belief, they are a less secure basis than Jesus' words/teaching (cf. 20:29).[7] Whether the official does not understand Jesus or cannot bring himself to the level of trust that Jesus implicitly requires is unclear, but the urgency of the situation causes him to repeat his plea that Jesus come to Capernaum (to perform a miracle) (4:49).

Whereas the official first *asked* Jesus to come with him (4:47), he now uses an imperative, 'Sir, *come down* before my child dies' (4:49). In turn, Jesus also uses an imperative, '*Go*; your son lives.' The official wants the physical presence of Jesus (perhaps because miracle workers usually interact directly with the ill person), but Jesus indicates that this is not necessary.[8] The verb *zaō* ('to live', 'to be alive') that Jesus uses, refers elsewhere in John's gospel always to eternal or divine life (4:10–11; 5:25; 6:51, 57–58; 7:38; 11:25–26; 14:19). John thus draws attention to Jesus' life-giving word (cf. 6:63, where Jesus says that his words are eternal/divine life [*zōē*]).[9] As Resseguie comments, 'The efficacy of his word is what is important, not his physical appearance at Capernaum.'[10] The official recognizes Jesus' authority and responds well when he believes, i.e. accepts, Jesus' life-giving word and leaves (4:50).[11] Hence, the royal official, one used to being in authority, now submits himself to Jesus' authority.

On his way home (without Jesus), his 'faith' is honoured or validated when his slaves bring him the good news of the child's recovery. He immediately inquires of them the precise hour when his son has begun to recover (4:51–52). Their reply makes the official realize (literally, 'know') that it was the same time when Jesus has said to him that his son would live.[12] His initial belief is thus justified and has become knowledge, and on this basis he expresses further belief – probably a saving belief in Jesus (4:52–53).[13] While the official's 'belief' in 4:50 may simply have been to trust or to take Jesus at his word, his 'belief' in 4:53 most likely denotes a saving

---

[6] Cf. Ridderbos who remarks that Jesus' words are not so much an accusation as a challenge (*Gospel*, 176).

[7] Bennema, *Power*, 145–7. Cf. G.H. Twelftree, *Jesus the Miracle Worker: A Historical & Theological Study* (Downers Grove: IVP, 1999), chs 7–8.

[8] M.L. Coloe, 'Households of Faith (Jn 4:46–54; 11:1–44): A Metaphor for the Johannine Community', *Pacifica* 13 (2000): 330.

[9] Cf. Collins, 'Figures', 20; Beck, 'Function', 151.

[10] Resseguie, *Strange Gospel*, 132.

[11] Cf. Beirne, who calls this a test of the official's faith, which he passes brilliantly (*Women*, 60).

[12] If the official left for Capernaum immediately after Jesus had spoken to him, and if the slaves left Capernaum soon after the boy's recovery, the official would have met his slaves halfway between Capernaum and Cana – the day after his encounter with Jesus.

[13] For the Johannine dialectic between knowledge and belief, in which both stimulate and inform one another, see Bennema, 'Christ', 122–4. Whereas we detect a development in the official's belief-responses, Coloe observes a development in the royal official's status: from a courtier used to having authority, to a human being stripped of his royal status ('man' in 4:50), to a father in relationship with his household (4:53) ('Households', 332–3).

belief.[14] Besides, his entire household (including the slaves) comes to believe in Jesus (4:53).[15] This implies that the official has shared the experience with his family and other members of his household. He thus acts as a witness like the Samaritan woman who testified to her fellow people. Like the Samaritans in 4:41–42, the royal official also believes in Jesus because of his word – without a drawn-out struggle for understanding.[16]

Conclusion

The royal official proves to be more than a flat character. He has multiple traits: (i) his willingness to come to Jesus in person and submit to his authority illustrates humility; (ii) he is persistent, not deterred by Jesus' mild rebuke in 4:48; (iii) his inquiry and his deduction about the efficacy of Jesus' word shows that he is meticulous and analytical; (iv) he is a persuasive witness to his household. The official shows a little character development in that the reader may be surprised that a high-ranking (perhaps Gentile) official comes personally to a Jewish itinerant preacher, rather than sending a slave, and submits quite willingly to his authority. His understanding of the efficacy of Jesus' word in 4:53 (literally, 'the father knew') gives insight into his thought process or inner life.

The royal official shows remarkable development of faith in his interaction with Jesus. First, the man knew about Jesus' ability to perform miracles – either because he had been to the Passover festival described in 2:23 or because he had heard it from the Galileans who had been there – and on this basis, he approaches Jesus to heal his deadly ill son. Perhaps we can call this an incipient signs-faith. Then, Jesus challenges him to move beyond a belief that is merely based on miraculous signs or requires his physical presence. The official responds to the challenge by 'believing' what Jesus said – probably not a saving belief in the Johannine sense but at least showing that he trusted Jesus' word. Finally, after his tentative trusting Jesus' word, his 'belief' was attested and became knowledge based

[14] Cf. Krafft, 'Personen', 21; Bultmann, *Gospel*, 208–9; Schnackenburg, *Gospel*, 1:467–8; Barrett, *Gospel*, 248. Moloney, however, claims that the official already reached authentic Johannine belief in 4:50 (*Gospel*, 154–5, 161–2; cf. Beirne, *Women*, 60–61). Beck correctly points out that if there is a difference in belief in 4:50 and 4:53, it is not inherent within the two occurrences of *pisteuein* but must be inferred from the context (*Discipleship*, 81). There is no intrinsic difference in meaning in *pisteuein* followed by the dative in 4:50 and the absolute use of *pisteuein* in 4:53 (Bennema, *Power*, 130 n. 91; *idem*, 'Christ', 128).

[15] Some see a parallel with the conversion of Gentile households in Acts (e.g. Lincoln, *Gospel*, 188). Consequently, Brodie views this story as representing the arrival of the Gentiles into God's household (*Gospel*, 233).

[16] Koester perceptively comments that 'his faith was confirmed by a sign, not based upon a sign' (*Symbolism*, 52). Brown, however, argues that Jesus did not lead the official away from a faith based on signs but toward a signs-faith that recognizes Jesus as the life-giver (*Gospel*, 1:195).

on which he reached an adequate belief in Jesus. The royal official, then, represents those who initially believe in Jesus on the basis of his signs but are able to progress towards a more secure basis for faith – dependent less on signs and more on Jesus' life-giving words/teaching.

The story of the royal official is a fitting climax to the series of encounters that people have with Jesus in the 'from-Cana-to-Cana' section (John 2 – 4).[17] Comparing the characters of Nicodemus (see ch. 9), the Samaritan woman (see ch. 10) and the royal official, we observe that Nicodemus, the top theologian of Israel and presumably the insider, is outclassed by two despised outsiders: a female Samaritan outcast and a royal official, who may have been a Gentile or a Jewish collaborator. After their respective encounters with Jesus, both the Samaritan woman and the royal official reach an adequate belief in Jesus and testify to others, who in turn come to a saving belief. On a scale of religious prominence there is a decline: from the prominent Jewish theologian to a Samaritan woman and finally a possible Gentile. On the scale of belief-responses, however, there is a progression: from ambiguity and no response, to a slow progression towards faith after a struggle to understand, to an almost instant belief based on Jesus' word.

The Royal Official		
Appearances	References	4:46; 4:49
Identity	Titles given	'royal official'
	Gender	male
	Age	–
	Marital status	married
	Occupation	a member of the Herodian family or in service of Herod Antipas – either as a Jewish civil officer or a Roman army officer
	Socio-economic status	prominent, well-to-do
	Place of residence/operation	Capernaum
	Relatives	son
	Group affiliation	Jewish or Gentile, part of the royal court

[17] B. Lindars argues that John's story of the royal official is an adaptation of a similar narrative in the Synoptics (Matt. 8:5–13; Luke 7:1–10) ('Capernaum Revisited: John 4,46–53 and the Synoptics', in *The Four Gospels 1992: Festschrift Frans Neirynck* [ed. F. Van Segbroeck et al.; BETL 100; Leuven: Leuven University Press, 1992], 1985–2000). Although these narratives show many similarities, there are also striking differences: (i) in the Synoptic story Jesus entered Capernaum rather than being in Cana; (ii) the main character is a Roman centurion, who in Matthew comes himself to Jesus while in Luke he sends Jewish elders to Jesus; (iii) in Matthew, the centurion's child or slave (*pais*) is paralysed; in Luke, his slave (*doulos*) is deadly ill; in John, the royal official's son/child (*huios/paidion/pais*) is deadly ill; (iv) in the Synoptic versions, Jesus is willing to go to the Roman centurion's home, but the centurion objects, whereas in the Johannine version, the royal official wants Jesus to come but Jesus refuses. Cf. Bultmann, *Gospel*, 204–6; Carson, *Gospel*, 233–4; Beasley-Murray, *John*, 71; Keener, *Gospel*, 631–2.

The Royal Official		
Speech and actions	In interaction with Jesus	from being in authority to submitting to Jesus' authority; from a belief based on Jesus' signs to a belief based on Jesus' word
	In interaction with others	testifies to his household
Character classification	Complexity	little complex; multiple traits: humble, persistent, meticulous, analytical, being a witness
	Development	little
	Inner life	little
Degree of characterization		towards personality
Response to Jesus		adequate: from incipient signs-faith to a tentative belief in Jesus' word to a saving belief in Jesus

The Invalid at the Pool – A Lame Response

'Prolonged idleness paralyses initiative' — Anonymous

Leaving the royal official and the section 'from Cana to Cana' (John 2 – 4) behind, we enter another major section, John 5 – 12, where Jesus faces increasing opposition from the religious leaders in Judaea and Jerusalem. The first character in John 5 is an invalid man, whose encounters with Jesus and 'the Jews' in 5:1–16 precipitate the first main confrontation between Jesus and 'the Jews'. The majority of scholars adopt a negative reading of the story, suggesting that the invalid was dull, passive, and did not respond to Jesus with belief but betrayed him to 'the Jews'.[1] Some scholars, however, propose a positive reading, arguing that the man was daring, opposed the Jewish authorities and defended Jesus.[2] The positive reading has not won much support or been considered adequately.[3] We shall listen to both sides of the argument and demonstrate that this character is not as straightforward or 'flat' as most scholars assume.

Regarding the man's identity, we are simply presented with an unnamed man who has been ill for thirty-eight years (5:5). Although his illness is not specified, 5:8–9 seems to indicate that he is paralysed or lame. More importantly, the man is marginalized since his illness has kept him from participating in the socio-religious life of his day. He is confined to the portico around a pool called Bethesda, which was reputed to have mystical

---

[1] E.g. Krafft, 'Personen', 21–2; Culpepper, *Anatomy*, 137–8; Collins, 'Figures', 21–3; *idem*, 'John', 364–5; Lee, *Narratives*, 102, 109–10, 123; Ridderbos, *Gospel*, 186–90; Koester, *Symbolism*, 52–4; Keener, *Gospel*, 643–4; S.M. Bryan, 'Power in the Pool: The Healing of the Man at Bethesda and Jesus' Violation of the Sabbath (Jn. 5:1–18)', *TynB* 54 (2003): 7–22; Köstenberger, *John*, 180–83; Howard, 'Significance', 71–3. Although P.D. Duke argues that the invalid's main characteristic is his passivity, he remains equivocal whether the man praises or betrays Jesus ('John 5:1–15', *RevExp* 85 [1988]: 539–42).

[2] J.L. Staley, 'Stumbling in the Dark, Reaching for the Light: Reading Character in John 5 and 9', *Semeia* 53 (1991): 55–80; J.C. Thomas, '"Stop Sinning Lest Something Worse Come Upon You": The Man at the Pool in John 5', *JSNT* 59 (1995): 3–20; O'Day, *Gospel*, 578–80; Resseguie, *Strange Gospel*, 134–8. Cf. Beck, 'Function', 151; *idem*, *Discipleship*, 89–90.

[3] For example, Lee mentions Staley in some footnotes but does not get to the heart of his case (*Narratives*, 102 n. 4, 110 n. 5). Bryan simply dismisses Staley and Thomas in a footnote ('Power', 17 n. 26).

healing powers (5:2–4),[4] and is probably dependent on others for food and shelter. According to Jewish law, he is probably prohibited to worship in the temple. Mishnah *Hagigah* 1:1, for example, states that '[a]ll are liable for *an appearance offering [before the Lord]* (Exod. 23:14, Deut. 16:16) except for . . . the lame . . . and one who cannot go up on foot.'[5]

The Man's First Interaction with Jesus

John 5:5–6 describes how Jesus zeroes in on this marginalized person. The narrator's comment that Jesus 'knew' that the man had been there a long time might well be the result of Jesus' knowledge of people and situations rather than from asking the lame man (cf. 1:48; 2:25; 5:42; 6:64; 13:11; 16:30; 21:17).[6] At first glance, Jesus' question to the man, 'Do you want to become well?', seems absurd but perhaps Jesus wants to clarify what the man really wants.[7] After thirty-eight years the man may have resigned to his illness and healing would mean new, perhaps unwanted, responsibilities.[8]

The invalid's lament in 5:7 reveals that he does not understand how Jesus could help him, or perhaps he does not dare to believe that Jesus could do for him what that the pool was unable to for thirty-eight years.[9]

---

[4] There is considerable debate about the precise location and name of the pool (cf. J. Jeremias, *The Rediscovery of Bethesda: John 5:2* [Göttingen: Vandenhoeck & Ruprecht, 1966]; Bryan, 'Power', 12–4). The tradition about the pool's mystical powers has been preserved in some late documents (the earliest textual evidence comes from the fifth century) as verses 3b–4, which translate, '[3b] waiting for the stirring of the water. [4] For an angel of the Lord used to come down to the pool at certain times and stir up the water. The first person then who stepped in after the movement of the water was made well no matter what sort of disease he once had.' Although most scholars agree that 5:3b–4 is not part of the original text, the explanation may not be too wide of the mark when we consider 5:7, which appears to indicate that something mystical happened when the water was stirred up. Z.C. Hodges makes a compelling case for accepting 5:3b–4 as both authentic and original ('The Angel at Bethesda – John 5:4', *BibSac* 136 [1979]: 25–39; cf. Bryan, 'Power', 9), but see the challenge by G.D. Fee, 'On the Inauthenticity of John 5:3b–4', *EvQ* 54 (1982): 207–18.

[5] Although the Mishnah is compiled around 200 CE, it reflects earlier rabbinic tradition.

[6] Cf. Thomas, '"Stop Sinning"', 8–9.

[7] In the light of the use of *holos* ('whole') in 7:23, Thomas suggests that *hugiēs* in 5:6 is an example of double entendre, evoking misunderstanding – the invalid understands it as a question whether he wants to be *healed* by the pool, whereas Jesus intends to know whether the man wants to be *whole* ('"Stop Sinning"', 10). Attractive as this suggestion may be, it does not work since 7:23 employs both words: 'because I [Jesus] made the whole [*holon*] man well [*hugiēs*]'.

[8] Cf. Duke, 'John 5:1–15', 541. Contra T. Thatcher, who suggests that Jesus attempts to manipulate a weak man and assert his own authority and power over the lame man ('The Sabbath Trick: Unstable Irony in the Fourth Gospel', *JSNT* 76 [1999]: 70–71).

[9] Based on the alleged double entendre in 5:6, Thomas argues that the man is not complaining in 5:7 but simply misunderstands Jesus ('"Stop Sinning"', 10–11). However, the man misunderstands Jesus not because of the assumed double meaning of *hugiēs* (see n. 7, above) but simply because he does not know who Jesus is and can only think in categories known to him –

This complaint that there is no one who can help him to get into the water when it is stirred up is also ironic since the reader knows from John 4 that the real 'healing' water can be found in Jesus himself.[10] Whereas the pool was reputed to heal the first person who got in, Jesus is continually available to everyone as the source of 'living water'. Duke perceptively points out that the pool of Bethesda is, in fact, a cruel place of competitive healing since '[i]t advertises mercy and so appeals to the weak – but it favors the strong.'[11] Put differently, the invalid's reply points to an understanding of God as one who periodically infuses the pool with impersonal power, which is accessed in a purely arbitrary way.[12]

Thus, the invalid does not know the identity of the one who is speaking to him or what to expect. Nevertheless, Jesus apparently takes the man's complaint in 5:7 as an implicit request for help, and heals him of his illness (5:8–9a).[13] Duke observes that this story is almost as much about raising the dead as about healing the sick since Jesus' command to the man 'to get up' (*egeirō*) is also used to refer to the resurrection of the dead to eternal life (5:21).[14]

John's concise statement that 'immediately the man was made well' (5:9a) indicates to the reader that the focus should not be on the mechanics of the miracle but on how the character responds to Jesus.[15] By now we should be sufficiently conditioned to look for the man's response to Jesus and to evaluate it, but we find none – at least not at this point – the man simply walks away (5:9a). Although this miracle is not identified as a sign, it may function as such, intending to direct the man's attention to the true identity of Jesus.[16] Instead, the man seems disinterested or inert in knowing his benefactor (but see our examination of 5:13 below).

There is, however, another possible interpretation. Although the reader will only learn later that all this happened on the Sabbath (5:9b), both Jesus and the invalid would have been aware of it. The implication is that Jesus knowingly commanded the invalid to 'work' on the Sabbath, and the invalid knowingly and willingly became a Sabbath-breaker. This view raises various

---

someone to help him to get into the pool in time (cf. L.Th. Witkamp, 'The Use of Traditions in John 5.1–18', *JSNT* 25 [1985]: 24).

[10] Cf. Culpepper, *Anatomy*, 138.

[11] Duke, 'John 5:1–15', 539.

[12] Bryan, 'Power', 11, 14.

[13] Thatcher is off the mark when he asserts that Jesus is frustrated by the man's response in 5:7 and hence directly manipulates the ill man by ordering him to be well in 5:8. He concludes that Jesus has not displayed God's love and that 'his dominating use of power against another to achieve his own purposes does not live up to his own standard of self-sacrificial love (15.13)' ('Sabbath Trick', 72).

[14] Duke, 'John 5:1–15', 540. Cf. Resseguie, *Strange Gospel*, 135–6.

[15] Staley suggests that picking up his mat and walking was the means to being healed rather than the result ('Stumbling', 59 n. 13).

[16] Bryan also perceives the healing as a sign, albeit to show in the following discourse that Jesus' actions must be understood as the actions of God himself ('Power', 21).

questions. Why did the man obey Jesus rather than pointing out that Jesus' command was not lawful? Was the man perhaps not as dull, disinterested, passive or naive as some scholars contend? Perhaps the man obeyed Jesus' command because he would rather get well and violate the Sabbath than keep the law and remain ill.[17] Willing to face the consequences, he believes Jesus' word and obeys.

Staley, for example, asserts that the narrator's belated reference to the Sabbath in 5:9b comes as a surprise and forces the reader to re-evaluate the behaviour of the characters. Consequently, Staley views Jesus' command to the invalid to work on the Sabbath negatively, while the ill man proves to be a daring and risk-taking individual, unquestioningly accepting Jesus' Sabbath-breaking command.[18] However, it is unnecessary to interpret Jesus' Sabbath-breaking command negatively when, in the light of the entire chapter, we realize that Jesus intentionally 'works' on the Sabbath to show that he is on a par with God. The healing of the lame man on the Sabbath is a foil for the Sabbath controversy between Jesus and 'the Jews' in the remainder of the narrative. The intention of John 5 is that the invalid and 'the Jews' (as well as the reader) should recognize that Jesus works legitimately and continually on God's behalf – even on the Sabbath.[19]

The Man's First Interaction with 'the Jews'

The narrator's revelation that this happened on the Sabbath (5:9b) hints at the first clash between Jesus and the Jewish religious leaders. Although 'the Jews' were unaware of the miracle, they readily notice the healed man carrying his mat on the Sabbath, a deemed offence (5:10). The oral tradition of the Pharisees painstakingly spelled out what could and could not be done on the Sabbath. The Mishnah, which reflects this oral tradition, mentions for instance that '[t]he generative categories of acts of labor [prohibited on the Sabbath] are forty less one: . . . (39) he who transports an object from one domain to another' (*m. Shabbat* 7:2; cf. Neh. 13:19; Jer. 17:21).

In response to the accusation, the man quickly shifts the blame, saying that the man who healed him had commanded him to take up his mat (5:11).[20] However, if the man knowingly and willingly violated the Sabbath, his reply was defiant, opposing the authority of 'the Jews', rather than timid, putting the blame on Jesus. Staley argues that the invalid was indeed standing up to the Jewish authorities, juxtaposing the legal authority of 'the Jews' and the authority of the charismatic healer. The invalid would then

---

[17] Cf. Thatcher, 'Sabbath Trick', 74.

[18] Staley, 'Stumbling', 60.

[19] Cf. Bennema, *John's Gospel*, 69–70. Bryan's excellent article makes precisely this point ('Power', esp. 14–21).

[20] Cf. Barrett, *Gospel*, 255; Culpepper, *Anatomy*, 138; Carson, *Gospel*, 245.

be saying that the charismatic healer who has power to heal also has the power to abrogate Sabbath law.[21] Thomas also regards the man's reply positively, where he appears to set the authority of the one who has power to heal (and hence has power over the law) against the halakic authority of 'the Jews'.[22] Thus, the invalid may be suggesting that a man who has sufficient authority to heal also has authority to issue a Sabbath-breaking command.[23]

When 'the Jews' ask who gave him those instructions, the invalid cannot answer since he does not know his benefactor's identity. Therefore 'the Jews' cannot pursue the issue further (5:12–13). Until this moment, the invalid perceives Jesus only as 'the man who healed him'. It must be noted that 5:13 indicates that the invalid is ignorant of Jesus' identity not because of his assumed passivity but because Jesus had slipped out of the pool precincts and disappeared into the crowd. Therefore, 5:9 does perhaps not suggest that the man had simply walked away, unconcerned about Jesus' identity. Nevertheless, the man, in a critical situation, confesses ignorance of who Jesus is.[24] Indeed, the man's reply is a non-confession and he fails as a witness – unlike the Samaritan woman in John 4 and the blind man in John 9.

The Man's Second Interaction with Jesus

Jesus later finds the man in the temple and says to him, 'See, you have been healed. Sin no longer so that nothing worse may happen to you' (5:14). It is likely Jesus seeks out the man because he needs more than physical healing. Like his other encounters with people, in this encounter too Jesus' aim is to elicit a belief-response. Jesus' healing of the man's physical disability is intended to obtain a belief-response – a 'spiritual healing' so to speak. Therefore, in 5:14, Jesus moves to a spiritual level by introducing the concept of sin.

The physical healing has already contributed to holistic healing since Jesus finds the man *in the temple*, indicating that the man has started to participate in the socio-religious life again. In 7:23, while referring to the incident in John 5, Jesus says that he had healed 'the *whole* man'. Indeed, Jesus' healing of the man has more than one benefit. However, Jesus' exhortation to the man indicates that he needs more than physical and socio-religious restoration.

Many scholars contend that Jesus' exhortation to the man suggests a relation between the man's illness and (his) sin, and that Jesus is providing

[21] Staley, 'Stumbling', 61–2.

[22] Thomas, '"Stop Sinning"', 13.

[23] Cf. Lindars, *Gospel*, 216; Resseguie, *Strange Gospel*, 137; Bryan, 'Power', 17–8.

[24] Collins, 'John', 365.

corrective advice.[25] Even so, this does not imply that illness is always caused by personal sin – in a later episode, Jesus explicitly objects to such an over-simplification, denying a relation between a man's blindness and (his) sin (9:1–3). More importantly, however, Jesus' admonition does not necessarily imply that the man's lengthy illness was *caused* by his sin; he merely cautions the man that continuing in sin may precipitate 'something worse' than his previous illness.[26]

It is not clear what Jesus' admonition is about. First, the text does not indicate what sin Jesus is referring to, although the Greek present imperative suggests that the man's sinning was ongoing or habitual. Second, does the 'something worse' refer to a worse illness than he previously had or to some calamity? The proponents of the positive reading have difficulties explaining this verse. Thomas suggests that the phrase 'See you have been made whole. Stop sinning' means that the man should not continue sinning when his sins have just been forgiven, indicated by the use of 'whole'.[27] However, Thomas's interpretation, suggesting that the man had come to faith in Jesus and was now committing post-conversion sin, goes beyond what we can legitimately infer from the text – there is no indication that the man had come to belief in Jesus in the full Johannine sense. Staley also fails to explain 5:14 satisfactorily. His tentative suggestion that the man's 'sin' was the failure to reveal the identity of his benefactor to the Jewish authorities (and hence the corrective action in 5:15) seems far-fetched.[28] Moreover, Jesus could hardly be warning the man that 'something worse' (than his previous illness) would occur if he continues to provide an inferior testimony.

I suggest another interpretation. John views sin primarily as unbelief (16:9; cf. 8:24), so 5:14 can be understood as a reprimand not to continue in unbelief. So far, the man has been unresponsive to Jesus and hence unbelieving – at least from a Johannine perspective. Jesus admonishes the man to discontinue in sin/unbelief and adopt an attitude of belief.[29] For John, the attitude of someone who has experienced an extraordinary action or revelation of Jesus but fails to understand the true identity of Jesus and to respond adequately, is considered sin. The 'something worse' than thirty-eight years of illness would be not knowing who Jesus really is, not receiving the divine life that he gives but experiencing divine judgement instead (cf. 3:18, 36; 5:24).[30]

---

[25] Krafft, 'Personen', 21; Collins, 'Figures', 22 n. 65; Thomas, '"Stop Sinning"', 16–7; Lincoln, *Gospel*, 195.

[26] Bryan, 'Power', 17 n. 25. Cf. Barrett, *Gospel*, 255.

[27] Thomas, '"Stop Sinning"', 14–5. Schnackenburg also assumes that the man's healing includes the forgiveness of his sin (*Gospel*, 2:97).

[28] Staley, 'Stumbling', 62–3.

[29] Cf. Collins, 'Figures', 23 n. 65; *idem*, 'John', 364.

[30] Cf. Thatcher, 'Sabbath Trick', 75; Bryan, 'Power', 16–7; Koester, *Symbolism*, 54.

The Man's Second Interaction with 'the Jews'

The man, seemingly unable to accept Jesus' reprimand, and perhaps out of spite, goes to 'the Jews' and reports that Jesus is the man who healed him (5:15). That we should interpret the man's action negatively is clear from the following verse: 'And *for this reason* "the Jews" started persecuting Jesus' (5:16). Even though 'for this reason' looks forward ('the Jews' started to persecute Jesus *because* he was doing these things on the Sabbath) rather than backward (to the man's action in 5:15), it is clear that 'the Jews' could only target Jesus because the invalid had identified him. The man's report to the Jewish authorities sets off this persecution.

The advocates for the positive reading continue to struggle with these verses. According to Staley, the man's action in 5:15 should be understood positively – by supplying the name of the healer the man hopes 'the Jews' will be impressed. Thus, the man serves in his own way as a faithful witness.[31] However, the man must have realized from his previous conversation with 'the Jews' in 5:10–12 that they wanted to charge Jesus with violating the Sabbath and that his report would cause trouble for his benefactor.[32] Others interpret the man's action in 5:15 positively because the term *anangellein* ('to proclaim', 'to inform') is always used positively in John.[33] However, these scholars make too much of *anangellein*; the term simply denotes 'to announce, proclaim' or 'to inform, report' and the literary context determines whether there are positive or negative connotations. In this context, we contend that the invalid's action should be understood negatively – he either intentionally betrays Jesus or is guilty of inexcusable dullness if he did not consider the repercussions of his action.[34]

Conclusion

Having compared the negative and positive readings of 5:1–16, we contend that both readings are legitimate and convincing, and both readings face difficulties.[35] The character of the invalid is much more complicated and

[31] Staley, 'Stumbling', 62–3.

[32] The issue was not so much that Jesus performed a miracle but that he had done it *on the Sabbath*. As Bryan points out, at issue is the legitimacy of using *God's* power on the Sabbath, and whether Jesus could be regarded as exercising God's power in a way that violated God's will ('Power', 14–6).

[33] Thomas, '"Stop Sinning"', 18; Resseguie, *Strange Gospel*, 138. Cf. van Tilborg, *Love*, 218–9, who even calls the man's proclamation a confession of faith.

[34] Krafft ('Personen', 22) and Lee (*Narratives*, 110) interpret the man's action as betrayal, while Brown (*Gospel*, 1:209) and Culpepper (*Anatomy*, 138) contend the man is guilty of persistent naivety.

[35] Although Beck realizes the ambiguity of the man's portrayal, he allows his previously established paradigm of anonymous characters who respond positively to Jesus' word (based on Jesus' mother, the Samaritan woman and the royal official) to shape his understanding of the invalid (as he himself admits) (*Discipleship*, 88–91). Thus, Beck gives more importance to

ambiguous than most scholars have recognized. There is, however, one tool left to assist us in making up our minds. As most scholars have recognized, John wants his readers to compare the response of the man at the pool in John 5 with that of the man born blind in John 9 (see ch. 16).[36]

There are many parallels between the two stories: (i) both men had been disabled for a long time and excluded from the socio-religious life of their day; (ii) both were healed by Jesus on the Sabbath; (iii) in both stories there is the mention of a pool; (iv) 'the Jews' investigate both healings; (v) in both stories, Jesus later finds the healed person in order to offer spiritual healing. Despite these remarkable similarities, their responses are rather different – both to the Jewish authorities and to Jesus. For one, the invalid eventually betrays Jesus to the authorities, whereas the blind man persistently defends Jesus before the authorities, to the extent that he also is persecuted. Second, the invalid appears unresponsive – he is unable to digest Jesus' warning, does not progress in his knowledge of him, and there is no indication that he comes to faith in Jesus. In contrast, even as he stands up to the Jewish religious leaders, the man born blind progresses in his knowledge of Jesus, and, when Jesus later finds him, he is keen to respond in faith. Both men need physical and spiritual healing, but while the man who was blind also gains spiritual sight, the man who was lame gives a 'lame' response to Jesus – he does not take any steps to gain knowledge about Jesus.

In the final analysis, we side with the majority reading, which evaluates the invalid negatively, for three reasons. First, while the invalid may have responded positively in 5:9a (he daringly and knowingly accepts Jesus' Sabbath-breaking command) and in 5:11 (he tentatively sets Jesus' authority over against that of 'the Jews'), we cannot view 5:14–16 positively. In the end, the man appears to side with 'the Jews', reporting Jesus as the Sabbath-breaker, knowing that it would create trouble for Jesus. In his betrayal of Jesus, the man displays the characteristic of a traitor, a 'Judas'. Second, for John, an adequate belief-response and evidence of discipleship are necessary characteristics of a saving relationship with Jesus. The invalid fails to show these characteristics. He fails to testify to 'the Jews' about Jesus – unlike the Samaritan woman to her people, the royal official to his household, and the blind man to 'the Jews'. The man also fails to produce a belief-response to Jesus. Third, John intentionally creates a contrast between the invalid in John 5 and the blind man in John 9, in which the latter outclasses the former. Nevertheless, although the invalid's attitude and response to Jesus falls short of John's ideal, it is not as gloomy as the proponents of the negative reading suggest, so the positive reading provides a corrective.

his paradigm than to the text. Besides, he hardly grapples with the issues in 5:14–16 but merely refers to some arguments from van Tilborg, *Love*, 218 and Staley's article. It is also unclear why he does not consider the comparison to the blind man in John 9 more seriously.

[36] Cf. Bultmann, *Gospel*, 329; Martyn, *History*, 72–6; Culpepper, *Anatomy*, 139–40; Collins, 'Figures', 21; Lee, *Narratives*, 105–7. Contra Koester, who states that the invalid is the royal official's counterpart (*Symbolism*, 52–3).

Regarding his traits, the man appears to be obedient, daring, cooperative, defiant, ignorant, ambiguous, unresponsive and disloyal. He shows some character development in that it is surprising that, after he seemingly chooses Jesus' side in 5:9–11, he is unable or unwilling to accept Jesus' warning and becomes disloyal and betrays Jesus to 'the Jews' (5:14–15). The narrator reveals a little of the man's inner life in that he is ignorant of Jesus' identity (5:13).

The lame man was in a pitiful condition: he was not merely physically disabled but also a social-religious outcast, economically dependent (perhaps on begging), and in need of spiritual healing. Jesus initially heals him at a physical and socio-economic level – the man can walk again, gain economic independence, go to the temple and participate in worship. Unfortunately, he is unable to receive the spiritual healing that Jesus also offers him. John 5:1–47 is an integrated story in which the healing of the invalid in 5:1–18 functions as 'sign', informing the following discourse of 5:19–47. In this discourse, Jesus expounds his statement in 5:17, revealing that he is on a par with God because he has authority to give life and to judge, both divine prerogatives. Jesus wants to give life to the invalid by healing the whole man (cf. 7:23), but the man essentially rejects it so he will experience Jesus' other divine function – judgement (cf. 5:14, 24).[37]

The lame man, with his negative or ambiguous response, serves as an example of what must be avoided. While he appears to side with Jesus at first, willingly accepting Jesus' Sabbath-breaking command and challenging the authority of 'the Jews', later he seems unwilling to accept Jesus' reprimand and sides with 'the Jews', betraying Jesus. He seems a passive person – disinclined to learn the true identity of his benefactor and (hence) unable to respond appropriately.[38] He even resembles a 'Judas', betraying his benefactor to the enemy. For John, miracles are 'signs' – revealing something of Jesus' true identity – that aim to elicit an adequate belief-response (cf. 20:30–31). However, as Culpepper succinctly puts it, 'the lame man represents those whom even the signs cannot lead to authentic faith.'[39] When the lame man was restored by Jesus, he could produce no more than a lame response.

---

[37] Cf. Witkamp, 'Use', 34; Lee, *Narratives*, 98, 105, 114–8, 123. Although Bryan also notices that the healing functions as a sign followed by a discourse, it is not clear for him how the healing of the invalid functions as a sign that Jesus gives life ('Power', 21). Bryan concentrates on explaining that Jesus' activities are one with those of God and appears to neglect Jesus' divine tasks – to give life and to judge – and how they are linked to the invalid.

[38] Cf. Duke, who calls the man 'passivity incarnate' and although Duke contends that the man's passivity is excusable, he admits that 5:14 stands as Jesus' admonition to passive people who have not responded to his gracious initiative ('John 5:1–15', 540–42).

[39] Culpepper, *Anatomy*, 138. Cf. Howard, 'Significance', 72. Contra Beck, who asserts that *all* anonymous characters in John produce a faith response, modelling the paradigm of discipleship – including the lame man at the pool ('Function', 145, 151, 155).

The Invalid at the Pool		
Appearances	References	throughout 5:1–16
Identity	Titles given	–
	Gender	male
	Age	–
	Marital status	–
	Occupation	–
	Socio-economic status	marginalized
	Place of residence/operation	the pool at Bethesda in Jerusalem
	Relatives	–
	Group affiliation	–
Speech and actions	In interaction with Jesus	first sides with Jesus but then turns against him
	In interaction with others	first challenges the authority of 'the Jews' but eventually chooses their side by betraying Jesus to them
Character classification	Complexity	complex; multiple traits: obedient, daring, defiant, cooperative, ignorant, ambiguous, unresponsive, disloyal
	Development	some
	Inner life	little
Degree of characterization		towards personality
Response to Jesus		eventually inadequate

The Crowd – A Faceless, Divided Mass

'The man who follows the crowd will usually get no further than the crowd' — *Alan Ashley-Pitt*

The crowd is not an obvious character – it has received virtually no attention from Johannine scholarship – but it comprises the largest number of people.[1] The crowd has a dominant presence only in John 6 – 7 (60% of all occurrences) and in John 12 (30% of all occurrences).[2] Although the crowd occurs in different geographical locations (Galilee in John 6; Jerusalem in John 7 and 12) and has different referents (common people in John 6 and 7; 'the Jews' in John 12), we treat the crowd as a single, corporate character.[3]

The Galilean Crowd

John 6 contains the account of Jesus miraculously feeding the crowd and the subsequent discourse in which he reveals himself as the true bread from heaven who gives life to the world. The setting for the story is Galilee, where this new character – the crowd – gets a positive introduction (6:1–2). Seeing the crowd following Jesus because of his miraculous signs reminds us of the 'believing' group in 2:23 (although 2:24–25 reveals the inadequacy of its 'belief'). Besides, John frequently uses the verb 'to follow' to suggest discipleship, thus creating the expectation that this crowd might come to believe in Jesus and become true followers. What is important for John is that people not only come to Jesus but also stick with him in discipleship.

With the miraculous feeding of the crowd in 6:10–15, Jesus begins to test its willingness or ability 'to follow'. Jesus performs this miracle not simply to provide a free meal but to reveal something of his identity and mission – that if he can miraculously provide physical food he can also provide spiritual

---

[1] Except for Culpepper (*Anatomy*, 131–2) and Koester (*Symbolism*, 54–62), no one deals with the crowd. Resseguie even contends that the crowd is part of the setting rather than a character in its own right (*Narrative Criticism*, 125). We understand a crowd to be a large gathering of people, whereas a mob or throng denote particular types of crowd.

[2] The only references to the crowd outside John 6 – 7, 12 are in 5:13 and 11:42.

[3] The setting of John 7 and 12 as a Jewish festival that requires a pilgrimage to Jerusalem makes it highly likely that the 'Jerusalem' crowd includes Jews from all over Palestine.

nourishment. The crowd builds on its promising start by recognizing something of Jesus' identity – he is the Prophet like Moses of Deuteronomy 18:15–18 (6:14). However, their intention to make him some sort of national leader is too worldly 'from below' – and causes Jesus to withdraw (6:15).

Jesus escapes to the other side of the Sea of Galilee but the crowd keeps following him (6:22–25). Although this appears commendable, Jesus knows their intentions are still worldly – they simply want another free lunch (6:26). Even to have continued seeking Jesus because of his signs, as they initially did (6:2), would have been more spiritual; hence, their faith hardly seems 'faith' at all. Typically, Jesus moves from a material to a spiritual level but the crowd misunderstands him (6:27–29). The crowd is stuck at an earthly level, thinking of Jesus merely as a miracle worker and demanding a greater miracle, similar to what Moses did (6:30–31). Nevertheless, the crowd does progress in understanding by setting the feeding and the bread within the theological framework of the manna in the wilderness (6:31).

In 6:32–33, Jesus corrects the crowd's misinterpretation of the true bread from heaven but they continue to think at an earthly level, hoping for a continual supply of this miraculous bread (6:34). Jesus then explains that he is the bread of life who will sustain those who believe in him, knowing all the while that the crowd will not believe (6:35–36; cf. 2:24–25).

From 6:41 onwards, the debate between Jesus and his audience intensifies and becomes hostile. It is important to note that the term 'the Jews' is used in 6:41, 52 instead of 'the crowd'. While it is possible that the crowd consists of 'the Jews', it is more likely that from among the crowd of common Galileans a group of 'the Jews' emerges and becomes openly hostile towards Jesus.[4] Although 'the Jews' start out as part of the crowd, their emerging from it and their increased hostility demand that they be distinguished from the crowd.[5] The crowd disappears into the background. Although this crowd initially shows (signs-)faith and potential discipleship, it follows Jesus for the wrong reasons, is slow to understand and eventually fails to believe.

The Jerusalem Crowd

The Jerusalem crowds in John 7 and 12 are distinct but seem to behave like the Galilean one. Nonetheless, although these crowds largely reject Jesus, he is able to penetrate them and some individuals respond positively.[6]

---

[4] These 'Jews' in 6:41, 52 are either Pharisees from Jerusalem or, more likely, Pharisees residing in Galilee (see ch. 4). Contra Koester, who states that John identifies the crowd as 'the Jews' in 6:41, 52 (*Symbolism*, 57–8).

[5] There is probably also a shift in location, from the shore of Capernaum in 6:25–40 to its synagogue in 6:41–59.

[6] Besides the crowd in John 7, Koester surprisingly also considers the audience in John 8 as the Jerusalem crowd (whereas 8:12–59 clearly presents an audience of Pharisees and 'the Jews') but ignores John 12, where a Jerusalem crowd is present (*Symbolism*, 59–62).

The Jerusalem Crowd in John 7

The setting for John 7 is the temple during the Feast of Tabernacles – one of the three great Jewish festivals that required Jews to make a pilgrimage to Jerusalem. Hence, besides local residents, the crowd probably includes Jews from all over Palestine. Throughout John 7, Jesus' audience is a mix of the crowd (the common people), 'the Jews' (the particular Torah- and temple-loyalists), and the leaders of 'the Jews' – the Pharisees, the chief priests or 'rulers/authorities', and the temple police. The crowd is clearly distinct from 'the Jews' and their leaders because 7:11–13 mentions the former's fear of the latter, then in 7:26 common Jerusalemites distinguish themselves from the religious authorities, and finally in 7:49 the Sanhedrin authorities contemptuously label the crowd as ignorant rabble.[7]

Before Jesus appears on the scene, the crowd is already divided on who he is but they are too afraid of 'the Jews' to discuss the issue publicly (7:12–13). Like 'the Jews' in 6:41, the crowd grumbles (7:12, 32) and it resembles Israel's grumbling in the wilderness (Exod. 15:24; 16:2–12; Num. 14:26–27). Jesus' teaching is met with incomprehension and aggravation (7:20). In fact, the crowd comes close to siding with 'the Jews' when it accuses Jesus of being demon-possessed (cf. 7:20; 8:48, 52). The crowd claims to know Jesus' origin (7:25–27) but he firmly refutes this claim saying they lack knowledge of God – and hence of him (7:28–29).[8] Jesus' reply causes division: some try to arrest Jesus while others believe in him, reasoning that Jesus' miraculous signs prove that he is the Messiah (7:30–31). However, this 'belief' may be viewed with caution because a similar miracle-based belief of a Jerusalem 'crowd' was deficient (2:23–24). Jesus' invitation on the last day of the festival (7:37–38) seems attractive but once again causes division in the crowd (7:40–43).

Thus, throughout John 7, the crowd remains divided, unable to make up its mind about Jesus (7:12, 30–31, 40–43). Nevertheless, this division shows that Jesus is able to penetrate the crowd with his teaching and elicit some positive (though inadequate) responses. The crowd is a microcosm of humanity, and the reactions and divisions in the crowd represent the responses of acceptance and rejection that humankind can make (cf. 1:10–13; 3:18, 36). Although the crowd in John 7 is primarily a divided one, it also shows an unflattering resemblance to 'the Jews': (i) both 'the Jews' and the crowd grumble about Jesus (6:41; 7:12, 32); (ii) both accuse him of being demon-possessed (7:20; 8:48, 52).

The Jerusalem Crowd in John 12

Whereas the crowds in John 6 and 7 consist of common people, John 12 presents a different one. It is not a crowd of common Jerusalemites because

---

[7] Cf. Bultmann, *Gospel*, 310–11 n. 5; R. Meyer, '*Ochlos*', in *TDNT*, 5:589–90.

[8] Although the term 'Jerusalemites' rather than 'crowd' is used in 7:25, they probably belong to the crowd since they distinguish themselves from 'the authorities' in 7:26.

John identifies this crowd as 'the great crowd of "the Jews"' (12:9). Nor is it a crowd of the religious authorities because the crowd in 12:9 is contrasted with the religious authorities in 12:10–11, 18–19.[9] The crowd in 12:9 is more likely a great crowd of Judaean Torah- and temple-loyalists, corresponding to the 'many people from the countryside' who went up to the Passover feast of 'the Jews' in Jerusalem (11:55).[10] Although initially this crowd of 'the Jews' is favourable to Jesus (12:12–19), soon its attitude changes and ultimately it responds with rejection and unbelief (12:27–40) – typical of 'the Jews' throughout (cf. ch. 4). In fact, this crowd displays an attitude similar to the Galilean crowd. We will elaborate.

Just as in 6:14, 26, 30, the crowd of 'the Jews' is focused on the spectacular: they have come to see the controversial Jesus and the resurrected Lazarus (12:9, 18). The Jewish authorities are afraid that seeing Lazarus, the crowd may believe in Jesus – just as many of 'the Jews' did when Lazarus was raised – therefore they plan to kill Lazarus too (12:10–11; cf. 11:45). When the crowd hears that Jesus is approaching Jerusalem, it hails him as the long-awaited messianic king (12:12–13). Jesus is given this rousing welcome because of the raising of Lazarus (12:17–18). While the crowd expects Jesus to be a political messianic leader who would liberate them from Roman oppression, Jesus' action in 12:14–15 serves to correct their misunderstanding. Against the backdrop of Zechariah 9:9–10, Jesus is depicted not as a warrior-king but as a king who will destroy Israel's war tools (including the war horse), and establish peace. Hence, the devotion and expectations of the crowd seem rather misplaced (cf. 6:14–15).

Jesus attempts to help the crowd overcome their misunderstanding and unbelief (12:29–30) but in vain. When he speaks of his impending, salvific death, the crowd is scandalized but once again Jesus urges the crowd to understand and believe in him lest the darkness overtake them (12:31–36; cf. 1:5; 8:12; 11:9–10). Finally, Jesus withdraws and John reveals that for all Jesus' admonitions and miraculous signs, the crowd at large does not believe in him (12:37; cf. 6:36). The crowd's unbelief fulfils the prophecy in Isaiah 53:1, which speaks of the messianic Servant who is rejected (12:38). John then reveals in 12:39–40 the reason for the crowd's unbelief: The closed minds of 'the Jews' prevent understanding, repentance and salvation, and by rejecting Jesus and his message they remain blind, or, are plunged further into darkness (cf. 9:39–41).[11]

Nevertheless, John mentions that while the crowd at large is unbelieving, many from the crowd 'believe' in Jesus (12:42). However, this 'belief' appears

[9] John 12:17–18 depicts different crowds: the crowd in 12:17 is the same as in 11:42, whereas the crowd in 12:18 has only *heard* of the miracle and corresponds to the crowd in 11:55; 12:9, 12, 29, 34 (cf. Meyer, 'Ochlos', 5:588–9; *pace* Bultmann, *Gospel*, 419).

[10] Cf. the crowd in 11:42, which certainly consists of 'the Jews' who had come to console Mary and Martha (11:19, 31, 33, 36, 45). However, the crowd in 11:42 is different from the one in 12:9 (see n. 9, above).

[11] Bennema, *John's Gospel*, 135–6; *idem*, *Power*, 131.

inadequate. First, it is a 'secret' belief since the fear of expulsion from the synagogue prevents them from publicly confessing their belief (12:42). John implicitly criticizes such an attitude in John 9, by contrasting the bold testimony of the formerly blind man before the religious authorities with the denial of his fearful parents. Second, these 'secret believers' are more concerned with winning human praise than God's (12:43). Such an attitude, Jesus points out to 'the Jews' in 5:44, is an obstacle to true faith.

Thus, the crowd in John 12 as a whole is ultimately an unbelieving crowd. They move from enthusiasm to misunderstanding to aggravation to rejection and unbelief. This is not surprising since this crowd consists of 'the Jews', who primarily represent the attitude of hostility and disbelief. The crowd makes no appearance beyond John 12.

Conclusion

Even though John presents different crowds – a Galilean crowd of common people in John 6, a Jerusalem crowd of common people in John 7, and a Jerusalem crowd of the particular religious partisans in John 12 – they have similar characteristics and emerge as a consistent, corporate character. The Galilean crowd makes a promising start, giving the impression that they will become true disciples (6:2), but this expectation is short-lived as it becomes clear that it follows Jesus for the wrong reasons, misunderstands him (6:25–34), and as Jesus foretells, fails to believe (6:36). Out of this crowd, a group of hostile 'Jews' appears (6:41–59). In John 7, the Jerusalem crowd of commoners is divided about Jesus (7:12, 30–31, 40–43). This divided crowd is a microcosm of the world – representing the responses of acceptance and rejection that humankind can make. At the same time, this crowd mimics the negative attitude of 'the Jews' in that they grumble and accuse Jesus of being demon-possessed (7:12, 20, 32). In John 12, we encounter a crowd of 'the Jews'. Although this crowd is initially enthusiastic about Jesus (12:12–19), it proves to be motivated by a desire for the spectacular (12:9, 18). Besides, its expectations are misplaced because it has misunderstood the nature of Jesus' mission (12:13–14). This continued misunderstanding eventually leads to rejection and unbelief because this crowd is 'blind' (12:27–40; cf. 6:36).

John 6 thus depicts an unbelieving crowd, out of which the hostile 'Jews' emerge; John 7 presents a divided crowd which shares characteristics with 'the Jews'; John 12 portrays an unbelieving crowd of 'Jews'. Although the crowd and 'the Jews' are distinct characters, the crowd closely resembles 'the Jews'.[12] It thus appears that the crowd as a group or corporate character

---

[12] Contra those who argue that John has blurred the distinctions between the crowd and 'the Jews' (Fuller, '"Jews"', 32–3; Koester, *Symbolism*, 59–62; R. Hakola, *Identity Matters: John, the Jews and Jewishness* [NovTSup 118; Leiden: Brill, 2005], 160–62, 226–31).

remains in darkness and chooses to respond with unbelief.[13] The crowd's main trait is its divisibility, while displaying various sub-traits: it is sympathetic, patriotic, enthusiastic, even sensationalist (6:14–15; 7:31, 40–41a; 12:9, 12–13, 18) and shows potential for belief and discipleship; yet, it also displays misunderstanding, dismissiveness, rejection and unbelief. Regarding the crowd's 'inner life', Jesus reveals that it desires the spectacular, will not believe and does not know him (6:26, 36; 7:28), while the crowd itself claims to know Jesus' origins (7:27). Sometimes, the crowd's style of speaking is comparable to a soliloquy – an 'inner monologue' (7:12, 40–42).

Despite the crowd's negative attitude overall, Jesus is able to break through and elicit positive responses – even belief – from some. And while the crowd has a cognitive problem – it does not understand Jesus and his teaching – and develops a hostile and unbelieving attitude, it can nevertheless think theologically (6:14, 28–31; 7:25–27, 31, 40–43; 12:34) – though the religious authorities, ironically, consider them incapable of doing so (7:49). However, the belief-responses do not stand scrutiny. In 7:31, the 'belief' of many in the crowd is perhaps just that Jesus is a miracle worker – and Jesus has already been critical of such belief of the crowd (2:23–25). Next, though many from the crowd believe in Jesus (12:42), John is critical of these so-called 'secret believers' who are afraid to confess publicly. Nevertheless, though the 'belief' of individuals in the crowd is questionable, the point is that the crowd is not uniform in its response to Jesus; some responses can be designated as 'positive' (though inadequate).[14]

The crowd as a character has not received much attention because, typically, it seems a mass of 'grey', faceless people. So also in life, many people prefer to remain anonymous, moving with the crowd. The Johannine crowd embarks on a negative course. Though Jesus is able to penetrate this group with his teaching, causing controversy and division, and elicit positive responses, these appear inadequate. For John, a true believer is someone who publicly confesses belief in Jesus, so remaining in the crowd as a 'secret believer' is inadequate.

---

[13] In Jewish antiquity, the crowd was also perceived negatively. Josephus mentions the crowd's desire for the spectacular (*Antiquities* 7:286–287; cf. John 6:26; 12:9, 18), its susceptibility to deception (*Antiquities* 20:160, 167; cf. John 7:12b), its ignorance (*Against Apion* 2:224; cf. John 7:49), and its function as a hiding place (*Antiquities* 2:255; cf. John 5:13). Philo speaks negatively of the crowd as 'a misguided multitude of ordinary careless people' (*Who is the Heir of Divine Things* 1:303), unstable (*On the Life of Moses* 1:197; *Allegorical Interpretation* 1:67), easily deceived (*On Abraham* 1:22), lazy, disorderly, erring and blameable (*On Rewards and Punishments* 1:20), and unable to produce wisdom or pursue what is genuine (*On Joseph* 1:59[–66]).

[14] Cf. Culpepper's conclusion that '[t]he crowd represents the struggle of those who are open to believing, but neither the scriptures nor the signs lead them to authentic faith' (*Anatomy*, 132).

The Crowd		
Appearances	References	5:13; 6:2, 5, 22, 24; 7:12 (2x), 20, 31, 32, 40, 43, 49; 11:42; 12:9, 12, 17, 18, 29, 34
Identity	Titles given	–
	Gender	–
	Age	–
	Marital status	–
	Occupation	–
	Socio-economic status	–
	Place of residence/operation	Galilee, Jerusalem
	Relatives	–
	Group affiliation	common people, 'the Jews'
Speech and actions	In interaction with Jesus	enthusiastic, divided, misunderstanding, unbelieving
	In interaction with others	afraid of 'the Jews'
Character classification	Complexity	complex; multiple traits: divided, enthusiastic, patriotic, sympathetic, sensationalist, potential for belief/discipleship, undiscerning, dismissive, rejective, unbelieving.
	Development	none
	Inner life	some
Degree of characterization		corporate personality
Response to Jesus		inadequate: as crowd it disbelieves; individuals make positive but still inadequate responses

The Twelve – Slow but Sticky

'The person who renders loyal service in a humble capacity
will be chosen for higher responsibilities' — B.C. Forbes

The term 'the Twelve' occurs four times in John's gospel (6:67, 70, 71; 20:24), referring to Jesus' inner circle of disciples, but nowhere does John provide a list of their names. We shall examine the Twelve as a collective character, while other chapters in this book study individual disciples from among the Twelve.[1] We must keep in mind that John uses the term 'disciple' for others who follow Jesus apart from the Twelve (4:1; 6:60–66; 7:3; 8:31; 9:28; 19:38) – though many of them are unable to sustain their discipleship. Sometimes John's description of a person's speech and actions indicates that she or he functions as a disciple: for example, the Samaritan woman, the royal official, the man born blind, the Lazarus family and Mary Magdalene. John's understanding of who is a disciple of Jesus is broader than 'the Twelve' and includes everyone who follows Jesus and stays with him.[2]

The Identity of the Twelve

Regarding the composition of the Twelve, we shall first look at the Gospel of John before considering the Synoptics. John explicitly mentions three disciples who belong to the Twelve: Simon Peter (6:67–68), Judas Iscariot (6:71) and Thomas (20:24). It seems reasonable to assume that the disciples present with Jesus during the farewell discourses in John 13 – 17 also belong to the Twelve, and hence we can add the so-called Beloved Disciple (13:23), Philip (14:8–9) and Judas not Iscariot (14:22). Andrew most probably also belongs to the Twelve because: (i) he is one of the first of Jesus' disciples (1:40); (ii) he brings his brother Peter, one of the Twelve, to Jesus (1:41–42); (iii) he often appears with Philip who probably belongs to the Twelve (6:5–9; 12:22). Consequently, if three of the four named disciples in 1:35–51 belong to the Twelve (Andrew, Peter, Philip), then perhaps Nathanael does

---

[1] Only a few treat the Twelve as a collective character (Culpepper, *Anatomy*, 115–9; Edwards, *John*, 98–9, 102–3).

[2] Cf. the extensive discussion in Köstenberger, *Missions*, 144–53.

too (1:45), but this is more tentative (see ch. 7). This idea may be supported by the parallelism of 1:35–42 and 1:43–51, in which Andrew finds Peter, and Philip finds Nathanael. The final two named disciples that can be counted among the Twelve are 'the sons of Zebedee' in 21:2, undoubtedly referring to the brothers James and John (see below). Since 21:7 mentions the Beloved Disciple, who must have been one of the seven disciples in 21:2, he is either one of the sons of Zebedee or one of the two unnamed disciples. The two unnamed disciples in 21:2 could be Andrew and Philip because if those whom they found are present in 21:2 (Peter and Nathanael), then it is plausible the finders are there as well. In which case, the Beloved Disciple would be a son of Zebedee (see ch. 21). It is therefore possible that all seven disciples in 21:2 belong to the Twelve.

We therefore suggest that the Twelve includes: Simon Peter, his brother Andrew, James and John of Zebedee, Philip, Thomas, Judas Iscariot and Judas not Iscariot. Besides, we tentatively suggest that Nathanael was also among the Twelve. Since 'the Beloved Disciple' is short for 'the disciple whom Jesus loved' rather than a proper name, we cannot count him as a *named* member of the Twelve. Besides, the identity of the Beloved Disciple is not relevant for the identity of the Twelve but for when we study the Beloved Disciple himself (see ch. 21). Therefore, depending on whether we include Nathanael, John's gospel mentions eight or nine of the Twelve by name.

The term 'the Twelve' is not unique to John but also occurs frequently in the Synoptics to designate Jesus' inner circle of disciples (e.g. Matt. 10:1; 26:14; Mark 3:16; 4:10; 6:7; 9:35; Luke 8:1; 9:1; 18:31). Hence, there is no reason to assume that 'the Twelve' in John's gospel is a different group from the one portrayed in the Synoptics. Besides, since the Synoptics provide all the twelve names, a comparison with those that John provides would be in order. The Synoptics name the Twelve as: Simon Peter, Andrew his brother, James son of Zebedee, John brother of James, Philip, Bartholomew, Thomas, Matthew the tax collector, James son of Alphaeus, Thaddaeus or Judas of James, Simon the Canaanite/Zealot, Judas Iscariot (Matt. 10:2–4; Mark 3:16–19; Luke 6:14–16).[3] We quickly recognize that of the named disciples in John's gospel, seven find a direct parallel with those mentioned in the Synoptics: Peter, Andrew, James and John, Philip, Thomas and Judas Iscariot. Regarding Judas not Iscariot, the most likely candidate seems to be Judas of James, also called Thaddaeus. If Nathanael belongs to the Twelve (which is by no means certain), most scholars contend that he is Bartholomew, but Hill makes a convincing case for identifying him with James son of Alphaeus (see ch. 7).[4]

---

[3] I assume that the Synoptics refer to the same twelve disciples, and hence Thaddaeus and Judas of James are the same person.

[4] Although the Synoptics provide the names of all the twelve disciples, they only give roles to Peter, James and John, and Judas, whereas John describes all the eight or nine disciples that he mentions.

The Character of the Twelve

Even though the term 'the Twelve' only occurs four times, the phrase 'his disciples' occurs frequently and mostly refers to Jesus' twelve disciples, or at least includes them (2:2, 11–12, 17, 22; 3:22; 4:2, 8, 27; 6:3, 8, 12, 16–17; 9:2; 12:16; 16:17, 29; 18:1; 20:26; cf. 11:7, 54; 13:5). Occasions where (some of) the Twelve are present include: the disciples who headed for Capernaum in a single boat in 6:16–17 are probably the Twelve mentioned in 6:67; the mention of Peter, Philip, Thomas, Judas Iscariot, Judas not Iscariot and the Beloved Disciple in the farewell discourses (John 13 – 17) implies the presence of the Twelve. In 6:60–71 we come across a larger group of Jesus' disciples, including the Twelve. Many from this group turn out to be pseudo-disciples who stop following because they find Jesus' teaching too demanding or difficult (6:60–66) but the Twelve stick to Jesus (6:67–69). Therefore, where Jesus' disciples refers to a larger group, the Twelve could be included, so we must investigate those passages that mention 'disciples' in order to determine the character of the Twelve. Conversely, the passages where the Twelve or individual members are explicitly mentioned are expected to reveal aspects of discipleship. Thus, *the Twelve are representative of discipleship in general.*

The Twelve are placed firmly on Jesus' side right from the beginning. In 1:35–51 we learn of five people (Andrew and an unnamed person, probably the Beloved Disciple [see ch. 21], Peter, Philip and Nathanael) who come to and remain with Jesus. Besides, the confessions of Andrew, Philip and Nathanael (1:41, 45, 49) indicate that all five have understood true aspects of Jesus' identity. Then, at the wedding at Cana, the disciples respond to Jesus' first sign with belief (2:11), which indeed is the response that John desires to see (20:30–31). On two other occasions the Twelve confirm their understanding and belief: (i) 6:67–69 mentions Peter's confession on behalf of the Twelve; (ii) in 16:30 the Twelve affirm their knowledge of and belief in Jesus. Besides, Jesus himself indicates that the Twelve have understood and believed him (17:6–8; cf. the plural use in 3:11).

We shall now examine two features of the Twelve that stand out: (i) their frequent misunderstanding of Jesus and (ii) their following of Jesus (except for Judas Iscariot).

Misunderstanding

The Twelve frequently struggle to understand Jesus, compelling him to provide further revelation and explanation. In 4:32–33, for example, the disciples misunderstand Jesus' talk of 'food', which he then explains (4:34–38). In 6:5–9, Jesus tests Philip (and Andrew) but they fail to think 'from above' (see ch. 5). The Twelve also misunderstand Jesus' statement that he will 'wake' Lazarus who had 'fallen asleep', so Jesus explains again (11:11–

14). Later, they do not understand the crowd's enthusiasm towards Jesus and his corrective action at the end of his ministry (12:12–16). Again, during the farewell discourses, when Jesus gives private instruction to the Twelve in order to prepare them for his departure and their mission, they struggle to understand what Jesus does and says: see Peter in 13:6–10, 36–38; the Twelve in 13:28–29 and 16:17–18; Thomas in 14:5; Philip in 14:8; and Judas not Iscariot in 14:22. In 18:10–11, it becomes clear that Peter has still not understood the nature of Jesus' mission. Even after the cross, the misunderstanding continues: Peter and the Beloved Disciple do not understand the significance of the empty tomb and perhaps believe Mary Magdalene's report that Jesus' body has mysteriously disappeared (20:2, 8–10). Even when Mary provides a corrected report after her encounter with the risen Jesus (20:18), the Twelve possibly struggle to accept it – why else are they behind locked doors in 20:19? Then, in 21:2–3, some of the Twelve appear to have returned to their old profession, perhaps misunderstanding their mission (cf. 20:21), so the miraculous catch of fish that Jesus provides serves as a symbolic reminder of their mission (21:4–14).

We must examine *why* the Twelve (and others) frequently misunderstand Jesus. One reason is that people belong to the world, which is enveloped in an epistemic darkness – they do not know God (1:5, 10). The divine response to this epistemic darkness is light or epistemic illumination. The Logos-Light came into the dark world to enlighten people by revealing the Father (1:4–5, 9, 18), that is, Jesus brought life-giving revelation of God. However, Jesus' revelation only produces life if it is understood and accepted – and that is where a further problem arises. Frequently, the language of the Johannine Jesus is enigmatic or ambiguous.

Sometimes Jesus uses the literary technique of double entendre, where a word can have two meanings, and often Jesus has one meaning in mind and his audience chooses the other, causing misunderstanding. In case of the Twelve, the verb *koimaomai* in 11:11 can mean either 'to sleep' (as the disciples understand it [11:12]) or 'to be dead' (as Jesus meant it [11:13–14]). At other times, Jesus uses metaphors, which are misunderstood when taken literally: for instance, in 4:32–33, the disciples misunderstand Jesus' metaphorical use of 'food' because they think of literal food. On other occasions, some disciples are victims of irony, revealing their ignorance of another reality: Nathanael's comment in 1:46 in response to Philip's revelation about Jesus shows his lack of understanding and is ironic in the light of his confession in 1:49; Thomas's remark in 11:16 about dying at the hands of 'the Jews' (which ironically comes true for Jesus himself) shows he misunderstood Jesus' reasons for returning to Judaea; Peter's response in 13:37 is ironic because he has not yet understood the true meaning of following and laying down his life, as Jesus points out in 13:38.[5] Thus, Jesus' teaching is often enigmatic or ambiguous because he uses literary devices such as double

---

[5] Cf. Culpepper, *Anatomy*, 170–79.

entendre, metaphors, symbolism and irony, which are prone to misunderstanding. In 16:25a, Jesus even refers to his revelation as being 'veiled' (*paroimia* denotes 'veiled language' or 'figure of speech').

The following picture emerges. Although the disciples are placed firmly on Jesus' side and stick with him throughout, they often fail to understand Jesus' revelation and actions. Even though cognitive dullness is not unique to the Twelve – many people in John's gospel have the same problem – we would nevertheless expect Jesus' closest circle of followers to better understand him, his teaching and mission.[6] When Jesus provides further revelation in response to the Twelve's misunderstanding, they often make little or no cognitive progress (but see 6:68–69; 16:29–30). This raises the following questions: Will the Twelve overcome their cognitive dullness about Jesus and his teaching? And how can they be expected to carry on Jesus' ongoing mission in the world? John explains that further divine assistance is available from the Spirit as a cognitive agent.[7]

The Spirit, according to John's gospel, is instrumental in bringing people towards knowledge/understanding and belief. First, the Spirit provides Jesus with revelatory wisdom and knowledge that forms the basis for his life-giving teaching/revelation (see 1:32–34; 3:34–36).[8] From 3:1–15; 4:10–14; 6:63 and 7:38–39 we learn that the Spirit actively reaches out to people *through* Jesus' teaching, mediating this saving wisdom/knowledge to people so that they might come to an adequate understanding and belief-response.[9] The Twelve are explicitly assured of the Spirit's aid in John 13 – 17. Jesus promises that after his departure, the Spirit-Paraclete will mediate or reveal to his disciples (and by implication later generations of believers) the life-giving truth present in Jesus' teaching (16:12–15) in order to equip them for their mission in the world (15:26–27). Thus, the Spirit-Paraclete acts as a cognitive agent, assisting the disciples in understanding Jesus' teaching.[10]

[6] John presents many people who misunderstand Jesus: Nicodemus misunderstands the spiritual birth 'from above' that Jesus speaks of; the Samaritan woman struggles to understand the nature of the living water and Jesus' identity; the crowd and 'the Jews' frequently misunderstand what Jesus is talking about in John 5 – 12; the man born blind needs a second encounter with Jesus before he truly understands his benefactor's identity (9:35–38); Pilate is sympathetic towards Jesus but does not understand him.

[7] Elsewhere I have elaborated on the epistemic darkness of people and the twofold divine assistance in the form of Jesus' providing life-giving revelation and the Spirit's aiding people to grasp the meaning of this revelation (Bennema, 'Christ', 110–20).

[8] The coming and remaining of the Spirit on Jesus in 1:32 probably alludes to Isa. 11:2, which describes the Messiah as being empowered with the Spirit of wisdom, understanding, knowledge and liberating power. Subsequently, 3:35 explains that God has given the entire revelation to Jesus, and 3:34 clarifies that Jesus can provide this revelation because he is empowered with the Spirit. See further Bennema, *Power*, 161–7.

[9] Bennema, *Power*, 167–212 or, briefer, Bennema, 'Christ', 116–8.

[10] The role of the Spirit as a cognitive agent is elucidated in Bennema, *Power*, chs 4–5; *idem*, 'Christ', 116–20. This role of the Spirit was already known in Judaism (C. Bennema, 'The Strands of Wisdom Tradition in Intertestamental Judaism: Origins, Developments and Characteristics', *TynB* 52 [2001]: 61–82; *idem*, *Power*, ch. 2).

We are now also able to understand what Jesus refers to when he promises to speak 'plainly' in the future (16:25b). I suggest that he refers to the time of the coming of the Spirit-Paraclete for two reasons. First, the Paraclete will cause the disciples to remember the things Jesus said (14:26). Second, when Jesus says in 16:12, 'I still have many things to say to you, but you cannot bear them now', he refers to the future teaching of the Paraclete (explained in 16:13–15). Hence, from 14:26 and 16:12–15 we conclude that the Paraclete will explain everything that Jesus has said, in such a way that Jesus' words become plain. Thus, Jesus presents God's life-giving revelation in a 'veiled' way and the Spirit-Paraclete has the task of revealing to the believer the meaning and significance of this revelation. Indeed, John records a few instances where the disciples are brought to an understanding of Jesus' revelation after the resurrection through remembrance (2:17, 22; 12:26; 16:4) – very likely the result of the Spirit-Paraclete's anamnesis.[11] In addition, 16:29–30 gives us a preview of the 'plain' revelation that is to come, for suddenly the disciples grasp the meaning of Jesus' words.

To sum up, during Jesus' ministry, the Twelve's intellectual grasp of Jesus' teaching, mission and actions fluctuate between understanding (1:41, 45, 49; 6:68–69; 16:30; 17:7–8), misunderstanding and failure to understand. In response to their cognitive dullness, Jesus often provides further revelation. One reason for the Twelve's misunderstanding of Jesus is that his revelation is veiled and at times ambiguous, and needs to be penetrated cognitively in order to be understood. The Spirit is the designated interpreter *par excellence* who will assist the Twelve (and later believers) to understand the meaning and significance of Jesus' 'veiled' teaching. At the level of narrative, misunderstanding functions as a hermeneutical device – the misunderstanding of the character in the story often results in further explanation of Jesus, which benefits the reader. In the process of reading (and interpreting), the reader also enjoys the assistance of the Spirit as the hermeneutical key to unlock Jesus' revelation.

Remaining with Jesus as a Disciple

John's understanding of discipleship is not simply coming to Jesus but also *remaining* with him. In John's gospel we find examples of people who appear

---

[11] In 2:17, 22 and 12:16, the Greek uses the passive form 'to be reminded' rather than the active 'to remember', which implies that an *agent* is involved in the reminding. In the light of the work of the Spirit-Paraclete (14:26; 16:7, 13), I suggest that the disciples were reminded of Jesus' action and able to understand its significance because of the Spirit-Paraclete. Although Culpepper also highlights the disciples' understanding after Jesus' death and resurrection, he does not connect this understanding with the work of the Spirit. Besides, Culpepper seems to suggest that understanding could *only* come after Jesus' death and resurrection (*Anatomy*, 117–9). However, we have seen that the disciples already had an adequate understanding of Jesus before the cross, and that their positive belief-responses include a certain cognizance of Jesus' identity and mission (see also Bennema, 'Christ', 122–4).

to be disciples but are unable to sustain their discipleship or confess it openly. For example, when Jesus is in Jerusalem, many people believe in him because they see his miraculous signs (2:23), but Jesus, knowing people's inner thoughts and motivations, perceives that their 'belief' is deficient (2:24–25).[12] Similarly, in 6:2 John mentions that a large crowd follows Jesus because of his miraculous signs. The verb 'to follow' in John carries the idea of following *as a disciple*, and hence it creates the expectation that this crowd has the potential for discipleship. However, it soon becomes clear that the crowd follows Jesus for the wrong reasons, misunderstands him and fails to believe, thus unable to realize its potential for discipleship (6:25–36). Besides, Jesus' teaching is apparently so difficult to understand and accept that even many of his disciples stumble over it, deciding to stop following Jesus (6:60–66).

On another occasion, many 'Jews' believe in Jesus after they hear his teaching (8:30). However, when Jesus probes further, their 'belief' proves to have no substance and they turn violent (8:31–59). In 8:31, Jesus makes a crucial point regarding discipleship: 'If you *remain* in my word, you are truly my disciples', implying that a *continual* adherence to Jesus' teaching is a demonstration of authentic discipleship. Elsewhere Jesus makes a similar point to his disciples, urging them to remain in fellowship with him and to adhere to his teaching (15:4–10). To stick to Jesus and his teachings thus demonstrates genuine discipleship.

Joseph of Arimathea is described as a 'secret' disciple of Jesus because of his fear of 'the Jews' (19:38). Reading John's gospel, it appears that John is critical of such kind of discipleship. In John 9, for example, the fearful attitude of the parents of the formerly blind man when they are interrogated by the Jewish leaders is contrasted with the bold attitude of their son who defends Jesus before the authorities. The so-called 'fear of the Jews' affects many people since those who confess Jesus as the Messiah are threatened with excommunication, resulting in exclusion from the socio-religious life of their day (7:13; 9:22; 12:42; 19:38; 20:19). Despite the harsh reality of this threat, John encourages people to confess their belief openly, so 'secret discipleship' is no option (see further ch. 23).

The Twelve are able to continue in discipleship. John 1:35–40 recounts the event where two of John's disciples left him in order to follow Jesus. Their 'staying' with Jesus demonstrates their desire to discover more about him. The verb used is literally 'to remain', which in John frequently means to remain in fellowship with Jesus or to remain with him as a disciple. On another occasion, when there is a sifting of Jesus' disciples (6:60–66), Jesus asks the Twelve whether they also want to quit, to which Peter, as the spokesperson for the Twelve, affirms that Jesus is worth following (6:67–69).

---

12 Indeed, from this group Nicodemus comes forward, and his dialogue with Jesus reveals the deficiency of Nicodemus's 'belief' (and that of the people in 2:23): he was not born 'from above' (cf. ch. 9).

In the farewell discourses, Jesus urges the Twelve *inter alia* to remain in fellowship with him and to adhere to his teaching (14:15–24; 15:1–17). Jesus especially implores Peter to follow him (13:36) – and he eventually will (21:19–22).

The Spirit-Paraclete, who Jesus promises to the Twelve (and by implication to any disciple) (14:16–17; 15:26), plays an important role in sustaining people's discipleship. First, the Spirit-Paraclete will explain the meaning and significance of Jesus' teaching to a disciple thereby enabling the disciple to remain in Jesus and his words (14:26; 16:12–15). Second, the Spirit will inform and empower the disciple's testimony to the world (15:26–27; 16:7–11). Third, the Spirit will mediate to the believer the intimate fellowship with Jesus and the Father (14:23; cf. 1 John 1:3; 3:24; 4:13) and consequently sustain the unity between the believer, Jesus and the Father that 17:21–23 speaks of. Fourth, based on 17:6–19, I have tentatively suggested elsewhere that the Spirit-Paraclete may also protect the disciples against the hate and persecution of the world, and sanctify them for their mission in the world.[13]

In sum, for John, a genuine disciple is one who remains in fellowship with Jesus, adheres to his teaching and commandments, and openly testifies to the world. At the same time, Jesus' teaching appears to be a testing ground for authentic discipleship since it often causes misunderstanding or offence, frequently preventing people from becoming disciples or causing them to discontinue their discipleship. In case of the Twelve, their frequent misunderstanding of Jesus' words does not result in defection or an inadequate belief-response.[14] They have a sufficient grasp of Jesus' true identity, mission and intimate relationship with God, and are able to stick with Jesus. The Spirit plays a crucial role in both bringing people to Jesus and sustaining their relationship with him in discipleship.

Conclusion

Jesus apparently teaches in 'veiled' language, interlaced with double entendre, symbolism, metaphors and irony, which are prone to misunderstanding. Jesus does this for two reasons. First, he wants people to think 'from above' in order to develop spiritual insight into the things of God. Second, Jesus' 'veiled' teaching, which needs to be 'unveiled' or penetrated cognitively in order to be understood, forms a testing ground for discipleship. While the Twelve continue to stick with Jesus despite their frequent misunderstandings, others find Jesus' teaching too difficult or demanding and it becomes a stumbling block for them (e.g. 6:60–66; 8:30–59). The Spirit

---

[13] Bennema, *John's Gospel*, 185–9. For an extensive treatment of the role of the Spirit-Paraclete, see Bennema, *Power*, ch. 5.

[14] Cf. Culpepper, *Anatomy*, 118.

functions as a decoder, decrypting or unlocking Jesus' revelation, thereby enabling discipleship.

We have seen that the Twelve have both an individual and a corporate dimension. On the one hand, the Twelve make up Jesus' inner circle of disciples, and John identifies eight or nine by name. We have studied these individual characters in other chapters of this book, but this chapter concentrated on the corporate dimension – how the Twelve function as a group. As a collective character, 'the Twelve' represents Johannine discipleship, being characterized as 'slow but sticky'. The Twelve are 'slow' in understanding Jesus' revelatory teaching but they are 'sticky' in remaining firmly on Jesus' side.[15] There is hope for their dullness with Jesus' promise of the coming of the Spirit-Paraclete, who will aid them in understanding Jesus' teaching. For John, the Spirit is primarily a cognitive agent enabling the disciple to think 'from above' and access divine realities.

The Twelve display multiple traits: perceptiveness (1:41, 45, 49; 6:68–69; 16:30; 17:7–8), belief (2:11; 6:69; 16:30), loyalty (they stick with Jesus), misunderstanding/dullness, zeal (11:16; 13:37), remembrance (2:22; 12:16).[16] John's gospel shows an extensive inner life of the Twelve. Frequently, the narrator reveals aspects of their inner life: the disciples remember certain things (2:17, 22; 12:16), are amazed (4:27), afraid (6:19; 20:19), make assumptions (11:13; 13:29), are at a loss (13:22), do not understand (12:16; 13:28; 21:4), and lack courage (21:12). Once, Jesus exposes the sorrow of the Twelve (14:1; 16:6), and elsewhere they discuss amongst themselves something Jesus has said, comparable to a soliloquy or 'inner monologue' (16:17). We may even speak of character development regarding the Twelve. Their understanding of and belief in Jesus, and their ability to stick with him despite frequent misunderstanding is somewhat surprising and are traits that can cause tension, especially since misunderstanding often prevents adequate belief (e.g. Nicodemus and 'the Jews') or even results in defection (the disciples in 6:60–66). The Twelve may represent the believer or disciple in general, who although firmly at Jesus' side also struggles to understand.[17]

---

[15] Peter's denial of his discipleship in 18:15–27 is only a temporary defection, as 21:15–19 clarifies.

[16] Cf. the different list in Tolmie, *Farewell*, 135.

[17] Cf. Culpepper, *Anatomy*, 115; Edwards, *John*, 111. U.C. von Wahlde's case to view the disciples as 'the exemplars of belief in Jesus' is overstated ('The Witnesses to Jesus in John 5:31–40 and Belief in the Fourth Gospel', *CBQ* 43 [1981]: 399–404 [quotation from p. 399]). We contend that their faith, understanding and discipleship are not perfect but *realistic* of the believer's general experience. On the one hand, the tremendous claims to knowledge among the Johannine believers (e.g. 1 John 2:20, 27 and the frequent phrase '[by this] we/you know that') seem to indicate that with the coming of the Spirit misunderstanding no longer occurs. On the other hand, the possibility of blindness, darkness and lack of knowledge (1 John 2:11; 4:8), the urge for (Spirit-provided) discernment (1 John 4:1–6), and the problem of defecting believers (1 John 2:19; 4:1), seems to imply that misunderstanding is still possible. Köstenberger argues extensively that the original disciples function as representatives and models for later believers (*Missions*, 149–53). For other aspects of discipleship, see Köstenberger, *Missions*, ch. 4; Bennema, *Power*, 139–41, 154–5.

The Twelve		
Appearances	References	6:67; 6:70; 6:71; 20:24
Identity	Titles given	'the Twelve'
	Gender	male
	Age	–
	Marital status	–
	Occupation	various
	Socio-economic status	–
	Place of residence/operation	various
	Relatives	Peter and Andrew are brothers, and so are James and John, Nathanael is an acquaintance of Philip
	Group affiliation	Peter, Andrew, James, John, Philip, Thomas, Judas Iscariot, Judas not Iscariot and possibly Nathanael are named members of the group
Speech and actions	In interaction with Jesus	adequate belief, frequent misunderstanding, stick with Jesus
	In interaction with others	minimal
Character classification	Complexity	little complex; multiple traits: believing, loyal, perceptive, undiscerning/dull, zealous, able to remember
	Development	little
	Inner life	much
Degree of characterization		moving towards corporate personality
Response to Jesus		adequate but needs enhancement (which the Spirit provides)

Judas Iscariot – The Black Sheep of the Family

'To betray you must first belong' — *Harold Philby*

Judas Iscariot has certainly made a mark in history. According to the Oxford English dictionary, a Judas is 'a person who betrays a friend' – a traitor. None of the Gospels has drawn such a devastating picture of Judas as the Gospel of John, where he is described variously as 'a devil' (6:71), a thief (12:4) and 'the son of perdition' (17:12). Traditionally, Judas is infamous for having betrayed Jesus but William Klassen challenges this view.[1] According to Klassen, the verb *paradidōmi*, which is virtually always translated 'to betray' in connection with Judas's act, *never* connotes 'betray' in Greek literature – whether in classical Greek, the Septuagint, Josephus or the New Testament – but simply means 'to hand over'.[2] Klassen argues that Judas's act of 'handing over' was not one of betrayal but of informing the temple authorities – an act authorized by Jesus in line with God's purposes.[3] Is Judas then the reviled betrayer or the victim of betrayal? For example, the character Judas in the popular rock opera *Jesus Christ Superstar* exclaims:

My God I'm sick, I've been used
And you knew all the time God!
I'll never know why you chose me for this crime.
You have murdered me! You have murdered me![4]

The Identity of Judas Iscariot

In the Gospel of John the name of Judas appears in three forms: (i) Judas (13:29; 18:2–5); (ii) Judas (the) Iscariot (12:4); (iii) Judas, son of Simon Iscariot (6:71; 13:2, 26). Judas, the Greek variant of the Hebrew Judah, one of the patriarchs of the twelve tribes of Israel, was a popular name in first-century

---

[1] W. Klassen, *Judas: Betrayer or Friend of Jesus?* (Minneapolis: Fortress Press, 1996). The recently uncovered *Gospel of Judas* (found in the 1970s but restored and translated in 2006 is dated around 300 CE) seems to support Klassen's case.

[2] Klassen, *Judas*, 47–58.

[3] Klassen, *Judas*, 62–74.

[4] Cited in Klassen, *Judas*, 7.

Palestine.[5] There is more uncertainty about the term 'Iscariot'. Most scholars hold that it refers to Judas's hometown Kerioth, presumably in Judaea but some have suggested Moab.[6] Others have suggested that 'Iscariot' indicates Judas was one of the Sicarii or 'dagger-men' – urban assassins who attacked the Jewish aristocracy.[7] However, the Sicarii only surfaced in the 50s and became prominent during the first Jewish war – too late for Judas to have belonged to this group. A few have argued that 'Iscariot' is an Aramaic occupational surname, meaning '(red) dyer'.[8] This divergence of theories prevents us from inferring too much about Judas's identity.[9] What clues we have to Judas's identity reveal that he belonged to Jesus' inner group of disciples, called 'the Twelve' (6:71; 12:4), and within this group, he was the treasurer (12:6; 13:29).

Judas's Act – Betrayal or Handing Over?

Central to Klassen's case, challenging the traditional view that Judas's act in Gethsemane was an act of betrayal, is his discussion on the meaning of the verb *paradidōmi*, arguing that it never means 'to betray' but simply 'to hand over'.[10] A critique of Klassen's linguistic study of *paradidōmi* in Greek literature is beyond the scope of our study – and perhaps unnecessary; we only need to examine how the term is used in the Johannine narrative.[11] Although the basic lexical sense of *paradidōmi* is 'to give over, to hand over', we must determine how *John* uses the term and whether it has connotations of betrayal.

The verb *paradidōmi* occurs fifteen times in John's gospel. Once is it used in a neutral sense – in 19:30 to refer to Jesus' handing over the Spirit as his life-force. Four times, there are negative implications for Jesus but no sense of betrayal (18:30, 35, 36; 19:16a). The ten remaining occurrences, referring to Judas's act of handing Jesus over (6:64, 71; 12:4; 13:2, 11, 21; 18:2, 5; 19:11; 21:20), clearly have negative connotations with the force of 'to betray'. In 6:70–71, for example, Judas who will 'hand Jesus over' is designated a devil, and, in contrast to true disciples, is included in the category of those who do not believe (6:64). Jesus identifies the one who will 'hand him over'

[5] Klassen, *Judas*, 29–30.

[6] Culpepper, *Anatomy*, 124; Köstenberger, *John*, 222. Cf. the scholars mentioned by Klassen, *Judas*, 32–3.

[7] E.g. O. Cullmann, *Jesus and the Revolutionaries* (New York: Scribner's, 1970), 21–3.

[8] A. Ehrman, 'Judas Iscariot and Abba Saqqara', *JBL* 97 (1978): 572–3; Y. Arbeitman, 'The Suffix of Iscariot', *JBL* 99 (1980): 122–4.

[9] Klassen, *Judas*, 34.

[10] Klassen, *Judas*, 47–58. Cf. A. Cane, *The Place of Judas Iscariot in Christology* (Aldershot: Ashgate, 2005), 19–24.

[11] In fact, F.A. Gosling evaluates Klassen's lexicographical study and observes that the rendering 'betray' for *paradidōmi* is found in classical Greek, the Septuagint, Josephus and the New Testament ('O Judas! What Have You Done?', *EvQ* 71 [1999]: 117–25). Cf. Kim, *Apostasy*, 204.

as unclean (13:11) and thinking of him causes agitation (13:21). Judas's act of handing Jesus over to the Jewish temple police and a Roman cohort of soldiers obviously has negative consequences since the Jewish authorities have already plotted Jesus' death (11:47 53). In 19:11, when Jesus declares to Pilate that the one who 'handed him over' has a greater sin, Jesus probably means Judas.[12] Thus, contra Klassen, Judas's act of handing Jesus over to the Jewish and Roman authorities is depicted by John as a negative act – an act of betrayal. Even though *paradidōmi* does not mean 'to betray', *John* unmistakably attaches the nuance of betrayal to the verb when he uses it in connection with Judas's act.[13]

Judas a Devil

At a crucial time when many of his disciples start defecting (6:60–66), Jesus challenges 'the Twelve' on their loyalty to him. Peter assures him that they will stick with him as only he can give eternal life because he is intimate with the holy God (6:67–69; cf. ch. 6).[14] What Peter does not know, and Jesus reveals, is that even among 'the Twelve' there is a devil (6:70) – Judas who will betray Jesus, as the narrator clarifies (6:71).[15] The reference to Judas as a devil probably implies that his behaviour *resembles* that of the devil. The devil, as Jesus' main opponent, is described as the ruler of the realm below, whose main occupation is to lie and kill (8:44; 12:31). Similarly, Judas lies (12:5–6) and, through his betrayal, abets the killing of Jesus (John 18 – 19). The devil, who plants the idea of betraying Jesus, uses Judas as his instrument (13:2, 27).[16]

---

[12] Judas's sin is greater than Pilate's because unlike Pilate (19:11) Judas has no divine authority; rather, his 'authority' to betray Jesus comes from the devil (cf. 13:2, 27). Or, the reference is to 'the Jews' who hand Jesus over to Pilate (18:30, 35) (Jesus' use of the singular is perhaps generic) and/or to Caiaphas as the leader of 'the Jews' (although 'to hand over' is never used with reference to him, he is the leading voice in 11:47–53). However, the majority of occurrences of the verb refer to Judas.

[13] Cf. H.T. Fleddermann, 'Review of W. Klassen, *Judas: Betrayer or Friend of Jesus?* (Minneapolis: Fortress Press, 1996)', *CBQ* 59 (1997): 772.

[14] Seeing a parallel with Jesus' rebuke of Peter in Mark 8:33, Klassen suggests that John seeks to improve on Peter by putting an anti-Judas spin on this story (*Judas*, 140; cf. H.-J. Klauck, *Judas: Ein Jünger des Herrn* [Quaestiones Disputatae 111; Freiburg: Herder, 1987], 74–5). However, we have already rejected such an interpretation (see the section 'Peter's Confession' in ch. 6).

[15] Klassen's interpretation of 6:70–71 that Judas is an adversary in the legal sense at Jesus' right hand to present evidence, just as the *diabolos* did in Job 1, Zech. 3:1 and Ps. 108:6 (LXX) (*Judas*, 141) seems far-fetched. Considering 6:64, J.V. Brownson argues that Judas is even characterized as an unbelieving insider who rejects the christological claims regarding Jesus' divine identity and origin ('Neutralizing the Intimate Enemy: The Portrayal of Judas in the Fourth Gospel', *SBLSP* 31 [1992]: 50–51). Although 6:64 may simply indicate that Jesus knew those who did not believe *and* the one who was going to betray him, the juxtaposition of unbelief and betrayal suggests a relation between the two. Besides, if Jesus' reply in 6:70 implicitly corrects the 'we' in Peter's confession in 6:69, then Judas is marked by unbelief (cf. Kim, *Apostasy*, 154–5, 159; Klauck, *Judas*, 72, 74).

[16] Klauck's remark that Judas harboured his criminal plans from the beginning (i.e. when he joined Jesus) is unwarranted (*Judas*, 73).

Judas the Thief

During a dinner given in Lazarus's home in honour of Jesus, Mary's devotion is contrasted by the early stages of Judas's defection (12:1–8). Although we have known since 6:70–71 that Judas will betray Jesus, it is only in John 12 – 13 that the character and role of Judas emerge. After reminding his readers that Judas will betray Jesus (12:4), John says that Judas is a thief (12:6).[17] As the treasurer of the group, Judas would have preferred to receive the large sum of money that the perfume could fetch, so he could keep a part for himself (12:6). Learning that Judas *as the treasurer* is a thief highlights his dishonesty and disloyalty to the group – he betrays their trust. Besides, Judas is a liar or hypocrite – his question in 12:5 feigns a concern for the poor which the narrator quickly falsifies. In this Judas emulates the devil who is characterized as a liar (8:44). Jesus' reprimand in 12:7–8 reveals that Judas does not recognize Jesus' uniqueness and instead believes that Mary showed excessive devotion to Jesus.[18]

The word for 'thief' occurs only here and in 10:1, 8, 10, and perhaps John deliberately portrays Judas as a false shepherd whose intention is to steal, kill and destroy. It is unlikely, however, that Judas illegitimately found his way into Jesus' group of disciples and joined Jesus *as a thief*; he probably became one along the way. The point of comparison between the thief in John 10 and Judas in John 12 is probably the thief's *behaviour* of stealing, killing and destroying rather than his entry into the sheepfold.[19]

Judas the Apostate

In the Johannine context, apostasy is the defection from Jesus to the opposition – the devil. The narrator clearly informs the reader in 13:2 that Judas is going to betray Jesus (cf. 6:70–71; 12:4). What is less clear is whose 'heart' is in view in 13:2 – whether the devil had already decided in *his* heart that Judas should betray Jesus or that the devil had put it in *Judas's* heart to betray Jesus. We favour the latter interpretation because Jesus' comment to his disciples, 'And you are clean, but not all of you', should be understood in the light of Judas's betrayal – it suggests that Judas is not clean (13:10b–11).[20] But even if Judas was unaware of the devil's plan in 13:2,

---

[17] Klassen cannot accept John's allegation that Judas is a thief (*Judas*, 146). However, even the Synoptics hint at Judas's greed for money (Matt. 26:14–15; 27:3–10; Mark 14:10–11; Luke 22:3–5) (Schnackenburg, *Gospel*, 2:368; Kim, *Apostasy*, 171–2).

[18] Cf. Brownson, 'Enemy', 51; Kim, *Apostasy*, 168.

[19] O'Day also notes that Judas exhibits a lack of care – whether for the poor (12:6) or the sheep (10:13) (*Gospel*, 702).

[20] Cf. Bultmann, *Gospel*, 464 n. 2. Amongst those who favour the former interpretation, are Brownson, 'Enemy', 52; Moloney, *Gospel*, 378; Kim, *Apostasy*, 190–91. There is no suggestion that Judas was excluded from the footwashing – it simply did not benefit him. Klassen deals poorly

he quickly learned of it because his sudden departure in 13:30 indicates that he understood Jesus' gesture and comment in 13:26–27.

In 13:18, Jesus refers again to Judas's imminent betrayal. The literal phrase, 'The one who eats my bread has lifted his heel against me', is better translated as 'The one with whom I shared a close relationship has opposed me'. Jesus speaks of this event as a fulfilment of Psalm 41:9, where David speaks of being betrayed by an intimate friend whom he trusted and had table-fellowship with.[21] In 13:21–30, a similar scene is played out between Jesus and Judas. Besides serving to identify Judas as the betrayer, Jesus' gesture of sharing bread in 13:26 may also represent a last effort to restore fellowship.[22] In 13:1, John states that Jesus loves people to the end, and here, we see Jesus' showing his love for Judas until the very 'end', when Satan enters into Judas after he takes the piece of bread (13:27).[23] Judas's 'end' is then secured: not only does the devil prompt Judas (13:2), he also indwells him (13:27).[24] Judas, indwelled by the devil, stands in sharp contrast to the disciples, who are indwelled by the Father and Son (14:23; cf. 17:21–23). Judas has become a devil or his embodiment (cf. 6:70–71), a defector and apostate, switching his allegiance from Jesus to Satan.

After receiving the piece of bread from Jesus, Judas immediately leaves – literally, but also symbolically in leaving the fellowship of Jesus (13:30). The dramatic, abrupt sentence, 'And it was night', in 13:30 reinforces the solemnity: besides being a literal reference to late evening, it also refers to a spiritual reality, namely, the darkness caused by Satan in driving Judas to his act of betrayal (cf. 9:4; 11:10). Judas's being indwelled by the devil and leaving the presence of Jesus heralds the approaching darkness precipitated by the devil.

This passage records the tragic defection and apostasy of Judas in a context that promotes discipleship. While Jesus exhorts his disciples to emulate him and to exemplify humility and service (13:1–20), the devil prompts Judas to

---

with Judas's uncleanness, arguing that John, like the Essenes, views purity in broad terms as including financial matters and ritual purity (*Judas*, 151–2). The footwashing clearly has salvific overtones – it foreshadows Jesus' death on the cross and the completion of the disciples' spiritual cleansing. Judas, however, is not clean and will not partake in Jesus' salvific death. Although Cane perceptively raises the issue of how it is that Jesus' footwashing is unable to cleanse Judas from the devil's influence, his conclusion that Judas is either treated unjustly or evidence of a salvific failure (*Judas*, 36–7) seems unwarranted.

[21] Kim contends that John might have had in mind Ahithophel's betrayal of David, and he also sees an allusion to the 'heel' motif of Gen. 3:15 which prophesies the cosmic conflict between Satan and the Son of God (*Apostasy*, 183–8).

[22] Referring to ancient seating arrangements, Keener suggests that the Beloved Disciple and Judas held the honoured positions on either side of Jesus (*Gospel*, 915–6).

[23] Cf. Krafft, who states that Judas has twice witnessed acts of love – Mary's devotion of Jesus in John 12 and Jesus' footwashing in John 13 – but also twice closed himself from them ('Personen', 29–30).

[24] Contra Kim, who contends that Judas is not so much influenced by the devil to betray Jesus as he wilfully hardens his heart and invites the devil to work through him (*Apostasy*, 191–2).

defect and negate discipleship. Many of Jesus' disciples left him along the way (6:60–66) and now one of his closest disciples also leaves, to betray him. The character of Judas embodies the most negative of all responses to Jesus: defection, apostasy and betrayal. Judas's apostasy was the climax of a gradual, negative development rather than an abrupt turnaround, so he had opportunities to choose to do otherwise.[25]

Judas the Son of Perdition

In his prayer for the disciples, Jesus requests his Father to protect them from that day on (17:11). Until then, Jesus had protected them and not one of them was 'destroyed' except 'the son of destruction' – a reference to Judas – to fulfil Scripture (17:12).[26] This raises various questions. Was Judas (pre)destined to be lost, and how does it fulfil Scripture? If Jesus has insight into people (2:24–25; 6:15) – including Judas (6:70–71; 13:10–11, 21) – why did he choose Judas (6:70; cf. 17:6, 9)? How could Jesus lose someone when he says elsewhere that no one can snatch a person out of his hands (10:28)?

We believe Brownson is correct in understanding the term 'son of destruction' as a genitive of origin rather than a genitive of purpose ('son destined for destruction') or an adjectival genitive ('destroying son').[27] Brownson also argues that the Greek term *apōleia* ('destruction') probably stands for the Hebrew *Abaddon,* a term used for hell (Prov. 15:11; 27:20; 1QH 3:16, 19, 32) or hell personified, the devil (Job 28:22), and this reference to Judas as 'son of hell' is in keeping with similar phrases in Jewish apocalyptic and early Christian literature.[28] Indeed, the reference to Judas as 'son of destruction/hell' corresponds to the earlier description of Judas as 'devil' (6:70–71), and also evokes the image of the thief who comes to destroy in 10:10 (cf. the devil as a murderer in 8:44). Thus, Jesus' reference to Judas in 17:12 as 'son of destruction' implies that Judas is an agent of the devil, in that he belongs to the devil and acts like him. Whether Judas was (pre)destined for destruction was probably not an issue for John.[29]

---

[25] Contra Klassen's evaluation that 'Judas appears more like an automaton than a free, willing person' (*Judas*, 153).

[26] Contra Moloney, who contends that 'the son of perdition' refers to Satan (*Gospel*, 467, 470).

[27] Brownson, 'Enemy', 52. Cf. Klassen, *Judas*, 152. Contra those who interpret the term as Judas being (pre)destined for destruction (Brown, *Gospel*, 2:760; Barrett, *Gospel*, 508; Kim, *Apostasy*, 152, 178).

[28] Brownson, 'Enemy', 52. Cf. Klassen, *Judas*, 152–3, 158 n. 53; Klauck, *Judas*, 87–8; Carson, *Gospel*, 563.

[29] For the dialectic between God's sovereignty and human free will, see D.A. Carson, *Divine Sovereignty and Human Responsibility: Biblical Perspectives in Tension* (London: Marshall, Morgan & Scott, 1981), ch. 12.

Judas the Betrayer

John 18:1–12 describes Judas's act of betrayal, which leads to Jesus' arrest. We observe that his act is clearly premeditated. First, Judas uses his inside knowledge of Jesus' habits to reveal his whereabouts (18:2). Second, he brings with him a cohort of Roman soldiers and the temple police of the Jewish religious authorities to arrest Jesus (18:3). Judas thus aligns himself with 'the Jews' – Jesus' main opponents – and the Roman oppressors.[30] In fact, Judas and 'the Jews' are linked in that they are both controlled by the devil (8:44; 13:2, 27).

The failed attempts of the temple police to arrest Jesus (7:32, 44–45; cf. 7:30; 8:20, 59; 10:39) may explain why Judas brought an unusually large number of soldiers and police to arrest a single man. Jesus' arrest is successful not because of their large numbers but because his hour has arrived and he allows these men to arrest him. In fact, the arrest makes a mockery of the authorities since 18:4–6 reveals that Jesus is still in full control. Jesus' divine self-revelation, 'I am', causes them to step back and fall to the ground, demonstrating his power over the devil, whom Judas has come to embody.

Conclusion

Unlike Peter's temporary defection, Judas's defection is permanent and is a case of apostasy – he ceases to be a disciple of Jesus and joins the opposition, becoming a disciple of the devil. Judas mimics the characteristics and actions of the devil: he lies about his concern for the poor (12:5–6); he steals money from the treasury (12:6); he aids the killing of Jesus by precipitating Jesus' arrest, eventually leading to Jesus' death. Judas is an instrument and embodiment of the devil, in that the devil uses him for his evil purposes and indwells him.

Some scholars perceive Judas as a flat, one-dimensional character who shows no development,[31] but this is simplistic. Judas is a complex character whose dominant traits are betrayal and apostasy, but he also has secondary traits such as a lack of care, unreliability, dishonesty and disloyalty. Both the narrator and Jesus disclose aspects of Judas's inner life. The narrator reveals that Judas is indifferent and dishonest (12:6), influenced in his mind by the devil (13:2), going to betray Jesus (6:71; 12:4), and knows where Jesus normally goes (18:3). Jesus reveals that Judas is a devil (6:70), unclean (13:10) and will betray him (13:21).

---

[30] Judas who 'stood with them' (18:5) also indicates that he no longer was with Jesus, in contrast to those who 'stood with Jesus' (3:29; 19:25).

[31] E.g. Tolmie, *Farewell*, 142; Davies, *Rhetoric*, 332; Resseguie, *Narrative Criticism*, 159.

Judas shows significant development in that his behaviour shocks the reader and new traits replace old ones.[32] The revelation in 6:70–71 should shock the reader because it becomes evident that Judas will develop from being one of Jesus' intimate friends to a betrayer. When Jesus repeats this information in 13:21, the disciples are shocked, indicating that Judas has shown unexpected development.[33] Even when Jesus provides a clue to the identity of the betrayer in 13:26–27, the disciples are too stunned to grasp it (13:28–29). When the narrator mentions in 12:6 that Judas is a thief, we infer that he became a thief somewhere *along the way* rather than that he joined Jesus as a thief. A chapter later, we are privy to Judas's rapid development from being influenced by the devil (13:2) to being indwelled by the devil (13:27) to leaving the fellowship of Jesus and entering into the darkness (13:30) and eventually arranging Jesus' arrest – in short, the catastrophic development from being a disciple of Jesus to becoming a disciple of Satan. This negative development reveals that Judas is unreliable – he is a thief, a defector, a betrayer and a disciple of the devil.[34] The reader should also notice the replacement of traits signifying the change in Judas. Since 12:6 mentions that Judas was a thief while being the treasurer of the group (a position of trust), traits of honesty and reliability are being replaced by dishonesty and unreliability. Then, with the switch of allegiance from Jesus to Satan, traits of intimacy and following Jesus disappear, and alienation and defection emerge.

Judas's betrayal is not limited to the premeditated act of handing Jesus over to the judicial authorities at his arrest but is a behavioural pattern that emerged over time. As a thief and then as a defector and apostate, he betrays the trust of both Jesus and his fellow disciples. He belonged to Jesus' inner circle of disciples, had an intimate relationship with Jesus, but eventually chose to join the opposition. Judas's betrayal therefore includes deceiving Jesus and his fellow disciples, being disloyal and letting down his master, and finally handing him over to the opposition. It is as thief, apostate and the one who hands Jesus over to his enemies that Judas is the betrayer. At the heart of betrayal is relationship; you can only betray someone with whom you share a relationship. Since betrayal presupposes belonging, Judas is the betrayer *as an intimate friend and disciple of Jesus.*[35]

[32] Contra Klauck, who contends that the character of Judas does not show development since he harboured evil plans from the beginning (*Judas*, 73).

[33] Contra Klassen's view that 'the disciples are not bewildered by the announcement that someone will hand him over. They take it in stride . . . when Judas acted, he acted for everyone' (*Judas*, 150). John 13:22 indicates that the disciples were clearly 'at a loss' or 'in consternation' (cf. 13:28).

[34] In view of the many antichrists who left the Johannine community and went out into the dark world (1 John 2:18–19; 4:1), Culpepper characterizes Judas as 'the representative defector' (*Anatomy*, 124–5). Kim's contention that 'John deliberately alludes to the historical situation of the church in which apostate-disciples become henchmen of Satan in delivering Christian brothers into the hands of Synagogue authorities and think that they are offering a service to God (16:2)' (*Apostasy*, 211), seems unwarranted.

[35] Cf. Brownson, 'Enemy', 50.

This brings us to an important Johannine concept – 'family'. In keeping with his dualistic worldview, John identifies two families and their respective fathers: Jesus constitutes a new family that has God as Father, whereas the devil, the ruler of 'the world', is the father of those who belong to 'the world'. There exists a long-standing feud between these two families and Jesus' coming brings the reality of two mutually exclusive and opposing families into sharp focus (1:11–13; 8:12–59). At the heart of this 'family debate' is the question of which family one belongs to and who one's father is (see esp. John 7 – 10). Judas's betrayal and apostasy result in a transfer of allegiance from the family of God to the family of the devil. As the betrayer and apostate, Judas is the black sheep of the family.[36]

Judas Iscariot		
Appearances	References	6:71; 12:4; 13:2; 13:26; 13:29; 18:2; 18:3; 18:5
Identity	Titles given	Iscariot, 'a devil', 'son of perdition'
	Gender	male
	Age	–
	Marital status	–
	Occupation	perhaps a dyer, treasurer of 'the Twelve'
	Socio-economic status	–
	Place of residence/operation	perhaps from Kerioth
	Relatives	son of Simon
	Group affiliation	one of 'the Twelve' but ultimately joins the devil; he also becomes an ally of 'the Jews' and the Romans
Speech and actions	In interaction with Jesus	betrays Jesus by being dishonest, disloyal and bringing about Jesus' arrest
	In interaction with others	betrays the trust of his fellow disciples; assists the Jewish temple police and a Roman cohort to arrest Jesus
Character classification	Complexity	complex; multiple traits: dominant traits of betrayal and apostasy with secondary traits of dishonesty, indifference, unreliability, disloyalty
	Development	negative development: from one of 'the Twelve' to a thief, to one prompted by the devil, to one indwelled by the devil, to precipitating Jesus' arrest. Presumed earlier traits of intimacy, belonging and trust are replaced by dishonesty, disloyalty, betrayal and apostasy.
	Inner life	much
Degree of characterization		individual
Response to Jesus		inadequate: betrayal and apostasy

[36] Contra Klassen, who asserts that 'it may be time to . . . bury once and for all the belief that Judas was a thief or was motivated by demonic forces. Not for a moment does it seem credible that the Johannine portrait of Judas could be authentic' (*Judas*, 146).

The Man Born Blind – Once I Was Blind but Now I See

'The best vision is insight' — Malcolm S. Forbes

John 9 contains the well-known story of the blind man who came to see.[1] John provides few details about the man's identity. He is unnamed, blind from birth, and a beggar in the vicinity of the temple in Jerusalem (8:59 – 9:1; 9:8). He is possibly a young adult since the phrase 'he is of age' (9:21) indicates that he has passed his thirteen birthday and hence had the age of legal responsibility.[2] Jewish regulations very likely restricted his entry into the temple and participation in regular worship. The Mishnah, for example, mentions, 'All are liable for *an appearance offering [before the Lord]* except for . . . the blind' (*m. Hagigah* 1:1; cf. 4Q394 f8 3:19 – 4:4). Besides, the associations between blindness and sin probably left him stigmatized as a sinner (9:2, 34). In short, this blind beggar was an economic, social and religious outcast; living on the periphery of society.

Jesus' Encounter with the Man Born Blind

After a hostile clash with 'the Jews'/Pharisees in 8:12–59, Jesus leaves the temple and comes across the blind beggar (8:59 – 9:1).[3] The disciples' question in 9:2 reflects the common notion of that day that the man was blind because either he or his parents had sinned.[4] Jesus rejects both

---

[1] We shall not follow Martyn, who especially uses John 9 to read John's gospel as a two-level drama, in which the gospel stories really are the stories of the Johannine community (in conflict with post-70 CE synagogue Judaism). Although the majority of Johannine scholars have adopted Martyn's reading strategy, we contend that John's gospel is primarily the story of Jesus, and that the encounter in John 9 is authentic and historically reliable (cf. ch. 1). We thus reject a statement like '[t]he definitive interpretation of the significance of the blind man is Martyn' (Culpepper, *Anatomy*, 140).

[2] Beasley-Murray, *John*, 157; Brown, *Gospel*, 374.

[3] Narratologically, 9:1 follows on from 8:59 (the antecedent of 'he' in 9:1 is 'Jesus' in 8:59) and hence the events of John 9 probably occurred in or near the temple area.

[4] For the issue of parental sin and ante-natal sin in Judaism, see, Brown, *Gospel*, 1:371; Beasley-Murray, *John*, 154–5; Schnackenburg, *Gospel*, 2:240–41. Lee notes that John 9 begins

suggestions and corrects their presupposition, saying that the man's condition is simply an opportunity for God's redemptive work to be revealed (9:3). Jesus seems to convey to his disciples a sense of urgency to participate in the work God is doing in the world, while there is an opportunity (9·4; cf. 4:31–38; 5:17). Although Jesus declared in 8:12 that he is the life-giving light of the world, he was not given the opportunity to explain himself. In 9:5, Jesus reiterates that he is the light of the world and John 9 essentially clarifies how.

The stage is set and Jesus turns his attention to the blind man. The miracle is swiftly narrated in 9:6–7. Wordlessly, Jesus spits on the ground, makes mud with saliva, and anoints the man's eyes with the mud (9:6). He then gives the man a terse command (9:7) and disappears from the scene until 9:35.[5] 'Siloam' means 'Sent' and perhaps John wants to emphasize that Jesus as the Sent One (e.g. 3:17, 34; 5:36; 6:29; 7:29; 8:42) is the 'spiritual Siloam'; that although the blind man gains his sight when he washes in the pool of Siloam, he actually receives it through the power of the Sent One.[6] The actual miracle is described in very few words: 'So he went and washed and came back seeing' (9:7). Interestingly, Jesus does not heal the man instantaneously but asks him to do something, perhaps to test his willingness or 'faith'.[7] In previous healing miracles, Jesus also requires active participation – from the royal official in 4:50 and from the invalid in 5:8–9. Thus, it appears that Jesus intentionally requires the active involvement of a person in the miracle – not simply to participate in or even precipitate the miracle but to enhance or initiate faith, ultimately aimed at an adequate belief-response (although Jesus' intended purpose is not realized in case of the invalid at the pool).

It must be noted that the man did not come back to Jesus (cf. the invalid in John 5) – either Jesus had left or the man had gone straight home (cf. 9:8) – and it is only later that Jesus (on his own initiative) encounters him again (9:35). The reader may expect a confession from the man after 9:7 but his response is delayed.

---

and ends with the same theological issue of who is a sinner (*Narratives*, 170). The words 'to sin' and 'sinner' occur nine times (9:2, 3, 16, 24, 25, 31, 34, 41 [2x]), referring to the blind man, his parents, Jesus and the Pharisees.

[5] Jesus' command to the blind man recalls the story of Elisha telling Naaman to wash in the Jordan (2 Kgs 5:10–13), but in contrast to Naaman the blind man obeys without demur, which may hint at his readiness to believe (Schnackenburg, *Gospel*, 2:243). Cf. T.L. Brodie, 'Jesus as the New Elisha: Cracking the Code', *ExpTim* 93 (1981–82): 39–42. Contra Brown (*Gospel*, 1:380–82) and Collins ('Figures', 21), there is no allusion to baptism in this washing (cf. Schnackenburg, *Gospel*, 2:257–8; J. Painter, 'John 9 and the Interpretation of the Fourth Gospel', *JSNT* 28 [1986]: 44–6).

[6] Beasley-Murray, *John*, 155–6; Carson, *Gospel*, 365; Resseguie, *Narrative Criticism*, 149. B. Grigsby's argument that Jesus' command to the blind man should be understood symbolically as a universal command to all unbelievers to wash in the fountain of living waters at Calvary is far-fetched ('Washing in the Pool of Siloam – A Thematic Anticipation of the Johannine Cross', *NovT* 27 [1985]: 227–35).

[7] Cf. D.A. Farmer, 'John 9', *Int* 50 (1996): 61.

Although the physical healing of the blind man in 9:6–7 is a precursor to the broader topic of spiritual blindness and spiritual sight, Jesus is not solely concerned with 'spiritual' issues. He is also keen to deal with issues in the here and now. This blind beggar was living on the margins of society, and his physical healing had profound implications for his economic, social and religious status, showing Jesus' holistic approach to the human condition. Nevertheless, Jesus' physical healing of the blind man should ideally lead to his spiritual healing (see 9:35–38). Indeed, the blind man's physical healing is a sign pointing to Jesus as the giver of true sight and life.[8] Although he has experienced Jesus as the sight-giving Light, he must still experience him as the life-giving Light.

The Blind Man's Encounter with the Religious Authorities

John 9:8–12 is an interlude, describing what caused the man to be brought to the Pharisees in 9:13.[9] When the formerly blind man returns to his neighbourhood, those who know him are quite startled and confused (9:7b–9). When he confirms his identity, they want to know how he was healed (9:9b–10). The man then gives an accurate testimony, apparently aware that his benefactor was Jesus (9:11).[10] However, he does not know Jesus' whereabouts (9:12), because either Jesus had withdrawn or the man had not gone back to him. At another level, the issue of Jesus' 'whereabouts' – whether or not he is from God – is crucial to the narrative (9:16, 29, 33) – and indeed the entire gospel (cf. 1:38–39; 7:27–28; 8:14; 19:9; 20:2).[11] Although he knows the name of his benefactor (unlike the invalid in John 5), the formerly blind man does not know much else about him and is (like the invalid) questioned by the religious authorities.

The First Interrogation

Those who know the blind beggar are apparently not satisfied with the man's explanation, so they bring him to the religious authorities (9:13).[12]

---

[8] Although the word 'sign' only occurs in 9:16, the term 'works' in 9:3–4 is often used synonymously (e.g. 7:21; 10:37–38; 14:11) (cf. Lee, *Narratives*, 165–6).

[9] The man's interrogators are identified as the Pharisees in 9:13–17 and as 'the Jews' in 9:18–34. Since 'the Jews' call the man for *the second time* in 9:24, the implication is that 'the Jews' here are, or at least include, the Pharisees of 9:13–17.

[10] Although the man knows his benefactor's name, he has not yet seen Jesus; this only happens in 9:35 (Carson, *Gospel*, 366).

[11] Cf. J.W. Holleran, 'Seeing the Light: A Narrative Reading of John 9', *ETL* 69 (1993): 363–4; Resseguie, *Strange Gospel*, 142; P.S. Minear, '"We Don't Know Where . . ." John 20:2', *Int* 30 (1976): 130–33.

[12] Staley suggests that, in the light of 9:14, the neighbours' intentions were perhaps malicious. He also observes that both the healed man and the reader have been innocently caught: (i) the

John's aside in 9:14 that this healing happened on the Sabbath is significant for the rest of the story and reminds the reader of the angry reactions on the previous occasion (5:9b–16). Again, the real offence is not that Jesus performed a miracle but that he did so *on the Sabbath*.

This time, the investigation is more systematic and rigorous than in John 5. The religious leaders first question the healed man himself, asking him the same question as his neighbours (9:15). Staley convincingly argues that the man wants to protect Jesus because (i) he does not mention his name (protection of identity), and (ii) regarding the mud, he uses the verb 'put' rather than 'make' (9:6, 11), and he leaves out Jesus' command, 'Go and wash' (9:7, 11) (concealment of method).[13] Besides, unlike the invalid who carried his mat on the Sabbath, the blind man simply washed his face and did not violate the Sabbath himself.[14]

The man's testimony in 9:15 sparks off a debate amongst the Jewish leadership. One group of Pharisees argues that '[t]his man is not from God because he does not keep the Sabbath' (9:16a).[15] They operate on the premise that someone who breaks the law is not from God and is a sinner. In their view, Jesus is not authorized by God and makes illegitimate use of God's power (they do not deny the miracle) – a similar controversy as in John 5.[16] Another group asks, 'How can a sinful man perform such signs?' (9:16b), suggesting that only someone authorized by God could heal a man born blind, thus tentatively challenging the Sabbath understanding of their colleagues.[17] This causes division among Jesus' opponents (9:16c; cf. 7:43; 10:19).

Carson argues that the reasoning of the second group is theologically weak because miracles are not an infallible guide to spiritual authority (Deut. 13:1–5; Matt. 7:21–23), but they do hit upon the truth, however hesitantly expressed. The first group's argument is logically more compelling, *provided* their premise is correct. The reader, however, knows that Jesus is from God,

healed man faithfully testifies (9:11), getting himself into trouble; (ii) the reader has until 9:14 no idea that all this occurred on a Sabbath ('Stumbling', 66).

[13] Staley, 'Stumbling', 67. According to the Mishnah, kneading was forbidden on the Sabbath (*m. Shabbat* 7:2), and hence Jesus' making mud with saliva violated the Sabbath.

[14] Staley, 'Stumbling', 69.

[15] S. Pancaro points out that Jesus violates the Sabbath three times: (i) the kneading of mud; (ii) healing a person whose life is not in danger; (iii) using a substance which was not normally used to anoint eyes (*The Law in the Fourth Gospel: The Torah and the Gospel of Moses and Jesus, Judaism and Christianity according to John* [NovTSup 42; Leiden: Brill, 1975], 19–20). Staley suggests that the Pharisees know of Jesus' Sabbath violation from the man's neighbours since the man did not give this information ('Stumbling', 67). Hence, his neighbours betray the healed man. Pancaro, however, disagrees that the Sabbath is the motive for bringing the man to the authorities (*Law*, 19 n. 41).

[16] Cf. Bryan's article on Jesus' legitimate use of God's power on the Sabbath in John 5 ('Power', 7–22).

[17] Lee contends that 9:16b indicates that some of the Pharisees were at least open to belief in Jesus (*Narratives*, 173–4). We have also noted that Jesus' opponents could occasionally express sympathy and even 'belief' in Jesus (see ch. 4).

and hence the first group's deductions are wrong.[18] Where Nicodemus was able to reason that if Jesus performs such miracles he must be from God (3:2), his colleagues are unable to do so because they cling to the premise that Jesus is a sinner, and hence remain stuck in their darkness.

The formerly blind man's understanding of Jesus' identity progresses from 'the man called Jesus' (9:11) to 'a prophet' (9:17). This resembles the way the Samaritan woman advanced in her understanding of Jesus (cf. ch. 10), and makes the reader curious about how far this man will come in grasping the truth about Jesus. John keeps us in suspense, however, because 'the Jews' now summon his parents to testify to what happened (9:18–19).

The testimony of the parents in 9:20–23 is disappointing and the antithesis of the kind of witness John advocates. Although the parents most likely know what their son told the neighbours in 9:11, they claim to be ignorant and suggest that their son speak for himself (9:21). They avoid testifying because of their 'fear of the Jews' – 'the Jews' had decreed that anyone who confessed Jesus to be the Messiah would be expelled from the synagogue, which would mean social exclusion (9:22; cf. 7:13; 19:38; 20:19).[19] Despite the reality of this fear, John implicitly criticizes those who give in to it when he contrasts the parents' fearful testimony with their son's bold testimony.

The Second Interrogation

'The Jews' summon the healed man for further questioning (9:24). In this second interrogation, the man turns out to be a clever witness to the great annoyance of his interrogators. 'The Jews' begin by clarifying their position regarding Jesus: 'We know that this man is a sinner' (9:24; notice their pompous claim to knowledge). Whereas in 9:16 there was still a division amongst Jesus' opponents, in 9:24 they seem to stand unified – Jesus is a sinner. Perhaps the second group in 9:16b was silenced (cf. Nicodemus being silenced by his colleagues in 7:50–52); perhaps it has been convinced by the first group's argument; or perhaps only the first group was present at the second interrogation. The text does not provide sufficient information, but it is clear that the first group has prevailed.

With their aggressive assertion in 9:24, 'the Jews' probably hoped to intimidate the man into agreeing with them, but he courageously questions their presupposition (9:25a). 'Give glory to God' is, as in Joshua 7:19, an exhortation to tell the truth and confess one's sins before God,[20] and indeed the man does – but not by agreeing with his interrogators. Instead, the man

---

[18] Carson, *Gospel*, 368.

[19] The issue of expulsion from the synagogue in 9:22 has been long-debated but should not concern us. For an informed discussion, see W. Horbury, 'Extirpation and Excommunication', *VT* 35 (1985): 13–38; E.W. Klink III, 'Expulsion from the Synagogue? Rethinking a Johannine Anachronism', *TynB* 59 (2008): 99–118.

[20] Beasley-Murray, *John*, 158; Schnackenburg, *Gospel*, 2:251; Carson, *Gospel*, 372.

puts forward *his* empirical knowledge, namely, that once he was blind but now he can see (9:25b). When 'the Jews' repeat their question regarding the mechanics of the healing (cf. 9:26 and 9:15), the man refuses to cooperate further. Instead, he sharply reminds them that he has already given this information, and adds ironically, 'You do not want to become his disciples too, do you?' (9:27).[21] His tone upsets his interrogators and they start to insult him: they are disciples of Moses but he is the disciple of this man from who-knows-where (9:28–29).[22]

Instead of being intimidated, the man grows in confidence. Once more, he pits what he knows (9:30–33) against his opponents' claim to knowledge (9:29).[23] He even goes on the offensive, mocking his interrogators' lack of knowledge regarding Jesus' origins and logically concluding that Jesus must be from God (9:30–33).[24] This infuriates his interrogators – they accuse him of being born in sin (cf. 9:2), charge him of educating them, and eventually expel him (9:34).[25] Since the action of the authorities resembles the threat of expulsion from the synagogue in 9:22, they may have viewed the man's claim about Jesus as being equivalent to a confession that Jesus is the Messiah.[26]

A Further Encounter with Jesus

After the man's expulsion, Jesus comes in search of him (9:35; cf. 5:14 where Jesus seeks the invalid again).[27] We must assume that the man sees Jesus for the first time now but recognizes him by his voice. Jesus' question, 'Do you believe in the Son of Man?', is puzzling.[28] This title is used exclusively by Jesus himself, mostly referring to his death expressed as being 'lifted up'

[21] The 'too' suggests that the blind man now considers himself one of Jesus' disciples – and his interrogators certainly consider him as such (9:28) (Lee, *Narratives*, 176; Koester, *Symbolism*, 64). Apparently the man has been reflecting and resolving some things about Jesus since the first interrogation because he knows that Jesus is making disciples, and that those disciples are at odds with the religious authorities (M.F. Whitters, 'Discipleship in John: Four Profiles', *WW* 4 [1998]: 426).

[22] However, Moses is not Jesus' opponent but a witness to him and hence a witness against 'the Jews' who reject Jesus (5:45–47).

[23] Lee comments that the man 'is constrained by the logic of his own experience to move to a deeper understanding of Jesus' (*Narratives*, 177).

[24] While in 9:12 the man did not know Jesus' whereabouts, he has now worked out Jesus' origins – from God.

[25] The blind man, like Jesus, stands falsely accused of being a sinner (Lee, *Narratives*, 178). At the same time, the man will share in the life-giving light that Jesus is and spreads. Conway even remarks that the man's performance before the authorities closely resembles that of Jesus himself (*Men and Women*, 133). Perhaps the man's reply 'I am' in 9:9, paralleling Jesus' 'I am'-sayings, already hints at this 'identification' (cf. Holleran, 'Light', 361).

[26] Holleran, 'Light', 370.

[27] The man was first an outcast because of his blindness, and Jesus' physical healing allowed him to join normal life. Then, the expulsion by 'the Jews' made him an outcast again, and Jesus restores him once again – this time providing spiritual healing.

[28] The textual variant 'Son of God' in 9:35 is not well attested (cf. Lee, *Narratives*, 168 n. 3).

(3:14; 6:62; 8:28; 12:34), but it also denotes Jesus as mediator, the point of contact between heaven and earth (1:51; 3:13). In this capacity, Jesus offers the blind man an opportunity to encounter the divine reality.[29] The man is eager to believe in the Son of Man but he does not know who he is (9:36). Jesus then plainly reveals that he is the Son of Man (9:37; cf. 4:26).[30] The man responds promptly: he confesses, 'I believe, Lord!', and prostrates himself before Jesus (9:38).[31]

The man's twofold response of a verbal confession and a non-verbal act of worship is the climax of the story. Although the reader may have expected a confession after 9:7, the man was not ready to make an adequate belief-response to Jesus then because he did not know who he was.[32] Jesus' disappearance in 9:7 and the consequent delay of the man's response was necessary to allow him to develop his understanding of Jesus. The man's understanding of Jesus progresses from 'the man called Jesus' (9:11), to 'a prophet' (9:17), to 'a man from God' (9:33), to the climactic 'Lord' (9:38). Like the Samaritan woman in John 4, and contra the invalid in John 5, the man born blind reaches an adequate, saving belief in Jesus.

In 9:39, Jesus sums up the implications of his coming as the light of the world: those who lack spiritual sight may receive it, while those who claim to see may become or appear blind. The Pharisees, who claim to have spiritual insight, belong to the latter group – they reject the light when it comes and thus confirm their own blindness (9:40–41). If they had admitted to their blindness, they would not have been guilty and could have received spiritual sight, but their claim to have sight (and knowledge) only

---

[29] Painter's suggestion that John seeks to correct the inadequate Christology of the secret believers who understood Jesus as the Christ in terms of traditional Davidic messiahship (underlying 9:22) by a faith in the heavenly Son of Man (9:35) seems unwarranted ('John 9', 36–41). The confession of Jesus as the Christ seems adequate since it is the kind of belief-response John aspires (20:31). It is the failure to make such a confession publicly out of fear of the religious authorities that John finds wanting.

[30] Jesus' assertion to the man in 9:37 that he has seen the Son of Man is somewhat puzzling. Perhaps we can explain it as follows. The man's progressive understanding of Jesus is probably indicative of his developing belief, and since understanding and belief in John often results from a spiritual insight into Jesus' true identity, the man's emerging understanding and belief is evidence of his ability to 'see' (cf. Collins, 'John', 365; Painter, 'John 9', 43). For the two Johannine levels of seeing, see Bennema, *Power*, 124–5. Hence, while Lee perhaps ascribes too little faith to the man when she states that 'the man both sees and "sees" Jesus for the first time in the narrative' (*Narratives*, 179), M. Müller attributes too much, contending that the phrase 'you have seen him' indicates that the man is a believer prior to 9:37 ('"Have You Faith in the Son of Man?" [John 9.35]', *NTS* 37 [1991]: 293).

[31] *Kurios* in 9:38 clearly means 'Lord' rather than 'Sir' (as in 9:36). Besides, the verb *proskuneō* denotes 'to prostrate oneself before someone' and connotes here an act of worship (cf. Bultmann, *Gospel*, 339 n. 3). Although Schnackenburg (*Gospel*, 2:254) and Beasley-Murray (*John*, 159–60) contend that 9:38 conveys no Christological significance or formal adoration as we have in 20:28, they admit that the man perceives Jesus to be from God as the bringer of salvation.

[32] *Pace* Beck, who appears to say that the man's understanding of Jesus' identity develops rather than his faith (*Discipleship*, 92–3). We contend that the man's understanding of, and faith in, Jesus develops simultaneously.

causes them to stumble further into their darkness (9:41).[33] As the man becomes increasingly receptive and finally makes a full confession of faith, so the Pharisees become increasingly blind to Jesus, ending up in total darkness. In the end, the blind man receives physical and spiritual sight, while the Pharisees are left completely blind, spiritually.[34]

Conclusion

As the life-giving light, Jesus came to illuminate this dark world by revealing God. Blind spots in one's worldview (cf. the disciples in 9:2) or flawed logic (e.g. the reasoning of 'the Jews'/Pharisees) prove obstacles to clear vision. However, if people acknowledge their blindness, the light will illumine them and enable them to see. Those who 'see'/understand and accept the light will receive life and enter into God's family; those who reject or fail to understand the light will continue in blindness and darkness. The man born blind could represent humanity because everyone is spiritually blind from birth and needs illumination that only Jesus can give.[35]

John intends a threefold contrast in John 9. First, while the man starts out being blind and gains both physical and spiritual sight, the Pharisees claim to have spiritual sight but turn out to be blind. Second, while the man testifies boldly before the religious authorities in the face of persecution, his parents withhold their testimony out of fear. Third, the blind man progresses in his understanding of Jesus before the authorities and eventually reaches a saving faith, unlike the invalid in John 5 who faltered and betrayed Jesus (cf. ch. 12).

The blind man displays multiple traits: he is obedient (9:7b), courageous, intelligent, open-minded, willing to testify and take risks, and he remains loyal to Jesus throughout. The man also shows development. Despite his disadvantaged start in life and his marginalization in society, the blind man surprises the reader with his cognitive abilities and how he reaches an authentic understanding of Jesus – in the face of persecution.[36] Finally, there are glimpses into his inner life – he knows his own condition (9:25), he has knowledge of God (9:31) and he believes in Jesus (9:38).

---

[33] The notion of sin is thus turned radically on its head; the allegation of sin is transferred from the blind man and Jesus to 'the Jews'/Pharisees (Lee, *Narratives*, 181). J.M. Lieu remarks that sin is *defined* by the response to Jesus (rather than by any predeterminism reflected in 9:2, 34) ('Blindness in the Johannine Tradition', *NTS* 34 [1988]: 84).

[34] John 9 shows a double narrative movement wherein the man progresses from blindness to sight while the Pharisees move in the opposite direction (Lee, *Narratives*, 162).

[35] Bennema, 'Christ', 110–14. Cf. Barrett, *Gospel*, 356; Carson, *Gospel*, 361.

[36] Resseguie appears to speak of the man's character development mainly in terms of his developing understanding of Jesus (*Narrative Criticism*, 153; cf. Conway, *Men and Women*, 126). However, we should be careful not to confuse a character's progression in his/her understanding of Jesus with character development. Only when a character's progression *surprises* the reader, we can speak of character development (cf. Bennema, 'Theory', 403–4).

The bold witness of the man while facing a biased and vicious interrogation is an example of true discipleship and his situation approximates what believers can expect when they partake in the cosmic trial that Jesus is involved in (15:18 – 16:4a).[37] The formerly blind man displays a remarkable development in his understanding of Jesus and only needs Jesus' assistance for the last step to reach adequate belief. Although the man's progressive understanding of Jesus' identity and display of discipleship correspond to those of the Samaritan woman, the man attains this understanding not in a reflective encounter with Jesus but in a confrontation with the hostile religious authorities.[38] Amidst persecution (even because of it), the man is able to progress in faith and demonstrate true discipleship, and thus become an example for later generations.[39] He represents the person who is open to faith, defends Jesus before his accusers, and develops a saving understanding and belief *while* facing persecution.

The Man Born Blind		
Appearances	References	throughout 9:1–41
Identity	Titles given	–
	Gender	male
	Age	young adult
	Marital status	–
	Occupation	beggar
	Socio-economic status	socio-economic outcast
	Place of residence/operation	near the temple in Jerusalem
	Relatives	his parents
	Group affiliation	neighbours, 'the Jews'/Pharisees
Speech and actions	In interaction with Jesus	he responds well (9:7b, 38)
	In interaction with others	he testifies boldly about Jesus to his neighbours and to the authorities amidst persecution
Character classification	Complexity	complex; multiple traits: obedient, courageous, intelligent, open-minded, willing to testify, risk-taking, loyal
	Development	some
	Inner life	some
Degree of characterization		personality
Response to Jesus		adequate, saving belief-response

[37] Cf. Holleran, 'Light', 20; Koester, *Symbolism*, 64.

[38] Cf. Rensberger, *World*, 46. Cf. Beirne, who comments that the blind man's faith 'grows in inverse proportion to the hardening into blindness of his antagonists' (*Women*, 124).

[39] The hostile authorities end up playing a crucial role in his faith development (P.D. Duke, *Irony in the Fourth Gospel* [Atlanta: John Knox Press, 1985], 125; Lee, *Narratives*, 183). Indeed, the greatest irony of the narrative is that Jesus' opponents push the man towards Jesus (Lee, *Narratives*, 183).

Martha – The Ideal Johannine Confessor

'You believe easily that which you hope for earnestly' — Terence

Martha lives with her sister Mary and brother Lazarus in Bethany, a village about three kilometres south-east of Jerusalem (11:1–2, 18).[1] All three are perhaps unmarried and the text indicates that Jesus is a close friend of the family (11:3, 5, 11). The sisters send a message to Jesus that Lazarus is ill (11:3), and when Martha learns that Jesus is coming, she leaves the village to meet him on his way (11:20, 30). Martha's addressing Jesus as 'Teacher' (11:28) and 'Lord' (11:21) reflects the teacher-disciple relationship mentioned in 13:13, showing that she probably considers herself a disciple of Jesus.[2] The phrase that Jesus loves Martha (11:5) may also indicate that she is his disciple (cf. 13:34; 15:9).[3] After the raising of Lazarus, Martha appears once more, in a domestic role, serving at a thanksgiving dinner for Jesus (12:2).[4]

Martha's Interaction with Jesus

We know that Jesus has intentionally delayed his journey to Bethany by two days (11:6) and that Lazarus's illness has taken his life (11:14). From 11:17, 39 we learn that Lazarus has already been buried for four days. Since Jesus is in Bethany across the Jordan, in Peraea (10:40; 11:6–7), we must allow one day for the sisters' message to reach Jesus, one day for Jesus to travel to Bethany where Lazarus lived, plus the two extra days Jesus delayed, adding up to four days. Thus, Lazarus has died almost immediately after the sisters sent the message to Jesus – so Lazarus's death is *not* the result of Jesus' delay.[5]

---

[1] Our chapters 17–19, dealing with Martha, Mary and Lazarus, should be read together.

[2] S. Yamaguchi, *Mary and Martha: Women in the World of Jesus* (Maryknoll: Orbis, 2002), 120.

[3] Scott, *Sophia*, 200.

[4] Although the remark in 12:2 may resemble Luke 10:40, there are also significant differences between the Lukan and Johannine stories about Martha and Mary. It is unlikely to view Martha's service at the table as referring to the office of women deacons in the early church (contra Brown, 'Roles', 690–91; Yamaguchi, *Mary*, 121).

[5] Cf. Brown, *Gospel*, 1:431; Carson, *Gospel*, 407; I.R. Kitzberger, 'Mary of Bethany and Mary of Magdala – Two Female Characters in the Johannine Passion Narrative: A Feminist, Narrative-Critical Reader-Response', *NTS* 41 (1995): 573.

We can nevertheless understand that the sisters are upset that Jesus, a loving family friend, only turns up after four days, when others had already arrived to participate in the mourning process (11:19). Indeed, the identical words with which each approaches Jesus, 'Lord, if you had been here, my brother would not have died' (11:21, 32), suggests an implicit reproach.[6] However, the sisters' criticism is unfair and unrealistic because Lazarus was already dead (and buried) when Jesus received the sisters' message. At the same time, their reproach probably reveals an underlying belief in Jesus as a miracle worker who could have healed their brother. They may have heard about Jesus' miraculous signs or witnessed them for themselves (cf. 2:23). Lazarus's death, however, creates an opportunity for Jesus to move Martha and Mary beyond such belief and deepen their understanding of him (cf. 11:15).[7] We shall see that although Martha and Mary share the same starting point, their response to Jesus is very different (cf. ch. 18).

Martha's response in 11:21 goes beyond reproach when she expresses hope that God will give Jesus whatever he asks (11:22). Martha has already shown more initiative than Mary because she left Bethany to meet Jesus while her sister remained at home (11:20). Jesus' assurance to Martha that Lazarus will rise again does not startle her, although she does not grasp the full significance of Jesus' statement – she simply states her belief in the final resurrection (11:23–24). Martha understands Jesus' talk of Lazarus's resurrection ('he will rise' [11:23]) as a distant resurrection on the last day (cf. 6:39–40, 44, 54), whereas Jesus speaks of an event in the immediate future. As usual, a person's misunderstanding causes Jesus to provide further revelation, stating here that he is the resurrection and the life (*zōē*) (11:25a).[8]

This 'I am' saying and its development in 11:25–26 echoes 5:28–29, where Jesus promises that, at the end of time, believers will experience the resurrection into eternal life (cf. 6:39–40, 44, 54). Schneiders translates 11:25b–26 as, 'the believer who dies will live; the living believer will never die', indicating that the eternal life possessed by the believer in union with Jesus does not succumb to either physical death (though some believers will die) or 'eternal death'.[9] Jesus' revelation to Martha is that 'eternal life conquers death without abolishing it.'[10]

The added significance of Jesus' divine self-revelation here is that Lazarus need not wait until the last day but can rise *now* because of Jesus' presence.

---

[6] Ridderbos contends that Martha's disappointment was so intense because she expected so much from Jesus (*Gospel*, 395). O'Day adds that 'complaint belonged to the language of faith in Judaism (e.g. Psalms 4; 6; 13; 22)' (*Gospel*, 688).

[7] Cf. Lee, who states that Martha and Mary are the central characters and their moving to a deeper faith is the primary concern of the narrative (*Narratives*, 189).

[8] Koester remarks that with this 'I am' saying, Jesus brings together Martha's trust in him (expressed in 11:22) and her faith in future resurrection (expressed in 11:24) (*Symbolism*, 66).

[9] S.M. Schneiders, 'Death in the Community of Eternal Life: History, Theology, and Spirituality in John 11', *Int* 41 (1987): 52.

[10] Schneiders, 'Death', 55.

Jesus then probes to see whether Martha is able to grasp this (11:26). The text does not indicate whether Martha completely understands the significance of Jesus' revelation in 11:25–26, but she is able to respond in faith to Jesus and recognize him for who he is (11:27).[11] As Jesus intended, Martha's understanding and belief has developed from viewing him as a miracle worker to one who is able to provide resurrection life.[12] In fact, Martha's response that she believes Jesus is 'the Messiah, the Son of God' echoes the purpose of John's gospel in 20:31. The significance being that Martha produces the intended belief-response John has in mind.[13] After this ideal confession, Martha hurries home to tell her sister Mary, who then goes to Jesus (11:28–29). Martha's action resembles that of the Samaritan woman,

---

[11] Cf. Schneiders, who remarks that '[l]ike Peter, who did not fully understand the Bread of Life discourse, Martha believes not in *what* she understands but in the *one* who has the words of eternal life (cf. 6:68)' ('Death', 53 n. 26). Lee concludes that 'while the three titles signify a maturing faith, the precise meaning which Martha attaches to them is ambiguous. They cannot be said to imply full faith' (*Narratives*, 206). However, while Martha's faith may not be perfect (cf. 11:39), it seems adequate in the Johannine sense.

[12] Cf. Beirne, who states that Martha, who already has a partial faith in Jesus, is challenged to expand it (*Women*, 124). Scott remarks that Martha demonstrates true faith since it is expressed in response to Jesus' word *before* the sign occurred (*Sophia*, 202).

[13] Cf. Culpepper, *Anatomy*, 141; van Tilborg, *Love*, 192; Schneiders, 'Death', 53; Scott, *Sophia*, 204–6; M.W.G. Stibbe, 'A Tomb with a View: John 11.1–44 in Narrative-Critical Perspective', *NTS* 40 (1994): 47; Fehribach, *Women*, 105–6; Conway, *Men and Women*, 141–2; W.E. Sproston North, *The Lazarus Story within the Johannine Tradition* (JSNTS 212; Sheffield: SAP, 2001), 143–4; Koester, *Symbolism*, 66; Beirne, *Women*, 127, 130–31. Martha's confession also gains significance when we note the close resemblance to Peter's confession in Matt. 16:16 (Brown, 'Roles', 693; Yamaguchi, *Mary*, 120). Scott thus concludes that Martha represents the confessing believer in the Johannine community (*Sophia*, 203). Lee, however, adds that just as Peter makes the basic Christian confession and immediately after that stumbles (Mark 8:29, 32–33), so Martha falters after an equivalent confession (11:27, 39) (*Narratives*, 213 n. 2). Others contend that Martha's confession in 11:27 does not express adequate faith. Beck, for example, believes that neither Martha's response to Jesus in 11:27 nor her testimony to Mary is appropriate (*Discipleship*, 99–101). D. Burkett argues that the Lazarus narrative is made up of two distinct accounts, wherein Martha exhibits strong faith in 11:21–22, implying that Jesus can raise Lazarus even now, but weak faith in 11:23–27, where she hesitates at the thought of an immediate resurrection ('Two Accounts of Lazarus' Resurrection in John 11', *NovT* 36 [1994]: 219–20). However, Burkett's view that an alternative hypothesis is a single author who was 'either senile, incompetent, or unable to finish the work' ('Accounts', 230), is extreme. While Burkett detects too easily 'rough connections' in the text, many view John 11 as a unity (e.g. Lee, *Narratives*, 188; Stibbe, 'Tomb', 38–44). Besides, Burkett fails to recognize the strength of Martha's confession in 11:27. Similarly, F.J. Moloney believes that Martha's confession in 11:27 simply indicates her long-held beliefs (the perfect tense 'I have believed' is used), which fall short of true faith ('The Faith of Martha and Mary: A Narrative Approach to John 11,17–40', *Bib* 75 [1994]: 477–8; *Gospel*, 328, 339). However, Moloney fails to see the verbal parallel to John's ideal confession in 20:31. Besides, the tense of a verb primarily expresses verbal aspect, i.e. a perspective on an action, rather than time aspect (past, present, future). The function of the perfect tense is to depict the action as reflecting a given state of affairs, with the grammatical subject of the verb as its focus. This stative aspect carries more semantic weight than the other tenses (S.E. Porter, *Idioms of the Greek New Testament* [2d edn; Sheffield: JSOT Press, 1994], 20–21, 39–40). Martha's confession would thus mean something like 'I am in a believing state' or 'I have now arrived at the belief that'.

who went back to her fellow-villagers to testify about Jesus,[14] and that of Andrew and Philip, who went and testified to Peter and Nathanael.[15] Martha thus serves as an exemplary disciple in her belief-response and her testimony to Jesus.

This does not necessarily imply that her understanding of Jesus is perfect. When Jesus arrives at Lazarus's tomb and commands that the stone be removed from the entrance, Martha shows scepticism (11:39). Despite recognizing Jesus' true identity in 11:27, she may not have fully understood the significance of Jesus' revelation in 11:25–26 or its realized dimension. She probably believes that Jesus is able to provide resurrection life beyond death, but only then – on the last day. Alternatively, Martha's newfound or deepened belief may have cringed in the face of reality – a body that had been rotting for four days. Whatever causes her to make this remark, Jesus encourages her to continue to believe (11:40).[16]

Conclusion

Martha is presented as someone who takes initiative (she goes to meet Jesus) and responds appropriately to Jesus.[17] Initially, Martha welcomes Jesus with an implicit reproach mixed with hope. Then, in her interaction

[14] Kitzberger contends that Martha in 11:27 also answers the Samaritan woman's doubtful question, 'Can this be the Christ?' in 4:29 ('Mary', 574–5).

[15] Schüssler Fiorenza, *Memory*, 329.

[16] Contra Moloney, who sees Martha' reaction as evidence that she had never reached adequate faith ('Faith', 490–91). Conway notes that whereas 11:27 presents Martha as the disciple *par excellence*, her reaction in 11:39 introduces tension to her characterization and complicates it (*Men and Women*, 150; 'Ambiguity', 335). Van Tilborg, who first understands Martha's profession of faith in 11:27 positively, surprisingly labels it 'defective' when he arrives at 11:40 (*Love*, 192, 195). Beck puts it more strongly when he asserts that 'Martha verbally expresses her belief but is challenged to no act of faith' ('Function', 153). This is perhaps too harsh a judgement, but we agree with Conway's overall point that most Johannine characters are not perfectly stable or consistent. As in real life, people's faith is not always consistent or progressive; circumstances may generate critical questions, create doubt and cause a shifting faith. Lee sums it up nicely: 'Her doubt does not nullify her earlier confession. It means that, though her faith is centred on Jesus, she has not perceived its full implications. While she understands that Jesus is "resurrection and life" . . . [i]n the moment of crisis her faith wavers at the point of eschatology. She does not yet fully comprehend the "I am" of Jesus, the revelation of Jesus' gift of life in the present' (*Narratives*, 213; cf. Sproston North, *Lazarus*, 156). Similarly, Beirne comments that Martha is still on a journey of faith: '[t]he "sign" [Lazarus's raising] which will confirm that Jesus does indeed have power over life and death, becomes for her the means by which the faith she already possesses will be perfected' (*Women*, 134).

[17] If the sisters Martha and Mary in John 11:1 – 12:8 are the same as those in Luke 10:38–42, Mary comes out better than Martha in the Lukan story, whereas in John the reverse appears to be true (*pace* R. Bauckham, who, in our view, overestimates the consistency of characterization of the two sisters in Luke and John ['The Bethany Family in John 11–12: History of Fiction?' in *The Testimony of the Beloved Disciple: Narrative, History, and Theology in the Gospel of John* (Grand Rapids: Baker Academic, 2007), 177–9]).

with Jesus, Martha's understanding develops from his being a miracle worker to the one who can provide resurrection life. She considers herself Jesus' disciple (she addresses Jesus as 'Teacher' and 'Lord'; cf. Jesus' love for her), and functions as an exemplary disciple who (i) provides the ideal belief-response to Jesus, as John intends his readers to do (11:27 corresponds to 20:31); (ii) successfully testifies to her sister (11:28–29); (iii) provides practical service (12:2).[18] Nevertheless, her belief is not perfect and wavers when faced with the brutal reality of death. Without criticizing her, Jesus encourages Martha to continue in her newfound or enhanced belief.

Martha thus displays various traits: she shows initiative; is confident in what Jesus can do; is perceptive, able to progress cognitively in response to Jesus' revelation; she testifies to her sister; and she shows practical service. Martha also provides glimpses into her inner life: she claims theological knowledge (11:21–22, 24), and she believes (11:27). We can trace a subtle development in Martha. She displays initiative and confidence – she goes to meet Jesus first and professes her belief in Jesus' powers (11:20–22). Then, responding to Jesus' revelation, Martha's faith reaches a new depth with the ideal Johannine confession (11:27). However, her enhanced faith wavers when she is confronted with the prospect of a rotting corpse in 11:39. Although her reaction at the tomb does not necessarily nullify her earlier confession, this hesitation is surprising, and implies a subtle change between 11:27 and 11:39.

Martha		
Appearances	References	11:1, 5, 19, 20, 21, 24, 30, 39; 12:2
Identity	Titles given	–
	Gender	female
	Age	–
	Marital status	perhaps unmarried
	Occupation	–
	Socio-economic status	–
	Place of residence/operation	Bethany near Jerusalem
	Relatives	sister Mary and brother Lazarus
	Group affiliation	–
Speech and actions	In interaction with Jesus	an initial greeting of implicit reproach mixed with hope; after Jesus' revelation, she progresses in her understanding of him; facing the tomb, her deepened faith falters a bit; she serves/follows Jesus
	In interaction with others	testifies to her sister Mary, serves at a meal

[18] Regarding her service, Scott explains, in the light of 12:26, that a servant is one who truly follows, i.e. a disciple (*Sophia*, 213). Cf. D.E. Peters, who examines medieval sources and contends that 'Martha provides a model of the faithful servant, of one who professes the Christian gospel, and of a leader who sets an example through her piety and social concern' ('The Life of Martha of Bethany by Pseudo-Marcilia', *TS* 58 [1997]: 441–60).

Martha		
Character classification	Complexity	little complex; multiple traits: initiatory, confident, perceptive, able to testify, serving
	Development	little
	Inner life	some
Degree of characterization		type, towards personality
Response to Jesus		the ideal Johannine confession; true expressions of discipleship

Mary of Bethany – At Jesus' Feet

'Love is not to be purchased, and affection has no price' — St. Jerome

John 11:1 – 12:8 presents a story about a small family – Lazarus, Mary and Martha – in the village of Bethany, near Jerusalem.[1] Mary may be unmarried and reasonably wealthy, considering the cost of the perfume she uses to anoint Jesus' feet (12:3, 5). That Jesus loves her (11:5) probably indicates that she is his disciple (as are Martha and Lazarus [cf. chs 17, 19]). Her interactions with Jesus are recorded in two incidents – one before and one after Lazarus's resurrection.

Mary's Interaction with Jesus before Lazarus's Resurrection

Regarding their understanding of Jesus, both Mary and Martha start from similar positions: underlying their identically worded greeting, 'Lord, if you had been here, my brother would not have died' (11:21, 32), is most likely the belief that Jesus could work miracles. However, Mary shows less initiative than her sister who goes out to meet Jesus (11:20).[2] She hurries to Jesus only after Martha's testimony (11:29–30). Mary's falling at Jesus' feet and her implicit complaint (11:32), accompanied by weeping (11:33), probably indicate that she is still grieving, preoccupied with the loss of her brother.[3] Mary does not appear to share the hope that Martha has (cf.

---

[1] Mary of Bethany is distinct from Mary the wife of Clopas (19:25) and Mary Magdalene (19:25; 20:1–18).

[2] Contra Fehribach, who views Mary as 'the dutiful betrothed/bride who waits until her bridegroom calls her' (*Women*, 95).

[3] Contra those scholars who believe that Mary's falling at Jesus' feet denotes her devotion (Kitzberger, 'Mary', 576; O'Day, *Gospel*, 690; Conway, *Men and Women*, 145–6; Sproston North, *Lazarus*, 146). Mary's devotion only comes into view in 12:3. Moloney contends that Mary and not Martha portrays true faith ('Faith', 482–3; *Gospel*, 330, 340). However, he has overlooked the significance of Martha's confession in 11:27 (cf. ch. 17). Besides, his equating Mary's falling at Jesus' feet in 11:32 with that of the man born blind in 9:38 is erroneous because the man's act is accompanied by a belief-response *after* Jesus has revealed himself to him, while Mary's act comes before Jesus has spoken to her and seems to be an act of grief and despair rather than worship (cf. Edwards, *John*, 108–9). At the other extreme is the allegation that Mary's act denotes a lack of faith (so Schnackenburg, *Gospel*, 2:333). More likely, Mary shares a similar

11:22) nor does she progress in her understanding of Jesus as her sister does. Mary's association with 'the Jews' (11:31, 33, 45), who generally are portrayed negatively in the Gospel of John (see ch. 4), does not improve her characterization.[4]

Jesus' emotional distress or anger in 11:33, when he is confronted with the wailing Mary and 'the Jews' who accompany her, is difficult to explain. Some argue that he was agitated about the destructive effect of death (or Satan) in lives of people in general.[5] Others argue that Jesus was disturbed more specifically by the human response of Mary and 'the Jews' who are so preoccupied with death that they fail to grasp the life-giving potential of Jesus.[6] Lee seems to have a better interpretation. Without denying the misunderstanding of Mary and her grieving companions, she suggests that Jesus' anger and distress is caused by the recognition of the approaching 'hour' of his own death (cf. 12:27; 13:21) and the imminent rejection of people which will eventuate in his death (cf. 11:45–57).[7] Nevertheless, the text is ambiguous and the reader must struggle with the tension that results in a somewhat unclear characterization of Mary.[8]

We must not evaluate Mary too negatively.[9] She may have been slower in understanding Jesus than Martha, was perhaps more emotional than Martha and overwhelmed by grief, but Jesus seemingly did not get angry

---

faith in Jesus as her sister (cf. 11:21, 32) but Mary is so overcome with grief that she cannot bring herself to the hope that Martha expresses in 11:22 or progress as Martha does in 11:24, 27 (cf. Beasley-Murray, *John*, 192).

[4] Kitzberger notes that Mary is 'very emotional' because when she leaves the house, 'the Jews' think she is going to the tomb to weep (11:31), whereas when Martha left the house, nobody ascribed the same motivations to her ('Mary', 576). Ridderbos, however, does not see much difference between the two sisters (*Gospel*, 400–401).

[5] Brown, *Gospel*, 1:435; Schneiders, 'Death', 54; A. Robertson, 'John 11:1–53', *Int* 58 (2004): 176. Consequently, Schneiders evaluates Mary more positively, suggesting that Jesus shares in Mary's grief and legitimizes human agony in the face of death.

[6] Bultmann, *Gospel*, 406; Schnackenburg, *Gospel*, 2:336; Beasley-Murray, *John*, 193; Moloney, 'Faith', 486. Some of 'the Jews' seem to have shared Mary's belief in Jesus as a miracle worker (11:37).

[7] Lee, *Narratives*, 208–12. See also Sproston North, *Lazarus*, 147–53. Contra Moloney, who contends that Jesus' weeping in 11:35 rather than his anger in 11:33 expresses his frustration and disappointment that people will never understand him ('Faith', 487–8), and R. Hakola, who concludes that Jesus' emotions (11:4–6, 33–35) are inconsistent ('A Character Resurrected: Lazarus in the Fourth Gospel and Afterwards', in *Characterization in the Gospels: Reconceiving Narrative Criticism* [ed. D. Rhoads and K. Syreeni; JSNTS 184; Sheffield: SAP, 1999], 240–44). B. Lindars identifies behind 11:33 a Synoptic exorcism story where Jesus rebukes an unclean spirit ('Rebuking the Spirit: A New Analysis of the Lazarus Story of John 11', *NTS* 38 [1992]: 89–104).

[8] Conway, 'Ambiguity', 336. Conway also observes that 11:32 creates ambiguity: is Mary's faith weaker than Martha because she does not add Martha's firm affirmation of 11:22, or is she portrayed as having a deeper devotion than Martha because she falls at Jesus' feet? ('Ambiguity', 335–6).

[9] Contra Schnackenburg's impression of Mary as 'nothing but a complaining woman' (*Gospel*, 2:333). Brodie's view of Mary is also too gloomy (*Gospel*, 392–5).

at her lack of faith. Besides, when Jesus calls Mary in 11:28, it may echo the calling of his sheep in 10:3 – and she responds (11:29).[10] Then, in 11:31, Mary unintentionally leads 'the Jews' to Jesus – some of who will believe (11:45).[11] Finally, the prolepsis in 11:2 probably serves to inform the reader about her reappearance in 12:3, which shows her in a better light.[12]

Mary's Interaction with Jesus after Lazarus's Resurrection

Not long after Lazarus is raised, Jesus is in the home of Lazarus for a thanksgiving dinner (12:1–2).[13] During this dinner, we encounter an extraordinary demonstration of Mary's devotion to Jesus. While her attitude was not entirely positive or progressive in 11:28–33a, in 12:3 Mary is depicted as one who is totally devoted to Jesus. On both occasions (11:32 and 12:3), Mary is found at Jesus' feet, but here grief is replaced by devotion.[14]

Mary's act is extraordinary in three ways. First, it was extravagant. The pound of perfume made of pure nard was worth a year's wages according to Judas's estimation, assuming a labourer earned about one denarius per day (12:4–5).[15] Second, the anointing of the feet was extraordinary. The normal practice was to anoint one's head and wash one's feet, but Mary anoints Jesus' feet. Although Coakley demonstrates that the anointing of the feet was not unthinkable, it was certainly not an everyday occurrence in first-century Palestine.[16] Third, Mary's wiping of Jesus' feet with her hair is unusual. As Coakley appropriately remarks, the wiping up of the ointment follows naturally from the extravagant quantity that Mary uses, but it is unusual that she does it with her hair rather than a towel or her sleeve.[17] Her act of wiping Jesus' feet with her hair would certainly have raised a few eyebrows since a respectable woman was not supposed to have her

---

[10] Moloney, 'Faith', 480–81; O'Day, *Gospel*, 689; Lincoln, *Gospel*, 325.

[11] Conway, *Men and Women*, 143, 145.

[12] Schüssler Fiorenza hence argues that Mary articulates the right praxis of discipleship (*Memory*, 330–31).

[13] For a critical comparison of John 12:1–8, Mark 14:3–9 and Luke 7:36–50, see J.F. Coakley, 'The Anointing at Bethany and the Priority of John', *JBL* 107 (1988): 241–56. Kitzberger uses the Synoptic stories less judiciously, simply assuming that the first readers knew these texts ('Mary', 571, *passim*). However, the Synoptics cannot be used indiscriminately to interpret John.

[14] Culpepper, *Anatomy*, 141. Kitzberger aptly remarks that 12:2–3 presents *both* sisters in a servant role in relation to Jesus: Martha serves at the table and Mary anoints Jesus' feet ('Mary', 579).

[15] Lee comments that Mary responds to the cost of Jesus' love and self-giving in raising Lazarus (and to God's costly self-giving in Jesus [3:16]) with her own costly self-giving (*Narratives*, 222).

[16] Coakley, 'Anointing', 246–8.

[17] Coakley, 'Anointing', 249, 251.

hair loose in public.[18] For Mary, however, devotion takes precedence over convention.[19]

Mary has perhaps understood that Jesus will die soon because he clarifies that she had intended the perfume for his burial (12:7).[20] Her act of anointing Jesus prefigures his death and anticipates Nicodemus's act of embalming Jesus' body for his burial in 19:39–40. Nevertheless, we cannot assume that she had grasped the theological significance of Jesus' death; she may simply have heard of the resolution of the Jewish council (11:45–53, 57), and comprehended the serious threat to Jesus' life.[21] However, her under-standing of Jesus must have progressed because the second time – again at Jesus' feet – she shows no tears or grief but love and devotion.

Apart from a prophetic action pointing to Jesus' imminent death, Mary's act of loving service probably foreshadows Jesus' washing his disciples'

---

[18] Cf. Barrett, *Gospel*, 412; Fehribach, *Women*, 90. However, Coakley notes that a woman's letting down her hair applies only to a *married* woman (and Mary may have been unmarried) and *in public* (while 12:1–8 depicts a private occasion) ('Anointing', 250–52).

[19] Mary's act of love and devotion gains greater significance if we view it in contrast to Judas's defection, starting in 12:1–8.

[20] Cf. Beirne, who understands 12:7 as Mary's having kept the perfume for this day as a symbolic anticipation of Jesus' burial rather than keeping it for the actual burial (*Women*, 151). In contrast, Maccini contends that Jesus indicates in 12:7 that Mary might keep what oil she has left for the day of his burial (*Testimony*, 174). Van Tilborg detects sexual connotations in Mary's act and states that she must have been surprised when she heard Jesus' interpretation in 12:7, indicating that he distances himself from her (*Love*, 196–8, 208). However, Jesus' corrective in 12:7 is directed towards Judas rather than Mary's possible sexual intention. Fehribach explores the possible sexual overtones of Mary's act more fully and argues that she acts as a betrothed or bride of Jesus, the messianic bridegroom, on behalf of the Jewish people with whom she is connected in 11:31, 33, 45 (*Women*, 86–93). Although the act of anointing could occur in the context of both sexual intercourse and burial/mourning, Jesus indicates that the latter is in view (12:7) and hence there is no warrant for Fehribach's argument. Besides, Mary can hardly be a representative of 'the Jews' who are generally hostile to Jesus. Finally, Fehribach's conclusion that the purpose of Mary's portrayal as the betrothed/bride of Jesus is to establish a familial relationship between Jesus and Lazarus and between Jesus and those Jews who believed in him (*Women*, 107–8), is too reductionistic; Mary is important in her own right and representative of a particular kind of people – then and now.

[21] Contra scholars who attribute too much understanding to Mary. For example, Lee argues that Mary's prophetic act is more complete than Martha's confession at 11:27 because 'Mary acknowledges that, by bringing Lazarus back to life, Jesus has sacrificed his own life . . . Her action is a proclamation of Jesus' authority as *anastasis kai zōē* (11.25a)' and she perceives 'the death and raising of her brother as symbolic of the death of Jesus through which life is given to believers' (*Narratives*, 220–21). J.S. Webster contends that Mary's act confirms Jesus as the Messiah, the anointed one (*Ingesting Jesus: Eating and Drinking in the Gospel of John* [SBLAB 6; Atlanta: SBL, 2003], 94–7). Beirne claims that Mary recognizes the true nature of Jesus' kingship as a service of love (*Women*, 153). It is more likely that Mary was simply aware that raising Lazarus resulted in a serious threat to Jesus' own life and she anticipated that he would die. Instead of attributing the elevated christological meaning to Mary, we suggest it is the author who wants to communicate this truth to the reader. Besides, it is *Jesus* not Mary who marks the anointing as an indicator of his burial (Maccini, *Testimony*, 183). Nevertheless, even if Jesus assigned a deeper meaning to Mary's act than she intended, the anointing still testifies to her love for and devotion to Jesus.

feet in John 13, in which case, Mary proleptically displays the true nature of discipleship.[22]

Conclusion

Mary does not express the hope or insight into Jesus' identity that her sister does. The grim reality of death seems to cause overwhelming grief, hindering her understanding of Jesus and his potential. Her affiliation with 'the Jews' also contributes to a negative evaluation of her. Nevertheless, in an extraordinary act of devotion, she expresses her affection for and allegiance to Jesus. In both instances, we find Mary at Jesus' feet. However, while on the first occasion she appears emotional, overwhelmed with grief, and unable to respond adequately to Jesus (11:32–33), on the second occasion she shows love for and allegiance to Jesus. Her act not only points to Jesus' imminent death, but may also reflect the attitude of loving servanthood that Jesus expects from his disciples (cf. 13:12–17). It would be reasonable to assume that underlying her affectionate behaviour is an adequate understanding of, and belief in, Jesus.[23]

Mary thus displays multiple traits: she is emotional and affectionate; she can be passive but also show initiative; she displays difficulty as well as progress in understanding; and she has a serving attitude. Both sisters show similarities and dissimilarities. Both are loved by Jesus, serve Jesus and belong to him, but where Martha shows more cognitive progress and insight, Mary seems more emotional and affectionate.[24]

[22] Scott, *Sophia*, 209–12. Cf. E.E. Platt, 'The Ministry of Mary of Bethany', *TTod* 34 (1977): 36–7; Schneiders, 'Women', 43; Maccini, *Testimony*, 175–6; Conway, *Men and Women*, 152; Yamaguchi, *Mary*, 122–3; Beirne, *Women*, 160–61.

[23] Cf. Beirne, *Women*, 159. According to Lee, Mary's prophetic act in 12:3 functions as a faith-confession: at the feet of Jesus Mary no longer expresses grief and disappointment (11:32), but love and devotion – the marks of true faith and discipleship (*Narratives*, 219). Beck does not consider Mary to fit the paradigm of appropriate response to Jesus because (i) in John 11 she has no meaningful dialogue, response or witness, and (ii) in John 12 her witness by anointing is unrepeatable (*Discipleship*, 98). However, Beck has underestimated Mary's perception of Jesus underlying the anointing. Besides, although Mary's act is unrepeatable, her attitude of loving devotion and service are an example for later believers (cf. Matt. 26:13; Mark 14:9).

[24] Cf. Culpepper, who concludes that Martha represents the ideal of discerning faith and service, and Mary unlimited love and devotion (*Anatomy*, 142). Kitzberger asserts that Mary is characterized as more emotional and vulnerable than Martha, who seems more intellectual and rational ('Mary', 578). Edwards remarks that in 11:1–44 Martha is presented as active and outgoing, while Mary appears more passive and quieter (*John*, 108). However, in 12:2–3 we see a reversal of these roles.

Mary of Bethany		
Appearances	References	11:1, 2, 19, 20, 28, 31, 32, 45; 12:3
Identity	Titles given	–
	Gender	female
	Age	–
	Marital status	perhaps unmarried
	Occupation	–
	Socio-economic status	probably well-to-do
	Place of residence/operation	Bethany near Jerusalem
	Relatives	sister Martha and brother Lazarus
	Group affiliation	'the Jews'
Speech and actions	In interaction with Jesus	first: implicit reproach, emotional, lack of understanding; later: devotion, servanthood, progressive understanding
	In interaction with others	responds to Martha's testimony, maybe influenced by 'the Jews'
Character classification	Complexity	little complex; multiple traits: emotional, affectionate, passive/active, undiscerning/discerning, serving
	Development	none
	Inner life	none
Degree of characterization		type
Response to Jesus		initially inadequate but finally her loving devotion and service probably implies adequate understanding/belief

Lazarus – The Dead Shall Hear His Voice

'Where, O death, is your victory? Where, O death, is your sting?' — *1 Corinthians 15:55*

At first sight, Lazarus does not appear to agree with our definition of an 'active' character as one who interacts with Jesus and produces a response to him (see ch. 1). He never utters a word and appears entirely passive; his illness, death, burial and resurrection merely happen to him.[1] We shall show, however, that this is an inaccurate picture.

The Identity of Lazarus

Lazarus lived in Bethany, a village about three kilometres south-east of Jerusalem (11:1, 18).[2] His family may have been well-to-do, considering the very expensive perfume his sister Mary could afford (12:3, 5). Besides, Lazarus was probably buried in a private tomb or cave sealed with a stone (11:38). We shall gain more insight into Lazarus's identity by examining his relationship with 'the Jews' and with Jesus.

For seven days after a death in a Jewish family, the nearest relatives of the deceased would remain at home, grieving and receiving the condolences of extended family and friends.[3] Therefore, we must explain the somewhat awkward presence of 'the Jews' on the scene (11:19, 31, 33–37). I have argued elsewhere that 'the Jews' in John's gospel refers to a particular religious group within Judaism – the (strict) Torah- and temple-loyalists who are mainly (but not exclusively) located in Jerusalem and Judaea – with the chief priests as the main leaders and the Pharisees having an influential role.[4] I also argued that 'the Jews' in John 11 are either members of this particular group or their leaders, albeit not the chief priests and Pharisees of the Sanhedrin. They were perhaps the lay aristocracy or prominent noblemen who were an influential element within the Jerusalem/Judaean leadership.[5]

---

[1] Cf. Stibbe, 'Tomb', 48, 53–4; Keener, *Gospel*, 838; Yamaguchi, *Mary*, 124.

[2] 'Lazarus' means 'God helps' (Collins, 'Figures', 25; Hakola, 'Character', 235 n. 27).

[3] B.R. McCane, 'Burial Practices, Jewish', in *DNTB*, 175.

[4] Bennema, 'Identity'.

[5] Bennema, 'Identity', section 3.2.

I then suggested that Lazarus may have been a 'Jew', perhaps even a wealthy nobleman, which would explain fellow 'Jews' coming to mourn him. Although it is odd that Lazarus as a 'Jew' is identified as Jesus' friend (11:3, 11), 11:45 reveals that not every 'Jew' is hostile towards Jesus. In fact, 'the Jews' in John 11 are divided (11:36–37, 45–46) – and not for the first time (10:19–21). Thus, it is possible that a group of 'Jews' who are already divided on the issue of Jesus come to mourn their friend Lazarus, and when Jesus raises Lazarus it only reinforces their opinions about him – the hostile ones report him to the authorities (11:46); others who are open come to believe in him (11:45).[6]

Regarding Lazarus's relationship with Jesus, the text mentions that Jesus loves Lazarus (11:3, 5, 36) and calls Lazarus his friend (11:11). Jesus explains elsewhere that love and friendship are closely related in that love is the hallmark of friendship and finds its ultimate expression in the laying down of one's life for one's friends (15:13). Friendship is an important Johannine motif. Besides Lazarus, John (the Baptist) and the disciples are also called Jesus' friends (3:29; 15:14–15), and one of the disciples is identified as 'the one whom Jesus loved' (13:23) – the so-called 'Beloved Disciple'. As Jesus' friends, the disciples have inside knowledge of the Father and his business, and, unlike slaves, they have a permanent place in the Father's household or family (8:35; 15:15). Friendship and love also denote intimacy: the Father and Jesus have an intimate relationship characterized by love (1:18; 3:35; 5:20; 14:31; 15:9), and Jesus' friends participate in this relationship (14:23; 15:9). Friendship is closely connected to discipleship because the two are marked by sacrificial love (11:16; 13:37; 15:13).[7] Lazarus then is part of God's family since friends, like sons and in contrast to slaves, have a permanent place in God's household. Jesus' relationship with Lazarus is one of friendship, characterized by love, implying that Lazarus belongs to him.[8] This suggests that, earlier, Lazarus must have expressed adequate belief in Jesus and become his disciple.[9]

The Raising of Lazarus and His Interaction with Jesus

If Jesus is Lazarus's friend, how do we explain the deliberate delay of two days, mentioned in 11:6? O'Day points out that in Graeco-Roman antiquity

---

[6] Bennema, 'Identity', section 3.2 n. 46.

[7] Bennema, *Power*, 223–5. See also J.M. Ford, *Redeemer – Friend and Mother: Salvation in Antiquity and in the Gospel of John* (Minneapolis: Fortress Press, 1997); S.H. Ringe, *Wisdom's Friends: Community and Christology in the Fourth Gospel* (Louisville: WJK Press, 1999); G.R. O'Day, 'Jesus as Friend in the Gospel of John', *Int* 58 (2004): 144–57.

[8] There is no warrant to Fehribach's argument that Jesus' love for Lazarus was based on the love/betrothal relationship between Mary and Jesus (*Women*, 91–2). For the Lazarus family as prototypes for those whom Jesus loves, see P.F. Esler and R.A. Piper, *Lazarus, Mary and Martha: A Social-Scientific and Theological Reading of John* (London: SCM, 2006), ch. 4.

[9] Cf. Collins, 'Figures', 26.

friendship was not simply about affection but also about social roles and responsibilities; a friend was available in a time of crisis.[10] Wuellner thus remarks that Jesus' intentional delay violates the code of loving friendship.[11] It must be noted that this delay did *not* cause Lazarus's death.[12] We learn that when Jesus arrives, Lazarus has been buried for four days (11:17, 39). These four days can be accounted for: the sisters' message regarding their brother's illness took one day to reach Jesus (from Bethany near Jerusalem to Bethany in Peraea, where Jesus was hiding [10:40; 11:7]); Jesus stays for two more days in Peraea; and Jesus' journey to Lazarus's tomb would take another day. This would mean Lazarus died shortly after the sisters sent their message to Jesus, and hence Lazarus's death cannot be attributed to Jesus' delay. Jesus could not even have uttered a life-giving word, as with the royal official's son (4:50), because Lazarus is already dead (and buried) when the sisters' message reaches Jesus. Besides, from 11:11, 14 it is clear that Jesus foreknew that Lazarus was dead. We must yet find an explanation for Jesus' intentional delay.[13]

One explanation could be that in John's gospel, Jesus is in control of time and events, and does not succumb to people's demands (cf. 2:3–4; 7:6–10).[14] Alternatively, his delay allows the mourning process and the decay of Lazarus's body to get well under way, which would heighten the intended effect of his self-revelation and miracle. Scholars observe that according to rabbinic thought the soul lingers near the grave for three days, seeking to return to the body, after which death is irreversible.[15] Jesus' intentional delay of two days would get them past the three-day mark, adding to the significance of the miracle. Thus, Jesus' intentional delay is not a denial or violation of his friendship with Lazarus (and Martha and Mary), but demonstrates his control over time and events, aimed at revealing more about his identity and hence deepening the faith of his friends. Besides, since the raising of Lazarus precipitates the plot to kill Jesus (11:45–53; cf. 11:8), Jesus' return to Judaea is the ultimate demonstration of his love for Lazarus – an act of laying down his life for a friend (cf. 15:13).[16]

---

[10] O'Day, 'Jesus', 144–6.

[11] W. Wuellner, 'Putting Life back into the Lazarus Story and its Reading: The Narrative Rhetoric of John 11 as the Narration of Faith', *Semeia* 53 (1991): 116.

[12] Contra Koester, *Symbolism*, 65; Köstenberger, *John*, 328.

[13] The difficulty of 11:6b after 11:5–6a, implying that *because* Jesus loved the family he delayed going to visit them, causes Burkett to think that v.6b belongs to another account ('Accounts', 217). The thrust of Burkett's article is that two distinct sources are behind the Lazarus narrative. However, there is good reason to believe that 11:1–44 is a literary unity (Lee, *Narratives*, 188).

[14] Cf. Lee, *Narratives*, 199.

[15] Collins, 'Figures', 26; Beasley-Murray, *John*, 189–90; Lee, *Narratives*, 194 n. 3; O'Day, *Gospel*, 687; Coloe, 'Households', 331 n. 23.

[16] Culpepper, *Anatomy*, 141; Sproston North, *Lazarus*, 49–50. Jesus' delay has been understood symbolically as the delay of the Parousia and the problem this caused for the Johannine community, but Schneiders disputes this and contends that Jesus' delay follows the pattern

In the entire narrative Jesus addresses Lazarus just once, when he stands in front of the open tomb and cries out loudly, 'Lazarus, come out' (11:43). Lazarus's response is as dramatic as Jesus' command: still wrapped in burial cloth, he comes out (11:44). Apparently Lazarus hears Jesus' voice and obeys.[17] This only interaction between Jesus and Lazarus, brief as it is, evokes two earlier passages – 5:28–29 and 10:3–5.[18] In 5:28–29, Jesus speaks about the bodily resurrection of people at the end of time. The phrase 'all who are in their tombs will hear his voice and come out' in 5:28–29 is enacted in 11:43–44. Thus, Lazarus's resurrection is a powerful demonstration of Jesus' being the resurrection and the life (11:25) and a foretaste of what awaits those who believe in Jesus. Moreover, in 10:3–5, we read that Jesus' sheep hear his voice and follow him. Here, in Lazarus's case it becomes evident that even death cannot hinder his sheep from hearing the voice of the good shepherd. When Jesus calls, Lazarus, as one of Jesus' sheep, hears his voice and responds in obedience (cf. Mary in 11:28–29). In hearing Jesus' voice and obeying his command, Lazarus shows himself to be a true disciple and friend of Jesus (15:14).[19]

The 'Testimony' of Lazarus

The effect of Lazarus's resurrection is twofold: (i) it causes people to believe in Jesus; and (ii) it points believers to the future bodily resurrection. Let us clarify this. In 11:11, Jesus speaks enigmatically about Lazarus's condition since the Greek word *koimaomai* can either mean 'to fall asleep' or, figuratively, 'to be dead'. The disciples misunderstand Jesus, thinking that Lazarus has fallen asleep (11:12), whereas Jesus speaks of Lazarus's death (11:13–14). Although Jesus uses 'sleep' in 11:11–13 as a metaphor for death

that can be observed in Jesus' response to his mother in 2:4, to the royal official in 4:50, and to his brothers in 7:8–9, emphasizing Jesus' sovereign independence in relation to human initiative ('Death', 47).

[17] Contra Stibbe, who asserts that Lazarus's silence indicates a lack of response ('Tomb', 53–4). For John, it is clear that Lazarus was clinically dead – he had been buried four days and there was a noticeable decay of his body (11:39). Jesus' action, then, was not a resuscitation of a comatose Lazarus but the resurrection of a dead person whose body was rotting.

[18] Cf. Hakola, 'Character', 231, 235; Sproston North, *Lazarus*, 158–9. There are also intentional allusions to Jesus' own resurrection in John 20 (cf. Lee, *Narratives*, 214–6; Hakola, 'Character', 232–3). However, while Lazarus is still bound by the grave clothes and thus not fully freed from the power of death, Jesus will leave the grave clothes and death behind (20:5–7) (Collins, 'Figures', 26–7; Culpepper, *Anatomy*, 141; Sproston North, *Lazarus*, 159–60). According to Schneiders, John 11 – 12 as a whole symbolically portrays Jesus' execution (11:47–53), burial (12:1–8), resurrection (11:1–44) and glorification (12:12–13) ('Death', 45).

[19] Cf. J.N. Suggitt, 'The Raising of Lazarus', *ExpTim* 95 (1983–84): 107. Contra Beck, who asserts that 'Lazarus' response to Jesus' command is not the faith response of a human being but the reanimation of one who had lost his capacity to believe or respond' ('Function', 153; cf. *idem, Discipleship*, 97).

to indicate that death is temporary, a passage to life, he also asserts in 11:14 that 'sleep' is not a euphemism for the harsh reality of death.[20] Jesus then declares that Lazarus's death is aimed at evoking belief (11:15). This incident can elicit faith because Jesus shows, in his capacity of being 'the resurrection and the life', his power over death by raising Lazarus.[21]

Jesus' comment in 11:15 is somewhat puzzling because (i) it is directed to his disciples but nowhere do we read that they respond in faith after Lazarus is raised; and (ii) the disciples have already responded to Jesus in faith (cf. 2:11; 6:68–69). I suggest that Martha's interaction with Jesus provides a clue to understanding 11:15. Her initial remarks to Jesus reveal her belief that Jesus could have healed her terminally ill brother and prevented him from dying (11:21). Jesus, however, wants Martha to move beyond a belief in him as a miracle worker towards a deeper or more mature understanding of him. When Jesus reveals a new aspect of his identity, namely that he has power over life and death, Martha is able to grasp Jesus' revelation and respond with the ideal Johannine confession (11:23–27). If Jesus had healed Lazarus and prevented his death, it would have simply affirmed what Martha already believed Jesus could do. Now, however, Lazarus's death and Jesus' delay have deepened the crisis and created an opportunity for Jesus to reveal to Martha (and by extension to the disciples) a new aspect of his identity, enhancing an already *existing* belief.[22]

Jesus' raising of Lazarus also elicits *initial* faith. Jesus repeats what he says in 11:15, but now in the presence of 'the Jews' who had come to mourn, that the raising of Lazarus is intended to elicit belief (11:42). Indeed, many of 'the Jews' believe in Jesus when they witness the miracle (11:45). Although this 'belief' may not be adequate belief in the Johannine sense and merely a belief in Jesus as a miracle worker, it is a step in the right direction.[23] Lazarus thus is or provides an implicit testimony that evokes belief (12:11; cf. 17:20). At the same time, Lazarus's testimony also has a negative effect in that the chief priests, after deciding to kill Jesus, now plan to kill Lazarus too because he caused some of their fellow 'Jews' to defect to Jesus' side (11:53; 12:10–11; cf. the world's reaction towards the disciples in 15:18 – 16:4a).

In sum, Lazarus's death provided an opportunity for Jesus to reveal an aspect of his identity – that he is 'the resurrection and the life' with power over life and death – in order to elicit belief. The incident bears results in that Jesus is able to evoke both initial faith (in case of 'the Jews') and deepen existing faith (in case of Martha and by implication the disciples).

---

[20] Schneiders, 'Death', 49.

[21] Jesus' comment that Lazarus's illness 'is not to death' (11:4) probably means that death will not have the final say.

[22] Cf. Jesus' exhortation to move beyond signs-faith towards a belief based on his words in 4:48 and 20:29.

[23] John 11:45 could perhaps indicate an enhancement of existing faith. Since 11:37 indicates that some of 'the Jews' already perceive Jesus as a miracle worker, witnessing the resurrection of Lazarus may well have enhanced their 'faith'.

Lazarus's resurrection had a strong effect on the original audience in Jesus' time but should also have an effect on the reader – whether in John's time or now. Lazarus exemplifies the true disciple, in that he hears Jesus' voice and follows him even through death. This, as we mentioned, foreshadows the experience of all believers at the end of time. Thus, Lazarus's obedience provides hope for all believers and should strengthen their faith. The good shepherd goes ahead of his sheep – even in death and resurrection – and the believer who dies in Christ will one day hear the shepherd's voice and rise from the dead to the abundant, eternal life.[24] Although it has been suggested that John 11 seeks to address the questions, faced by the Johannine community, regarding the delay of the Parousia and the fate of believers who die before this event (cf. 1 Thess. 4:13–17; Rev. 6:10; 14:13), Schneiders contends that the delay of the Parousia is not the primary issue in John 11:

> The problem is not that Christians die too soon (i.e. before the last day) but that they die at all . . . If Jesus is truly present, as he promised in the last discourses, indwelling his disciples as a principle of eternal life, death is an anomaly. Death it would seem, can only mean that Jesus is absent . . . The theological concern of the Lazarus story, therefore, is not the delay of the parousia but the real meaning of death and life, of the absence and presence of Jesus. It is the problem of death in the community of eternal life.[25]

Conclusion

Jesus' relationship with Lazarus is characterized by friendship and love, indicating that Lazarus is Jesus' disciple and part of God's family. Lazarus proves his discipleship when he hears Jesus' voice from the tomb and obeys – he comes out of the grave. In the light of John 5 and 10, Lazarus, by hearing Jesus' voice, confirms that he belongs to Jesus' flock since his sheep hear his voice. Lazarus's response epitomizes obedience and shows that nothing (not even death) need be an obstacle for hearing and obeying Jesus. Lazarus thus functions as a paradigmatic disciple, showing that true disciples will continually hear Jesus' voice and follow him – even through death.

[24] Cf. Schneiders, who understands John 11 as a story for the Johannine community to help them understand how the death of believers can be understood and faced. The answer John provides is derived from Jesus' own resurrection and its efficacy in the experience of believers, and the raising of Lazarus is a powerful vehicle for presenting this theology ('Death', 47). The early church also recognized the raising of Lazarus as an example that testifies to the corporeal resurrection of the dead (Irenaeus, *Adversus Haereses* 5.13.1; Tertullian, *De Resurrectione Carnis* 53.3–4) (Hakola, 'Character', 249).

[25] Schneiders, 'Death', 47–8 (quotation from p. 48). Cf. Coloe, who states that Martha and Mary (representing the post-Easter Christian community) have a faith that requires Jesus' physical presence as the means of life and that falters by the arrival of death. Jesus challenges them (and later generations of believers) to trust in his efficacious word that is powerful to overcome death – even when he is absent ('Households', 332–5). Others who understand the Lazarus narrative to speak to later Christian communities who felt the consternation when believers died during Jesus' absence are Collins, 'Figures', 26; Koester, *Symbolism*, 65; Esler and Piper, *Lazarus*, ch. 5.

Lazarus also exemplifies discipleship indirectly in that his raising provides a testimony with a twofold effect: (i) it evokes initial belief (11:45; 12:11; cf. 17:20) and deepens existing belief (11:27, albeit proleptically of Lazarus's raising); (ii) it triggers off a hostile reaction from the religious authorities who plan to kill Lazarus (12:10–11). Jesus foretells that his disciples (and later generations of believers) will face similar responses: the believer's testimony is expected to elicit faith (17:20) as well as hostile reactions from the world (15:18 – 16:4a). Thus, Lazarus is far from a passive character.

Lazarus		
Appearances	References	11:1, 2, 5, 11, 14, 43; 12:1, 2, 9, 10, 17
Identity	Titles given	Jesus' friend, the one whom Jesus loves
	Gender	male
	Age	–
	Marital status	–
	Occupation	–
	Socio-economic status	perhaps a nobleman and part of 'the Jews'
	Place of residence/operation	Bethany near Jerusalem
	Relatives	sisters Martha and Mary
	Group affiliation	'the Jews'
Speech and actions	In interaction with Jesus	he hears Jesus' voice and is obedient
	In interaction with others	his raising is instrumental in producing belief in others
Character classification	Complexity	uncomplicated; few traits: obedience, providing testimony
	Development	none
	Inner life	none
Degree of characterization		type
Response to Jesus		as Jesus' disciple, he hears his voice and obeys, and becomes a testimony

THOMAS – LET ME SEE AND TOUCH

'Yes, I do touch. I believe that everyone needs that' — *Diana, former Princess of Wales*

Thomas is popularly known by his nickname 'doubting Thomas', which comes from his demand for tangible evidence in order to believe Jesus is alive (20:25). Indeed, the Oxford English Dictionary defines a 'doubting Thomas' as 'a person who refuses to believe something without proof'. We must examine whether this is a true portrait. Regarding his identity, John only provides two clues. First, Thomas was one of 'the Twelve' (20:24). Second, the name 'Thomas' corresponds to the Aramaic word for 'twin' ('Didymus' is its Greek equivalent) (11:16; 20:24; 21:2), but there is no evidence that Thomas had a twin. This could lead one to interpret the name symbolically – of Thomas being double-minded or in two minds – in line with his supposed main trait of doubt. However, if John does not portray Thomas as a doubter, this symbolic interpretation will fail.

Thomas's Misunderstandings

One of the main characteristics of 'the Twelve' is their misunderstanding or failure to understand Jesus (cf. ch. 14) – and Thomas is no exception. In the first instance, Jesus is in Bethany in Peraea, having escaped the latest murderous attempts of 'the Jews', (10:31, 39–42). When Jesus suggests that they should return to Judaea to visit his ill friend Lazarus, his disciples naturally are alarmed because Bethany is close to Jerusalem – the political-religious headquarters of 'the Jews' – but Jesus insists that they go (11:7–15). Thomas's exclamation, 'Let us also go, that we may die with him' in 11:16 reveals that he misunderstands Jesus, fearing that 'the Jews' would kill them all. Despite the misunderstanding, Thomas's declaration speaks of courage, loyalty and the willingness to die with Jesus (cf. 15:13).[1] Thomas seems prepared, perhaps more than Peter in 13:37, to lay down his life for

---

[1] Cf. Carson, *Gospel*, 410. Contra Bultmann, who contends that Thomas's remark 'signifies a resignation to the fate that threatens alike the disciples and Jesus' (*Gospel*, 400; cf. Krafft, 'Personen', 27).

his master since Jesus does not comment on Thomas's suggestion (unlike with Peter).[2]

The second instance of Thomas's failing to understand Jesus is recorded in 14:5. With his departure imminent, Jesus informs his disciples that he will go to his Father's house to prepare a home for them and he assures them that they know the place where he is going (14:1–4). Thomas's exclamation, 'Lord, we do not know where you are going. How can we know the way?', shows that he does not grasp what Jesus says, and the use of a plural suggests that he speaks on behalf of the other disciples.[3]

The last recorded misunderstanding of Thomas has to do with his demand to see and touch the risen Jesus in order to believe (20:25). Although Jesus graciously fulfils Thomas's request (20:27), he encourages him (and others) towards a belief that is less dependent on the tangible (20:29). Thomas, like Mary Magdalene in 20:17 (see ch. 24), may not have understood Jesus' teaching in 14:18–23 where he says he will continue to be present with them after his return to the Father. Jesus' statements 'I will not leave you orphaned; I am coming to you' (14:18) and 'In a little while . . . you will see me' (14:19) do not refer to Jesus' resurrection appearances (otherwise the disciples would be orphaned again after the ascension) or to the Parousia (otherwise the disciples would be orphans until then). Rather, they refer to Jesus' coming back to the disciples through the Spirit-Paraclete, whom he promised them in 14:16–17. After his departure from this world, Jesus will continue to be with his disciples through the Spirit-Paraclete. Consequently, Jesus, in 14:23, is most likely saying that the Father and he will indwell the believer by means of the Spirit, i.e. the Spirit will mediate to the believer the presence of Jesus and the Father. Thomas, however, has not understood that Jesus' ongoing presence would be a spiritual rather than a physical presence. His misunderstandings thus betray a perspective 'from below'.[4]

Thomas's Interaction with Jesus

John 20 describes the resurrection of Jesus (20:1–10) and his appearances to Mary Magdalene (20:11–18), the disciples (20:19–23) and Thomas (20:24–29). The common element in all three encounters is that a tangible experience with the risen Jesus leads to greater faith.

---

[2] Contra Stibbe, who contends that Thomas, like Peter, shows false bravado and discipleship ('Tomb', 46).

[3] Hence, it is unfair to single out Thomas as the one who does not understand Jesus (so Krafft, 'Personen', 27).

[4] Cf. W. Bonney, who characterizes Thomas as one who betrays an earth-bound or worldly point of view (*Caused To Believe: The Doubting Thomas Story at the Climax of John's Christological Narrative* [BIS 62; Leiden: Brill, 2002], 137–41).

For reasons unknown to us, Thomas is absent on Sunday evening when Jesus appears to the disciples (20:24). When the others report to him that they have seen the risen Lord, Thomas replies that he will have to see and touch Jesus for himself in order to believe (20:25). This reply has earned him the nickname 'doubting Thomas' – perhaps unfairly. First, it is possible that the other disciples did not accept Mary's testimony that she had seen the risen Lord (20:18–19).[5] Second, in 20:25, Thomas only asks to see Jesus' hands and side – the same marks that Jesus had earlier shown the other disciples (20:20).[6] Third, Jesus' 'rebuke' in 20:29 is certainly not harsh, and it seems that all the characters in John 20 – Mary Magdalene, the disciples, Thomas – need a tangible experience with the risen Lord to confirm a saving relationship with him.[7] Nonetheless, Thomas's proviso that he see and touch the risen Jesus reveals unbelief/scepticism and misunderstanding. First, he is sceptical about the testimony of the other disciples that Jesus has been resurrected (20:25).[8] Second, like Mary Magdalene, Thomas's desire for a tangible presence of Jesus indicates that he has not understood that Jesus' ongoing presence with his disciples will be *by means of the Spirit* – as Jesus had mentioned to his disciples in 14:17–23 (see the previous section).[9]

Then, a week later, Thomas has his encounter with the risen Lord in a similar fashion and location as the other disciples (cf. 20:19–23). In the same house, with the doors again shut, again Jesus appears supernaturally and greets Thomas with the greeting he greeted the others, 'Peace be with you' (20:26). Then, Jesus invites Thomas to examine the physical scars as he had requested, and encourages him to discontinue his unbelief and to believe (20:27). The text does not clarify whether Thomas did touch Jesus (the sight of Jesus may have been sufficient), but his reply, 'My Lord and my God!' (20:28), certainly expresses adequate belief.[10] Thomas's recognition of Jesus'

---

[5] The Synoptics also record that all the disciples struggle with Jesus' resurrection (Matt. 28:17; Mark 16:11, 14; Luke 24:10–11, 36–43).

[6] Cf. Lee, who stresses that Thomas's determination to see and touch the risen Lord is positive ('Partnership', 43).

[7] See also S. Harstine, 'Un-Doubting Thomas: Recognition Scenes in the Ancient World', *Perspectives in Religious Studies* 33 (2006): 435–47.

[8] Cf. Bonney, *Caused To Believe*, 159–60.

[9] Cf. Lee, 'Partnership', 43.

[10] Cf. Lee, 'Partnership', 46. Bonney contends that it is Jesus' knowledge of Thomas's thoughts (20:27a echoes 20:25b) that causes Thomas to believe (*Caused To Believe*, 165–6). Krafft comments that whereas Thomas previously did not understand that Jesus' humiliation will lead to his exaltation (11:16; 14:5), now he realizes that the humiliated one is, at the same time, the exalted one ('Personen', 27–8). The personal aspect of '*my* Lord and *my* God' indicates the intimacy of Thomas's saving relationship with Jesus (cf. Mary Magdalene's '*my* Lord' [20:13] and '*my* Teacher' [20:16] and Jesus' reply of '*your* Father and *your* God' [20:17]). Chennattu remarks that Thomas declares and accepts publicly the covenant God ('*my* God and *your* God') that Jesus announced to Mary in 20:17 (*Discipleship*, 166). However, Thomas addresses *Jesus* as his Lord and God. J.A. Glancy observes that Thomas's exclamation ascribes authority and sovereignty not to the one who imposed the marks (Pilate) but to the marked man (Jesus) ('Torture: Flesh, Truth, and the Fourth Gospel', *BibInt* 13 [2005]: 131–5). At a secondary level, Thomas's confession

deity is the christological climax of the entire gospel. Nowhere in the gospel is Jesus called 'God', except for the Prologue where John identifies the Logos as (being in nature) God (1:1).[11]

The Beatitude of Believing without Seeing

Jesus' response in 20:29 should be considered as a mild rebuke directed at Thomas and as an exhortation for later generations of believers to progress towards a belief that is less dependent on sight or signs (cf. our comments on 4:48 in ch. 11). Jesus cannot have been condemning the request for a sign, otherwise John's statement in 20:30–31 that he has recorded Jesus' signs in order to evoke belief would not make sense. Besides, in all three encounters with the risen Jesus in John 20, the characters do not perform ideally and need a tangible experience to confirm their faith.[12] Mary pursues an 'earthly' quest for Jesus, then mistakes Jesus for the gardener, and only recognizes him when he calls her by name. The disciples are behind locked doors, gripped by a fear of 'the Jews', when Jesus miraculously appears, showing them his scars and insufflating them with the Spirit. Thomas simply demands what the others got – a first-hand experience of the risen Jesus – and it is graciously granted to him. Considering John's stated purpose for writing his gospel in 20:31, Thomas's belief is certainly adequate.[13] Nevertheless, Jesus encourages people to adopt a different approach – one of belief without sight. In other words, a belief that is less dependent on sight or the tangible, and more on Jesus' word or a truthful eyewitness testimony, is more reliable and stable.[14]

counters Roman emperor worship, especially that of Domitian, who claimed divinity (Keener, *Gospel*, 1211–2; Köstenberger, *John*, 579–80).

[11] John's concept of 'God' takes on a binitarian form, in which Jesus, as the Son, is included in the Godhead (R. Bauckham, *God Crucified: Monotheism and Christology in the New Testament* [Carlisle: Paternoster, 1998], 25–42).

[12] Even the Beloved Disciple is portrayed ambiguously: the nature of his 'belief' in 20:8 is unclear, and even if it is resurrection faith, he does not testify and has no narrative impact (see ch. 21).

[13] Cf. Collins, 'Figures', 37–8. Contra Beck, who contends that Thomas's faith is inadequate because it requires seeing (*Discipleship*, 122–3). Bauckham perceptively comments that even the recommended believing that is not based on seeing is still based on the seeing and believing of reliable *eye*witnesses (*Jesus*, 367).

[14] Cf. Bennema, *Power*, 145–7. Barrett remarks that the contrast is not between seeing and touching, but between seeing, and believing apart from seeing, between Thomas who saw and later believers who did not (*Gospel*, 573). Brown comments that the comparison is not between seeing and not-seeing as such but between seeing and not-seeing *beyond the signs* offered as a means of faith (*Gospel*, 2:1050–51). Beirne's explains Jesus' contrasting reactions to Mary ('do not touch me') and Thomas ('touch me') as being responses to different stages of faith development (*Women*, 214). Maccini contends that 20:29 applies neither to Mary Magdalene nor to the disciples or to Thomas because none of them came to believe without seeing (*Testimony*, 225).

The real issue in the Thomas pericope is not simply the difficulty of believing that Jesus had risen but of believing *someone else's testimony* that Jesus had risen.[15] Thomas's struggle represents the struggle of subsequent generations to believe in the risen Jesus without having seen, to believe on the basis of other's testimony.[16] However, can Thomas, who was eventually granted a tangible experience of the risen Jesus, really be representative of future believers who have to believe without seeing? If adequate belief appears to require an authentic encounter with the risen Jesus (as the three instances in John 20 indicate), how can Jesus urge people to believe without seeing? I suggest that in the believer's testimony – whether oral or written (as is the case with John's gospel) – people can encounter the risen Jesus for themselves.

I have explained elsewhere that adequate belief is based on sensory perception followed by cognitive perception, in which sensory perception can refer to seeing Jesus and his signs (or to touching Jesus, as Thomas prefers), or to hearing Jesus' teaching.[17] After Jesus' departure from this world, appropriate belief should be based on his word rather than signs or sight. Nevertheless, sensory perception is still required as the first step – either by hearing Jesus' word (e.g. in preaching or testimony) or by 'seeing' Jesus' word (e.g. in reading John's gospel or the Bible). The believer's testimony is a valid basis for true faith because it is based on Jesus' teaching, informed and empowered by the Spirit, and expected to elicit belief (14:26; 15:26–27; 16:12–15; 17:20). To draw on 6:63 where Jesus states that his words are 'Spirit and life', the force of 17:20 is that the believer's words are 'Paraclete and life'. When people are confronted with the believer's Spirit-imbued testimony, they are essentially confronted with the life-giving words of Jesus himself. John's gospel, for instance, is the reliable Spirit-inspired *written* testimony of the Beloved Disciple, aimed at evoking adequate belief by providing an authentic encounter with the risen Jesus (19:35; 20:30–31; 21:24–25). Just as John records encounters of various characters with Jesus, the reader of this gospel can also encounter the risen Jesus – and reach adequate faith. As Thomas (and others) could have a tangible experience with the risen Lord, so future believers can encounter him through oral or written testimony to reach adequate faith.[18]

[15] K.S. O'Brien, 'Written That You May Believe: John 20 and Narrative Rhetoric', *CBQ* 67 (2005): 284.

[16] Cf. Lee, 'Partnership', 47–8.

[17] Bennema, *Power*, 126–33; *idem*, 'Christ', 115–20.

[18] Cf. O'Brien, who argues that the Gospel of John provides the possibility of a *substitute* experience of the risen Lord for the reader ('Written', 285, 296, 302). See also Bonney, *Caused To Believe*, 169–71; Bauckham, *Jesus*, 367, 405. The testimony of the other disciples to Thomas in 20:25 failed either because Thomas was unwilling to accept their testimony and/or because their testimony was not yet Spirit-empowered – in 20:22, the disciples had received the Spirit as salvation but not yet as the empowerment for mission since Jesus had not yet left (16:7) (see Bennema, 'Giving', 195–213). In contrast, the Samaritans believed on the basis of the woman's testimony (4:39).

Conclusion

Instead of a doubter or someone in two minds, we find a character who displays traits of courage, loyalty and discipleship (willing to lay down his life for his master) (11:16).[19] Nevertheless, Thomas misunderstands Jesus, but in that he is not unique. Thomas is a realist, displaying a down-to-earth, and sometimes sceptical, faith in Jesus. His realism or pragmatism essentially reveals a view 'from below', needing correction or improvement, which takes place in 20:24–28, where his faith eventually transforms into a climactic resurrection faith in Jesus as 'Lord and God'.[20]

Thomas represents the pragmatic person who needs a tangible or personal experience of Jesus in order to believe adequately but who is encouraged to progress towards a belief that is not completely dependent on such an experience of Jesus.[21] Thomas represents the struggle of later generations of believers who have not witnessed the resurrection of Jesus and must depend on other's testimony.[22] Future believers are encouraged to 'see', i.e. encounter, the risen Lord in the eyewitness account of John's gospel and believe (19:35; 20:30–31; 21:24).[23] Many people today may still identify with Thomas's demand to see and touch Jesus – and Jesus may still graciously grant such requests. However, they are encouraged to a steadier faith that is less dependent on the concrete, touchable and physical and more rooted in the trustworthy eyewitness testimony of John's gospel (and indeed the entire Bible as God's word) and the assurance of the indwelling presence of the Father and Son by means of the Spirit (14:23). The desire for a personal, sensory experience of Jesus is valid and natural (perhaps even essential for adequate faith), but people are encouraged to have this encounter through the oral testimony of other believers or the written testimony of the Bible's authors.[24]

[19] Contra Brodie, who sees doubt in Thomas wherever he occurs (*Gospel*, 570).

[20] Cf. Koester, who remarks that Thomas moves from scepticism to true faith (*Symbolism*, 72). Contra evaluations of Thomas as a depressed unbeliever (Beasley-Murray, *John*, 369), as sceptical, pessimistic, obstinate, 'the spokesman of apostolic doubt' (Brown, *Gospel*, 2:1024–33), or as unenlightened and ambiguous (J.H. Neyrey, *The Resurrection Stories* [Wilmington: Glazier, 1988], 78).

[21] Cf. Edwards, who describes Thomas as 'a model of a faith that grows but requires strong evidence' (*John*, 100). However, we disagree with Edwards that Thomas is set in contrast to the Beloved Disciple who believes without even seeing the risen Jesus (20:8) (see ch. 21). Culpepper describes Thomas as a realist who embraces the earthly Jesus but does not understand the risen Christ (*Anatomy*, 123–4). However, Thomas eventually does embrace the risen Jesus (20:28) – even though Jesus needs to help him (like the other disciples and Mary).

[22] Cf. Koester, *Symbolism*, 72.

[23] The 'we have seen his glory' (1:14) and 'we know that his [the Beloved Disciple's] testimony is true' (21:24) may also show the effectiveness of John's gospel as testimony for its readers/hearers (contra Bauckham, *Jesus*, 369–81, who argues that 'we' is a substitute for 'I' – the Beloved Disciple).

[24] Where this is not possible (such as in strict Muslim countries or where people are illiterate), we sometimes hear reports that people directly experience Jesus through visions.

Thomas		
Appearances	References	11:16; 14:5; 20:24; 20:26; 20:27; 20:28; 21:2
Identity	Titles given	Didymus or Twin
	Gender	male
	Age	–
	Marital status	–
	Occupation	–
	Socio-economic status	–
	Place of residence/operation	–
	Relatives	–
	Group affiliation	'the Twelve'
Speech and actions	In interaction with Jesus	misunderstanding, courage, commitment, belief, realism
	In interaction with others	disbelieves the other disciples' testimony (20:25)
Character classification	Complexity	little complex; multiple traits: courageous, loyal, realistic, misunderstanding/undiscerning, unbelieving, believing
	Development	none
	Inner life	none
Degree of characterization		type
Response to Jesus		eventually adequate belief

The Beloved Disciple – The Unique Eyewitness

'What you don't see with your eyes, don't witness with your mouth' — *Jewish proverb*

In the second half of the gospel, we meet a new character – 'the disciple whom Jesus loved' (13:23; 19:26; 20:2; 21:7, 20), better known as the Beloved Disciple. The Beloved Disciple is an enigmatic and intriguing character, and his network of relationships is complex. His presence in John 13 (presumably throughout John 13 – 17) and in John 21, and the constant companionship of Peter, would suggest that he was one of the Twelve or closely associated with them. The Beloved Disciple is also familiar with the high priest and facilitates Peter's entry into the courtyard (18:15–16).[1] Regarding Jesus' mother, although the Beloved Disciple may have met her as early as the wedding at Cana (we contend that the unnamed disciple in 1:35–40 is the Beloved Disciple), it is at the foot of the cross that he obtains a new relationship with her (19:26–27; cf. ch. 8). We now turn to the more significant relationships of the Beloved Disciple with Jesus and Peter, through which we learn most about his character and role.

The Beloved Disciple and Jesus

Jesus' relationship with the Beloved Disciple is defined by *love* and *intimacy*. Although Jesus loves all his disciples (13:1, 34), the Beloved Disciple is singled out as 'the disciple whom Jesus loved'. Besides, 13:23 describes the Beloved Disciple as reclining 'in the bosom' of Jesus. This phrase echoes 1:18, describing Jesus' being 'in the bosom' of the Father. It is a picture of intimacy. As the Father and Jesus have an intimate relationship character-ized by love (1:18; 3:35; 5:20; 14:31; 15:9), so the Beloved Disciple enjoys an

---

[1] The 'other' disciple in 18:15 is most likely the Beloved Disciple since 20:2 also mentions 'another' disciple, who is identified as the Beloved Disciple (again accompanied by Peter). Cf. Brown, *Gospel*, 2:822; Collins, 'Figures', 42; Beasley-Murray, *John*, 324; Quast, *Peter*, 76–81; R.A. Culpepper, *John, the Son of Zebedee: The Life of a Legend* (Columbia: University of South Carolina Press, 1994), 58. Bauckham does not think that 18:15 necessarily refers to the Beloved Disciple, but fails to consider 20:2 ('Beloved Disciple', 27, 34, 37).

especially close relationship with Jesus, which the other disciples apparently did not share – or not to the same extent.[2]

The Beloved Disciple is depicted as one who *follows* Jesus and *remains* with him.[3] In fact, he is present at key moments during Jesus' life. A good case can be made that the Beloved Disciple is the unnamed disciple in 1:35–40.[4] Having been a follower of John (the Baptist), he becomes one of the first followers of Jesus (at least in the Johannine narrative) and remains with him (1:37, 39). Later, when Jesus is arrested, the Beloved Disciple and Peter are the only disciples who follow him – the former is able to follow Jesus further than Peter since he knows the high priest (18:15).[5] Next, when Peter denies being a disciple of Jesus and stops following (temporarily) (18:15–27), the Beloved Disciple remains with Jesus as a true disciple. During Jesus' crucifixion, the Beloved Disciple is the only male disciple who sticks with Jesus (19:26; cf. 19:35). Perhaps this is the reason Jesus entrusts his mother into his care. After the resurrection, we find again that the Beloved Disciple follows Jesus, and Jesus makes an enigmatic statement about his continual remaining (21:20–22). It can hardly be a coincidence that the Beloved Disciple's first and last appearances are marked by the *inclusio* of the verbs 'follow' and 'remain' in 1:37–39 and 21:20, 22.

The Beloved Disciple is also *perceptive*. He probably perceives the significance of John's exclamation that Jesus is 'the Lamb of God' in 1:36, harking back to 1:29, because he and Andrew leave John and start following Jesus (1:37). Then, in reply to Jesus' summons 'come and you will see', he and Andrew investigate matters for themselves and remain with him (1:39). In 19:27, the Beloved Disciple grasps Jesus' directive since he immediately takes Jesus' mother in and cares for her. He is the first to recognize the risen Jesus when the disciples are out fishing (21:7). Although 20:7–8 also refers to the Beloved Disciple's perception, it is unclear what he comprehends. Most scholars contend that he reaches resurrection faith.[6] There are problems,

---

[2] Although Tovey (*Art*, 121) and Conway ('Ambiguity', 338) provide a corrective in stating that Jesus' love for the Beloved Disciple is neither exclusive nor unique since others also enjoyed Jesus' love (11:3, 5; 13:1), they overlook his being 'in Jesus' bosom' as being an exclusive and privileged position. Van Tilborg explains Jesus' intimate relationship with the Beloved Disciple against the backdrop of the classic philosophical ideal of the love between a teacher and his favourite disciple (*Love*, 77–103).

[3] In John, 'to follow' Jesus and 'remain' with him often denote following and remaining with him *as a disciple*.

[4] Brown, *Gospel*, 1:73; Bauckham, 'Beloved Disciple', 36; J.H. Charlesworth, *The Beloved Disciple: Whose Witness Validates the Gospel of John?* (Valley Forge: Trinity Press, 1995), 326–36; A.T. Lincoln, 'The Beloved Disciple as Eyewitness and the Fourth Gospel as Witness', *JSNT* 85 (2002): 15; Tovey, *Art*, 132. Tovey also draws attention to 15:27, where the Beloved Disciple is included in Jesus' words, implying that he must have been with Jesus from the beginning (*Art*, 133).

[5] Tovey notes that the Beloved Disciple has privileged access to both Jesus (13:23) and the high priest's house (18:15) (*Art*, 129).

[6] Bultmann, *Gospel*, 684; Brown, *Gospel*, 2:987; *idem*, 'The Resurrection in John 20 – A Series of Diverse Reactions', *Worship* 64 (1990): 197; Lindars, *Gospel*, 602; Schnackenburg, *Gospel*, 3:312; F.J. Matera, 'John 20:1–18', *Int* 43 (1989): 403; Moloney, *Gospel*, 520–21; Bauckham, 'Beloved

however, with this view. First, 20:9 provides a causal explanation for 20:(6–)8 – 'because they did not yet know (or, still did not know) the Scripture that he had to raise from the dead' – implying that the Beloved Disciple probably had not understood that Jesus has risen.[7] Second, if the Beloved Disciple believed that Jesus had risen, why did he not share this joyous news with Peter or the other disciples but simply return home (20:10)?[8] It is Mary Magdalene who brings the sensational news (20:17–18).[9] But if the Beloved Disciple's belief in 20:8 is not belief in Jesus' resurrection, then what is it? Some have suggested that he believes Mary Magdalene's report in 20:2 that Jesus' body has been taken away.[10] The weakness of this suggestion is the presence of the burial clothes in the tomb, for it seems unlikely that anyone would remove the wrappings and take a naked corpse. Charlesworth thus suggests that the Beloved Disciple believes that Jesus has gone to the Father, linking 20:8 back to 14:28–29.[11] Whichever way one interprets the Beloved Disciple's 'belief', the ambiguity in 20:8 causes some tension in his characterization.[12] Certainly in 13:24–29 the Beloved Disciple appears less than perceptive – while his special access to Jesus elicits further information, none of the disciples, including the Beloved Disciple himself, understands it.[13]

Disciple', 33, 38; Tovey, *Art*, 136; Beck, *Discipleship*, 116–7; Resseguie, *Strange Gospel*, 161. Quast contends that the Beloved Disciple reached resurrection faith but in the light of 20:9 this faith was not fully developed or formulated (*Peter*, 119). B. Byrne makes the best case for the Beloved Disciple's reaching resurrection faith ('The Faith of the Beloved Disciple and the Community in John 20', *JSNT* 23 [1985]: 83–97).

[7] Byrne explains 20:9 in that *up to now* (i.e. prior to seeing the evidence in 20:6–8) they had not understood the Scripture's witness that Jesus would rise from the dead ('Faith', 86, 89). However, the point is that *after* having seen the burial clothes, the Beloved Disciple and Peter *still* did not understand the Scripture's witness regarding Jesus' resurrection. Brown's view that, while the Beloved Disciple believed in Jesus' resurrection, 20:9 explains Peter's failure to understand ('Resurrection', 197–8) is untenable for the 'they' in 20:9 surely includes the Beloved Disciple. Others argue that even without the benefit of scriptural understanding, the Beloved Disciple believes nonetheless that Jesus has risen (Collins, 'Figures', 43; *idem*, 'John', 369 n. 35; Tovey, *Art*, 127). However, the Beloved Disciple's return home and the lack of indication that he shared his newfound belief with anyone leads us to understand that he did not believe that Jesus had risen. Besides, the point of 20:9 is most probably that he had not yet understood how *Old Testament* Scripture foretold Jesus' resurrection (cf. Matt. 16:21–23; 17:23; Luke 24:22–27).

[8] The Beloved Disciple has no narrative impact – his 'belief' affects no other character in the story – and his response falls short of authentic discipleship, which is to believe *and to testify* (Lee, 'Partnership, 39; O'Brien, 'Written', 296–7).

[9] It is even uncertain whether the disciples (including the Beloved Disciple) accepted Mary's report (cf. the locked doors and fear in 20:19). They may only have believed when they saw Jesus.

[10] Brown, *Gospel*, 987; Minear, 'John 20:2', 127–8; Conway, *Men and Women*, 191–2; *idem*, 'Ambiguity', 339; H.E. Hearon, *The Mary Magdalene Tradition: Witness and Counter-Witness in Early Christian Communities* (Collegeville: Liturgical Press, 2004), 164–5. Cf. Lee, 'Partnership', 39.

[11] Charlesworth, *Beloved Disciple*, 80–81. Cf. S.M. Schneiders, 'The Face Veil: A Johannine Sign (John 20:1–10)', *BTB* 13 (1983): 96–7.

[12] A statement that the Beloved Disciple reaches 'a resurrection faith in its purest state' (Collins, 'Figures', 43) is thus exaggerated.

[13] Conway, 'Ambiguity', 338; Beck, *Discipleship*, 113–4; Quast, *Peter*, 160–61; I. Dunderberg, 'The Beloved Disciple in John: Ideal Figure in an Early Christian Controversy', in *Fair Play:*

What then do we make of the Beloved Disciple being portrayed as especially close to Jesus, as perceptive, and remaining with Jesus as a loyal follower? Contra many scholars who assume that this characterization makes him the ideal disciple,[14] we contend that Bauckham has the better argument. According to him, John's gospel portrays the Beloved Disciple as *the ideal (eye)witness* to Jesus.[15] This needs clarification.[16] First, the Beloved Disciple makes an ideal eyewitness because he is loved by Jesus and enjoys a special position of intimacy. In 13:23–25, for example, his closeness allows him to draw out information from Jesus about the betrayer's identity. Second, the Beloved Disciple can be an ideal eyewitness because he is perceptive. Lincoln explains that the task of a witness is not so much to provide a 'factual', 'objective' account of events but to give a plausible account of past events that *reinterprets* those events, drawing out their *significance*, in order to persuade the readers of his perspective.[17] This would require the witness be perceptive. Third, the Beloved Disciple can be an ideal eyewitness because he is present at key moments in Jesus' ministry. He is present at the start of Jesus' ministry (1:29–39) and at the final meal and hence a recipient of Jesus' private instructions in John 14 – 17. He also witnesses Jesus' arrest, trial and crucifixion (18:15–16; 19:26–27, 19:35),[18] and is one of the first to arrive at Jesus' tomb on resurrection day (20:2–10). Finally, he witnesses the miraculous catch of fish, Peter's restoration and commission, and continues to remain with Jesus (21:7, 20–22). In sum, the Beloved Disciple is an ideal and unique eyewitness to Jesus' ministry because he enjoys a privileged position, is perceptive, and remains with Jesus from the start in 1:29 to the end in 21:22.[19]

Diversity and Conflicts in Early Christianity. Essays in Honour of Heikki Räisänen (ed. I. Dunderberg, C. Tuckett, and K. Syreeni; NovTSup 103; Leiden: Brill, 2002), 260. Even if the Beloved Disciple has special knowledge, he never (neither in 13:28 nor in 20:10) communicates it to others, except in 21:7 (Conway, *Men and Women*, 181–4, 189–90).

[14] E.g. Culpepper, *Anatomy*, 123; Collins, 'Figures', 45; *idem*, 'John', 367; Beck, 'Function', 153; Davies, *Rhetoric*, 341, 344; Tolmie, *Farewell*, 138.

[15] Bauckham, 'Beloved Disciple', 33–39. For a more extensive argument, see his *Jesus*, chs 14–15.

[16] Although the following argument is my own, I have been influenced by Bauckham, *Jesus*, 396–9.

[17] Lincoln, 'Beloved Disciple', 21; *idem*, *Truth*, 369–7.

[18] Most scholars contend that the eyewitness in 19:35 is the Beloved Disciple rather than, for instance, the soldier who pierced Jesus' side (Bauckham, 'Beloved Disciple', 39–40; Lincoln, 'Beloved Disciple', 12–4).

[19] Cf. Bauckham, 'Beloved Disciple', 28–32; *idem*, *Jesus*, 390–93; Lincoln, 'Beloved Disciple', 15–6; Resseguie, *Strange Gospel*, 155–63. Dunderberg characterizes the Beloved Disciple as the one who reliably documents and transmits Jesus' revelation of the Father to the audience of the gospel ('Beloved Disciple', 257–9). Similarly, S. Brown contends that the Beloved Disciple is the interpreter *par excellence* ('The Beloved Disciple: A Jungian View', in *The Conversation Continues: Studies in Paul and John* [ed. R.T. Fortna and B.R. Gaventa; Nashville: Abingdon, 1990], 376). To add a qualification, although the Beloved Disciple interprets the events to which he was a unique witness and draws out their significance, he writes his gospel from a

We must also determine how the Beloved Disciple responds to Jesus. Although we do not read of an explicit belief-response to Jesus, it is implied. First, he must have understood something when John called Jesus 'the Lamb of God (who takes away the sins of the world)' (1:29, 36), and perhaps the significance of the event in 1:29–34, since he leaves John and joins Jesus. Second, his following and remaining with Jesus are indicative of his discipleship. Indeed, he remains with Jesus even in difficult circumstances like the trial and crucifixion, which is a belief-response in itself. Third, the aim of testimony is to evoke belief (1:7; 17:20; 19:35), and this gospel, a written account of the Beloved Disciple's eyewitness testimony, also aims to produce belief (20:31). In which case, the Beloved Disciple must surely have done what he persuades his readers to do, namely believe in Jesus as the Messiah, the Son of God in order to partake in the divine life. In fact, this gospel *is* the belief-response of the Beloved Disciple.

The Beloved Disciple as Author or Source?

Having suggested that the Beloved Disciple is the ideal eyewitness to Jesus' ministry, we must now consider whether he is the author of this gospel or its authoritative source. Bauckham, in his early writings, makes a convincing case for the Beloved Disciple as the *author* of the gospel. First, he argues that according to 21:23, the Johannine school knew very well who the Beloved Disciple was. Second, 21:24–25 comes from the hand of a later editor, who speaks for himself in 21:25 and for the Johannine school in 21:24. Third, in 21:24, this editor distinguishes both himself and the Johannine school from the author of the gospel, who is identified as the Beloved Disciple to whom 21:22–23 refers. Fourth, 21:24 alludes to 19:35, with the difference that in 19:35 the author himself vouches for the truth of what he has seen, whereas in 21:24 the Johannine school vouches for the truth of his witness.[20]

Lincoln, however, based on his analysis of 21:24, argues that the Beloved Disciple is the authoritative *source* for the Johannine narrative. Understanding the Beloved Disciple's eyewitness as a literary device incorporated into the cosmic trial motif, Lincoln concludes that this device provides 'verisimili- tude and authoritative support for the writer's distinctive overall perspective on the significance of Jesus'. By clarifying that the Beloved Disciple is the trustworthy source of his gospel, the author adds to its reliability.[21] However,

post-Easter perspective in which *the Spirit* is the interpreter *par excellence* who guides him 'into all truth' (Bennema, *Power*, 228–34).

[20] Bauckham, 'Beloved Disciple', 28–31. Bauckham now argues that 21:23–25 is also written by the Beloved Disciple, whereby the 'we' in 21:24 is not a genuine plural but the 'we' of authoritative testimony which can be substituted by 'I' (*Jesus*, 364–81). Although we are not entirely persuaded by his later argument, his overall case for the Beloved Disciple's authorship remains convincing.

[21] Lincoln, 'Beloved Disciple', 3–26 (quotation from p. 19). Others who contend that the Beloved Disciple is the source for this gospel are Beasley-Murray, *John*, 415; Culpepper, *John*, 66, 71–2;

regarding 21:24, '[t]he meaning of *grapsas* [he has written] cannot plausibly be so extended as to make the beloved disciple less than the author'.[22] In sum, the Johannine narrative claims that the Beloved Disciple is (i) the ideal eyewitness (both Bauckham and Lincoln agree on this), and (ii) the author (with Bauckham contra Lincoln).[23]

Before closing, the gospel thus identifies the Beloved Disciple as its reliable eyewitness and author (21:24–25). John 21:24 parallels 19:35, reiterating that the Beloved Disciple is an eyewitness to the things written in this gospel. Lincoln's argument could help explain why 21:24–25 is added. By vouching for the truth of what the Beloved Disciple has written (in the light of 21:25, 'these things' in 21:24 probably refers to everything that the Beloved Disciple has witnessed[24]), the editor, on behalf of his community, endorses the reliability of the Beloved Disciple's witness. This increases the probability that his readers will accept his gospel as a true and trustworthy account of Jesus' life and come to believe in him. We also recall that the purpose of bearing witness is to evoke belief (1:7; 17:20; 20:31).[25] John 21:25 parallels 20:30, clarifying that this gospel is a selective (rather than an exhaustive) account of Jesus' life. The editor thus skillfully connects 21:24–25 with 19:35 and 20:30 (and 20:31 is nearby): stressing the authenticity of the Beloved Disciple's testimony on which this gospel is based, the editor implicitly urges the readers to accept the truth claim of this gospel, so that they may receive eternal life.

The Beloved Disciple and Peter

The Gospel of John portrays an enigmatic relationship between the Beloved Disciple and Peter (cf. ch. 6). In all passages featuring the Beloved Disciple, except for 19:26–27, Peter is also present, and their interaction points to some sort of rivalry, in which the Beloved Disciple outclasses Peter. First, the Beloved Disciple has a closer relationship with Jesus than Peter (13:23–25). Second, he is able to follow Jesus further than Peter (18:15–16).[26] Third, Peter

---

Charlesworth, *Beloved Disciple*, 24–6, 46; Moloney, *Gospel*, 561; Conway, *Men and Women*, 185. Surprisingly, Lincoln does not interact with Bauckham's work.

[22] Bauckham, 'Beloved Disciple', 29; cf. *idem*, *Jesus*, 358–63. Contra Tovey, who remarks that *grapsas* might mean that this witness '*caused* the narrative to be written rather than that he wrote it himself' (*Art*, 142 [emphasis added]; cf. Barrett, *Gospel*, 119). Bauckham remarks that even if 21:24 meant 'had it written by a secretary', the author using an amanuensis would still be the author.

[23] Others who contend that the Beloved Disciple is the author are Carson, *Gospel*, 683–5; Keener, *Gospel*, 83–112. Tovey is equivocal (*Art*, 138–43).

[24] Cf. Lincoln, 'Beloved Disciple', 10–11; Tovey, *Art*, 133; Bauckham, *Jesus*, 362.

[25] Just as the disciples' verbal testimony aims to evoke belief (17:20), so too does the Beloved Disciple's written testimony (20:31).

[26] There are significant parallels between 10:1–18 and 18:15–16: (i) the Greek word for 'courtyard' in 18:15 is used in 10:1, 16 to translate 'sheepfold'; (ii) in both accounts, there is a

denies Jesus and stops following (18:17–27), whereas the Beloved Disciple remains with Jesus (19:26–27, 35). Fourth, he outruns Peter on the way to the tomb (20:4).[27] Fifth, the Beloved Disciple proves more perceptive than Peter (20:8; 21:7).[28]

The 'rivalry' between Peter and the Beloved Disciple is most apparent towards the end of the gospel. After Jesus restores and commissions Peter for his mission, Peter notices the Beloved Disciple following them (21:15–20). Seeing him, Peter asks Jesus about his destiny, to which Jesus replies that it is none of Peter's business (21:21–22). Jesus' answer implies that there is no place for rivalry in his mission.[29] Bauckham perceptively remarks that the Beloved Disciple is already doing ('following' [21:20]), as he has done throughout the gospel, what Peter is now commanded to do ('follow me' [21:22]).[30]

Contra scholars who contend that the relationship between Peter and the Beloved Disciple presents a tension in John's own time, we suggest that the seeming rivalry between Peter and the Beloved Disciple arises from their having complementary rather than competitive roles. Although Peter may perceive himself to be in competition with the Beloved Disciple, Jesus' reprimand in 21:22 indicates that there is no place for such an attitude. While the Beloved Disciple is the paradigm of a loyal and credible witness to Jesus, Peter functions as an example of self-sacrifice in following Jesus. Peter is appointed as the 'chief under-shepherd'[31] of Jesus' flock and exemplifies sacrificial love in following Jesus and eventually laying down his life for him, while the Beloved Disciple is depicted as the perceptive witness, who is intimate with Jesus and present at key moments in Jesus' life.[32] Both the Beloved Disciple and Peter thus function as paradigms of discipleship, highlighting different characteristics of a true follower of Jesus.

---

gate and a gatekeeper (10:1–3, 7, 9; 18:16). The significance of the allusion to John 10 is that the Beloved Disciple, contra Peter, is depicted as the true or ideal disciple. The former can freely go in and out and stay close to Jesus (cf. 10:9), whereas Peter has to remain at the gate and can only get in with the help of the Beloved Disciple.

[27] Byrne's suggestion that the greater speed of the Beloved Disciple reflects a greater degree of love for Jesus ('Faith', 86) is without warrant.

[28] S.M. Schneiders' comments that 21:7 indicates the Beloved Disciple's role of proclamation in the community of disciples (whereas Peter's role is that of mission), and that John reaffirms the priority of love as the basis of the Beloved Disciple's spiritual insight ('John 21:1–14', *Int* 43 [1989]: 71, 73) are far-fetched.

[29] In his attempt to demonstrate that the focus of John 21 is steadily on Peter, Wiarda seemingly downplays the comparison between the Beloved Disciple and Peter ('John 21.1–23', 66, 68).

[30] Bauckham, 'Beloved Disciple', 35.

[31] The term is coined by Bauckham, 'Beloved Disciple', 38–9.

[32] Even the Beloved Disciple 'lays down his life' in a sense because in 21:23–24 he gives up his immortality as a character in the story and emerges as the author of the book – he dies a literary death in that he is killed by his own narration (Brant, *Dialogue*, 200).

The Identity of the Beloved Disciple

The sheer number of hypotheses aimed at solving the issue of the Beloved Disciple's identity prevents any detailed discussion. We will therefore consider a selection of arguments.[33] We contend that the Beloved Disciple was a real, historical figure rather than a fictional character.[34] However, the historicity of the Beloved Disciple does not preclude his being idealized in the interests of portraying him as ideally qualified to be the unique eyewitness or author.[35] Nevertheless, even if he has been idealized, this has not been exaggerated to make him perfect: (i) 13:28 indicates that even he did not understand Jesus' comment; and (ii) 20:8 is ambiguous about the nature of the Beloved Disciple's 'belief'.[36] We shall now consider some of the internal and external evidence.

Internal evidence. It seems that the author deliberately keeps the Beloved Disciple anonymous in the gospel.[37] By implication the Beloved Disciple cannot be any named disciple in the gospel – why would he be named at times and at other times simply be referred to as 'the disciple whom Jesus loved'? This would rule out any identification with, for example, Thomas,[38] Nathanael,[39] or Lazarus.[40] Nonetheless, while the gospel may use the literary device of anonymity, it does not want to conceal the identity of the Beloved Disciple. Whether 21:23 comes from the hand of an editor or from the author, it is clear that some of the first readers knew who the Beloved Disciple was. This does not imply, however, that *we* can know who he is. Besides, the title 'according to John' was probably included in the gospel from the outset, thereby strengthening the argument that some of the first

---

[33] For an extensive overview of scholars' suggestions, see Charlesworth, *Beloved Disciple*, 127–224. Other, less persuasive, proposals for the identity of the Beloved Disciple have not won much support: Matthias of Acts 1:15–26 (E.L. Titus, 'The Identity of the Beloved Disciple', *JBL* 69 [1950]: 323–8); the antitype of Benjamin of Deut. 33:12 (P.S. Minear, 'The Beloved Disciple in the Gospel of John', *NovT* 19 [1977]: 105–23). Cf. Culpepper, who sees the Beloved Disciple as the embodiment of the Paraclete – the Spirit-filled perceptive witness (*Anatomy*, 122–3; *John*, 84–5).

[34] Contra Bultmann, *Gospel*, 484–5; Davies, *Rhetoric*, 341, 344.

[35] Cf. Hengel, *Question*, 78–80; Bauckham, 'Beloved Disciple', 23

[36] For the Beloved Disciple as less than ideal/perfect, see esp. O'Brien, 'Written', 296–301.

[37] Bauckham, *Jesus*, 415.

[38] Contra Charlesworth, *Beloved Disciple*. For a critique of Charlesworth's position, see Beck, *Discipleship*, 127–31.

[39] Contra D. Catchpole, 'The Beloved Disciple and Nathanael', in *Understanding, Studying and Reading: New Testament Essays in Honour of John Ashton* (ed. C. Rowland and C.H.T. Fletcher-Louis; JSNTS 153; Sheffield: SAP, 1998), 69–92.

[40] Contra F.V. Filson, 'Who Was the Beloved Disciple?', *JBL* 68 (1949): 83–8; Stibbe, *Storyteller*, 78–80; Waetjen, *Gospel*, 57–60, 277, 280, 412. Lazarus is an attractive candidate: (i) he is the only man named as the object of Jesus' love in John's gospel (11:3, 5, 36); (ii) if Lazarus belongs to 'the Jews' (see ch. 19), it readily explains his connection with the high priest in 18:15; (iii) it would explain his knowledge of Jerusalem. For a critique, see Tovey, *Art*, 123–4; Beck, *Discipleship*, 109–10; Keener, *Gospel*, 86.

audience knew this John.[41] We also believe that Martin convincingly demonstrates that a character's anonymity in Graeco-Roman antiquity indicates his or her familiarity with the first readers.[42]

The appearance of the Beloved Disciple in 21:7 strongly suggests that he is one of the disciples mentioned in 21:2. Therefore, he must either be one of the two unnamed disciples or one of the sons of Zebedee. In chapter 14, I suggested that the two unnamed disciples could be Andrew and Philip because if the disciples they found (Peter and Nathanael) are present, then perhaps their finders are too. This would mean that the Beloved Disciple could be John the son of Zebedee.[43] Although the Beloved Disciple need not belong to the Twelve, if we consider his privileged and intimate relationship with Jesus (13:23) and his 'rivalry' with Peter, it seems likely that he is one of the Twelve. Besides, while John's gospel reveals a circle of disciples beyond the Twelve, in John 13 – 17 perhaps only the Twelve are present – there is no indication that even exemplary disciples such as the Samaritan woman, the man born blind, Lazarus or Mary Magdalene are included.[44]

External evidence. Although external evidence of the second century identifies John, a disciple of Jesus, as the author of the gospel, it is unclear which John is in view – John of Zebedee or John the Elder. The apostolic father Papias (70–155 CE) refers to two Johns – John (of Zebedee) and John the Elder – both of whom were the Lord's disciples (*Fragments of Papias* 1 and 6; cf. Eusebius, *Ecclesiastical History* 3.39.4), leading to some confusion.[45] Keener argues that Papias refers twice to the same John, who was still alive, and hence John the Elder is John of Zebedee.[46] However, most scholars contend that Papias refers to two distinct Johns. Charles Hill argues that Papias identifies John of Zebedee as the author of the gospel (Eusebius,

[41] Hengel, *Question*, 74–6; Tovey, *Art*, 118; R. Bauckham, 'Papias and Polycrates on the Origin of the Fourth Gospel', *JTS* 44 (1993): 65; *idem, Jesus*, 300–305, 415.

[42] Martin, 'Epithet', 63–73.

[43] Bauckham objects to such an argument. He argues that the Beloved Disciple has remained anonymous throughout the gospel, and this convention is not expected to be breached in 21:2, so the Beloved Disciple must be one of the two unnamed disciples. Moreover, if the unnamed disciple in 1:35–40 is the Beloved Disciple, John son of Zebedee, the presence of John *without* his brother James would be more surprising than the absence of John ('Beloved Disciple', 25). However, 21:2, 7 may not be an intentional attempt to reveal the Beloved Disciple's identity; the author perhaps felt safe enough to mention himself in the list of names in 21:2. Regarding 1:35–40, if Andrew appeared on his own and later found his brother Peter, the Beloved Disciple could have done likewise.

[44] Cf. the Synoptics, which only present the twelve disciples at the final meal (Matt. 26:20; Mark 14:17; Luke 22:14), and there is no indication that John deviated from this tradition. Others, however, contend that the Beloved Disciple was not one of the Twelve (Hengel, *Question*, 124–6; Bauckham, 'Beloved Disciple', 24; *idem, Jesus*, 402–3, 412–4). Cf. P. Parker, who provides twenty-one reasons why John of Zebedee is not the author of the gospel ('John the Son of Zebedee and the Fourth Gospel', *JBL* 81 [1962]: 35–43).

[45] Cf. Bauckham's extensive discussion of this passage (*Jesus*, 15–21).

[46] Keener, *Gospel*, 96–8. Cf. Hengel, *Question*, 127–32.

Ecclesiastical History 3.24.5–13), but this is disputed by Bauckham.[47] Based on evidence from Papias, Polycrates and Irenaeus, Bauckham argues that John the Elder, a Jerusalem disciple of Jesus but not one of the Twelve, is the Beloved Disciple.[48] The fact that the author of 2–3 John identifies himself as 'the elder' (2 John 1; 3 John 1) raises the possibility that the same author is behind the gospel. We wonder, however, whether Papias's first John – the son of Zebedee – could be the Beloved Disciple, as Eusebius himself claims (*Ecclesiastical History* 3.39.5–7), although, admittedly, this view has not won much support. Nevertheless, when Irenaeus (e.g. *Against Heresies* 3.1.1) and Eusebius speak of John the disciple/apostle of the Lord, often in a context where others from among the Twelve are mentioned, it seems natural to think of John son of Zebedee.

What then shall we conclude? First, we must realize that this gospel primarily emphasizes the *function* of the Beloved Disciple within the Johannine narrative (as the reliable eyewitness to Jesus) rather than his identity. The most important contribution of the Beloved Disciple has been the writing of this gospel where his testimony has been carefully preserved.[49] Second, we suggest that the external evidence allows for the possibility that the Beloved Disciple is either John the son of Zebedee or John the Elder, but that the internal evidence favours an identification with the former.[50] The difficulty, however, would be to explain how a Galilean fisherman is familiar with the high priest and has an extensive knowledge of Jerusalem. The most viable alternative is that the Beloved Disciple is John the Elder, a Jerusalem Jew but not one of the Twelve, a hypothesis best defended by Bauckham.[51] The difficulty of this position would be in explaining satisfactorily how the Beloved Disciple, while not one of the Twelve, enjoyed the most privileged position of all – 'in Jesus' bosom'.

Lincoln, who deals less with issues of historicity, does not try to decipher the identity of the Beloved Disciple. Believing that the Beloved Disciple remains an anonymous figure throughout the narrative, Lincoln argues that the emphasis of the Gospel of John as witness is on the written text and the community that acknowledges its truth rather than on the figure of the Beloved Disciple.[52] Although the testimony of the Beloved Disciple (in the form of this gospel) is more important than his identity, we nevertheless

---

[47] C.E. Hill, 'What Papias Said about John (and Luke): A "New" Papian Fragment', *JTS* 49 (1998): 582–629, and Bauckham's critique in *Jesus*, 433–7.

[48] Bauckham, *Jesus*, chs 16–17. Bauckham suggests that the two unnamed disciples in 21:2 may be Aristion and John the Elder mentioned by Papias (Eusebius, *Ecclesiastical History* 3.39.4) (*Jesus*, 419).

[49] Cf. Bauckham, *Jesus*, 367–8, 388.

[50] Cf. Carson, *Gospel*, 68–81; Keener, *Gospel*, 82–104; Köstenberger, *John*, 6–8. While Brown and Schnackenburg once held that the Beloved Disciple was John of Zebedee, they later abandoned this position (Brown, *Community*, 33–4; Schnackenburg, *Gospel*, 3:383–7).

[51] Bauckham, 'Papias', 24–69; *idem*, *Jesus*, chs 16–17.

[52] Lincoln, 'Beloved Disciple', 22–4. Tovey also argues that the Beloved Disciple is intentionally kept anonymous (*Art*, 124).

believe that Bauckham is correct in insisting that the first recipients of this gospel certainly knew the identity of the Beloved Disciple, otherwise 21:23 would not make sense.[53] Although Bauckham agrees with Lincoln that the identity of the Beloved Disciple cannot be discovered on the basis of internal evidence, contra Lincoln, he believes that the external evidence points to John the Elder.[54]

Conclusion

The Beloved Disciple functions as the ideal eyewitness to Jesus, and his testimony has been secured in the form of this gospel. He qualifies for this role because (i) he was intimate with Jesus and enjoyed a privileged position within the group of disciples; (ii) he was ready to follow and stick with Jesus; and (iii) he was present at key moments in Jesus' life. In short, he was a loyal, perceptive and credible eyewitness. However, while the Beloved Disciple enjoys a privileged status and appears an ideal disciple, the reader may be surprised that twice he 'falters' – a lack of understanding in 13:28 and an indeterminate 'belief' in 20:8.

The identity of the Beloved Disciple remains a debatable (and perhaps irresolvable) issue. Although we tentatively propose that John of Zebedee is the most likely candidate, John the Elder is a serious contender. Besides, we must bear in mind that the Beloved Disciple's role as eyewitness to Jesus and as author of this gospel is most important. Nevertheless, while the Beloved Disciple is depicted as the *unique* eyewitness – his role has become redundant since we have his legacy in the form of this gospel – he still functions as an exemplary disciple for later believers to emulate. For example, believers can be encouraged to develop an intimate relationship with Jesus, to remain with him, and to be perceptive about how God works in this world.

[53] Bauckham, 'Beloved Disciple', 29.

[54] Beck argues that the Beloved Disciple's anonymity erases the identity distinction of the name and instead enables the reader to fill the identity gaps in the narrative with her or his own identity, entering and accepting the paradigm of discipleship that the Beloved Disciple presents. Beck explains the reader's identification with the Beloved Disciple as being able to experience the risen Jesus through the anonymous Beloved Disciple ('Function', 147, 154–5; *Discipleship*, 135–6). However, the ability of experiencing the risen Jesus is not so much due to the Beloved Disciple's *anonymity* which supposedly draws the reader into a psychological experience of 'myself in the other' but due to his being an *eyewitness* to Jesus and having written it down. In fact, we have argued in chapter 20 that a personal experience of the risen Jesus occurs through the reading of the gospel.

Beloved Disciple		
Appearances	References	13:23; 19:26; 20:2; 21:7, 20
Identity	Titles given	'the disciple whom Jesus loved'
	Gender	male
	Age	–
	Marital status	–
	Occupation	perhaps a fisherman (if he is John of Zebedee)
	Socio-economic status	
	Place of residence/operation	
	Relatives	James his brother (if the Beloved Disciple is John of Zebedee)
	Group affiliation	the Twelve, mother of Jesus, high priest
Speech and actions	In interaction with Jesus	intimate, loyal, principal witness
	In interaction with others	outclasses Peter, takes care of Jesus' mother
Character classification	Complexity	uncomplicated; multiple traits: perceptive, loyal, credible
	Development	little (occasionally he is less than ideal)
	Inner life	none
Degree of characterization		type
Response to Jesus		adequate (his gospel is the ultimate belief-response)

Pilate – Securing a Hollow Victory

'Victory is by nature insolent and haughty' — *Marcus T. Cicero*

Pontius Pilate was Rome's representative in Judaea from 26 till 36/37 CE. Although Pilate is given no title in John's gospel, other sources designate him as 'procurator' (a financial officer of a province; Josephus, *Jewish War* 2:169; Philo, *Embassy to Gaius* 1:299), 'prefect' (a military commander; according to an inscription at Caesarea, discovered in 1961), and 'governor' (a generic title for a leader; Matt. 27:2; Luke 3:1; Josephus, *Antiquities* 18:55). As Rome's appointed agent in Judaea, Pilate was in charge of the Roman auxiliary troops, stationed in Caesarea (Galilee) with a detachment (one cohort) in Jerusalem. Although his headquarters were in Caesarea, he sometimes stayed in Jerusalem (e.g. during the Passover to ensure order). Pilate had the final say on cases of capital punishment, and could reverse death sentences that the Sanhedrin submitted to him for ratification. Pilate's verdict was legally binding and he was only accountable to the emperor.

Pilate has been variously characterized: from being weak, indecisive and accommodating to being tough, cruel and prone to flaunting his authority. This may be due to the seemingly disparate representations of Pilate in the Gospels (pathetic or sympathetic) and in Philo and Josephus (strong and able).[1] The writings of Josephus and Philo make it evident that Pilate did not like or understand the Jews. Although Pilate appears to have been a relatively competent governor, he provoked the Jews on various occasions. However, he may have done so unintentionally, being ignorant about and insensitive to the rigorous Jewish customs and laws. In his conflicts with the Jews, Pilate could stubbornly and wilfully resist the Jews but also give in – especially when his loyalty to the emperor was questioned. He could be decisive but also be non-committal, use brute force or show restraint.[2] We shall therefore examine whether the Johannine Pilate is indeed weak, indecisive and accommodating or more in keeping with the Pilate in Philo and Josephus.

---

[1] B.C. McGing, 'Pontius Pilate and the Sources', *CBQ* 53 (1991): 416–7; H.K. Bond, *Pontius Pilate in History and Interpretation* (SNTSMS 100; Cambridge: CUP, 1998), 174–5; Conway, 'Ambiguity', 333; Dunn, *Jesus*, 774–5.

[2] See especially McGing, 'Pilate', 416–38; Bond, *Pilate*, chs 2–3.

Jesus' Trial before Pilate

Since Pilate was the Roman prefect or procurator of Judaea, Jesus' trial in 18:28 – 19:16a is a trial before the Roman authorities, the greatest power of the then-known 'civilized' world. In line with the universal scope of John's gospel, Jesus' trial must unfold on the world stage because he was sent into the world and his saving act on the cross will have cosmic consequences. Structurally, this episode consists of seven rounds with Pilate moving in and out of his palace with each round. In rounds one, three, five and seven, Pilate comes *out of* his palace to interact with 'the Jews' (18:29; 18:38b; 19:4; 19:13); in rounds two, four and six, he goes *into* his palace to interact with Jesus (18:33; 19:1; 19:9).[3] We must examine whether the structure of the passage holds any significance.

Round One (18:28–32). While presenting Jesus to Pilate, 'the Jews' do not enter the palace since that would render them ritually unclean and disqualify them from participating in the Passover meal (18:28). Ironically, their actions concerning Jesus make them spiritually 'unclean' and prevent them from partaking in the real Passover meal on the cross (cf. 1:29; 6:51–55). When Pilate comes out to inquire about the charges (18:29), his question is surprising since he must have known why 'the Jews' bring Jesus to him.[4] The Roman cohort could only have been present at Jesus' arrest (18:3) with Pilate's consent, implying that 'the Jews' had contacted Pilate earlier and probably informed him about their scheme to kill Jesus (cf. 11:47–53).[5] The reply of 'the Jews' that Jesus is an evildoer is not a legal charge and reveals some of their perplexity about Pilate's question (18:30). Pilate does not, however, humour 'the Jews', and, knowing that they want Jesus' death, he taunts them, flaunting his authority (18:31).[6]

Round Two (18:33–38a). Entering his palace, Pilate asks Jesus whether he is the king of the Jews (18:33). Pilate's question reveals he had contact with 'the Jews' prior to Jesus' arrest, when they probably told him that Jesus claimed to be a king – a political charge of insurrection against Rome (cf. 19:12). This explains Jesus' counterquestion in 18:34, but Pilate is quick to distance himself from 'the Jews' (18:35). Pilate may have assisted 'the Jews' to arrest Jesus – any potential insurrection would need to be investigated – but he does not side with them and probably wants to examine the case for

---

[3] Many scholars have observed this structure. For an alternative structure, see C.H. Giblin, 'John's Narration of the Hearing before Pilate (John 18,28 – 19,16a)', *Bib* 67 (1986): 221–4. John's mention of the *praetorium* in 18:28 may well have been Herod's palace, adjacent to the temple.

[4] It is unclear whether Pilate's coming out indicates that he is forced from the beginning to comply with the demands of 'the Jews' (Culpepper, *Anatomy*, 142) or whether he shows tact and courtesy (Bond, *Pilate*, 175).

[5] Cf. Bond, *Pilate*, 167.

[6] Some claim that John is historically inaccurate in 18:31b since there is enough evidence that the Sanhedrin had the authority to hand down death sentences in case of offences against Jewish religious law prior to 70 CE (e.g. T. Horvath, 'Why Was Jesus Brought to Pilate?', *NovT* 11 [1969]: 176–9).

himself.[7] Going back to Pilate's earlier question about kingship, Jesus asserts that his kingdom is not from this world (18:36). This is a political statement because Jesus acknowledges that he has a kingdom – and hence is a king – and although his kingdom is 'from above' it exists and operates *in* this world. Besides, it is impossible to be loyal to both Jesus and his kingdom, and to the Roman emperor and his empire.[8] Although in Greek Pilate's question in 18:37 expects the answer 'yes', he has probably concluded that Jesus' kingdom is not a threat to Rome and hence his statement seems condescending, 'You are a king then!'[9] Perhaps knowing that Pilate searches for truth, Jesus extends an implicit invitation to discover truth – saving truth about the divine reality present in Jesus' teaching.[10] Pilate's 'What is truth?' is not an earnest question (for he leaves immediately) but a dismissive remark, indicating that he does not take Jesus seriously and is probably irritated with Jesus' responses and his own lack of success in cracking the case. Not understanding Jesus, Pilate implicitly rejects him and his invitation.

Round Three (18:38b–40). Coming out of his palace, Pilate informs 'the Jews' that the charges against Jesus are baseless (18:38b). Although Pilate appears honest, he is also taunting 'the Jews'. This becomes more evident in 18:39 where Pilate, by referring to Jesus as 'the king of the Jews', is most likely mocking 'the Jews' about their nationalistic hopes. He does not seriously seek Jesus' release. If he had seriously considered Jesus a king, he would never have offered to release him.[11] Pilate has known since before Jesus' arrest that 'the Jews' want Jesus' death (cf. 18:31) – and he uses this knowledge to taunt 'the Jews' and flaunt his authority. In desperation and frustration, 'the Jews' shout out not to release Jesus (18:40).

Round Four (19:1–3). Pilate, though not convinced that Jesus poses a threat to Rome, resorts to cruel and calculated measures to extract truth from Jesus (19:1). Glancy makes a good case for understanding the scourging as an act of judicial rather than punitive torture, a means of interrogation to extract truth.[12] Pilate may not know the truth (cf. 18:38a), but he thinks he can get it out of Jesus: using a *mastix*, a whip studded with lumps of bone or metal, Pilate has Jesus tortured in order to extract a confession.[13]

---

[7] Contra W. Carter who contends that Pilate has allied himself with 'the Jews' to remove Jesus (*Pontius Pilate: Portraits of a Roman Governor* [Collegeville: Liturgical Press, 2003], 141–2).

[8] Cf. Bennema, 'Sword', 54–7; *idem, John's Gospel*, 198–9.

[9] Cf. B.D. Ehrman, 'Jesus' Trial before Pilate: John 18:28 – 19:16', *BTB* 13 (1983): 128; T.W. Gillespie, 'The Trial of Politics and Religion: John 18:28 – 19:16', *Ex Auditu* 2 (1986): 71.

[10] For the concept of saving truth, see Bennema, *Power*, 121–2; *idem*, 'Christ', 114.

[11] Cf. Bond, *Pilate*, 181–2.

[12] Glancy, 'Torture', 107–36. Most scholars perceive the scourging to be punitive torture, aimed to inflict pain as punishment (e.g. Barrett, *Gospel*, 539; Culpepper, *Anatomy*, 142; Rensberger, *World*, 93; cf. the scholars mentioned by Glancy, 'Torture', 121–2 n. 48), but this is unlikely in the *middle* of the interrogation. Convinced that the scourging is punitive and hence should come after the trial is over, Lindars concludes that John is unhistorical and has deliberately displaced this scene (*Gospel*, 553–4, 563–4).

[13] Glancy, 'Torture', 121–2.

Round Five (19:4–7). Pilate is now convinced that there is no real case and that Jesus is innocent (19:4; cf. 18:38), but he also knows that 'the Jews' are determined to have Jesus killed. For those who view the scourging as a punishment, the phrase 'to let you know that I find no case against him' is problematic. However, Pilate's statement makes perfect sense when the flogging is seen as judicial torture to extract truth. Pilate demonstrates to 'the Jews' that despite having Jesus whipped he gets no admission of guilt, and hence Jesus' flogged body testifies to guiltlessness.[14] With his exclamation, 'See the man!', Pilate scoffs at 'the Jews' about this pathetic figure whom he considers innocent and harmless (19:5).[15] Aggravated, 'the Jews' demand Jesus' crucifixion but Pilate continues to taunt them (19:6). For the first time, 'the Jews' level a (religious) charge: Jesus has blasphemed by equating himself with God (19:7; cf. 5:18; 10:33) – a capital offence according to the Mosaic law (Lev. 24:16).[16]

Round Six (19:8–11). Pilate becomes rather afraid, perhaps driven by a superstitious belief about divine matters, and wants to know Jesus' origin (19:8–9).[17] Annoyed by Jesus' silence, Pilate tries to assert his authority and fails; instead, Jesus points out that Pilate's authority is God-given (literally, 'given from above') (19:10–11).[18] Jesus' remark that the one who handed him over to Pilate (either Judas or Caiaphas/'the Jews') is guilty of a greater sin does not mean Pilate himself is guiltless – he rejects Jesus, does not use his God-given authority to do justice and will hand Jesus over to 'the Jews' (19:16a).[19]

Round Seven (19:12–16a). A mixture of belief in Jesus' innocence, superstitious fear and Jesus' words in 19:11 drive Pilate to make his first real attempt

[14] Glancy, 'Torture', 125.

[15] John may allude to Jesus' humanity or to his title 'Son of Man'. Cf. Bond, *Pilate*, 185–6. D. Böhler understands the phrase as a royal proclamation echoing 1 Sam. 9:17 ('"Ecce Homo!" (Joh 19,5) ein Zität aus dem Alten Testament', *BZ* 39 [1995]: 104–8).

[16] D.W. Wead argues that 'the Jews' also accuse Jesus of being a false prophet who led people away from the Mosaic law, another offence warranting the death penalty (Deut. 13:1–5) ('We Have a Law', *NovT* 11 [1969]: 185–9).

[17] Cf. Bultmann, *Gospel*, 661; Stibbe, *Storyteller*, 108; Giblin, 'Narration', 231; Bond, *Pilate*, 187. 'Rather afraid' makes more sense than 'even more afraid' (NIV) or 'more afraid than ever' (NRSV) since Pilate has not shown fear previously. Moloney observes that Pilate asks 'the fundamental question of Johannine Christology: "Where are you from?"' (*Gospel*, 495).

[18] Jesus probably refers to the power God has given Pilate for this particular moment (Bultmann, *Gospel*, 662; Brown, *Gospel*, 2:892–3; Beasley-Murray, *John*, 339; Carson, *Gospel*, 601–2) rather than to a possible God-given authority of the state (cf. Rom. 13:1). For a critique of this latter concept, see J.H. Yoder, *The Politics of Jesus* (2d edn; Grand Rapids: Eerdmans, 1994), ch. 10. Ironically, Pilate presumes to have authority whereas in reality it is Jesus who does (1:12; 5:27; 10:18; 17:2).

[19] Judas is most often the subject of the verb 'to hand over' in John, including in 18:2, 5. Here, the reference could be 'the Jews' who hand Jesus over to Pilate (18:30, 35) (Jesus' use of the singular is perhaps generic) and/or to Caiaphas as the leader of 'the Jews' (although never related to the verb 'to hand over', he is the leading voice in 11:47–53). Whoever the subject, his/their sin is greater because while Pilate has God-given authority his/theirs comes from the devil (8:44; 13:2, 27).

to release Jesus. It comes too late, however, for 'the Jews' play their trump card. They skillfully manipulate Pilate by modifying their allegation from a religious (19:7) to a political one (19:12). By questioning Pilate's loyalty to the emperor, they corner him leaving him no option to release Jesus. Hearing their words, Pilate sits on the judge's bench to demonstrate his authority over 'the Jews'.[20] Pilate knows what 'the Jews' want and while he realizes they have forced his hand, he too has a card up his sleeve. He taunts them saying, 'See your king!', causing the exasperated 'Jews' to demand Jesus' crucifixion (19:14b–15a). Pilate now plays *his* trump card. With his 'Shall I crucify your king?', Pilate shrewdly manipulates 'the Jews' into admitting their allegiance to Rome and denying their religious loyalties (19:15).[21] Having secured this victory, Pilate hands Jesus over to 'the Jews' to be crucified (19:16a).

  Beyond the Trial. After Jesus' trial, Pilate's power play continues. In 19:19–22, Pilate mocks the nationalistic, messianic hopes of 'the Jews' with the inscription 'Jesus the Nazarene, the king of the Jews' on the cross. He then flaunts his authority by refusing the alteration 'the Jews' suggest. Pilate's power over the Jewish people is also apparent in 19:31, 38 when they need his consent on a religious matter.[22]

Conclusion

Pilate is probably the most complex character in the Johannine narrative. In his dealing with Jesus, Pilate seeks to uncover the truth in his own cruel and efficient way. He misunderstands and disparages Jesus' kingship and rejects the (saving) truth he has to offer, but he is also convinced that Jesus is harmless and innocent (18:38; 19:4, 6) and tries to release him (19:12). At the same time, he uses Jesus to manipulate and taunt 'the Jews'. In his politically motivated game of mocking and manipulating 'the Jews' to admit their allegiance to Rome, he chooses to sacrifice the truth/Jesus. Pilate does not use his God-given authority to mete out justice, instead he rejects the truth/Jesus and thus condemns himself (cf. 3:20–21).[23] He knows what is true and just – Jesus is innocent and should be released – but he

---

[20] Although it is possible to translate 19:13b as, 'and he [Pilate] seated him [Jesus] on the judge's seat', this is unlikely (cf. Bond, *Pilate*, 190; Conway, *Men and Women*, 161; contra O'Day, *Gospel*, 822).

[21] Cf. Culpepper, *Anatomy*, 143; Giblin, 'Narration', 233, 238; Bond, *Pilate*, 191–3; Conway, *Men and Women*, 162; Carter, *Pilate*, 150–51. As Schnackenburg observes, both 'the Jews' and Pilate sacrifice their convictions – 'the Jews' their theological convictions and Pilate his conviction of justice (*Gospel*, 3:266).

[22] Contra Culpepper, who contends that these are all Pilate's efforts to atone for his concession to 'the Jews' (*Anatomy*, 143).

[23] In fact, Pilate is on trial and condemns himself (Ehrman, 'Trial', 128; R.E. Brown, 'The Passion According to John: Chapters 18 and 19', *Worship* 49 [1975]: 129–30).

does not act accordingly. In the final evaluation, Pilate does not come to the light (cf. 3:20–21) and his response to Jesus falters and fails.[24]

Regarding 'the Jews', Pilate is cruel, taunting, condescending and manipulative. Knowing that they want to kill Jesus but need his approval, Pilate repeatedly taunts them and flaunts his authority. In return, 'the Jews' manage to manipulate Pilate when they realize he wants to release Jesus. Knowing he is cornered and must concede to their demands, Pilate extracts a high price – a declaration of their allegiance to Rome and a denial of their religious loyalties. A seemingly victorious Pilate becomes victim of his own political game because he too pays a price for his victory – denying and perverting truth and justice. Indeed, it is a hollow victory.[25]

In our reading of the Johannine Pilate we differ from the majority of scholars who portray Pilate as weak and indecisive.[26] While we generally agree with scholars who view Pilate as a strong character, they seem to overrate Pilate's control over the situation by downplaying the force of 19:12 where 'the Jews' finally get a grip on Pilate.[27] Pilate is a competent, calculating politician who wants to show 'the Jews' he is in charge while also trying to be professional in handling Jesus' case. But he is unable to achieve either aim because he underestimates the determination and shrewdness of 'the Jews'. He may have released the innocent Jesus had he not been manipulated into sacrificing the truth/Jesus to ensure his own political survival and triumph. He knows Jesus is innocent but does not use his God-given authority to bring justice for fear of losing the political game. Pilate ultimately chooses Caesar and the empire 'from below' instead of Jesus and his kingdom 'from above'.

The narrator reveals two aspects of Pilate's inner life: he is afraid (19:8) and he wants to release Jesus (19:12). Some scholars contend that the structure of the passage, in which Pilate alternately goes in and out of his palace, reflects his inner conflict – he goes back and forth in his mind, unable to take sides.[28] This picture seems incorrect. Pilate despises 'the Jews' and is clear about his strategy but he is also in search of truth about Jesus. Although he tries to play both sides and fails, he is not indecisive: he ultimately opts for the emperor and his own political survival at the expense of truth and justice. Nevertheless, Pilate does go back and forth in his mind, constantly weighing his political options and this is what the structure of the passage

---

[24] Culpepper concludes that 'although he [Pilate] seems to glimpse the truth, a decision in Jesus' favor proves too costly for him' (*Anatomy*, 143). Cf. O'Day, *Gospel*, 825–6.

[25] Culpepper, *Anatomy*, 143.

[26] E.g. Brown, *Gospel*, 2:864 (the honest, well-disposed man who adopts a middle position); Culpepper, *Anatomy*, 143 (Pilate avoids making a decision); Stibbe, *Storyteller*, 109 (Pilate is indecisive, representing the 'impossibility of neutrality').

[27] Rensberger, *World*, 94–5; Bond, *Pilate*, 190–92; Conway, *Men and Women*, 161; Carter, *Pilate*, 127, 150. O'Day presents a more balanced view (*Gospel*, 813–26).

[28] E.g. Stibbe, *Storyteller*, 106, 109. Earlier I also held this view (*John's Gospel*, 204).

probably emphasizes.[29] There are some indications of development in Pilate. First, although Pilate is convinced early on about Jesus' innocence, he does not attempt to release him but, surprisingly, he tries fervently to release him later. Second, it is rather surprising that Pilate, the calculating politician, is outmanoeuvred by 'the Jews' and forced to yield.

John's portrait of Pilate does not differ too much from those of Josephus and Philo.[30] In John's gospel, Pilate refuses to give in to the demands of 'the Jews' and mocks them but they find a way to pressure Pilate into yielding. Similarly, Josephus (*Jewish War* 2:169–174; *Antiquities* 18:55–59) and Philo (*Embassy to Gaius* 299–305) record incidents where Pilate provokes the Jews and refuses to give in to their wishes but eventually has to concede. Whether in John's gospel, Josephus or Philo, Pilate appears cruel, decisive, calculating and provocative. He appears to choose the course of action which is to his advantage and ensures his political survival.

Pilate		
Appearances	References	18:29, 31, 33, 35, 37, 38; 19:1, 4, 6, 8, 10, 12, 13, 15, 19, 21, 22, 31, 38 (2x)
Identity	Titles given	–
	Gender	male
	Age	–
	Marital status	–
	Occupation	Roman prefect or procurator of Judaea
	Socio-economic status	–
	Place of residence/operation	Herod's palace in Jerusalem
	Relatives	–
	Group affiliation	Rome
Speech and actions	In interaction with Jesus	searches for truth, cruel/efficient; once willing to release him but in the end handing him over to be crucified
	In interaction with others	taunts 'the Jews', flaunts his authority, eventually gives in to their pressure but manipulates them
Character classification	Complexity	complex; multiple traits: cruel, calculating, taunting, manipulative, provocative, afraid
	Development	some
	Inner life	some
Degree of characterization		towards individual
Response to Jesus		inadequate: misunderstanding, rejection, compromising truth and justice, choosing Caesar rather than Jesus

---

[29] Cf. Lincoln, *Gospel*, 458. Brodie connects the inside/outside contrast with the idea of revelation: inside the praetorium Jesus gives revelation; 'the Jews' outside are without revelation (*Gospel*, 521).

[30] Cf. McGing, 'Pilate', 437–8. Contra Davies, *Rhetoric*, 314–5.

Joseph of Arimathea – Faith and Fear

'Fear defeats more people than any other one thing in the world' — *R.W. Emerson*

Joseph of Arimathea is mentioned only once in John's gospel (19:38), in connection with the burial of Jesus (19:38–42). Despite this single appearance, Joseph plays an important, representative role because John identifies him as a secret, fearful disciple of Jesus (19:38). Belief coupled with fear is a prominent motif in John's gospel, which needs further explanation. Besides, in the act of burying Jesus, he is accompanied by the ambiguous Nicodemus, raising more questions. Finally, it is unclear whether Joseph is affiliated with 'the Jews' or Jesus. We will address these issues in an attempt to understand Joseph better.

The Identity of Joseph of Arimathea

In Joseph, we are presented with an enigmatic figure since the information in John's gospel (and other sources) seems contradictory. First, as a few scholars have noted, there is a tension between John 19:31 and 19:38.[1] According to 19:31, 'the Jews' ask Pilate to have the bodies removed from the cross before the Sabbath starts, whereas in 19:38, Joseph asks for the body. Similarly, according to Acts 13:27–29, the Jews took Jesus down from the cross and buried him, whereas the Synoptic Gospels attribute this act to Joseph (Matt. 27:57–60; Mark 15:42–46; Luke 23:50–53). Second, the Synoptic Gospels portray Joseph as a rich man from Arimathea, a town in Judaea, and a respected member of the Sanhedrin, who nonetheless disagrees with his colleagues' plan regarding Jesus (Matt. 27:57; Mark 15:43; Luke 23:50–51; cf. Nicodemus in John 7).[2] Joseph is apparently a good and righteous man, who waits expectantly for the Kingdom of God (Mark 15:43; Luke 23:50–51), and is even a disciple of Jesus (Matt. 27:57). The Gospel of John, however, only mentions that Joseph is a *secret* disciple of Jesus because of his fear of 'the Jews' (19:38). These disparate portraits of Joseph are difficult

---

[1] Brown, *Gospel*, 2:933, 938, 956; Schnackenburg, *Gospel*, 3:288, 296.

[2] The 'council' of which Joseph was a member is most probably the Jewish Supreme Council or Sanhedrin.

to reconcile. It is also unclear whether Joseph is affiliated with 'the Jews' or with Jesus.

Piecing together the available information, I suggest the following profile of Joseph of Arimathea.[3] Joseph is probably a wealthy, respected Jewish leader and a member of the Sanhedrin, making him either a notable Pharisee or a chief priest (cf. ch. 4). However, he apparently disagrees with the Sanhedrin's decision to have Jesus killed (11:47–53). Joseph probably disagrees with them because he is a disciple of Jesus, albeit a secret one because he fears his colleagues. When 'the Jews' want to have the bodies removed from the cross before the Sabbath starts, Joseph perhaps volunteers to go to Pilate and ask for permission. Joseph has a lot in common with Nicodemus. Nicodemus, a wealthy and prominent Pharisee, is also a member of the Sanhedrin (see ch. 9). Like Joseph, Nicodemus is sympathetic to Jesus (although we cannot call Nicodemus a disciple of Jesus). At an earlier meeting of the Sanhedrin, Nicodemus too disagrees with his colleagues' plans regarding Jesus. It is therefore not surprising that Nicodemus pairs up with Joseph at Jesus' burial.

Joseph the Secret Disciple – Belief Combined with Fear

John informs us that Joseph is a secret disciple of Jesus because he fears 'the Jews'. 'The fear of the Jews' is an important motif in John's gospel and is first mentioned in John 7. At the Feast of Tabernacles in Jerusalem, 'the Jews' are looking for Jesus (7:11), and when they realize the influence of Jesus' teaching on the crowd, they send the temple police to arrest him – but their attempts fail (7:28–32, 45–46). The crowd is divided about Jesus but does not speak openly about him because of the fear of 'the Jews' (7:12–13). The text, however, does not clarify why the crowd fears 'the Jews'.

The second time we read of people being afraid of 'the Jews', in John 9, we learn the reason for this fear. It is the Sabbath and Jesus has healed a man blind from birth. When the man's neighbours report the healing to 'the Jews'/Pharisees, they interrogate the healed man but when they fail to achieve the desired result they summon his parents (9:13–18). During the interrogation, the parents fail to testify about what had happened to their son (if the man had testified to his neighbours surely he would have told his parents too) because they are afraid of 'the Jews' (9:19–22). The reason for their fear is explicitly mentioned: 'the Jews' had agreed that anyone who confessed Jesus as the Messiah would be expelled from the synagogue

---

[3] I attempt not so much to understand Joseph of Arimathea on the basis of the Synoptic material as to resolve the tension that John himself has created in 19:31 and 19:38, with the help of the information that the Synoptics provide.

(9:22). Expulsion from the synagogue would mean exclusion from religious and communal life – becoming socio-religious outcasts.

At the end of Jesus' public ministry we read that 'even of the authorities, many believed in him [Jesus], but because of the Pharisees they did not confess in order not to be expelled from the synagogue' (12:42). Although fear is not explicitly mentioned, it is evidently in the background. I have argued elsewhere that these religious authorities are either chief priests or Pharisees, who are afraid that if the/other Pharisees become aware that they are sympathetic to Jesus, they will report it to the Sanhedrin or to the wider body of 'the Jews'.[4] John records two instances where something similar occurs. First, when Nicodemus raises a critical issue during a meeting of the Sanhedrin, his fellow-Pharisees sneer at him and silence him (7:50–52). Second, when some of 'the Jews' go to the Pharisees to report about Jesus' raising of Lazarus, another meeting of the Sanhedrin is convened where Jesus' death is plotted (11:46–53). The Pharisees thus seem influential and outspoken enough to cause trouble, to the extent that those authorities who believe in Jesus are secretive about it out of fear.[5]

There is one other group of people affected by this fear of 'the Jews'. When Jesus appears to his disciples on the evening of Resurrection Sunday, he finds them behind locked doors because of their fear of 'the Jews' (20:19). A week later, the disciples are in the same house – again behind locked doors (20:26).

It is thus clear that 'the fear of the Jews', specifically the fear of being excommunicated from the synagogue and thus becoming a socio-religious outcast, dominated the lives of many people. This fear affected common people (7:13; 9:22), the Jewish authorities (12:42) and the disciples (20:19, 26). Amongst those who are afraid of 'the Jews' is Joseph of Arimathea, whose fear causes him to be a secret disciple of Jesus (19:38). He could perhaps be one of the religious authorities mentioned in 12:42. This fear of 'the Jews' should not be underestimated since the consequences for professing openly that Jesus was the Messiah were severe. Jesus even warns his followers that they could be killed (16:2).[6] In some cases, people do not dare to speak publicly about Jesus (the crowd and the parents of the blind man), in others they do not dare to profess their belief in Jesus openly (some of the authorities and Joseph), and still others are afraid even to be seen (the disciples).

---

[4] Bennema, 'Identity', section 3.3.

[5] This fear of possible ostracism is further motivated by a desire for the praise of people rather than the praise of God (12:43) – an attitude that is a hindrance to adequate belief (5:44). Hence, the 'secret belief' of the authorities is not simply caused by fear but also by wrong motivation, and hence may not be belief in the true Johannine sense at all.

[6] Indeed, up to the present day history shows that Christians worldwide have experienced various kinds of threats and persecution because of their faith. These threats and persecution should not be disparaged – then or now.

There are indications that John is critical of such an attitude – not of fear *per se* but of fear that prevents a public confession of belief in or allegiance to Jesus. First, in John 9, John contrasts the attitude of the man born blind with that of his parents. Whereas the man born blind progresses in his knowledge and recognition of Jesus' identity *while* facing persecution from 'the Jews', the same pressure from 'the Jews' scares his parents and keeps them from testifying (cf. ch. 16). Thus, John implicitly criticizes the parents' attitude and applauds that of their son. A second indicator comes from Jesus' teaching. In 15:18 – 16:4a, Jesus spells out for his disciples the seriousness and severity of the persecution that awaits them. Nevertheless, he also encourages them to continue to testify and not to give up their belief. For precisely such situations, Jesus promises to send the Spirit-Paraclete as an aide to inform and empower the believer's testimony (14:16–18; 15:26–27). Besides, Jesus assures his followers of his peace to counter the effects of fear and persecution (14:27; 16:33; 20:19–21).

John thus implicitly challenges his readers not to give in to this kind of fear and threat of persecution.[7] When belief in Jesus is coloured by a fear of people's responses, the result is secrecy or anonymity – a failure to make a public confession of that belief. This, according to John, is inadequate. John advocates that people profess their belief openly, even when fear of persecution is a reality.

Joseph's Attitude: Bold or Fearful?

Joseph of Arimathea is described as a 'secret disciple' because he feared 'the Jews'. We explained that though this fear was understandable considering the possible consequences for those who publicly confessed Jesus as the Messiah, John nevertheless found this attitude unacceptable. John does, however, mention two actions of Joseph that may cause the reader to reconsider him: (i) he requests Pilate for Jesus' body (19:38), and (ii), together with Nicodemus, he buries Jesus (19:39–42).

Joseph apparently shows courage in petitioning Pilate for the body of Jesus – a man condemned and crucified as an insurrectionist – for his actions would certainly be reported to 'the Jews'.[8] However, if Joseph was one of the Jewish religious leaders (as we contend he is) who wanted the bodies removed from the cross before the start of the Sabbath (19:31), then he may simply have volunteered (or been deputed by his colleagues) to go to

---

[7] In his letter, John also states that perfect love, which Jesus commands all believers to seek (John 13:34–35; 15:12, 17), will cast out fear (1 John 4:18).

[8] Mark 15:43 mentions explicitly that Joseph went *boldly* to Pilate. Under Roman law, crucified persons were normally not buried but left on the cross to decay, but the Jews usually buried condemned criminals in a common grave (Carson, *Gospel*, 629; Beasley-Murray, *John*, 358; Keener, *Gospel*, 1157). 'The Jews' request to Pilate reflects this custom (19:31).

Pilate and make this request. 'The Jews' would thus have known of Joseph's actions, but they may not have known that he was a secret disciple of Jesus. Besides, 'the Jews' probably intended to bury Jesus, a crucified criminal, in a common grave, whereas Joseph courageously goes against the grain in giving Jesus an honourable burial.[9] Thus, Joseph's request and actions are courageous and demonstrate some identification with Jesus – even though it remains unclear whether it is open or secret.[10] To 'the Jews', it would appear that Joseph had simply volunteered, or was authorized, to carry out their wishes, but they were unaware of Joseph's secret desire to pay homage to Jesus. However, 'the Jews' would certainly have learned of the kind of burial Jesus received, so Joseph did risk the reprisal of his fellow 'Jews'.

Joseph's association with Nicodemus does not particularly help his image. In chapter 9, we pointed out that Nicodemus's participation in Jesus' burial could be understood positively or negatively, which only reiterates Nicodemus's basic trait – ambiguity. Narratologically, the joint actions of Joseph and Nicodemus in 19:40–42 show that they form a unity, even though Joseph made the request to Pilate and Nicodemus brought the spices. Hence, his association with the ambiguous Nicodemus only confirms the secrecy of Joseph's belief. Although burying a convicted criminal in an unused tomb with honour as Joseph and Nicodemus did is highly unusual, it remains uncertain whether their 'public' act of courage entirely removes their ambiguity and secrecy.[11]

Conclusion

Joseph of Arimathea is characterized as a fearful, secret disciple of Jesus, who eventually shows courage and takes risk in 'publicly' honouring Jesus after his death. Although it is a positive act, it may not count as an adequate public confession of Jesus that John would approve of. His association with the ambiguous Nicodemus only complicates matters. Nevertheless, Joseph's courage may surprise the reader and hint at a little character development. Through the characterization of Joseph, John informs his readers that anonymous discipleship or secret Christianity will not suffice. Some form of testimony, preferably a public confession that Jesus is the Christ, seems appropriate and necessary.

[9] Cf. Carson, *Gospel*, 629; Beasley-Murray, *John*, 358; Keener, *Gospel*, 1160–61.

[10] Keener probably exaggerates when he identifies Joseph's act as 'a positive model for discipleship' (*Gospel*, 1160).

[11] The burial according to the custom of 'the Jews' (19:40) may also indicate that Joseph and Nicodemus still side with 'the Jews'. In our view, some scholars decide too quickly that Joseph reveals himself here as a true disciple (Lindars, *Gospel*, 592; Ridderbos, *Gospel*, 625–6; O'Day, *Gospel*, 835; Moloney, *Gospel*, 510–12).

Joseph of Arimathea		
Appearances	References	19:38
Identity	Titles given	–
	Gender	male
	Age	–
	Marital status	–
	Occupation	probably a member of the Sanhedrin
	Socio-economic status	probably prominent and wealthy
	Place of residence/operation	Arimathea (a town in Judaea)
	Relatives	–
	Group affiliation	'the Jews' (and Nicodemus in particular)
Speech and actions	In interaction with Jesus	he pays homage to Jesus by burying him
	In interaction with others	he collaborates with Nicodemus
Character classification	Complexity	little complex; multiple traits: secretive, fearful, courageous, risk-taking
	Development	little
	Inner life	none
Degree of characterization		type
Response to Jesus		inadequate (but his boldness provides a glimmer of hope)

Mary Magdalene – Recognizing the Shepherd's Voice

'The best vision is insight' — Malcolm S. Forbes

Mary Magdalene makes her first appearance at the foot of the cross (19:25), and a second one at the empty tomb (20:1–2, 11–18). The epithet 'Magdalene' suggests that she probably came from Magdala, a town on the western shore of the Sea of Galilee.[1] This begs the question why she was in Jerusalem. From the Synoptics we learn that several Galilean women accompanied Jesus during his ministry and went up to Jerusalem during his passion, including Mary Magdalene (Matt. 27:55–56; Mark 15:40–41; Luke 8:1–3; 23:49). Her presence at the foot of the cross would therefore suggest that she is already Jesus' disciple rather than a mere spectator.[2] Going by the Synoptics, Mary Magdalene was probably affluent since these Galilean women provided for Jesus out of their resources (Matt. 27:55; Luke 8:3).

Mary Magdalene gains significance when she encounters Jesus at the empty tomb. Once she reaches Jesus' tomb and sees that the stone has been removed, she reports to Peter and the Beloved Disciple that Jesus' body is missing (20:1–2).[3] Other than the visit of Peter and the Beloved Disciple to the empty tomb (20:3–10), Mary is the main player in 20:1–18. The central theme is Mary's dismay at finding Jesus' body missing and her consequent search for it (20:2, 13, 15).[4]

---

[1] Cf. Beirne, *Women*, 206.

[2] Beirne's assessment of Mary Magdalene's appearance in 19:25 being indicative of her faith, courage and love (*Women*, 209) is probably more than the text warrants.

[3] Scholars are divided whether the darkness in 20:1 has symbolic significance (see Hearon, *Mary*, 152 n. 13; cf. Resseguie, *Strange Gospel*, 146). Her use of plurals in 'we do not know where they have laid him' (20:2) probably indicates that she had not gone alone to the tomb (cf. the Synoptics). Minear's suggestion that the plurals in 20:2 point to the tension between the Johannine church (we) and the Jewish synagogue (they) is far-fetched ('John 20:2', 126).

[4] Minear, 'John 20:2', 125; S.M. Schneiders, 'John 20:11–18: The Encounter of the Easter Jesus with Mary Magdalene – A Transformative Feminist Reading', in *'What is John?': Readers and Readings of the Fourth Gospel* (ed. F.F. Segovia; Atlanta: Scholars Press, 1996), 157–8; Hearon, *Mary*, 149, 158.

Mary Encounters the Angels

After Peter and the Beloved Disciple examine the tomb for themselves, they return home showing no progress in their understanding, until Mary brings another report (20:3–10, 18). Mary, meanwhile, remains at the tomb, giving vent to her grief (20:11a). Some see a parallel with another Mary weeping over a dead man in a tomb (11:33).[5] However, despite the remarkable parallels between John 11 and 20 (e.g. the death and raising of Lazarus fore-shadow Jesus' own death and resurrection), it is unclear how the actions of Mary, Lazarus's sister, shed light on that of Mary Magdalene. We contend that 16:19–22 is the better intertextual background to understand Mary's behaviour. Mary weeps because she does not know where Jesus is (cf. 16:19–20a and 20:11, 13), but her distress will soon turn into joy when she sees Jesus (cf. 16:20b–22 and 20:16, 18).[6] Thus, Mary, appropriately a woman (cf. 16:21), is the first one to see the risen Jesus.

We make two observations about Mary's encounter with the angels in 20:11–13. First, Peter and the Beloved Disciple are denied the opportunity to see the angels, while Mary, a woman, sees not only the angels but is also the first to see the risen Jesus (cf. the Synoptics). This confirms the importance that John gives to women in his gospel. Second, in the Synoptics, the angels reveal to Mary and the other women that Jesus is risen, whereas in John, the risen Jesus reveals himself to her (20:14–16). This should come as no surprise since, for John, Jesus is the Revealer *par excellence*.

Mary Encounters Jesus

Jesus' revelation to Mary unfolds gradually. At first, Mary sees Jesus but does not recognize him; she mistakenly assumes he is the gardener (20:14–15). The text does not indicate whether Jesus deliberately keeps her from recog-nizing him or if her tears blur her vision.[7] Interestingly, Jesus asks Mary the same question the angels did, 'Woman, why are you weeping?', but only Jesus as the Revealer has the privilege of resolving Mary's problem.

Jesus' question, 'Whom do you seek?' (20:15a), evokes the Johannine theme of the quest for Jesus. This quest, expressed by the verbs 'to seek' and 'to find', is essentially a quest for life or salvation. The disciples have embarked on the right path (1:38; 6:68–69), the crowd is sometimes/often on

---

[5] Hearon, *Mary*, 153.

[6] Cf. O'Day, *Gospel*, 841; Conway, *Men and Women*, 192–3. To infer that Mary is a faithful follower of Jesus because she weeps when she does not see him while the world rejoices (so Hearon, *Mary*, 154) appears overstated.

[7] L.D. George suggests that Mary's grief, expressed in her weeping, causes her to miss several clues, suggesting a kind of spiritual blindness (*Reading the Tapestry: A Literary-Rhetorical Analysis of the Johannine Resurrection Narrative [John 20 – 21]* [StBL 14; New York: Peter Lang, 2000], 79).

a wrong quest (6:24–26; 12:37), and 'the Jews' are on an entirely erroneous and fruitless quest (5:18, 44; 7:1, 18, 34).[8] Mary's quest for the missing body of Jesus (20:15b) is in essence a quest 'from below' and needs redirecting.[9]

Jesus reveals himself by calling Mary by her name, and she responds with 'My teacher', indicating that she has now recognized his voice and identity (20:16). Jesus' use of her name must be placed against the background of the good shepherd calling his sheep by name so that they may find life (10:3–4, 9; cf. 5:25; 11:43).[10] Therefore, Jesus' calling Mary by her name has salvific overtones signifying that she is one of Jesus' sheep – a follower.[11] Mary's reply 'Rabbouni', a heightened form of 'Rabbi', literally means '*my* Teacher' (cf. the '*my* Lord' in 20:13) and constitutes her belief-response – it reveals that she has a personal relationship with Jesus.[12] In short, against the background of John 10, Jesus' calling Mary by name and her response strongly indicate that she has (entered into) a saving relationship with the risen Jesus.[13] Schneiders observes that since Mary has already turned to face Jesus in 20:14, her second 'turning' in 20:16 indicates Easter conversion.[14] Besides, the message that Mary is to convey to the disciples that Jesus is about to ascend to *their* Father/God (20:17) is surely meant for her too.[15] We may thus infer that she is placed on the same level as the disciples and is firmly included within the family of God.

Mary Is Commissioned

In 20:17, Jesus commands Mary to stop an action already begun (indicated by the present imperative tense in Greek): 'Do not continue to touch me' or

---

[8] See also Stibbe, 'Christ', 19–37.

[9] Cf. Schneiders, who remarks that Mary's search for Jesus is 'a quintessentially positive enterprise in John's gospel, but her grief has spiritually blinded her' ('John 20:11–18', 162).

[10] Many have noticed this connection: e.g. Brown, *Gospel*, 2:1009–10; Barrett, *Gospel*, 564; Schnackenburg, *Gospel*, 3:316; Lee, 'Partnership', 44; O'Day, *Gospel*, 842; Conway, *Men and Women*, 195; George, *Tapestry*, 75; Hearon, *Mary*, 159–60.

[11] Cf. Brown, 'Roles', 694; Kitzberger, 'Mary', 583; Beirne, *Women*, 210.

[12] Others also connect 13:13–14 where Jesus says his followers are to use the titles 'Teacher' and 'Lord', with 20:2, 13, 16, 18 where Mary uses these titles, and infer that she must be a disciple (Maccini, *Testimony*, 224; Conway, *Men and Women*, 187, 195; Hearon, *Mary*, 160). This implies that Mary's use of 'teacher' is not inappropriate, inadequate or incomplete (contra Bultmann, *Gospel*, 686–7; Scott, *Sophia*, 230; Moloney, *Gospel*, 526).

[13] Cf. Fehribach, *Women*, 159–62. Differently, Collins contends that only *after* Jesus' explanation in 20:17 can Mary be counted among those who are truly believers ('Figures', 34–5). Similarly, Moloney contends that Mary only reaches full faith when she exclaims, 'I have seen the Lord' (20:18) (*Gospel*, 527).

[14] Schneiders, 'John 20:11–18', 159, 162–3. Cf. D.A. Lee, 'Turning from Death to Life: A Biblical Reflection on Mary Magdalene (John 20:1–18)', *Ecumenical Review* 50 (1998): 112–20; Resseguie, *Strange Gospel*, 149.

[15] Contra Davies, *Rhetoric*, 335.

'Do not hold on to me'.[16] Apparently Jesus is assuring Mary that there is no need to cling to him – he is not leaving just yet so there will be further opportunities to see him before he ascends to the Father.[17] More importantly, Jesus assigns Mary the task of informing the disciples of his imminent ascension to the Father (20:17).[18] As Schneiders explains, 'what Jesus is really doing is redirecting Mary's desire for union with himself from his physical or earthly body . . . to the new locus of his presence in the world, that is, the community of his brothers and sisters, the disciples'.[19] More precisely, Jesus has indicated in 14:18–23 that after his return to the Father he will be present among his followers by means of the Spirit-Paraclete.[20]

In searching for Jesus' body and clinging to him, Mary betrays a perspective 'from below' – she is preoccupied with the temporal. She fails to understand that Jesus must return to the Father (hence the message she is asked to convey) and that subsequently Jesus' presence with her and other believers will be through the Spirit. This explanation dovetails with our assertion that 16:19–22 is the background to Mary's behaviour. We have argued elsewhere that Jesus' enigmatic saying in 16:16, 'shortly, and you will no longer see me; again shortly, and you will see me', refers *both* to his temporary departure in death and return in the resurrection *and* to his permanent departure in the ascension and his return by means of the indwelling Spirit-Paraclete.[21] This dual reference may also be seen in Mary's story. First, she grieves over Jesus' death but rejoices when she sees the resurrected Lord. Then, correcting her desire to hold on to him, Jesus announces that he will depart again to be with his Father (cf. 20:17 and 16:17b), but will return to her (and others) in a more permanent way through the indwelling Spirit-Paraclete (cf. 14:23).

Scholars have recognized the covenantal overtones of Jesus' message 'I am ascending to my Father and your Father, to my God and your God' (cf. Ruth 1:16; Jer. 31:33; Ezek. 37:27).[22] Jesus' victorious cry at the cross, 'It is

---

[16] Cf. Schneiders, 'John 20:11–18', 164.

[17] Fehribach's interpretation that Mary *embraces* Jesus (*Women*, 160) is an *over*-interpretation. For a critique of those who contend that Jesus had already ascended before 20:17 (e.g. Schneiders, 'John 20:11–18', 165) or between 20:17 and 20:19 (e.g. Minear, 'John 20:2', 130; O'Day, *Gospel*, 842–3), see Bennema, 'Giving', 202–3.

[18] It is somewhat puzzling why Jesus commands Mary to tell the disciples about the ascension rather than the resurrection. Nevertheless, Mary's first words to the disciples are that she has seen the Lord (20:18).

[19] Schneiders, 'John 20:11–18', 164–5. Cf. Resseguie, *Strange Gospel*, 148.

[20] Bennema, *Power*, 222–3. Cf. Brown, *Gospel*, 2:1012; Schnackenburg, *Gospel*, 3:301; Scott, *Sophia*, 230; Lee, 'Partnership', 42; Köstenberger, *John*, 569–70. Conway reads Jesus' prohibition in 20:17 as a warning to Mary indicating that he is in some sort of sacred liminal state, different from when he meets the disciples and Thomas (*Men and Women*, 196–7). However, Jesus' prohibition has nothing to do with his state. It simply reveals Mary's misunderstanding of his future presence with her (and other believers) – namely, in the Spirit.

[21] Bennema, *John's Gospel*, 178–9. Cf. Bennema, *Power*, 222–3.

[22] Brown, *Gospel*, 2:1016–7; Schneiders, 'John 20:11–18', 166; T. Okure, 'The Significance Today of Jesus' Commission to Mary Magdalene', *IRM* 81 (1992): 182; van Tilborg, *Love*, 206;

finished' (19:30), signals the completion of his Father's work, i.e. the salvific mission for which he was sent into the world. Now it is possible for him to speak in New Covenantal language to his followers. Mary is to convey to the disciples that they (and she) can now relate to God the same way Jesus does, namely as Father (cf. 1:12–13).[23] Indeed, the disciples will soon have their salvation sealed or secured in the reception of the Spirit in 20:22.[24] Okure rightly remarks that Mary is not primarily commissioned to tell the disciples that Jesus had risen from the dead (although she does that too in 20:18) but to convey the *significance* of Jesus' resurrection for believers, namely their new status as children of God and as brothers and sisters of Jesus and one another (cf. 'go to my *brothers*' in 20:17).[25]

As the first (apostolic) witness to the risen Lord, Mary tells the disciples about her encounter (20:17–18).[26] Hearon points out that Mary's second report to the disciples, 'I have seen the Lord' (20:18), is a reversal of her first message, 'they have taken the Lord and I do not know where they have laid him' (20:2).[27] Her ignorance and distress have been replaced with insight and assurance.

Conclusion

As Hearon comments, '[t]he characterization of Mary is complex . . . she moves from distress to grief to confusion to insight'.[28] Mary represents the one who searches for Jesus in the realm below but responds in belief when the good shepherd calls her by name.[29] Many scholars assess Mary negatively, but this is unwarranted. Although she exhibits ignorance, distress, confusion and views events 'from below', she also shows traits of persistence, responsiveness to Jesus' revelation and obedience to Jesus' commission.[30] There are some glimpses into Mary's inner life: she claims not to know where Jesus' body is (20:2, 13), and the narrator reveals that she does not recognize

---

Lee, 'Partnership', 45; Chennattu, *Discipleship*, 154–5. Van Tilborg's suggestion that Jesus retreats from his relationship with Mary by rejecting her emotional, physical response in 20:17 in favour of the Beloved Disciple (based on 20:8, 29), seems unwarranted (*Love*, 206–8).

[23] Cf. Schneiders, 'John 20:11–18', 166–7; Okure, 'Significance', 182.

[24] Bennema, 'Giving', 208–9; idem, *John's Gospel*, 216–7.

[25] Okure, 'Significance', 184–5. Cf. Lee, 'Partnership', 46.

[26] Cf. Schneiders, 'John 20:11–18', 168. For Mary's quasi-apostolic role, see Brown, 'Roles', 692–3. Schüssler Fiorenza's characterization of Mary as 'the apostle of the apostles' (*Memory*, 332) is overstated. Maccini points out that Mary is the only person in the gospel who can testify to both the crucifixion (19:25) and the resurrection (20:16) (*Testimony*, 232).

[27] Hearon, *Mary*, 153.

[28] Hearon, *Mary*, 151.

[29] Cf. Collins, 'Figures', 35.

[30] Although George observes similar traits, he evaluates Mary's role as 'ambivalent at best' (*Tapestry*, 78–9), whereas we contend that Mary, though not perfect, shows a positive development.

('know') Jesus but supposes him to be the gardener (20:14b–15). In contrast to Peter and the Beloved Disciple who return home and hence remain ignorant, Mary remains at the tomb. Her persistence in searching for Jesus' body is rewarded when she becomes the first to see the risen Lord. Though her quest needs redirection, it is she who is commissioned to go to the disciples. Through her actions, she exemplifies aspects of true discipleship.[31]

Mary Magdalene		
Appearances	References	19:25; 20:1, 11, 16, 18
Identity	Titles given	Magdalene ('from Magdala')
	Gender	female
	Age	–
	Marital status	–
	Occupation	–
	Socio-economic status	possibly affluent
	Place of residence/operation	from Magdala in Galilee, possibly accompanied Jesus during his ministry
	Relatives	–
	Group affiliation	other female followers of Jesus (19:25) and the disciples
Speech and actions	In interaction with Jesus	distressed but persistent in her search for Jesus; she misunderstands Jesus but responds to his correction
	In interaction with others	persistent (contra Peter and the Beloved Disciple), and commissioned to bring Jesus' message to the disciples
Character classification	Complexity	complex; multiple traits: ignorant, confused, distressful/grieving, dull, insightful, persistent, responsive, obedient, able to testify
	Development	none
	Inner life	some
Degree of characterization		personality
Response to Jesus		adequate: despite her 'earthly' quest for Jesus, she recognizes Jesus and is depicted as belonging to him

[31] Cf. Hearon, *Mary*, 166–8. Contra Beck, who contends that Mary does not serve as an example to be imitated (*Discipleship*, 122) and Fehribach, who maintains that Mary is marginalized and unimportant in and of herself (*Women*, 163–4). Some scholars read, in our view, too much symbolism in Mary's portrayal. For example, Fehribach develops the character of Mary along the lines of female lovers in the Greek love-novels and/or the woman of Song of Songs – a single, frantic woman in search of her lover's body (*Women*, ch. 6; cf. van Tilborg, *Love*, 203–6; Schneiders, 'John 20:11–18', 161, 168). Waetjen sees in 20:11–18 the imagery of the new Adam (the resurrected Jesus) and the new Eve (Mary Magdalene) in the Garden of Eden (*Gospel*, 414–20; cf. Schneiders, 'John 20:11–18', 161).

Conclusion

'Characters resemble people . . . we even go so far as to identify with the character' — Mieke Bal

In our introduction, we stated that John's strategy to achieve the stated purpose of his gospel – to evoke and strengthen belief in Jesus among his readers (20:30–31) – is to present an array of characters who encounter Jesus. The task of this book has been to study these characters and their responses to Jesus within a comprehensive theoretical framework. Our aim was to examine whether the majority of scholars is correct in viewing most Johannine characters as 'flat' or types, or whether they are more complex, developing and 'round'. In keeping with John's aim, we also intended to challenge the readers to identify with one ore more of the characters and evaluate their stance regarding Jesus. We will summarize what we have done, make our conclusions, and finally point to what still needs to be done.

What Have We Done?

We started with a critical examination of the contribution of contemporary scholarship to Johannine character studies and identified four major lacunae that we would address in this book. First, while Johannine scholars have either studied a few characters in detail or many characters cursorily, we have examined comprehensively all the Johannine characters who interact with and respond to Jesus. Second, the absence of a comprehensive theory of character in either literary or biblical criticism shows up in the lack of consensus on how to analyse, classify and evaluate characters. Using a comprehensive, non-reductionist theory of character, we have analysed and classified the Johannine characters along the dimensions of complexity (in terms of traits), development and inner life. We then plotted each character on a continuum of degree of characterization – from type to personality to individual. Finally, we analysed and classified each character's response to Jesus in the light of John's evaluative point of view as expressed in 20:30–31. Third, many scholars who have studied the Johannine characters have limited themselves to the text, while we have attempted to ground our study more in the social-historical world of first-century Judaism. Fourth,

Conway has argued in her 2002 article that many Johannine characters are ambiguous, unstable and produce responses to Jesus that resist or undermine the gospel's binary categories of belief and unbelief. We have not yet addressed this issue but shall do so in the section 'The Characters' Responses and John's Dualistic Worldview' below.

What Can We Conclude?

The Classification of John's Characters and Their Responses

Up to this point we have examined all the Johannine characters that interact with Jesus independently. Now we need a comparative analysis of all the characters and their responses to arrive at a more coherent understanding of how characterization works within this gospel. Most scholars have studied the Johannine characters without or with a minimal (often reductionist) theoretical framework, concluding that most (if not all) Johannine characters are 'flat' or types. We have used a comprehensive, non-reductionist theory of character that studies the characters on their own terms and examines their typical response to Jesus. Table 1 shows the various Johannine characters classified according to three dimensions (complexity, development, inner life), and their degree of characterization (type, personality, individual). We observe that many Johannine characters are more complex or 'round' than Johannine scholarship has made out, showing in a higher degree of characterization.

Table 1: Classification of the Johannine Characters

Character	Complexity	Development	Inner Life	Degree of Characterization
Lazarus	0	0	0	type
Mother of Jesus	–	0	0	type
Nathanael	–	0	–	type
Andrew & Philip	–	–	0	type
Beloved Disciple	–	–	0	type
Joseph of Arimathea	–	–	0	type
Thomas	–/+	0	0	type
Mary of Bethany	–/+	0	0	type
John (the Baptist)	–/+	0	–	type/personality
World	–/+	0	++	type/personality
Royal official	–/+	–	–	type/personality
Martha	–/+	–	+	type/personality
Twelve	–/+	–	++	type/personality
Invalid at the pool	+	+	–	type/personality
Crowd	++	0	+	personality
Mary Magdalene	++	0	+	personality

Character	Complexity	Development	Inner Life	Degree of Characterization
'the Jews'	++	–	++	personality
Samaritan woman	+	+	–	personality
Nicodemus	++	+	–	personality
Man born blind	+	+	+	personality
Pilate	++	+	+	personality/individual
Judas Iscariot	++	+	++	individual
Peter	++	++	+	individual

0 = none, – = little, + = some, ++ =much

We must also classify the belief-responses of the various characters to Jesus. To begin with, table 2 indicates the main aspects of each character's response and how we have evaluated their response according to John's point of view.[1] We conclude that it is not the character that should be seen as a 'type' (table 1 shows that this would be unattainable) as much as the character's *response* to Jesus in that it represents the response of a particular group of people – both then and now. Although many Johannine characters themselves cannot be reduced to 'types', their belief-responses function as such. John's evaluative point of view only allows for two categories of responses – adequate and inadequate – since John has a dualistic framework within which all his characters operate.

Table 2: Classification of the Responses to Jesus

Character	Response to Jesus	John's Evaluation
John (the Baptist)	provides testimony about Jesus, directs other to Jesus, loyalty	adequate
World	as 'world'/system: opposition, hostility, rejection, unbelief; some individuals: acceptance and belief	inadequate adequate
'the Jews'	as a group: opposition, hostility, rejection, unbelief; some individuals: positive, even 'belief'-responses	inadequate probably inadequate
Andrew & Philip	come to and remain with Jesus, testify about Jesus, introduce others to Jesus; think 'from below'	adequate inadequate
Peter	belief, loyalty, shows love; misunderstanding, temporary defection	adequate inadequate
Nathanael	confession of Jesus' true identity, belief	adequate
Mother of Jesus	catalyst, directs others to Jesus, remains with Jesus	adequate
Nicodemus	sympathetic, 'signs-faith', ambiguous, no open commitment	inadequate
Samaritan woman	cooperative, cognitive progress, belief, testifies about Jesus	adequate
Royal official	submits to Jesus' authority, progressive belief, testifies about Jesus	adequate

[1] Contra Brant, who argues that John does not invite the readers to evaluate the characters (see our critique on p. 10).

Character	Response to Jesus	John's Evaluation
Invalid at the pool	first obedient and sides with Jesus but then turns against him	inadequate
Crowd	as a group: enthusiastic, divided, misunderstanding, fear, dismissive, unbelief; some individuals: positive, even 'belief'-responses	inadequate probably inadequate
Twelve	belief, misunderstanding, remaining with Jesus	adequate
Judas	dishonesty, disloyalty, betrayal, apostasy	inadequate
Man born blind	cooperative, obedient, testifies about Jesus, progressive understanding, belief	adequate
Martha	progressive understanding, belief, servanthood	adequate
Mary of Bethany	progressive understanding, devotion, servanthood	adequate
Lazarus	hears Jesus' voice, obedient, becomes a testimony to Jesus	adequate
Thomas	misunderstanding, courage, commitment, belief	adequate
Beloved Disciple	intimate, loyal, remains with Jesus, testifies about Jesus	adequate
Pilate	sympathy, cruelty, misunderstanding, rejection, compromise	inadequate
Joseph of Arimathea	secret belief, fearful but with elements of boldness	inadequate
Mary Magdalene	persistent, seeks Jesus, misunderstanding, hears Jesus' voice, responsive	adequate

We can then organize the various responses into the main categories 'adequate' and 'inadequate', and identify those characters who typify them.[2]

Table 2a: Adequate Responses to Jesus

Type of Response	Characters Who Typify This Response
acceptance (of Jesus and his revelation)	Andrew, Philip, Nathanael, the Samaritan woman (and her kinsfolk), the royal official (and his household), Peter, the man born blind, Martha, Thomas, Mary Magdalene
bearing fruit (causing others to come to Jesus)	John (the Baptist), the Samaritan woman, the royal official, Lazarus, the Beloved Disciple (through his gospel)
belief based on Jesus' word	the royal official, Martha, [the Samaritans in 4:42]
cooperation	the Samaritan woman, the royal official, the invalid at the pool (at first), the man born blind
devotion, affection, love	Mary of Bethany, Peter, Mary Magdalene
following Jesus	the Twelve (Andrew, Philip, Nathanael, Peter, Beloved Disciple), the mother of Jesus, the crowd (initially)
hearing Jesus' voice	Lazarus, Mary Magdalene
intimate with Jesus	the Beloved Disciple, Lazarus
introducing/directing people to Jesus	John (the Baptist), Andrew, Philip, the mother of Jesus, the Samaritan woman, the royal official, the Beloved Disciple (through his gospel)
loyalty/commitment	John (the Baptist), Peter, the Beloved Disciple

[2] Tables 2a and 2b are sorted alphabetically and contain a few characters in square brackets that we have not discussed but who also typify a particular response.

Type of Response	Characters Who Typify This Response
obedience	the Samaritan woman, the invalid at the pool (at first), the man born blind, Lazarus
open/public confession	John (the Baptist), Andrew, Philip, Nathanael, the Samaritan woman [and the Samaritans in 4:42], Peter (on behalf of the Twelve), the man born blind, Martha, Thomas
persistence	the royal official, Mary Magdalene
remaining with Jesus	the Twelve (Andrew, Philip), [the Samaritans in 4:40–42], the mother of Jesus, the Beloved Disciple
seeking Jesus	Andrew, Mary Magdalene, [the Greeks in 12:21]
servanthood	Mary of Bethany, Martha
signs-faith	as their starting position: the royal official, Martha, Mary of Bethany. Possibly Thomas, [the disciples in 2:11].
submitting to Jesus' authority	the royal official
sympathy	Nicodemus, the crowd, Pilate
testifying about Jesus	John (the Baptist), the Samaritan woman, the royal official, the man born blind, Martha, Lazarus (indirectly), Mary Magdalene, the Beloved Disciple (through his gospel)
understanding (with or without struggle)	the Twelve, the Samaritan woman, the man born blind, Martha, Mary of Bethany

Table 2b: Inadequate Responses to Jesus

Type of Response	Characters Who Typify This Response
alignment with the devil	'the Jews', Judas
ambiguity	Nicodemus, Joseph of Arimathea
apostasy	Judas
betrayal	Judas, the invalid at the pool
compromise	Pilate, the invalid at the pool
defection/disloyalty	Judas, Peter (temporarily), [the disciples in 6:60–66]
dishonesty	Judas
division	the crowd, 'the Jews' (6:52; 9:16; 10:19–21)
fear	the crowd (7:13), the authorities in 12:42, Joseph of Arimathea, the disciples (20:19), [the parents of the man born blind]
hostility	'the Jews', the world
misunderstanding	the crowd, Pilate, the Twelve (Peter, Thomas), Mary Magdalene
murder	'the Jews', Pilate
no open commitment	Nicodemus, Joseph of Arimathea, the authorities in 12:42
no response/apathy	the invalid at the pool
opposition	'the Jews', the world
pseudo-belief	'the Jews' (8:30–31; 12:42), some in the crowd (7:31), [the people in 2:23]
pseudo-devotion	the crowd (6:14–15; 12:12–19)
rejection	'the Jews', the world, the crowd, Pilate, the invalid at the pool
secrecy	Joseph of Arimathea, the authorities in 12:42, possibly Nicodemus
signs-faith	Nicodemus (3:2), 'the Jews' (11:45), [the people in 2:23]
thinking 'from below'	Andrew, Philip, Nicodemus, Mary Magdalene
unbelief	'the Jews', the world, the crowd, [Jesus' biological brothers in 7:5]

We make four observations. First, a typical response is not necessarily restricted to one person (e.g. the response of defection is seen in some disciples in 6:60–66, Peter and Judas), nor is a person restricted to one type of response (e.g. Peter responds both adequately and inadequately). Second, misunderstanding Jesus in terms of his identity, mission and teaching is a frequent response but misunderstanding itself does not determine whether the character's overall response is adequate or inadequate – other aspects are responsible for that. For instance, the crowd's frequent misunderstanding of Jesus together with being divided, fearful, dismissive and unbelieving cause the overall response to be inadequate. On the other hand, the Twelve frequently misunderstand Jesus but remain at his side; the Samaritan woman and the man born blind also struggle to understand but are open-minded and eventually reach sufficient understanding to make an adequate belief-response to Jesus. Hence, it is possible to arrive at a saving but less than perfect understanding of Jesus.[3]

Third, from his evaluative point of view expressed in 20:31, it appears that John wants the reader to evaluate primarily the character's response rather than the character. John is not warning us to dissociate from Nicodemus as a character as much as his response to Jesus. Nor should we judge Peter too harshly. Peter is far from perfect, shifting between adequate responses (his confessions in 6:68–69 and 21:15–17) and inadequate ones (his misunderstandings in 13:6–10 and 18:10–11; his denial; his petulant query about the Beloved Disciple in 21:20–22), but he is (and remains) firmly at Jesus' side (cf. his restoration in 21:15–19 after his temporary defection). Admittedly, it would be difficult in the cases of Judas and 'the Jews' to differentiate between character and response since both are negative/inadequate throughout the gospel with almost no glimmer of hope. Thus, we cannot always clinically distinguish between the characters and their responses (we explain this further in the next section). Fourth, we refrain from plotting the characters' responses along a continuum of faith because that would assume some sort of rating. Can we possibly decide whether testifying about Jesus, following him or remaining with him is closer to the ideal, or whether antipathy is worse than apathy?[4]

The Johannine Characters as Representative Figures

It was Raymond Collins who, in 1976, dubbed the characters in the Gospel of John as 'representative figures'. Collins argued that John has definitely typecast the various characters (they have characteristic traits) in order to

---

[3] The Spirit has a continual role in helping people (believers and unbelievers) to overcome their misunderstanding of Jesus but there is no guarantee that this will happen (see esp. Bennema, *Power*, chs 3–5 or, briefer, Bennema, 'Christ', 115–22).

[4] This is the difficulty we have with Culpepper's taxonomy, ranking the various belief-responses of the characters (*Anatomy*, 146–8).

represent a particular type of faith-response to Jesus.[5] Culpepper has perhaps brought out best the paradigmatic function of John's characters.[6] Although Collins and Culpepper have rightly noticed the representative value of the Johannine characters, they have wrongly assumed or concluded that John reduces his characters to their belief-responses and hence makes them types. We have demonstrated that many Johannine characters are complex, able to change, and show personality or even individuality. Besides, a particular type of response can be made by characters displaying entirely different traits (e.g. defection by Peter and Judas; misunderstanding by the Twelve and the crowd).

Even so, we do affirm the representative value of the Johannine characters but it is the totality of the character – traits, development *and* response – that is representative across cultures and time. We cannot separate characters from their responses – a character's response corresponds to who that character is. The Johannine characters are representative figures in that they have a symbolic or illustrative value beyond the narrative but not in a reductionist, 'typical' sense. The reader is invited to identify with (aspects of) one or more of the characters, learn from them and then make his or her own response to Jesus – preferably one that John approves of. Conversely, the reader may already have made a response to Jesus and can now evaluate that response against those of the characters.

Table 3 indicates the paradigmatic function of each Johannine character for the twenty-first century rather than the first century. We will therefore not mention, for example, that Nicodemus represents the Jewish authorities who are attracted to Jesus but make no clear belief-response and are still seeking, or that the Samaritan woman and her kinsfolk signify the inclusion of non-Jews into the community of faith in early Christianity – this has already been pointed out in the respective chapters above.[7] Instead, we shall highlight each character's representative value for today. We will not revisit all the character's traits and responses, lest we appear to be searching for the exact, modern *doppelgänger* for each Johannine character – we merely sketch a general (hopefully not too general) profile.

---

[5] Collins, 'Figures', 8.

[6] Culpepper, *Anatomy*, 101–48.

[7] Since we did not support a reading of John's gospel as a document written by and for a so-called 'Johannine community', we have not attempted to discover historical referents for the Johannine characters in John's own time and setting (contra Brown, *Community*, 59–91; Martyn, *History*, 145–67). Instead, we have indicated the representative value of the Johannine characters for a general reader in that time. Most recently, Klink also emphasizes this kind of representative importance of the Johannine characters, advocating readers to find a 'market niche' for each character, although he limits himself to the first-century scenario (*Sheep*, 187–203).

Table 3: The Contemporary Representative Value of the Johannine Characters

Character	Representative Value
John (the Baptist)	those who realize that testifying about Jesus is not optional and is done in (rather than apart from) the various roles they have; those whose testimony leads others to Jesus; those who continually direct others away from themselves to Jesus because they know that Jesus is greater
World	people who form a hostile environment for Jesus and his followers through opposition, hate and rejection; nevertheless, some may come to accept Jesus
'the Jews'	religious fanatics who claim to belong to God but oppose and reject the gospel, persecute and are capable of killing Jesus' followers
Andrew & Philip	those who are inquiring, resourceful in finding people and introducing them to Jesus, but who must hone their skills by learning to think more 'from above'
Peter	those who are outspoken, impulsive, zealous and devoted to Jesus but sometimes fail miserably; in general, Peter represents many Christians in-the-making but, more specifically, budding Christian leaders who must learn to give themselves up to Jesus and to those who are entrusted to them; Peter also offers hope for those who have turned their backs on Jesus but wish to return
Nathanael	those who are initially sceptical about Jesus but remain open-minded, are willing to investigate, perceptive and respond adequately to further revelation; more specifically, Nathanael may represent the messianic Jews
Mother of Jesus	those who, with good intentions, try to use Jesus for their own ends but find themselves drawn into his plan; those who are practical, observant and take initiative; catalysts who can direct people to obey Jesus or bring about events that advance the cause of Jesus
Nicodemus	those who are religious, sympathetic and attracted to Jesus ('seekers') but whose allegiance to Jesus remains ambiguous
Samaritan woman	the marginalized or outsiders who prove to have a keen religious interest, are open-minded, responsive and willing to testify about Jesus to their kinsfolk
Royal official	those who have incipient signs-faith, progress to trusting Jesus' words when challenged, and eventually come to a saving belief in Jesus after verifying facts; those who testify about Jesus within their circle of influence
Invalid at the pool	those who are needy, initially responsive and daring to defy others, but who cringe when Jesus corrects them and ultimately leave him showing no clear commitment
Crowd	those who are enthusiastic, show potential for discipleship but are drawn by the sensational, are divided and undiscerning, and eventually reject Jesus; some make positive, but inadequate, responses
Twelve	those whose allegiance to Jesus is firm despite often misunderstanding him or his teaching; however, the Spirit's continual assistance promises progress
Judas	those who belonged to Jesus but have defected and joined the opposition – the devil; those who are disloyal and betray the trust of Jesus and others
Man born blind	those who gradually gain understanding about Jesus while facing opposition, who are willing to stand by him despite the outcome; those who are witty and bold
Martha	those who have incipient signs-faith and progress towards more mature faith in response to revelation; those who show initiative, are confident in Jesus' abilities, perceptive and willing to testify and serve Jesus
Mary of Bethany	those who have incipient signs-faith, whose emotions may hinder progress towards mature faith but whose devotion and service to Jesus indicate they belong to him

Character	Representative Value
Lazarus	those who obey Jesus when they hear his voice despite adverse or difficult circumstances thereby providing testimony that leads others to Jesus; Lazarus provides hope for believers who die in that Jesus will be waiting on the other side
Thomas	those who are pragmatic and want a tangible experience of Jesus in order to believe; loyal pragmatists who desire tangible experiences but who are encouraged to a steadier faith that is less dependent on the concrete and physical
Beloved Disciple	those who are loyal, perceptive and have a close relationship with Jesus, and whose life, words and work are a credible testimony to Jesus, leading others to believe in him
Pilate	those in positions of authority who compromise truth and justice to safeguard their career and ensure survival; those who start well on a quest for truth but eventually abandon it because other things (career, image, etc.) take precedence
Joseph of Arimathea	those who secretly believe in Jesus but whose fear of others prevents an open confession of their allegiance; some may show courage and take risks, providing hope that eventually they will make a public confession
Mary Magdalene	those who persistently seek Jesus but too often in human or 'worldly' categories, but they respond positively when Jesus redirects their quest

The Characters' Responses and John's Dualistic Worldview

Colleen Conway has argued that the ambiguity and instability of many Johannine characters result in responses to Jesus that resist or undermine the gospel's binary categories of belief and unbelief.[8] We must now address the issue of how these characters, and their responses, fit into John's dualistic worldview. We had argued that John's evaluative point of view corresponds to both the soteriological purpose of his narrative (20:31) and his dualistic worldview in which there is scope for only two responses to Jesus – acceptance or rejection. John's evaluative point of view therefore allows for two options – adequate and inadequate. However, we have seen that the characters' responses to Jesus form a broad spectrum, which raises an important question: How do the characters' responses coordinate with John's dualistic scheme? Can such diverse responses fit into the binary categories of belief and unbelief, adequate and inadequate?

I suggest that the characters' responses do fit into John's dualistic worldview as follows: the Johannine characters reflect the *human* perspective, representing the gamut of responses that people make in life, while from a *divine* perspective these responses are ultimately evaluated as acceptance or rejection. The divine reality is that the world and its people are enveloped in darkness and do not know God – they are 'from below' (cf. 1:5; 8:23). In order to dispel people's darkness or lack of divine knowledge, Jesus came to the world to reveal God and to bring people into an everlasting, life-giving relationship with himself and God. People who encounter Jesus may

---

8 Conway, 'Ambiguity', 328–41.

reject or accept him, and consequently remain part of the world below or enter the world above through a spiritual birth. The human reality is that people respond to Jesus in a number of ways – instantly or gradually, positively or negatively, consistently or haphazardly, ambiguously or evidently. Faced with this reality we must attempt to evaluate what John thinks would qualify someone for the new birth that brings people into the realm of God, what kind of responses would bring and keep people in a life-giving relationship with Jesus. In table 2 above, we presented the array of responses to Jesus and John's evaluation of each response.

Conway's article shows clearly that the so-called 'minor' Johannine characters are often unstable, complex and ambiguous (contra most scholars), moving up and down on a spectrum of negative to positive faith responses. We agree with Conway when she warns against flattening the Johannine characters into a particular type. We disagree, however, with her conclusion that the minor characters, as a group, challenge or undermine John's dualistic worldview which has only scope for belief/acceptance and unbelief/rejection. Life is complex, unstable and ambiguous and so are people. Those who make an adequate belief-response to Jesus and enter into a saving relationship with him and God rarely make consistent or stable belief-responses throughout their lives. People have doubts, struggles, fluctuations or lapses in faith, and may even defect. Likewise, the various Johannine characters present a broad spectrum of responses, but because they operate within John's dualistic framework, their responses will eventually (but perhaps only at the Parousia) be distilled or crystallize to two basic categories – acceptance and rejection. People have either accepted or rejected Jesus and his teaching, they are either from below or from above, they belong either to God's family or to the devil's.

In our view, ambiguity, polyvalence and shifting in a person's character and faith can take place within a world of absolutes that allows only light or darkness, acceptance or rejection, belief or unbelief. The Twelve, for example, are firmly on Jesus' side from the beginning, but they often misunderstand him and fail to grasp important aspects of discipleship. While Peter also remains on Jesus' side, he is unstable, shifting between adequate and inadequate responses. In real life, a believer's relationship with Jesus rarely shows neat, linear development. The complexity (and sometimes apparent absurdity) of life forces or causes people to shift or change, perhaps by acquiring new traits, adding to or replacing existing ones. Someone's faith is often not consistent or progressive; circumstances may generate critical questions, create doubt and cause a shift in faith. Since characters resemble people, John's array of characters and their responses to Jesus correspond to people and their choices in real life in any culture and time. We have thus underlined how the Gospel of John seeks to challenge its readers, past and present, about where they stand in relation to Jesus.

The Modern Reader and a Jesus Encounter

In the Gospel of John, various characters encounter Jesus – and respond to him. Likewise, the reader of John's gospel can also encounter Jesus – and respond to him. But how does the modern reader encounter Jesus in this way? John 20 is instructive. From the encounters of Mary Magdalene, the disciples and Thomas with the risen Jesus, we learned that one needs a tangible experience of the risen Lord to reach adequate faith. However, Jesus' exhortation to later generations to believe without seeing (20:29) seems to contradict this. We suggest the following solution for this paradox. John's gospel is the Beloved Disciple's trustworthy, written eyewitness account of Jesus' life and teaching, which aims at evoking adequate belief (19:35; 20:30–31; 21:24–25). John, through his record of the encounters of various characters with Jesus, implicitly challenges his readers to evaluate and learn from these encounters. Consequently, the modern reader can also have an authentic, tangible encounter with the risen Jesus – and reach adequate faith.

The purpose of the Gospel of John is to evoke belief amongst its readers. John's strategy to achieve this purpose is to put various characters on the stage who, in their encounter with the protagonist (Jesus), produce a broad spectrum of responses. John also evaluates these responses, so as to guide readers in their own response to Jesus. As Culpepper states, '[t]he shape of the narrative and the voice of the narrator lead the reader to identify or interact variously with each character',[9] and, in Iser's words, '"identification" is not an end in itself, but a stratagem by means of which the author stimulates attitudes in the reader.'[10] John's technique of constructing these characters and his description of their encounters with Jesus is thus aimed at his readers – both the original readers, who were most likely general readers in the early Christian movement, and subsequent generations of readers.[11] The Gospel of John is uniquely timeless: readers of this gospel, in any generation and culture, will encounter Jesus and must decide where they stand. Even today, we can see the Nicodemuses, Peters, Marthas, Pilates, and so on of this world. Today, the reader of John's gospel, like the characters in the story, is also confronted with this Jesus – and has to respond. So, the question 'Where do you stand in relation to Jesus?' is perhaps the most crucial question a person has to face and answer in his or her lifetime.

---

[9] Culpepper, *Anatomy*, 148.

[10] W. Iser, *The Implied Reader: Patterns of Communication in Prose Fiction from Bunyan to Beckett* (Baltimore: Johns Hopkins University Press, 1978), 291.

[11] Bauckham (*Gospels, passim*) and Klink (*Sheep*, chs 2–4) provide the most substantial case to date for the audience of John's gospel being a general audience, consisting of various geographic communities in early Christianity.

What Still Needs to Be Done?

Our study is obviously not the final word on Johannine character and we have two suggestions for further study. First, it must be investigated whether our theory of character needs refinement. The number of dimensions or continua to analyse characters may be extended to include, for instance, the dimension of stability or consistency.[12] Second, our theory of character can presumably be extended to the Synoptic Gospels and Acts, but will need testing. Besides, a comparative analysis of the characters in the Synoptics and John would reveal the degree of continuity in character portrayal between these writings.

---

[12] Baruch Hochman has suggested the most comprehensive model for classifying characters to date, consisting of eight continua upon which a character may be located (*Character in Literature* [Ithaca: Cornell University Press, 1985], 86–140). D.B. Gowler, for example, utilizes Hochman's model in his character study of the Pharisees in Luke-Acts, although he admits that this model is not entirely adequate to evaluate character in ancient narrative (*Host, Guest, Enemy and Friend: Portraits of the Pharisees in Luke and Acts* [ESEC 2; New York: Peter Lang, 1991], 53–4, 306–17, 321). Although Conway refers to Hochman's classification, she does not utilize it herself (*Men and Women*, 58).

Bibliography

Allison, D.C. 'Mountain and Wilderness'. Pages 563–6 in *Dictionary of Jesus and the Gospels*. Edited by J.B. Green, S. McKnight, and I.H. Marshall. Downers Grove: InterVarsity Press, 1992.

Anderson, R.T. *The Keepers: An Introduction to the History and Culture of the Samaritans*. Peabody: Hendrickson, 2002.

Arbeitman, Y. 'The Suffix of Iscariot'. *Journal of Biblical Literature* 99 (1980): 122–4.

Ashton, J. 'The Identity and Function of the *IOUDAIOI* in the Fourth Gospel'. *Novum Testamentum* 27 (1985): 40–75. Repr. as 'The Jews in John'. Pages 36–70 in *Studying John: Approaches to the Fourth Gospel*. Edited by J. Ashton. Oxford: Clarendon Press, 1994.

—. *Understanding the Fourth Gospel*. Oxford: Clarendon Press, 1991.

Barrett, C.K. *The Gospel according to St John: An Introduction with Commentary and Notes on the Greek Text*. 2d edn. London: SPCK, 1978.

Barton, S.C. *The Spirituality of the Gospels*. London: SPCK, 1992.

Bassler, J.M. 'The Galileans: A Neglected Factor in Johannine Community Research'. *Catholic Biblical Quarterly* 43 (1981): 243–57.

—. 'Mixed Signals: Nicodemus in the Fourth Gospel'. *Journal of Biblical Literature* 108 (1989): 635–46.

Bauckham, R. 'The Beloved Disciple as Ideal Author'. *Journal for the Studies of the New Testament* 49 (1993): 21–44.

—. 'The Bethany Family in John 11 – 12: History or Fiction?' Pages 173–89 in *The Testimony of the Beloved Disciple: Narrative, History, and Theology in the Gospel of John*. Grand Rapids: Baker Academic, 2007.

—. *God Crucified: Monotheism and Christology in the New Testament*. Didsbury Lectures 1996. Carlisle: Paternoster, 1998.

—, ed. *The Gospels for All Christians: Rethinking the Gospel Audiences*. Grand Rapids: Eerdmans, 1998.

—. *Jesus and the Eyewitnesses: The Gospels as Eyewitness Testimony*. Grand Rapids: Eerdmans, 2006.

—. 'Nicodemus and the Gurion family'. *Journal of Theological Studies* 47 (1996): 1–37.

—. 'Papias and Polycrates on the Origin of the Fourth Gospel'. *Journal of Theological Studies* 44 (1993): 24–69.

Beasley-Murray, G.R. *John*. WBC 36. Milton Keynes: Word, 1991.

Beck, D.R. *The Discipleship Paradigm: Readers and Anonymous Characters in the Fourth Gospel*. BIS 27. Leiden: Brill, 1997.

—. 'The Narrative Function of Anonymity in Fourth Gospel Characterization'. *Semeia* 63 (1993): 143–58.

Beirne, M.M. *Women and Men in the Fourth Gospel: A Genuine Discipleship of Equals*. JSNTS 242. London: Sheffield Academic Press, 2003.

Bennema, C. 'The Character of John in the Fourth Gospel'. *Journal of the Evangelical Theological Society* 52 (2009): 271–84.

—. 'Christ, the Spirit and the Knowledge of God: A Study in Johannine Epistemology'. Pages 107–33 in *The Bible and Epistemology: Biblical Soundings on the Knowledge of God*. Edited by M. Healy and R. Parry. Milton Keynes: Paternoster, 2007.

—. *Excavating John's Gospel: A Commentary for Today*. Delhi: ISPCK, 2005. Repr., Eugene, OR: Wipf & Stock, 2008.

—. 'The Giving of the Spirit in John's Gospel – A New Proposal?' *Evangelical Quarterly* 74 (2002): 195–213.

—. 'The Identity and Composition of *hoi Ioudaioi* in the Gospel of John'. *Tyndale Bulletin* 60 (forthcoming 2009).

—. *The Power of Saving Wisdom: An Investigation of Spirit and Wisdom in Relation to the Soteriology of the Fourth Gospel*. WUNT 2/148. Tübingen: Mohr Siebeck, 2002. Repr., Eugene, OR: Wipf & Stock, 2007.

—. 'Religious Violence in the Gospel of John: A Response to the Hindutva Culture in Modern India'. In *Violence and Peace – Creating a Culture of Peace in the Contemporary Context of Violence*. Edited by F. Fox. Delhi: CMS/UBS/ISPCK, forthcoming 2009.

—. 'Spirit-Baptism in the Fourth Gospel. A Messianic Reading of John 1,33'. *Biblica* 84 (2003): 35–60.

—. 'The Strands of Wisdom Tradition in Intertestamental Judaism: Origins, Developments and Characteristics'. *Tyndale Bulletin* 52 (2001): 61–82.

—. 'The Sword of the Messiah and the Concept of Liberation in the Fourth Gospel'. *Biblica* 86 (2005): 35–58.

—. 'A Theory of Character in the Fourth Gospel with Reference to Ancient and Modern Literature'. *Biblical Interpretation* 17 (2009): 375–421.

Blaine, B.B. *Peter in the Gospel of John: The Making of an Authentic Disciple*. SBLAB 27. Leiden: Brill, 2007.

Boer, M.C. de. 'Narrative Criticism, Historical Criticism, and the Gospel of John'. *Journal for the Studies of the New Testament* 45 (1992): 35–48.

Boers, H. *Neither on This Mountain nor in Jerusalem: A Study of John 4*. SBLMS 35. Atlanta: Scholars Press, 1988.

Böhler, D. '"Ecce Homo!" (Joh 19,5) ein Zität aus dem Alten Testament'. *Biblische Zeitschrift* 39 (1995): 104–8.

Bond, H.K. *Pontius Pilate in History and Interpretation*. SNTSMS 100. Cambridge: Cambridge University Press, 1998.

Bonney, W. *Caused to Believe: The Doubting Thomas Story at the Climax of John's Christological Narrative*. BIS 62. Leiden: Brill, 2002.

Botha, J.E. *Jesus and the Samaritan Woman: A Speech Act Reading of John 4:1–42*. NovTSup 65. Leiden: Brill, 1991.

Brant, J.A. *Dialogue and Drama: Elements of Greek Tragedy in the Fourth Gospel*. Peabody: Hendrickson, 2004.

Brodie, T.L. *The Gospel according to John: A Literary and Theological Commentary*. New York: Oxford University Press, 1993.

—. 'Jesus as the New Elisha: Cracking the Code'. *Expository Times* 93 (1981–2): 39–42.

Brower, K.E. 'Holiness'. Pages 477–8 in *New Bible Dictionary*. Edited by D.R.W. Wood. 3d edn. Leicester: InterVarsity Press, 1996.

Brown, R.E. *The Community of the Beloved Disciple*. London: Chapman, 1979.

—. *The Gospel according to John*. AB 29. 2 vols. London: Chapman, 1971.

—. 'The "Mother of Jesus" in the Fourth Gospel'. Pages 307–10 in *L'Evangile de Jean: Sources, redaction, théologie*. Edited by M. de Jonge. BETL 44. Leuven: Leuven University Press, 1987.

—. 'The Passion According to John: Chapters 18 and 19'. *Worship* 49 (1975): 126–34.

—. 'The Resurrection in John 20 – A Series of Diverse Reactions'. *Worship* 64 (1990): 194–206.

—. 'Roles of Women in the Fourth Gospel'. *Theological Studies* 36 (1975): 688–99.

Brown, R.E., K.P. Donfried, J.A. Fitzmyer, and J. Reumann, eds. *Mary in the New Testament: A Collaborative Assessment by Protestant and Roman Catholic Scholars*. Philadelphia: Fortress Press, 1978.

Brown, S. 'The Beloved Disciple: A Jungian View'. Pages 366–77 in *The Conversation Continues: Studies in Paul and John*. Edited by R.T. Fortna and B.R. Gaventa. Nashville: Abingdon, 1990.

Brownson, J.V. 'Neutralizing the Intimate Enemy: The Portrayal of Judas in the Fourth Gospel'. *Society of Biblical Literature Seminar Papers* 31 (1992): 49–60.

Bryan, S.M. 'Power in the Pool: The Healing of the Man at Bethesda and Jesus' Violation of the Sabbath (Jn. 5:1–18)'. *Tyndale Bulletin* 54 (2003): 7–22.

Bultmann, R. *The Gospel of John*. Translated by G.R. Beasley-Murray. Philadelphia: Westminster Press, 1971.

Burkett, D. 'Two Accounts of Lazarus' Resurrection in John 11'. *Novum Testamentum* 36 (1994): 209–32.

Burridge, R.A. *What Are the Gospels?: A Comparison with Graeco-Roman Biography*. 2d edn. Grand Rapids: Eerdmans, 2004. Orig. SNTSMS 70. Cambridge: Cambridge University Press, 1992.

Byrne, B. 'The Faith of the Beloved Disciple and the Community in John 20'. *Journal for the Studies of the New Testament* 23 (1985): 83–97.

Cane, A. *The Place of Judas Iscariot in Christology*. Aldershot: Ashgate, 2005.

Carson, D.A. *Divine Sovereignty and Human Responsibility: Biblical Perspectives in Tension*. London: Marshall, Morgan & Scott, 1981.

—. *The Gospel according to John*. Leicester: InterVarsity Press, 1991.

Carter, W. *Pontius Pilate: Portraits of a Roman Governor*. Collegeville: Liturgical Press, 2003.

Catchpole, D. 'The Beloved Disciple and Nathanael'. Pages 69–92 in *Understanding, Studying and Reading: New Testament Essays in Honour of John Ashton*. Edited by C. Rowland and C.H.T. Fletcher-Louis. JSNTS 153. Sheffield: Sheffield Academic Press, 1998.

Charlesworth, J.H. *The Beloved Disciple: Whose Witness Validates the Gospel of John?* Valley Forge: Trinity Press, 1995.

Chatman, S. *Story and Discourse: Narrative Structure in Fiction and Film*. Ithaca: Cornell University Press, 1978.

Chennattu, R.M. *Johannine Discipleship as a Covenant Relationship*. Peabody: Hendrickson, 2006.

Coakley, J.F. 'The Anointing at Bethany and the Priority of John'. *Journal of Biblical Literature* 107 (1988): 241–56.

Coggins, R.J. *Samaritans and Jews*. Oxford: Blackwell, 1975.

Collins, R.F. 'From John to the Beloved Disciples: An Essay on Johannine Characters'. *Interpretation* 49 (1995): 359–69.

—. 'Mary in the Fourth Gospel: A Decade of Johannine Studies'. *Louvain Studies* 3 (1970): 99–142.

—. 'Representative Figures'. Pages 1–45 in *These Things Have Been Written: Studies on the Fourth Gospel*. LTPM 2; Louvain/Grand Rapids: Peeters Press/ Eerdmans, 1990. Repr. from *Downside Review* 94 (1976): 26–46; 95 (1976): 118–32.

Coloe, M.L. *Dwelling in the Household of God: Johannine Ecclesiology and Spirituality*. Collegeville: Liturgical Press, 2007.

—. 'Households of Faith (Jn 4:46–54; 11:1–44): A Metaphor for the Johannine Community'. *Pacifica* 13 (2000): 326–35.

Conway, C.M. *Men and Women in the Fourth Gospel: Gender and Johannine Characterization*. SBLDS 167. Atlanta: Society of Biblical Literature, 1999.

—. 'Speaking through Ambiguity: Minor Characters in the Fourth Gospel'. *Biblical Interpretation* 10 (2002): 324–41.

Cotterell, F.P. 'The Nicodemus Conversation: A Fresh Appraisal'. *Expository Times* 96 (1984–5): 237–42.

Cotterell, P., and M. Turner. *Linguistics & Biblical Interpretation*. Downers Grove: InterVarsity Press, 1989.

Crown, A.D., ed. *The Samaritans*. Tübingen: Mohr Siebeck, 1989.

Cullmann, O. *Jesus and the Revolutionaries*. New York: Scribner's, 1970.

Culpepper, R.A. *Anatomy of the Fourth Gospel: A Study in Literary Design*. Philadelphia: Fortress Press, 1983.

—. 'The Gospel of John and the Jews'. *Review and Expositor* 84 (1987): 273–88.

—. *John, the Son of Zebedee: The Life of a Legend*. Columbia: University of South Carolina Press, 1994.

Davies, M. *Rhetoric and Reference in the Fourth Gospel*. JSNTS 69. Sheffield: Sheffield Academic Press, 1992.

Day, J.N. *The Woman at the Well: Interpretation of John 4:1–42 in Retrospect and Prospect*. BIS 61. Leiden: Brill, 2002.

Droge, A.J. 'The Status of Peter in the Fourth Gospel: A Note on John 18:10–11'. *Journal of Biblical Literature* 109 (1990): 307–11.

Duke, P.D. *Irony in the Fourth Gospel*. Atlanta: John Knox Press, 1985.

—. 'John 5:1–15'. *Review and Expositor* 85 (1988): 539–42.

Dunderberg, I. 'The Beloved Disciple in John: Ideal Figure in an Early Christian Controversy'. Pages 243–69 in *Fair Play: Diversity and Conflicts in Early Christianity. Essays in Honour of Heikki Räisänen*. Edited by I. Dunderberg, C. Tuckett, and K. Syreeni. NovTSup 103. Leiden: Brill, 2002.

Dunn, J.D.G. *Jesus Remembered*. Vol. 1 of *Christianity in the Making*. Grand Rapids: Eerdmans, 2003.

Edwards, R. *Discovering John*. London: SPCK, 2003.

Ehrman, A. 'Judas Iscariot and Abba Saqqara'. *Journal of Biblical Literature* 97 (1978): 572–3.

Ehrman, B.D. 'Jesus' Trial before Pilate: John 18:28 – 19:16'. *Biblical Theology Bulletin* 13 (1983): 124–31.

Esler, P.F., and R.A. Piper. *Lazarus, Mary and Martha: A Social-Scientific and Theological Reading of John*. London: SCM, 2006.

Farmer, D.A. 'John 9'. *Interpretation* 50 (1996): 59–63.

Fee, G.D. 'On the Inauthenticity of John 5:3b–4'. *Evangelical Quarterly* 54 (1982): 207–18.

Fehribach, A. *The Women in the Life of the Bridegroom: A Feminist Historical-Literary Analysis of the Female Characters in the Fourth Gospel*. Collegeville: Liturgical Press, 1998.

Filson, F.V. 'Who Was the Beloved Disciple?' *Journal of Biblical Literature* 68 (1949): 83–8.

Fitzmyer, J.A. *The Dead Sea Scrolls and Christian Origins*. Grand Rapids: Eerdmans, 2000.

Fleddermann, H.T. 'Review of W. Klassen, *Judas: Betrayer or Friend of Jesus?* (Minneapolis: Fortress Press, 1996)'. *Catholic Biblical Quarterly* 59 (1997): 771–2.

Ford, J.M. *Redeemer – Friend and Mother: Salvation in Antiquity and in the Gospel of John*. Minneapolis: Fortress Press, 1997.

Fuller, R. 'The "Jews" in the Fourth Gospel'. *Dialog* 16 (1977): 31–7.

Gaventa, B.R. *Mary: Glimpses of the Mother of Jesus*. Edinburgh: T&T Clark, 1999.

George, L.D. *Reading the Tapestry: A Literary-Rhetorical Analysis of the Johannine Resurrection Narrative (John 20 – 21)*. StBL 14. New York: Peter Lang, 2000.

Giblin, C.H. 'John's Narration of the Hearing before Pilate (John 18,28 – 19,16a)'. *Biblica* 67 (1986): 221–39.

Gillespie, T.W. 'The Trial of Politics and Religion: John 18:28 – 19:16'. *Ex Auditu* 2 (1986): 69–73.

Glancy, J.A. 'Torture: Flesh, Truth, and the Fourth Gospel'. *Biblical Interpretation* 13 (2005): 107–36.

Gosling, F.A. 'O Judas! What Have You Done?' *Evangelical Quarterly* 71 (1999): 117–25.

Gowler, D.B. *Host, Guest, Enemy and Friend: Portraits of the Pharisees in Luke and Acts*. ESEC 2. New York: Peter Lang, 1991.

Grassi, J.A. 'The Role of Jesus' Mother in John's Gospel: A Reappraisal'. *Catholic Biblical Quarterly* 48 (1986): 67–80.

Grigsby, B. 'Washing in the Pool of Siloam – A Thematic Anticipation of the Johannine Cross'. *Novum Testamentum* 27 (1985): 227–35.

Hakola, R. 'A Character Resurrected: Lazarus in the Fourth Gospel and Afterwards'. Pages 223–63 in *Characterization in the Gospels: Reconceiving Narrative Criticism*. Edited by D. Rhoads and K. Syreeni. JSNTS 184. Sheffield: Sheffield Academic Press, 1999.

—. *Identity Matters: John, the Jews and Jewishness*. NovTSup 118. Leiden: Brill, 2005.

Harstine, S. 'Un-Doubting Thomas: Recognition Scenes in the Ancient World'. *Perspectives in Religious Studies* 33 (2006): 435–47.

Harvey, A.E. *Jesus on Trial: A Study in the Fourth Gospel*. London: SPCK, 1976.

Hearon, H.E. *The Mary Magdalene Tradition: Witness and Counter-Witness in Early Christian Communities*. Collegeville: Liturgical Press, 2004.

Hengel, M. *The Johannine Question*. London: SCM, 1989.

Hill, C.E. 'The Identity of John's Nathanael'. *Journal for the Studies of the New Testament* 67 (1997): 45–61.

—. 'What Papias Said about John (and Luke): A "New" Papian Fragment'. *Journal of Theological Studies* 49 (1998): 582–629.

Hochman, B. *Character in Literature*. Ithaca: Cornell University Press, 1985.

Hodges, Z.C. 'The Angel at Bethesda – John 5:4'. *Bibliotheca Sacra* 136 (1979): 25–39.

Holleran, J.W. 'Seeing the Light: A Narrative Reading of John 9'. *Ephemerides Theologicae Lovanienses* 69 (1993): 5–26, 354–82.

Horbury, W. 'Extirpation and Excommunication'. *Vetus Testamentum* 35 (1985): 13–38.

Horvath, T. 'Why Was Jesus Brought to Pilate?' *Novum Testamentum* 11 (1969): 174–84.

Howard, J.M. 'The Significance of Minor Characters in the Gospel of John'. *Bibliotheca Sacra* 163 (2006): 63–78.

Iser, W. *The Implied Reader: Patterns of Communication in Prose Fiction from Bunyan to Beckett*. Baltimore: Johns Hopkins University Press, 1978.

Jeremias, J. *Jerusalem in the Time of Jesus*. London: SCM, 1969.

—. *The Rediscovery of Bethesda: John 5:2*. Göttingen: Vandenhoeck & Ruprecht, 1966.

Jonge, M. de. 'Nicodemus and Jesus: Some Observations on Misunderstanding and Understanding in the Fourth Gospel'. Pages 29–47 in *Jesus: Stranger from Heaven and Son of God. Jesus Christ and the Christians in Johannine Perspective*. Edited and translated by J.E. Steely. SBLSBS 11. Missoula: Scholars Press, 1977.

Keener, C.S. *The Gospel of John: A Commentary*. Peabody: Hendrickson, 2003.

Kierspel, L. *The Jews and the World in the Fourth Gospel: Parallelism, Function, and Context*. WUNT 2/220. Tübingen: Mohr Siebeck, 2006.

Kim, D. *An Exegesis of Apostasy Embedded in John's Narratives of Peter and Judas against the Synoptic Parallels*. SBEC 61. Lewiston: Edwin Mellen Press, 2004.

Kitzberger, I.R. 'Mary of Bethany and Mary of Magdala – Two Female Characters in the Johannine Passion Narrative: A Feminist, Narrative-Critical Reader-Response'. *New Testament Studies* 41 (1995): 564–86.

Klassen, W. *Judas: Betrayer or Friend of Jesus?* Minneapolis: Fortress Press, 1996.

Klauck, H.-J. *Judas – Ein Jünger des Herrn*. Quaestiones Disputatae 111. Freiburg: Herder, 1987.

Klink III, E.W. 'Expulsion from the Synagogue? Rethinking a Johannine Anachronism'. *Tyndale Bulletin* 59 (2008): 99–118.

—. *The Sheep of the Fold: The Audience and Origin of the Gospel of John*. SNTSMS 141. Cambridge: Cambridge University Press, 2007.

Koester, C.R. 'Messianic Exegesis and the Call of Nathanael (John 1.45–51)'. *Journal for the Studies of the New Testament* 39 (1990): 23–34.

—. *Symbolism in the Fourth Gospel: Meaning, Mystery, Community*. 2d edn. Minneapolis: Fortress Press, 2003.

Köstenberger, A.J. *John*. BECNT. Grand Rapids: Baker Academic, 2004.

—. *The Missions of Jesus and the Disciples according to the Fourth Gospel: With Implications for the Fourth Gospel's Purpose and the Mission of the Contemporary Church*. Grand Rapids: Eerdmans, 1998.

Krafft, E. 'Die Personen des Johannesevangeliums'. *Evangelische Theologie* 16 (1956): 18–32.

Lee, D.A. 'Partnership in Easter Faith: The Role of Mary Magdalene and Thomas in John 20'. *Journal for the Studies of the New Testament* 58 (1995): 37–49.

—. *The Symbolic Narratives of the Fourth Gospel: The Interplay of Form and Meaning.* JSNTS 95. Sheffield: JSOT Press, 1994.

—. 'Turning from Death to Life: A Biblical Reflection on Mary Magdalene (John 20:1–18)'. *Ecumenical Review* 50 (1998): 112–20.

Lieu, J.M. 'Blindness in the Johannine Tradition'. *New Testament Studies* 34 (1988): 83–95.

—. 'The Mother of the Son in the Fourth Gospel'. *Journal of Biblical Literature* 117 (1998): 61–77.

Lincoln, A.T. 'The Beloved Disciple as Eyewitness and the Fourth Gospel as Witness'. *Journal for the Studies of the New Testament* 85 (2002): 3–26.

—. *The Gospel according to Saint John.* BNTC 4. London: Continuum, 2005.

—. *Truth on Trial: The Lawsuit Motif in the Fourth Gospel.* Peabody: Hendrickson, 2000.

Lindars, B. 'Capernaum Revisited. Jn 4,46–53 and the Synoptics'. Pages 1985–2000 in *The Four Gospels 1992: Festschrift Frans Neirynck.* Edited by F. Van Segbroeck et al. Leuven: Leuven University Press, 1992.

—. *The Gospel of John.* NCB. London: Oliphants, 1972.

—. 'Rebuking the Spirit: A New Analysis of the Lazarus Story of John 11'. *New Testament Studies* 38 (1992): 89–104.

Maccini, R.G. *Her Testimony is True: Women as Witnesses according to John.* JSNTS 125. Sheffield: Sheffield Academic Press, 1996.

Marrow, S.B. '*Kosmos* in John'. *Catholic Biblical Quarterly* 64 (2002): 90–102.

Martin, T.W. 'Assessing the Johannine Epithet "the Mother of Jesus"'. *Catholic Biblical Quarterly* 60 (1998): 63–73.

Martyn, J.L. *History and Theology in the Fourth Gospel.* 3d edn. Louisville: Westminster John Knox Press, 2003.

Matera, F.J. 'John 20:1–18'. *Interpretation* 43 (1989): 402–6.

Matthews, C.R. *Philip: Apostle and Evangelist. Configurations of a Tradition.* NovTSup 105. Leiden: Brill, 2002.

Maynard, A.H. 'The Role of Peter in the Fourth Gospel'. *New Testament Studies* 30 (1984): 531–48.

McCane, B.R. 'Burial Practices, Jewish'. Pages 173–5 in *Dictionary of New Testament Background.* Edited by S.E. Porter and C.A. Evans. Downers Grove: InterVarsity Press, 2000.

McGing, B.C. 'Pontius Pilate and the Sources'. *Catholic Biblical Quarterly* 53 (1991): 416–38.

McKay, K.L. 'Style and Significance in the Language of Jn 21.15–17'. *Novum Testamentum* 27 (1985): 319–33.

Mead, A.H. 'The *basilikos* in John 4.46–53'. *Journal for the Studies of the New Testament* 23 (1985): 69–72.

Meeks, W.A. 'The Man from Heaven in Johannine Sectarianism'. *Journal of Biblical Literature* 91 (1972): 44–72.

Meyer, R. '*Ochlos*'. Pages 582–90 in volume 5 of *Theological Dictionary of the New Testament.* Edited by G. Kittel and G. Friedrich. Translated by G.W. Bromiley. 10 vols. Grand Rapids: Eerdmans, 1964–76.

Michaels, J.R. 'Baptism and Conversion in John: A Particular Baptist Reading'. Pages 136–56 in *Baptism, the New Testament and the Church: Historical and*

Contemporary Studies in Honour of R.E.O. White. Edited by S.E. Porter and A.R. Cross. JSNTS 171. Sheffield: Sheffield Academic Press, 1999.

Minear, P.S. 'The Beloved Disciple in the Gospel of John'. *Novum Testamentum* 19 (1977): 105–23.

—. '"We Don't Know Where . . ." John 20:2'. *Interpretation* 30 (1976): 125–39.

Moloney, F.J. *Belief in the Word – Reading the Fourth Gospel: John 1 – 4.* Minneapolis: Fortress Press, 1993.

—. 'The Faith of Martha and Mary: A Narrative Approach to John 11,17–40'. *Biblica* 75 (1994): 471–93.

—. *The Gospel of John.* Sacra Pagina 4. Collegeville: Liturgical Press, 1998.

Motyer, S. 'Method in Fourth Gospel Studies: A Way Out of the Impasse?' *Journal for the Studies of the New Testament* 66 (1997): 27–44.

—. *Your Father the Devil?: A New Approach to John and 'the Jews'.* Carlisle: Paternoster, 1997.

Moule, C.F.D. 'A Note on "Under the Fig Tree" in John 1.48, 50'. *Journal of Theological Studies* 5 (1954): 210–11.

Müller, M. '"Have You Faith in the Son of Man?" (John 9.35)'. *New Testament Studies* 37 (1991): 291–4.

Munro, W. 'The Pharisee and the Samaritan in John: Polar and Parallel'. *Catholic Biblical Quarterly* 57 (1995): 710–28.

Neyrey, J.H. *The Resurrection Stories.* Wilmington: Glazier, 1988.

—. 'The Sociology of Secrecy and the Fourth Gospel'. Pages 79–109 in *What is John? Vol. II: Literary and Social Readings of the Fourth Gospel.* Edited by F.F. Segovia. Atlanta: Scholars Press, 1998.

O'Brien, K.S. 'Written That You May Believe: John 20 and Narrative Rhetoric'. *Catholic Biblical Quarterly* 67 (2005): 284–302.

O'Day, G.R. *The Gospel of John.* NIB 9. Nashville: Abingdon Press, 1995.

—. 'Jesus as Friend in the Gospel of John'. *Interpretation* 58 (2004): 144–57.

Okure, T. *The Johannine Approach to Mission: A Contextual Study of John 4:1–42.* WUNT 2/31. Tübingen: Mohr Siebeck, 1988.

—. 'The Significance Today of Jesus' Commission to Mary Magdalene'. *International Review of Mission* 81 (1992): 177–88.

Painter, J. 'Johannine Symbols: A Case Study in Epistemology'. *Journal of Theology for Southern Africa* 27 (1979): 26–41.

—. 'John 9 and the Interpretation of the Fourth Gospel'. *Journal for the Studies of the New Testament* 28 (1986): 31–61.

—. *The Quest for the Messiah: The History, Literature and Theology of the Johannine Community.* 2d edn. Edinburgh: T&T Clark, 1993.

Pancaro, S. *The Law in the Fourth Gospel: The Torah and the Gospel of Moses and Jesus, Judaism and Christianity according to John.* NovTSup 42. Leiden: Brill, 1975.

Parker, P. 'John the Son of Zebedee and the Fourth Gospel'. *Journal of Biblical Literature* 81 (1962): 35–43.

Perkins, P. *Peter: Apostle for the Whole Church.* Edinburgh: T&T Clark, 2000.

Peters, D.E. 'The Life of Martha of Bethany by Pseudo-Marcilia'. *Theological Studies* 58 (1997): 441–60.

Platt, E.E. 'The Ministry of Mary of Bethany'. *Theology Today* 34 (1977): 29–39.

Porter, S.E. *Idioms of the Greek New Testament.* 2d edn. Sheffield: JSOT Press, 1994.

Quast, K. *Peter and the Beloved Disciple: Figures for a Community in Crisis*. JSNTS 32. Sheffield: JSOT Press, 1989.

Rensberger, D.K. *Overcoming the World: Politics and Community in the Gospel of John*. London: SPCK, 1988.

Renz, G. 'Nicodemus: An Ambiguous Disciple? A Narrative Sensitive Investigation'. Pages 255–83 in *Challenging Perspectives on the Gospel of John*. Edited by J. Lierman. WUNT 2/219. Tübingen: Mohr Siebeck, 2006.

Resseguie, J.L. *Narrative Criticism of the New Testament: An Introduction*. Grand Rapids: Baker Academic, 2005.

—. *The Strange Gospel: Narrative Design and Point of View in John*. BIS 56. Leiden: Brill, 2001.

Rhees, R. 'The Confession of Nathanael, John i.45–49'. *Journal of Biblical Literature* 17 (1898): 23–8.

Ridderbos, H.N. *The Gospel according to John: A Theological Commentary*. Translated by J. Vriend. Grand Rapids: Eerdmans, 1997.

Rimmon-Kenan, S. *Narrative Fiction: Contemporary Poetics*. New York: Methuen, 1983.

Ringe, S.H. *Wisdom's Friends: Community and Christology in the Fourth Gospel*. Louisville: Westminster John Knox Press, 1999.

Robertson, A. 'John 11:1–53'. *Interpretation* 58 (2004): 175–7.

Ryken, L. et al. 'Path'. Pages 630–32 in *Dictionary of Biblical Imagery*. Downers Grove: InterVarsity Press, 1998.

Saldarini, A.J. *Pharisees, Scribes and Sadducees in Palestinian Society: A Sociological Approach*. Grand Rapids: Eerdmans, 2001. Orig., Wilmington: Glazier, 1988.

Sasse, H. '*Kosmeō, ktl.*' Pages 867–98 in volume 3 of *Theological Dictionary of the New Testament*. Edited by G. Kittel and G. Friedrich. Translated by G.W. Bromiley. 10 vols. Grand Rapids: Eerdmans, 1964–76.

Schnackenburg, R. *The Gospel according to St John*. 3 vols. London: Burns & Oates, 1968–82.

Schneiders, S.M. 'Born Anew'. *Theology Today* 44 (1987): 189–96. Repr. as 'Born Anew (John 3:1–15)'. Pages 117–25 in Schneiders, *Written*.

—. 'Death in the Community of Eternal Life: History, Theology, and Spirituality in John 11'. *Interpretation* 41 (1987): 44–56. Repr. as 'The Community of Eternal Life (John 11:1–53)'. Pages 171–83 in Schneiders, *Written*.

—. 'The Face Veil: A Johannine Sign (John 20:1–10)'. *Biblical Theology Bulletin* 13 (1983): 94–7. Repr. as 'Seeing and Believing in the Glorified Jesus (John 20:1–10)'. Pages 202–10 in Schneider, *Written*.

—. 'Inclusive Discipleship (John 4:1–42)'. Pages 126–48 in Schneiders, *Written*.

—. 'John 20:11–18: The Encounter of the Easter Jesus with Mary Magdalene – A Transformative Feminist Reading'. Pages 155–68 in *'What is John?': Readers and Readings of the Fourth Gospel*. Edited by F.F. Segovia. Atlanta: Scholars Press, 1996. Repr. as 'Encountering and Proclaiming the Risen Jesus (John 20:11–18)'. Pages 211–23 in Schneiders, *Written*.

—. 'John 21:1–14'. *Interpretation* 43 (1989): 70–75. Repr. as 'Contemplation and Ministry (John 21:1–14)'. Pages 224–9 in Schneiders, *Written*.

—. 'Women in the Fourth Gospel and the Role of Women in the Contemporary Church'. *Biblical Theology Bulletin* 12 (1982): 35–45. Repr. as 'Women in the Fourth Gospel'. Pages 93–114 in Schneiders, *Written*.

—. *Written That You May Believe: Encountering Jesus in the Fourth Gospel*. New York: Herder & Herder, 1999.

Schüssler Fiorenza, E. *In Memory of Her: A Feminist Theological Reconstruction of Christian Origins*. London: SCM, 1983.

Scott, M. *Sophia and the Johannine Jesus*. JSNTS 71. Sheffield: JSOT Press, 1992.

Smith, T.V. *Petrine Controversies in Early Christianity*. WUNT 15. Tübingen: Mohr Siebeck, 1985.

Snyder, G.F. 'John 13:16 and the Anti-Petrinism of the Johannine Tradition'. *Biblical Research* 16 (1971): 5–15.

Sproston North, W.E. *The Lazarus Story within the Johannine Tradition*. JSNTS 212. Sheffield: Sheffield Academic Press, 2001.

Staley, J.L. 'Stumbling in the Dark, Reaching for the Light: Reading Character in John 5 and 9'. *Semeia* 53 (1991): 55–80.

Stegemann, H. *The Library of Qumran: On the Essenes, Qumran, John the Baptist, and Jesus*. Grand Rapids: Eerdmans, 1998.

Stibbe, M.W.G. 'The Elusive Christ: A New Reading of the Fourth Gospel'. *Journal for the Studies of the New Testament* 44 (1991): 19–37.

—. *John*. Sheffield: JSOT Press, 1993.

—. *John as Storyteller: Narrative Criticism and the Fourth Gospel*. SNTSMS 73. Cambridge: Cambridge University Press, 1992.

—. *John's Gospel*. London: Routledge, 1994.

—. 'A Tomb with a View: John 11.1–44 in Narrative-Critical Perspective'. *New Testament Studies* 40 (1994): 38–54.

Suggitt, J.N. 'The Raising of Lazarus'. *Expository Times* 95 (1983–4): 106–8.

Sylva, D.D. 'Nicodemus and His Spices (John 19.39)'. *New Testament Studies* 34 (1988): 148–51.

Taylor, J.E. *The Immerser: John the Baptist within Second Temple Judaism*. Grand Rapids: Eerdmans, 1997.

Thatcher, T. 'Jesus, Judas and Peter: Character by Contrast in the Fourth Gospel'. *Bibliotheca Sacra* 153 (1996): 435–48.

—. 'The Sabbath Trick: Unstable Irony in the Fourth Gospel'. *Journal for the Studies of the New Testament* 76 (1999): 53–77.

Thomas, J.C. '"Stop Sinning Lest Something Worse Come Upon You": The Man at the Pool in John 5'. *Journal for the Studies of the New Testament* 59 (1995): 3–20.

Tilborg, S. van. *Imaginative Love in John*. BIS 2. Leiden: Brill, 1993.

Titus, E.L. 'The Identity of the Beloved Disciple'. *Journal of Biblical Literature* 69 (1950): 323–8.

Tolmie, D.F. *Jesus' Farewell to the Disciples: John 13:1 – 17:26 in Narratological Perspective*. BIS 12. Leiden: Brill, 1995.

Tovey, D. *Narrative Art and Act in the Fourth Gospel*. JSNTS 151. Sheffield: Sheffield Academic Press, 1997.

Trites, A.A. *The New Testament Concept of Witness*. SNTSMS 31. Cambridge: Cambridge University Press, 1977.

Trudinger, L.P. 'An Israelite in Whom There Is No Guile: An Interpretative Note on John 1:45–51'. *Evangelical Quarterly* 54 (1982): 117–20.

Turner, M. 'Historical Criticism and Theological Hermeneutics of the New Testament'. Pages 44–70 in *Between Two Horizons: Spanning New Testament*

Studies and Systematic Theology. Edited by J.B. Green and M. Turner. Grand Rapids: Eerdmans, 2000.

—. *The Holy Spirit and Spiritual Gifts – Then and Now.* Rev. edn. Carlisle: Paternoster, 1999.

Twelftree, G.H. *Jesus the Miracle Worker: A Historical & Theological Study.* Downers Grove: InterVarsity Press, 1999.

VanderKam, J.C. *The Dead Sea Scrolls Today.* Grand Rapids: Eerdmans, 1994.

Vanhoozer, K.J. *Is There a Meaning in This Text?: The Bible, the Reader and the Morality of Literary Knowledge.* Leicester: Apollos, 1998.

Von Wahlde, U.C. '"The Jews" in the Gospel of John: Fifteen Years of Research (1983–1998)'. *Ephemerides Theologicae Lovanienses* 76 (2000): 30–55.

—. 'The Johannine "Jews": A Critical Survey'. *New Testament Studies* 28 (1982): 33–60.

—. 'The Witnesses to Jesus in John 5:31–40 and Belief in the Fourth Gospel'. *Catholic Biblical Quarterly* 43 (1981): 385–404.

Waetjen, H.C. *The Gospel of the Beloved Disciple: A Work in Two Editions.* New York: T&T Clark, 2005.

Watt, J.G. van der. *Family of the King: Dynamics of Metaphor in the Gospel according to John.* BIS 47. Leiden: Brill, 2000.

Wead, D.W. 'We Have a Law'. *Novum Testamentum* 11 (1969): 185–9.

Webster, J.S. *Ingesting Jesus: Eating and Drinking in the Gospel of John.* SBLAB 6. Atlanta: Society of Biblical Literature, 2003.

Whitters, M.F. 'Discipleship in John: Four Profiles'. *Word and World* 4 (1998): 422–7.

Wiarda, T. 'John 21.1–23: Narrative Unity and Its Implications'. *Journal for the Studies of the New Testament* 46 (1992): 53–71.

—. *Peter in the Gospels: Pattern, Personality and Relationship.* WUNT 2/127. Tübingen: Mohr Siebeck, 2000.

Williams, D.J. 'Bride, Bridegroom'. Pages 86–8 in *Dictionary of Jesus and the Gospels.* Edited by J.B. Green, S. McKnight, and I.H. Marshall. Downers Grove: InterVarsity Press, 1992.

Williams, R.H. 'The Mother of Jesus at Cana: A Social-Science Interpretation of John 2:1–12'. *Catholic Biblical Quarterly* 59 (1997): 679–92.

Wink, W. *John the Baptist in the Gospel Tradition.* SNTSMS 7. Cambridge: Cambridge University Press, 1968.

Witherington III, B. *The Many Faces of the Christ: The Christologies of the New Testament and Beyond.* New York: Crossroad, 1998.

Witkamp, L.Th. 'The Use of Traditions in John 5.1–18'. *Journal for the Studies of the New Testament* 25 (1985): 19–47.

Wuellner, W. 'Putting Life back into the Lazarus Story and its Reading: The Narrative Rhetoric of John 11 as the Narration of Faith'. *Semeia* 53 (1991): 113–32.

Yamaguchi, S. *Mary and Martha: Women in the World of Jesus.* Maryknoll: Orbis, 2002.

Yoder, J.H. *The Politics of Jesus.* 2d edn. Grand Rapids: Eerdmans, 1994.

Index of Authors